Post- and Transhumanism

BEYOND HUMANISM: TRANS- AND POSTHUMANISM
JENSEITS DES HUMANISMUS: TRANS- UND POST-HUMANISMUS

Edited by / Herausgegeben von Stefan Lorenz Sorgner

VOL./BD. 1

Zu Qualitätssicherung und Peer Review der vorliegenden Publikation

Die Qualität der in dieser Reihe erscheinenden Arbeiten wird vor der Publikation durch den Herausgeber der Reihe geprüft.

Notes on the quality assurance and peer review of this publication

Prior to publication, the quality of the work published in this series is reviewed by the editor of the series.

Robert Ranisch / Stefan Lorenz Sorgner (eds.)

Post- and Transhumanism

An Introduction

Bibliographic Information published by the Deutsche Nationalbibliothek
The Deutsche Nationalbibliothek lists this publication in the Deutsche Nationalbibliografie; detailed bibliographic data is available in the internet at http://dnb.d-nb.de.

Library of Congress Cataloging-in-Publication Data
Post- and transhumanism : an introduction / Robert Ranisch, Stefan Lorenz Sorgner (eds.). -- 1 [edition].
pages cm. -- (Beyond humanism: trans- and posthumanism, ISSN 2191-0391 ; vol. 1 = Jenseits des Humanismus: trans- und posthumanismus, ISSN 2191-0391 ; Bd. 1)
Includes bibliographical references and index.
ISBN 978-3-631-60662-9 (alk. paper)
1. Humanism. 2. Philosophical anthropology. I. Ranisch, Robert, editor.
B821.P585 2014
144--dc23

2014035180

Cover Photo:
Antibodies of Surveillance / Pangender Cyborg – Metaformance
by Jaime del Val - Reverso - in Festival Alterarte Murcia, Spain, 2008;
Photo: Alterarte.

ISSN 2191-0391
ISBN 978-3-631-60662-9 (Print)
E-ISBN 978-3-653-05076-9 (E-Book)
DOI 10.3726/978-3-653-05076-9

Peter Lang – Frankfurt am Main · Bern · Bruxelles · New York · Oxford · Warszawa · Wien

This publication has been peer reviewed.
www.peterlang.com

Contents

Ontologies of Becoming

Paragone of the Arts

Introducing Post- and Transhumanism

Robert Ranisch & Stefan Lorenz Sorgner

Scientific and technological advances have questioned predominant doctrines concerning the human condition. *Transhumanism* and *posthumanism* are among the most recent and prominent manifestations of this phenomenon. Debates on trans- and posthumanism have not only gained a considerable amount of academic and popular attention recently, but have also created a widespread conceptual confusion. This is no surprise, considering their recent dates of origin, their conceptual similarities, and their engagements with similar questions, topics, and motifs. Furthermore, trans- as well as posthumanism frequently question their relationship to humanism[1] and reconsider what it means to be human. In this regard both movements are streaming *beyond humanism*. What this means, however, is far from clear and shall be subject of discussion in this volume.

In order to make sense of these two approaches and to investigate their interrelationship, a clarification of these concepts is necessary. As a first approximation, transhumanism can be seen as a stance that affirms the radical transformation of human's biological capacities and social conditions by means of tech-

---

1 We will not be able to address the complex histories and varieties of humanism in this chapter. Yet, the following must be noted: The word "humanism" (*Humanismus*) was coined in 1808 by the German theologian and philosopher Friedrich I. Niethammer in the context of educational curricula, as it is derived from the Latin word *humanitas*. This word has a variety of meaning but has strongly been identified with the Greek word *paideia* (παιδεία), e.g., i.) in Cicero's *De Oratore* (I, 71) the meaning of the concept *humanitas* corresponds to that of the concept *paideia*; ii.) in the text *Noctes Acticae* (XIII, 17) by the Latin author Aulus Gellius, who lived in the 2nd century, an explicit identification of *paideia* and *humanitas* can be found. The word *humanitas* within this tradition has both ontological as well as ethical elements. A categorical dualist ontology, which implies the special status of human beings, has been associated with the notions of *paideia* (e.g. Plato's analogy of the divided line) and *humanitas* (e.g. Cicero's affirmation of an immortal soul). Such dualist ontology, however, is absent in some of the recent humanist traditions, e.g. atheist, secular, evolutionary or naturalist versions of humanism. Post- and transhumanists distance themselves from the categorical dualist ontology, too. Concerning the ethical dimension, *paideia* and *humanitas* imply strong perfectionist concepts of the good, which are represented best by Plato's philosopher king as well as by the Stoic sage. There is no simple relationship between beyond humanist movements and humanism with respect to their ideals of perfection. Some traces of a stronger concept of perfection can also be found within transhumanism (e.g., the Renaissance ideal). Such ideals, however, are absent in posthumanism. For an overview on humanism, see Davies (1997). Soper (1986) and Seubold (2001) focus on the 20th Century discourses on (anti-) humanism, which have influenced contemporary posthumanism in particular.

nologies. These transformations are widely perceived as *human enhancement* or augmentation which might be so fundamental that they bring about life forms with significantly different characteristics as to be perceived as other than human. The result of such technologically induced version of evolution is referred to as the *posthuman*. However, there is no commonly shared conception of what posthumans are, and visions range from the posthuman as a new biological species, a cybernetic organism, or even a digital, disembodied entity. The link between the human and the posthuman is the *transhuman*, an abbreviation for a transitional human, to which transhumanism owes its name. In this regard, transhumanism can be understood as a *transhuman*-ism. By the same token, transhumanism, according to its self-understanding, is a contemporary renewal of humanism. It embraces and eventually amplifies central aspects of secular and Enlightenment humanist thought, such as belief in reason, individualism, science, progress, as well as self-perfection or cultivation.

While transhumanism presents a more or less coherent set of techno-optimist ideas, advocated by numerous distinguished transhumanist institutions and authors, *posthumanism* is a highly ambiguous notion. If transhumanism is seen as an intensification of humanism, a type of hyper-humanism, it may help to analyze posthumanism as a break with humanism; it is a *post*-humanism. In recent years "posthumanism" served as an umbrella term for a variety of positions that reject basic humanist concepts and values. Above all, the construction of "human beings" is deemed to be ideologically laden, insufficient, dangerous, or paternalistic. While there is certainly not *one* humanism, which could be identified as a common target of posthumanist criticisms, there are persistent concepts and dualities in Western culture, such as nature/culture, man/woman, subject/object, human/animal, or body/mind, which are deeply rooted in the Western tradition and which get challenged by posthumanist thinkers. Yet, not every criticism of these concepts must be seen as a posthumanist one (see Hayles 1999, 4). Feminism, postcolonial theory, and other postmodern theories have already questioned many of these historical constructs. Posthumanism, as we understand it here, is characterized by a specific focus on (emerging) technologies. The predominant concept of the "human being" is questioned by thinking through the human being's engagement and interaction with technology. It is this peculiar aspect that has caused confusion concerning the meaning of the concepts of trans- and posthumanism. Both philosophical approaches consider the question of human coevolution with technology, and both, post- as well as transhumanist thinkers, sometimes employ the motif of the "posthuman". However, in posthumanism the concept serves as a label for a new narrative, which may replace that of "the human", rather than one for a radically enhanced human being. Transhumanism, on the other hand, is characterized by a straightforward affirmation of technological augmentations and visions of an enhanced posthumanity.

This sketch of transhumanism and posthumanism is certainly vague and far from capturing all facets of both discourses. However, this initial attempt to characterize both ways of thinking shall give us some guidance for exploring central discourses beyond humanism. Before moving on and providing an overview on the topics of this volume, some further remarks on fundamental aspects of transhumanism and posthumanism are necessary.

Transhumanism

The terms "transhumanism" and "posthuman" have an ambiguous origin[2] and ideas of human perfection can be found throughout the history of ideas.[3] However, contemporary transhumanists emphasize their roots in Enlightenment thought and their commitment to secular humanism (see Hughes 2010). Furthermore, they frequently associate the notion "transhumanism" with Julian Huxley (1887-1975).[4] Darwin's bulldog, Thomas Henry Huxley (1825-1895), was his paternal grandfather. The author of the novel *Brave New World*, Aldous

2 For an overview on the word "transhumanism" and "posthuman(ism)", see Krüger (2004, 107-112).

3 The most comprehensive study on the history of human perfectibility has been written by Passmore (2000). A well-known history of transhumanist thought has been brought forward by Bostrom (2005) and Wiesing (2008) focuses on the medical history of ideas on human enhancement. Miah (2008) and Capurro (2012) outline the history of transhumanism alongside with posthumanism. The 20th Century history of transhumanism has been analyzed by Hughes (2004, 155-184) and More (2013). Since the most recent history of transhumanism is only documented in the internet, it is difficult to find reliable references.

4 Not only the coinage of "transhumanism" is associated with Julian Huxley. Recent studies have pointed to the early 20th Century roots of transhumanism in the intellectual milieu of Huxley. Huxley's friends, J. B. S. Haldane (1892-1964) and J. D. Bernal (1901-1971) can reasonable count as early forerunners of current transhumanism, too (see Bashford 2013; Tirosh-Samuelson 2012). Another contemporary of Huxley is worth further investigations with regard to the history of transhumanism: the Jesuit priest and paleontologist Pierre Teilhard de Chardin (1881-1955). Huxley, who contributed a forward to Teilhard's posthumously published *The Phenomenon of Man* (1955), is not the first to consider "trans-human" conditions. Teilhard referred to similar concepts before Huxley. In an unpublished essay from February 1949 entitled *The Essence of the Democratic Idea*, he suggests some biological definitions of central democratic concepts. As for "liberty" he states that this is "the chance offered to every man […] of 'trans-humanising' himself by developing his potentialities to the fullest extent" (Teilhard de Chardin 1964 [1949], 241).

Huxley (1894-1963), was his brother. Their lesser-known half-brother Andrew Huxley (1917-2012) won the Noble Prize in Physiology or Medicine. Julian Huxley was not only the first director-general of the UNESCO but also president of the British Eugenics Society. In 1957,[5] he coined the term "transhumanism" in *New Bottles for New Wine*, where he maintains:

> "The human species can, if it wishes, transcend itself – not just sporadically, an individual here in one way, an individual there in another way, but in its entirety, as humanity. We need a name for this new belief. Perhaps *transhumanism* will serve: man remaining man, but transcending himself, by realizing new possibilities of and for his human nature.
>
> 'I believe in transhumanism': once there are enough people who can truly say that, the human species will be on the threshold of a new kind of existence, as different from ours as ours is from that of Peking man. It will at last be consciously fulfilling its real destiny" (Huxley 1957, 17).

The meaning of "transhumanism", however, has changed after Huxley. While he still believed that "man" will be "remaining man" and associated transhumanism with "creating a more favorable social environment" as well as "techniques of spiritual development" (ibid., 16-17), "transhumanism" soon became the keyword for the transgression of human's biological boundaries by means of technologies.

The futurist Fereidoun M. Esfandiary (1930-2000), who later changed his name to FM-2030, is often said to have introduced the term "transhuman" in its current sense. During the mid-1960s, while he was teaching at the New School for Social Research in New York, he founded a futurist group, called the Up-Wingers and popularized speculative ideas about future human conditions (see Hughes 2004, 161). While FM-2030 seems to have used the term at least since the 1970s (see Esfandiary 1974), his non-academic book *Are You Transhuman?* (1989) explicitly addresses transhumanist ideas in greater length. Unlike Huxley, FM-2030 believed that the "most urgent problem facing us is not social – economic – political" (ibid., 161) but rather the brute fact of our biological limitations, namely human mortality. FM-2030 predicted that by the end of the 20th Century "monumental breakthroughs" would fix this flaw and transform the human species. Transhumans are "the earliest manifestations of new *evolutionary* beings", playing a "bridging role in evolution" (ibid., 205). The "transhuman" is an abbreviation for transitional human, the link between the human and posthuman.

Today FM-2030 is regarded as a forerunner of contemporary transhumanism. He was particularly influential for the American wing of contemporary

5 Some sources wrongly date the first use of the term "transhumanism" to Julian Huxley's *Religion without Revelation* (1927).

transhumanism, including Natasha Vita-More (born as Nancie Clark), who drafted a *Transhuman Manifesto* in 1983 (see More 2013). Nevertheless, in comparison to current transhumanist visions, FM-2030's depiction of the transhuman conditions seems rather odd: His transhumanist checklist includes factors such as having a pacemaker, having acted as a surrogate mother, or having died and being resuscitated (see ibid., 202-203). FM-2030 hoped for his own resuscitation: his body has been cryogenically preserved after his death in 2000, thirty years before his hoped-for 100th birthday.

Perhaps the best known figure speculating about the possibilities of cryonics is Robert Ettinger. He is frequently regarded as another pioneer of the transhumanist movement. In particular in *Man into Superman* (1972), he emphasizes the role of cryonics for transhumanity. Since cryonic freezing might be the only chance for most living beings to benefit from future transhuman technologies, the question of longevity is of central importance for most transhumanists. It is no surprise that a prominent figure of the contemporary transhumanist movement, Max More (born as Max O'Connor), husband of Natasha Vita-More, is director of one of the biggest cryonics organizations, the Alcor Life Extension Foundation. Furthermore, it is sometimes maintained, notably by the author himself, that Max More introduces the "-ism" into transhumanism and thus coined the name of the current movement.[6]

Most recent technological advances of the 1980s, and the increasing relevance of science fiction in mainstream culture brought about a broader interest in reflections on the technological future of humanity. Before the hype concerning gene technologies of the recent two decades, the techno-futurist discourse during this time was particularly interested in artificial intelligence, robotics, and nanotechnology. Seminal works of this time period include Marvin Minsky's *The Society of Mind* (1986), Eric Drexler's *Engines of Creation* (1986), Hans Moravec's *Mind Children* (1988), and Ray Kurzweil's *The Age of Intelligent Machines* (1990) just to name a few. While their work does not yet have the conceptual framework of current transhumanism, they reflected on future impacts of possible technologies and were a common source of inspiration for the current generation of transhumanists.

---

6 See, e.g., Humanity+ (n.d.) and Bostrom (2005). More claims to have provided the first definition of transhumanism in the current sense in his 1990 article *Transhumanism: Toward a Futurist Philosophy*. There he describes transhumanism as: "Philosophies of life [...] that seek the continuation and acceleration of the evolution of intelligent life beyond its currently human form and human limitations by means of science and technology, guided by life-promoting principles and values" (as cited in More 2013, 3).

Only when the internet established a broader world wide connectivity, transhumanism as a movement gained momentum. During the 1990s various institutions and local groups were founded and contributed to the dissemination of transhumanist ideas. The World Transhumanist Association (WTA) is particularly well known, also for providing a widely recognized definition of transhumanism, in the *Transhumanist FAQ,* firstly drafted in 1998. Even though this definition has been dropped in the recent version (3.0) of the FAQ, it still sums up the core elements of transhumanism. There transhumanism is defined as:

> "The intellectual and cultural movement that affirms the possibility and desirability of fundamentally improving the human condition through applied reason, especially by developing and making widely available technologies to eliminate aging and to greatly enhance human intellectual, physical, and psychological capacities" (Humanity+ n.d.).

Transhumanism today is a slogan for a variety of cultural, political, philosophical or digital movement, promoting techno-futuristic visions about the transgression of human biology. While transhumanism cannot be identified with a single movement or set ideas, some transhumanists are organized in the non-profit organization Humanity+ (H+), which popularizes transhumanist ideas. Current chair of H+ is Natasha Vita-More. The organization emerged out the World Transhumanist Association (WTA) and the Extropy Institute (see Humanity+ n.d.). The Extropy Institute was founded in the early 1990s by Max More and Tom Morrow. Both edited a journal of transhumanist ideas called *Extropy* together since 1988.

Nick Bostrom and David Pearce founded the WTA in 1998 (see Bostrom 2005, 12). Before Bostrom turned away from the mainstream transhumanist movement in recent years, he was the leading academic voice of transhumanism of the previous decade. In his role as director of the Future of Humanity Institute at the University of Oxford he made transhumanism accessible for a broader academic audience. Together with James Hughes, Bostrom also founded the Institute for Ethics & Emerging Technologies (IEET) in 2004. Today the IEET is one of the most important transhumanist platforms, promoting a liberal-democratic form of transhumanism, which they call *technoprogressivism* (see Hughes 2004). The IEET also publishes a peer-reviewed online journal, the *Journal of Evolution and Technology* (formally known as *Journal of Transhumanism*), which is one of the most prominent academic organs for transhumanist ideas.

Apart from H+ there are a number of other institutions which are associated with transhumanist ideas (see Tirosh-Samuelson 2011, 52), including the Machine Intelligence Research Institute (formally know as Singularity Institute), the Foresight Institute, or the Beyond Humanism Network. The Mormon Transhumanist Association, which is affiliated to Humanity+, is the rare instance of a religious foundation which is supporting transhumanism.

Transhumanist ideas are also an issue of growing importance in academic biomedical ethics. Quite a few liberal bioethicists, often with sympathies for utilitarian ethics, sometimes referred to as *bioliberals*, share many of transhumanists' aspirations. During the previous two decades an increasing amount of literature has been concerned with the ethical and legal questions of non-therapeutic uses of biomedical technologies. This includes questions like healthy patients using psychopharmacological drugs to increase or maintain cognitive functions or parents selecting their offspring for certain genetic traits. This so-called "human enhancement debate" bears similarities to transhumanist discourses (see, e.g., Savulescu/ Bostrom 2010). Even though the radical transformation of humanity is not the primary focus of all bioliberals (see, e.g., Agar 2010), some openly embrace the use of cutting-edge enhancement technologies and even regard their use as moral duty (see, e.g., Harris 2007).

While transhumanists as well as authors being associated with transhumanist ideas are not a homogenous group, they all share the belief in the desirability of technologically supported human enhancement procedures. Transhumanism, as we have seen already, owes its name to the fact that it affirms human enhancements technologies, aiming for trans- and finally posthumanity. However, in recent years the motif of the transhuman or posthuman has more and more disappeared from the transhumanist agenda, a trend which might be related to the rebranding of the WTA to Humanity+.

Regardless of the labeling, in current discourses the aspiration stays the same. Based on a neo-Darwinian wordview, it is upheld that humans should take evolution into their own hands and undertake broad-scale attempts to incorporate technologies into their lives. These projects aim for a radical increase of bodily functions (e.g. healthspan, longevity), cognitive and emotional capacities (e.g. intellect, memory), physical traits (strength, beauty), and behavior (e.g. morality). On the basis of the affirmation of specific traits, there is the promise that technologies promote the common good and individual happiness. For realizing these aims, transhumanists have a firm confidence in scientific progress. Transhumanism is not limited to specific technologies but embraces all kinds of means to realize their visions, including established ones like education and vaccinations. Their primary focus today is on emerging and converging technologies, such as nanotechnology, biotechnologies and means of artificial reproduction, information technologies and cognitive sciences (see Roco/ Bainbridge 2003).

Posthumanism

Transhumanism can be described as a techno-optimist discourse. Ideas, concepts and reflections associated with transhumanism are brought forward by philosophers – mainly from the analytic and utilitarian tradition –, bioliberal thinkers, bioethicist, engineers, computer scientists as well as futurists. It has been shown, that advocates of transhumanism are sometimes organized in institutions, which provide the movement with a certain political leverage. By contrast, it is difficult to identify a coherent posthumanist movement. We rather see disagreement concerning history, concepts as well as objectives of posthumanism.

While it was possible to identify historical roots of transhumanism, it is much more difficult to present a coherent history of these set of ideas that are associated with posthumanism.[7] It has sometimes been argued that the "history of posthumanism has no obvious beginning, middle or end point in philosophical thought" (Miah 2008, 89). By contrast, Stefan Herbrechter (2013, 31-33) suggests that posthumanism is a reaction to Nietzsche's revaluation of values and Neil Badmington (2000, 4-7) suggests Marx's rejection of a natural human essence outside social relations and Freud's discovery of the power of unconscious forces as beginning of posthumanism. Pramod K. Nayar (2014, 11-34) finds the origin of posthumanism in three recent critiques of humanism: Foucauldian poststructuralism, feminism, and technoscience studies.

Whereas there is evidently a significant amount of disagreement about the origins of posthumanism, most analysis locates its origin in a different context than transhumanism. Posthumanism is associated with postmodern and continental philosophy, science and technology studies, cultural studies, literary theory and criticism, poststructuralism, feminism, critical theory and postcolonial studies. In these contexts "posthumanism" serves as an umbrella term for ideas that explain, promote or deal with the crisis of humanism. So far, however, no common name for these critical discourses has been established. Sometimes "posthumanism" is used in a broad sense, encompassing transhumanism as a form of *technological* posthumanism, too (see, e.g., Miah 2008). Then specifications, such as *critical* posthumanism are used to distinguish those critical discourses from techno-utopian discourses (see, e.g., Braidotti 2013; Herbrechter 2013; Nayar 2014). Sometimes a difference is drawn between *cultural* and *philosophical* posthumanism (see, e.g., Miah 2008; Tirosh-Samuelson in this volume), highlighting different disciplines where posthumanist thinking is an issue. The concept "posthuman studies" might be even more promising to refer to a discipline which deals with post- and transhumanist questions, as the concept

---

7 Different histories and genealogies of posthumanism can be found in Herbrechter (2013, 31-73), Nayar (2014, 11-34), and Wolfe (2010, xi-xxxiv).

"posthuman" is employed in both traditions, even though the meaning of this term is employed in different ways. Thereby, the word "posthuman" serves in an integrative way. By being concerned with it's meaning, members of both movements step outside of the limited borders of their own discourses and get acquainted with different perspectives.

While there are different concepts of "posthumanism" and the "posthuman" in a variety of contexts, it is widely agreed that the term "posthumanism" has been coined by postmodern philosopher Ihab Hassan in 1977.[8] In his essay *Prometheus as Performer: Towards a Posthumanist Culture*, based on a presentation delivered for a symposium on postmodern performance in 1976, Hassan talks about this "dubious neologism", as he puts it, whereby he maintains:

> "We need first to understand that the human form – including human desire and all its external representations – may be changing radically, and thus must be re-visioned. We need to understand that five hundred years of humanism may be coming to an end, as humanism transforms itself into something that we must helplessly call posthumanism" (Hassan 1977, 843).

This transformation becomes evident when we consider experiences of journeys through space, artificial intelligence and "those Bionic Women from the German Democratic Republic" at the Olympic Games (ibid., 846). Nevertheless, Hassan's announcement of posthumanism has little to do with the posthuman in transhumanism. Similar to Foucault's (2002 [1966]) proclaimed "end of man", posthumanism does not mean "the literal end of man but the end of a particular image of us" (Hassan 1977, 845). In other words, for these theorists, our biological nature may remain unchanged, but the self-concept of the human changes, in particular when we consider the integration of technology in our life.

This aspect has been the source of conceptual confusions concerning the relationship between transhumanism and posthumanism. This confusion was also intensified by the fact that leading proponents of posthumanism, Donna Haraway and N. Katherine Hayles present metaphors of the "cyborg" and the "posthuman", which resemble concepts that can also be found in transhumanism. In her seminal work *A Cyborg Manifesto* (1991), firstly drafted during the mid-1980s, Haraway introduces the cyborg as "a matter of fiction and lived experience that changes what counts as women's experience in the late twentieth century" (Haraway 1991, 149). She employs the metaphor of the cyborg to question persisting binaries in the Western tradition. Our high-tech culture challenges dualisms such as mind/body, animal/human, organism/machine, culture/nature, male/female etc., and "ironically" from our "fusions with animals

8 Wolfe (2010, xii) presents an alternative genealogy and points to the Macy conferences on cybernetics from 1946-1953.

and machines" we can learn "how not to be Man, the embodiment of Western logos" (ibid., 173).

Another landmark posthumanist work is N. Katherine Hayles' *How We Became Posthuman: Virtual Bodies in Cybernetics, Literature, and Informatics* (1999). Hayles makes clear that the posthuman is a construction just like the human is and also that a "biologically unaltered *Homo sapiens* counts as posthuman" (ibid., 4). There again, the "posthuman" does not mean the end of humanity. Instead, it signals…

> "[…] the end of a certain conception of the human, a conception that may have applied, at best, to that fraction of humanity who had the wealth, power, and leisure to conceptualize themselves as autonomous beings exercising their will through individual agency and choice" (Hayles 1999, 286).

For Hayles it is not the question "whether we will become posthuman", because "posthumanity is already here". The question is, "what kind of posthumans we will be" (ibid., 246). While she has sympathies with the deconstruction of the liberal humanist subject in the technological age, she rejects transhumanist "fantasies of unlimited power and disembodied immortality" (ibid., 5), which she identifies with Moravec (1988) in particular. At best we can resist the temptation of post-biological phantasies and "put back into the picture the flesh that continues to be erased in contemporary discussions about cybernetic subjects" (Hayles 1999, 5). At worst we will bring about a culture "inhabited by posthumans who regard their bodies as fashion accessories rather than the ground for their being" (ibid.).

Even though, it is difficult to ascribe a common position to Haraway, Hayles and other posthumanist thinkers, it can be stressed that posthumanists reject the humanist belief that "man is the measure of all things" and that a dualist account of human beings is an appropriate starting point for further academic investigations. According to posthumanists, humanism has lost its credibility and the "crisis in humanism is happening *everywhere*", as Badmington (2000, 9) points out. Posthumanism, however, is not only a critical enterprise, but also entails positive consequences (see Braidotti 2013, 51). There are several emancipatory impulses, and political standpoints, which can clearly be associated with posthumanism, e.g. feminist positions or the attempt to transcend anthropocentric views or speciesism. Still, in most cases, the normative dimension of posthumanism is being stressed in a critical manner rather than in an explicit affirmative one, which is a further central difference from the transhumanist approach that is usually associated with an immediate and explicit normative standpoint.

About this Volume

Freeing human beings is the main objective of transhumanism and posthumanism. Transhumanism aims at liberating humans from their biological limitation. As part of this enterprise transhumanists might partly reinstall humanist concepts. Posthumanism, by contrast, can be identified with a critical approach that hopes to liberate humans from the harmful effects of the established humanist paradigm by debunking its false assumptions. While both traditions celebrate the "end of human beings" and reconsider and reinterpret what it means to be human, this happens on the basis of a different theoretical framework. While in some sense transhumanism can be seen as an *intensification* of humanism (see Wolfe 2010, xv), posthumanism can be analyzed as a criticism of humanism. Yet, both views have in common that they regard the humanist "human" as outdated, be it in physiological or conceptual terms. Hence, transhumanism as well as posthumanism try to move beyond humanism.

The relationship between both approaches, however, is intricate and deserves much further attention. We certainly do not do justice to both, if we weave these currents together, without acknowledging their direction of thrust. At the same time, too often a sharp line between transhumanism and posthumanism is drawn. Proponents of both movements are particularly eager to dissociate themselves from each other. The *Transhumanist FAQ*, for instance, suggests that posthumanism contributes to the "corruption of the original meaning" of the term "posthuman" (Humanity+ n.d.). Posthumanist authors such as Hayles (2011) recently confirmed their rejection of transhumanism and Haraway wishes to distance herself from the "blissed out [...] transhumanist techno-enhancement" (Gane/ Haraway 2006, 140). Cary Wolfe, in his introduction to posthumanism, even argues that his version of "posthumanism is the *opposite* of transhumanism" (Wolfe 2010, xv). Yet, this collection might also reveal that the differences between these two approaches are less significant than the above comments seem to suggest. It might be the case that mutual misunderstandings are related to a difference of style, which is being used in both traditions. Posthumanists employ a more metaphorical, artistic, dialectical and literary style, while transhumanists are much more closely associated with a linear, analytic and pragmatic way of thinking and expressing themselves.

As a matter of fact, far too little attention has been paid, to the connecting moments of both movements. While a remarkable and growing body of work has recently analyzed transhumanism[9] as well as posthumanism[10], no study has

9 See, e.g., Gordijn/ Chadwick (eds.) (2008), Hanssel/ Grassie (eds.) (2011), More/ Vita-More (eds.) (2013), Savulescu/ Bostrom (eds.) (2010), Tirosh-Samuelson/ Mossman (eds.) (2012).

juxtaposed both with regard to common foundations, topics, and sources of influences.[11] This volume seeks to remedy this shortcoming by exploring the connecting and diverging factors of transhumanism and posthumanism and by investigating how both contribute to the reconsideration of human conditions in the technological age.

Confessions

In *Pedigrees* Stefan Lorenz Sorgner provides a general philosophical map of both post- as well as transhumanism. Hereby, he relates the philosophical foundations of these movements to the ones from modernity and postmodernity. The article refers to selected strengths and weaknesses of both approaches and explains in what way they can benefit from each other, which promotes thinking in between (meta) both approaches: metahumanism. Thereby, problems concerning inappropriate ways of self-understanding get revealed, too. By recognizing the challenges related to the various approaches, the philosophical traces of the pedigrees of post- and transhumanism become clearer as well as the potential to benefit from each other due to the fact that both movements have more in common than is often being acknowledged.

In *Religion* Hava Tirosh-Samuelson investigates the role of religious beliefs in post- and transhumanism. After providing an in-depth analysis of different forms of philosophical, cultural, and technological posthumanisms, she turns to the role of religion in these currents. While Derrida affirms a negative theology, a widespread suspicion towards religion has to be noticed according to the author in posthumanist thinking, which is partly due to its Nietzschean roots. While transhumanists regard themselves as a secular movement and in opposition to religious beliefs, too, Tirosh-Samuelson points to the religious roots of transhumanism, in particular in the thinking of Julian Huxley. She argues, that there is actually no conflict between transhumanism and traditional religions. Some religious movements even endorse transhumanist ideas and forms of human enhancement. Furthermore, she argues that transhumanism shares many elements of religious thinking, e.g. eschatological concepts such as the Singularity. According to Tirosh-Samuelson, it might even be beneficial for transhumanists to define themselves as religious.

---

10 See, e.g., Badmington (ed.) (2000), Badmington (2004), Braidotti (2013), Graham (2002), Halberstam/ Livingstone (ed.) (1995), Herbrechter (2013), Nayar (2013), Pepperell (2003), Toffoletti (2007), Wolfe (2010).

11 A recent exception is Sharon (2014), who provides a systematic analysis of different types of discourses on trans- and posthumanism.

It is no surprise that the mythological figure of Prometheus is a recurring motif in transhumanist and posthumanist discourses. The Titan helped in the creation of mankind by bringing them fire and was eventually punished severely by Zeus for his deeds. In *Prometheus* Trijsje Franssen analyses how the ambiguity of this myth manifests itself in contemporary receptions. She stresses that for transhumanists Prometheus is a symbol of progress and expresses the will to evolve and overcome limitations, whereby he does not only manifest the characteristic of becoming better but also expresses the humanist roots of transhumanism. At the same time, this celebration of a Promethean drive to mastery is supposed to be a target of the critics of transhumanism. A different aspect of Prometheus is being received by posthumanists who not only emphasize the hubris associated with Prometheus, but also employ the myth to reject humanism and destruct its believe in anthropocentrism and human dichotomies, as Franssen explains further.

Criticisms of humanism have most prominently been expressed by German philosopher Friedrich Nietzsche. His diagnoses of Western culture as well as his call for human self-overcoming makes him a prominent ancestor for post- and transhumanist reflections, as Yunus Tuncel points out in his article *Nietzsche.* By rejecting humanist ideals such as human rationality, subjectivity, and consciousness, Nietzsche has been a major source of inspiration for the postmodern philosophical tradition (e.g. Deleuze and Foucault) that influences posthumanism as well as contemporary posthumanists (e.g. Hayles). In contrast to this tradition, Tuncel points out that many transhumanists are reluctant to be associated with Nietzsche's ideas, in particular his vision of the overhuman (*Übermensch*) as well as his politics. While Nietzsche defends an anti-liberal politics, transhumanists frequently stress their liberal (sometime libertarian) roots. Nevertheless, Tuncel sees some striking parallels between Nietzsche and transhumanism. Even though Nietzsche would have been critical with transhumanist beliefs in scientific objectivity and techno-progressivism, Tuncel argues that both appreciate a similar Renaissance ideal when it comes to questions of human self-overcoming.

Lands of Cockaygne

In his article *Utopia* Michael Hauskeller deals with utopian dimensions of trans- and posthumanism. He argues that transhumanism in particular has a distinguished utopian outlook and expresses a far-reaching enthusiasm about a technologically enhanced future. Its faith in posthumanity, where our descendants would eventually find never-ending bliss or even salvation, resembles well know motifs from the utopian tradition. In this regard Hauskeller sees transhumanism's roots in Renaissance humanism, above all, in Pico's idea that humans have no fixed nature but the unique capacity to shape themselves and realize a Godlike potential. By contrast posthumanism, while rejecting techno-utopianism, still welcomes the incorporation of technologies in our everyday life, he stresses, as technologies help undermine structures of domination. Thus technology may support the posthumanist liberationist visions of a redistribution of power, which in itself is an idea that has utopian traits as Hauskeller argues.

Among the most prominent dystopias in technological discourses is that of *Brave New World.* This motif is based on Aldous Huxley's novel with the same title, which Curtis D. Carbonell interprets in his article with regard to post- and transhumanism. It is no surprise that the infamous "brave-new-world"-argument is a common reference for critics of transhumanism, who see the novel as a prediction for the future of mankind. Transhumanists, by contrast, stress a different reading of the novel, according to which Huxley's work is rather a warning-sign than a depiction of a transhuman future. Carbonell, while having little sympathy for the missuse of *Brave New World* by "bioluddites", presents an interpretion of the novel as a transhumanist critique. For him, the novel does not only illustrate the dangers of biotechnologies but also admits the need for advances by a humanistic use of science and technology. Concerning posthumanist discourses, it has to be noted that *Brave New World* did not get much attention so far. Carbonell, however, shows that in particular in Adorno we find an interpretation according to which the novel presents the dehumanizing processes of Americanization. Carbonell stresses that this reading reveals post- and antihumanist elements in *Brave New World.*

Many transhumanists see aging as a disease and have the goal to promote a health span extension, which lies at the top of their list of priorities. Sascha Dickel and Andreas Frewer discuss this topic in the chapter *Life Extension.* By considering different suggested methods of life extension they portrait this debate as yet another instance of a familiar utopianism, updated with a particular technological emphasis. According to the authors, discourses on technological life extension or even immortality are characterized by science fiction fantasies and belief in fringe science. Nevertheless, these debates are vigorous, because here central characteristics of modernity, such as individuality, never-ending improvement, and progress are exaggerated. These promises of modernity are responsible for the attraction of transhumanism, too, as Dickel and Frewer argue. By contrast, the cultural framework of modernity has been critically examined by posthumanism. By incorporating posthumanist's perspectives, both authors point towards a "speculative posthumanism", which draws some transhumanist visions of life extension into question.

Neo-Socratic Reflections

In the article *Politics*, James Hughes investigates in social and political dimensions of the debates and shows transhumanists' commitment to individual liberty, together with their agreement on techno-optimism and a non-anthropocentric personhood. Apart from these common thoughts in transhumanism, based on a number of surveys that Hughes conduced, he shows the plurality of political views in the transhumanist movement. His remarks also make clear that contemporary transhumanism is mainly split into two camps: libertarians and left-leaning transhumanists. This plurality of positions becomes even clearer considering the great variety of posthumanist thinkers, to which Hughes ascribes a political diffidence. Still some posthumanists are seen as united in their rejection of transhumanists' position on the question of moral status and citizenship as reproducing humanist prejudices concerning human superiority. Hughes concludes that in particular in the current transition to a post-gender society transhumanists and posthumanists can benefit from each other.

General questions of norms and values in post- and transhumanism are being discussed by Robert Ranisch in the chapter *Morality*. By identifying ten elements of transhumanist morality, he points to a particular tension between their commitment to morphological and reproductive freedom on the one hand, and the transhumanist ideal of human perfection on the other hand. According to the author, it is necessary to dissolve this tension in order not to legitimize authoritarian politics or eugenics. By discussing transhumanist ideas of enhancing morality and the moral status of persons, political and moral questions of these attempts are being analyzed. The possibility of a superior moral and legal status of enhanced persons, i.e. post-persons, is being considered as a specific practical and theoretical challenge for transhumanists. Ranisch argues that posthumanist's criticism of human exceptionalism, which he sees as central to the humanistic framework of transhumanism, could contribute to resolve this issue. For the time being, however, he holds that most posthumanist authors have failed to bring forward a distinguished normative agenda that could help solving moral questions concerning the use of new technologies.

Ontologies of Becoming

Enlightenment humanism is characterized by a dualistic ontology, which is still influential in contemporary Western thinking and perpetuated in social and legal definitions of the "human". In the chapter *Ontology* Thomas D. Philbeck deals with transhumanist and posthumanist attitudes towards these dominating dualisms as well as their own (implicit) ontological frameworks. While both movements consider the techno-human integration and human dependence on technology, their ontologies are quite different. According to the author, transhumanism embraces a humanist metaphysics and the Enlightenment belief in rational progress. Transhumanist dualism becomes apparent when prominent visions such as mind uploading are being taken into consideration, i.e. the separation of the mind from the body, which, for Philbeck, reaffirms the dualistic ontological framework of humanism. By contrast, posthumanism actively tries to overcome the predominant dualistic paradigm and seeks for a new ontological framework. Nevertheless, Philbeck regards both movements as unsatisfactory with regard to their ontological reflections. In this context, it must be noted that the author refers to a posthumanist understanding of the posthuman, which differs from the use of the concept in the rest of the collection.

Ontological questions are also analyzed by Martin G. Weiss in the chapter *Nature*. By discussing Heidegger and Agamben, two authors whom he sees as particularly influential for contemporary posthumanist philosophies, Weiss presents their critique of traditional definitions of human nature. After analyzing how both philosophers scrutinize traditional anthropologies and beliefs concerning the essence of human nature, Weiss exposes how transhumanist authors challenge the biological side of human nature. Manipulation and enhancement of human nature, which so far has been deemed to be unchangeable, are seen as liberation and emancipation from our current biological constraints. In this regard Weiss sees transhumanism as confirming the humanist paradigms, which sees self-perfection as an essential characteristic of human nature. This view has been attacked by bioconservatives, who regard our common nature as the basis for human dignity, rights and equality. Since manipulation of human nature threatens our nature, from a bioconservatives perspective, human enhancement technologies need to be banned.

A rigid distinction between post- and transhumanism is being revealed in the chapter *Evolution* by Steve Fuller. He presents Peter Singer as representative of posthumanist thinking on the topic of evolution, and Ray Kurzweil as transhumanist protagonist. Fuller analyzes both of their responses to four central questions: 1. What is their attitude towards humanism? 2. What is the source of conflict between science and religion? 3. What is the meaning of human beings in the process of evolution? 4. Is there a normatively desirable intentional relationship between a successor species and their ancestors? Fuller reveals that post- and transhumanists put forward radically different answers to all of these four questions. He himself is in broad agreement with transhumanist perspectives, but not with posthumanist ones.

In the chapter *The Body* Francesca Ferrando focuses on the shifting ontological and epistemological perceptions of the "human" as an embodied being in the technological age. She reflects on the construction of the "human" by drawing on historical instances of the recognition and denial of human status, e.g., she exposes how the concept of the "human" has been formed by the construction of the "Other" in Nazi Germany. In the Western tradition the "human" as well as the human body has been unequivocally white and male, she argues. Posthumanism provides a radical deconstruction of the "human", and considers alternative forms of embodiment. This includes the human extension into the digital realm as well as a fusion with technologies. Transhumanism is interested in these alternative forms of embodiment, too. According to Ferrando, however, transhumanists lack a critical reflection on historical configurations of the human body and see it as a mere "outfit". Consequently, transhumanism is supposed to be more interested in the radical change of this outfit in accordance to individual desire rather than understanding the embodied (post)human as situated in the world and as a result of social-political interactions.

Paragone of the Arts

The fairly new artistic field of *Bioart* is being dealt in an article with the same title by Andy Miah. He both presents works of leading protagonists in the field like Stelarc, Kac, Damien Hirst or Bill Viola as well as tackles highly challenging issues such as a definition of the term bioart, reasons for rejecting the term and various ways of how works of bioart can be interpreted both from a trans- as well as an posthumanist perspective. Kac's fluorescent bunny represents a particularly helpful case, at which both trans- as well as posthumanists elements of bioart can be explained, from Miah's perspective, because it disrupts biological boundaries but at the same time locates the potential of genetic alteration technologies in a social context.

A related concept to that of bioart is the one of *New Media Art*. In an article entitled such, Evi Sampanikou, is concerned both with the genealogy of new media arts as well as with some current trends and their relationship to the various beyond humanism movements. By drawing upon historical developments, she describes the heritage of conceptual art within posthumanist works, whereby she focuses on the works of Beuys, Nam June Paik, Bill Viola and Shirin Neshat and William Kentridge. In this context, she also analyses the relevance of philosophical and theoretical reflections for the shifts which had taken place. Concerning transhumanist works, Stelarc, Orlan, Patricia Piccinini and Eduardo Kac are being recognized in particular.

In the chapter *Literature* Marcus Rockoff analyzes how themes of post- and transhumanist thinking can be found in literature. By focusing on transhumanism, he shows which traces of this paradigm can be found in selected pieces of works. For this sake the author distinguishes three classes of references in literature: 1. References to technologies that are central for the transhumanist project (e.g. Gibson's *Neuromancer*). 2. References to transhumanist motifs and themes (e.g. Shelley's *Frankenstein*). 3. Explicit references to the transhumanist movement (e.g. Brown's *Inferno*). While transhumanists as well as its critics frequently try to find support for their positions in works of literature, Rockoff expresses doubt whether this attempt could be successful. He rather stresses the plurality of plausible interpretations, which could support even contradicting theories. The author finally reveals the importance of different interpretations, whereby depending on the reading, a work could also be seen as portraying both transhumanist and posthumanist insights (e.g. Houellebecq's *The Elementary Particles*).

The genre of *Science Fiction Literature* is being considered by Domna Pastourmatzi. It is most probably the oldest genre in which post- and transhumanist issues have been described, interpreted and developed. A hermeneutic analysis of theoretical (from Haraway and Hayles to Dvorsky and Young) and practical (from the use of science fiction to the trans- and the posthuman condition in science fiction) issues of this topic provides the outline of her detailed insights concerning specific issues. Her description of some recent historical developments in the genre (in particular the previous 40 years) permanently recognizes the relevance of intellectual reflections from various traditions. Continental thinkers with posthumanist associations (Jean Baudrillard, Gilles Deleuze, Rosi Braidotti) are being referred to in the same way as thinkers who in some way are being linked to transhumanist thinking (Aubrey de Grey, John Harris).

Well known to a wider audience are post- and transhumanist issues in the *Movies*. Dònal P. O'Mathùna, is concerned with prominent beyond humanist themes in this artistic domain. The topics of understandings of technologies (*Star Trek*), anthropocentrism (*Blade Runner Bicentennial Man, I, Robot*), problems related to technologies (*Metropolis*), controlling evolution (*Dr. Jeckel and Mr. Hyde, I am Legend, 2001: A Space Odyssee, Avatar*), injustice (*The Time Machine, Brave New World, Gattaca*) and embodiment (*Surrogates, Vanilla Sky*) are focused on in particular such that the reader becomes familiar with some of the most central beyond humanism themes. The article makes clear that even though the amount of movies with both post- as well as transhumanist themes is enormous, it is quite challenging to identify specific movies as post- or transhumanist ones.

In contrast to the movies, the field of *Music* is rarely being considered when post- and transhumanist issues are being analyzed, even though these themes are of central relevance for many musically relevant perspectives, as Stefan Lorenz Sorgner shows. Thereby, he explains how such issues turn up in musical and operatic works (e.g. by Michael Nyman, Philip Glass, Richard Wagner or Sven

Helbig), how technologies are being used for compositional purposes (e.g. *The Eyeborg* by Neil Harbisson), how traditional boundaries between composing, and performing get blurred (e.g. Jaime del Val), and why and in what way emerging technologies get used within musical pieces (e.g. Kraftwerk or Björk). In all the various cases the ontological and ethical challenges at issue get tackled.

Bibliography

Agar, N. (2010): Humanity's End: Why We Should Reject Radical Enhancement. Cambridge(MA) et al.: MIT Press.

Badmington, N. (ed.) (2000): Posthumanism. New York: Palgrave.

Badmington, N. (2004): Alien Chic: Posthumanism and the Other Within. London et al.: Routledge.

Bashford, A. (2013): Julian Huxley's Transhumanism. In: Turda, M. (ed.): Crafting Humans: From Genesis to Eugenics and Beyond. Göttingen et al.: V&R Unipress & National Taiwan University Press, 153-67.

Bostrom, N. (2005): A History of Transhumanist Thought. In: Journal of Evolution and Technology 14(1), 1-25

Braidotti, R. (2013): The Posthuman. Cambridge: Polity Press.

Capurro, R. (2012): Beyond Humanisms. In: Journal of New Frontiers in Spatial Concepts 4, 1-12. http://ejournal.uvka.de/spatialconcepts/archives/1362 (accessed May 26, 2014).

Davies, T. (2008): Humanism. London et al.: Routledge.

Drexler, K.E. (1986): Engines of Creation: The Coming Era of Nanotechnology. New York et al.: Anchor Books.

Esfandiary, F.M. (1974): Transhumans-2000. In: Tripp, M. (ed.): Woman in the Year 2000. New York: Arbor House, 291-298.

Ettinger, R.C.W. (1972): Man into Superman. New York: St. Martin's Press.

FM-2030 (1989): Are You Transhuman? Monitoring and Stimulating Your Personal Rate of Growth In a Rapidly Changing World. New York: Warner Books.

Foucault, M. (2002 [1966]) The Order of Things: An Archaeology of the Human Science. London et al.: Routledge.

Gane, N./ Haraway, D. (2006): When We Have Never Been Human, What Is to Be Done? Interview with Donna Haraway. In: Theory, Culture & Society 23(7-8), 135-158.

Gordijn, B./ Chadwick, R. (eds.) (2008): Medical Enhancement and Posthumanity. New York: Springer.

Graham, E.L. (2002): Representations of the Post/Human. New Brunswick: Rutgers University Press.

Halberstam, J./ Livingston, I. (eds.) (1995): Posthuman Bodies. Bloomington et al: Indiana University Press.

Hansell, G.R./ Grassie, W. (eds.) (2011): H±: Transhumanism and Its Critics. Philadelphia: Metanexus Institute.

Haraway, D. (1991): A Cyborg Manifesto: Science, Technology, and Socialist-Feminism in the Late Twentieth Century. In: Haraway, D.: Simians, Cyborgs, and Women: The Reinvention of Nature. New York: Routledge, 149-181.

Harris, J. (2007): Enhancing Evolution: The Ethical Case for Making Better People. Princeton et al.: Princeton University Press.

Hassan, I. (1977): Prometheus as Performer: Towards a Posthumanist Culture? In: The Georgia Review 31(4), 830-850.

Hayles, N.K. (1999): How We Became Posthuman: Virtual Bodies in Cybernetics, Literature, and Informatics. Chicago et al.: The University of Chicago Press.

Hayles, N.K. (2011): Wrestling with Transhumanism. In: Hansell, G.R./ Grassie, W. (eds.): H±: Transhumanism and Its Critics. Philadelphia: Metanexus Institute, 215-226.

Herbrechter, S. (2013): Posthumanism: A Critical Analysis. London et al.: Bloomsbury.

Hughes, J. (2004): Citizen Cyborg: Why Democratic Societies Must Respond to the Redesigned Human of the Future. Boulder: Westview Press.

Hughes, J. (2010): Contradictions from the Enlightenment Roots of Transhumanism. In: Journal of Medicine and Philosophy 35(6), 622-640.

Humanity+ (n.d.): Transhumanist FAQ: 3.0. http://humanityplus.org/philosophy/transhumanist-faq/ (accessed December 3, 2013).

Huxley, J. (1957): Transhumanism. In: Huxley, J: New Bottles for New Wine. London: Chatto & Windus, 13-17.

Krüger, O. (2004): Virtualität und Unsterblichkeit: Die Vision des Posthumanismus. Freiburg im Breisgau: Rombach.

Kurzweil, R. (1990): The Age of Intelligent Machines. Cambridge(MA): MIT Press.

Miah, A. (2008): A Critical History of Posthumanism. In: Gordijn, B./ Chadwick, R. (Eds.): Medical Enhancement and Posthumanity. New York: Springer, 71-94.

Minsky, M. (1986): The Society of Mind. New York: Simon & Schuster.

Moravec, H. (1988): Mind Children: The Future of Robot and Human Intelligence. Cambridge(MA): Harvard University Press.

More, M. (2013): The Philosophy of Transhumanism. In: More, M./ Vita-More, N. (eds.): The Transhumanist Reader: Classical and Contemporary Essays on the Science, Technology, and Philosophy of the Human Future. Chichester: Wiley-Blackwell, 1-17

More, M./ Vita-More, N. (eds.) (2013): The Transhumanist Reader: Classical and Contemporary Essays on the Science, Technology, and Philosophy of the Human Future. Chichester: Wiley-Blackwell.

Nayar, P.K. (2013) Posthumanism. Cambridge et al.: Polity Press.

Passmore, J. (2000): The Perfectibility of Man. Indianapolis: Liberty Fund.

Paul, D. (2005): Genetic Engineering and Eugenics: The Uses of History. In: Bailie, H.W./ Casey, T.K. (eds.): Is Human Nature Obsolete? Genetics, Bioengineering, and the Future of the Human Condition. Cambridge(MA) et al.: MIT Press, 123-151.

Pepperell, R. (2003): The Posthuman Condition: Consciousness Beyond the Brain. Bristol et al.: Intellect Books.

Roco, M.C./ Bainbridge, W.S. (eds.) (2003): Converging Technologies for Improving Human Performance: Nanotechnology, Biotechnology, Information Technology and Cognitive Science. Dordrecht: Kluver Academic Publishers.

Savulescu J./ Bostrom N. (eds.): Human Enhancement. Oxford: Oxford University Press.

Seubold, G. (2001): Die Freiheit vom Menschen: Die philosophische Humanismusdebatte der Nachkriegszeit. Alfter et al.: DenkMal Verlag.

Sharon, T. (2014): Human Nature in an Age of Biotechnology. The Case for Mediacted Posthumanism. Dordrecht et al.: Springer.

Soper, K. (1986): Humanism and Anti-Humanism. London et al.: Hutchinson.

Teilhard de Chardin, P. (1964 [1949]): The Essence of the Democratic Idea: A Biological Approach. In: Teilhard de Chardin, P. (1964): The Future of Man. London: Collins, 238-243.

Tirosh-Samuelson, H. (2011): Engaging Transhumanism. In: Hansell, G.R./ Grassie, W. (eds.): H±: Transhumanism and Its Critics. Philadelphia: Metanexus Institute, 19-52.

Tirosh-Samuelson, H. (2012): Science and the Betterment of Humanity: Three British Prophets of Transhumanism. In: Tirosh-Samuelson, H./ Mossman, K.L. (eds.) (2012): Building Better Humans? Refocusing the Debate on Transhumanism. Frankfurt a. M. et al.: Peter Lang, 55-82.

Tirosh-Samuelson, H./ Mossman, K.L. (eds.) (2012): Building Better Humans? Refocusing the Debate on Transhumanism. Frankfurt a. M. et al.: Peter Lang

Toffoletti, K. (2007): Cyborgs and Barbie Dolls: Feminism, Popular Culture and the Posthuman Body. London et al.: I.B.Tauris

Wiesing, U. (2008): The History of Medical Enhancement: From *Restitutio ad Integrum* to *Transformatio ad Optimum?* In: Gordijn, B./ Chadwick, R. (eds.): Medical Enhancement and Posthumanity. New York: Springer, 9-24.

Wolfe, C. (2010): What is Posthumanism? Minneapolis et al.: University of Minnesota Press.

Pedigrees

Stefan Lorenz Sorgner

There is a great variety of thinkers, movements and cultural and scientific issues which are being associated with the "beyond humanism" debates. Not all concepts have a clear, concise and unified meaning yet. The posthuman of the transhumanist debates is different from the posthuman of the posthumanist discourses. The relationship between post-, trans- and metahumanism is unclear, too. Some regard posthumanism as a more generic term, under which transhumanism can be subsumed; others hold that these concepts refer to two separate social and cultural movements which have radically different goals, origins and genealogies. In this article, I am attempting to provide some initial guidelines concerning pedigrees of various ways of transcending humanism. The notion "pedigree" captures central motifs of the debates, because it does not only refer to ancestry, origin and family tree, but it is also widely employed in the discipline of zoology, in particular with respect to the line of descent, the genealogical record and the background. By employing this notion in the field of posthuman or in other words beyond humanism discourses, the central element of these discourses gets highlighted: human beings are no longer seen as coronation or categorically separate entity with respect to other natural beings, but are seen as merely gradually different from other natural beings; hence, in comparison to Christian and Kantian types of humanism, the various beyond humanist approaches plead for a new modesty, because we no longer see us as infinitely superior to all other natural beings.

Humanism is another concept with an enormous multiplicity of meanings. There is an ancient humanism, a Renaissance humanism, a Christian humanism, a Kantian humanism, but also a secular humanism. When, humanism is mentioned in the context of the beyond humanism debates, I take it that a specific version of humanism is referred to, namely a version which affirms a dualist ontology of the world. Even though, this assumption is appropriate for the majority of thinkers who attempt to move beyond humanism, it is not valid for all of them, e.g. there are Mormon transhumanist's who, most probably, believe in a metaphysical world, e.g. a transcendent world which is categorically separate from our sensual world concerning ontological qualities. However, my attempt to provide a general map of the debates includes the need to overgeneralize. Thereby, relationships and tendencies can be hinted at which otherwise would remain hidden.

Transhumanism

The great majority of transhumanists have a this-worldly, materialist, naturalist, relationalist or immanent understanding of the world (see Hughes 2014). The theory of evolution plays a central role in their understanding of human beings. They take evolution seriously and plausibly infer that it is highly likely that what has come into existence will develop further eventually. In addition, they take the possibilities of techniques seriously, too. Their anthropology can also serve as a basis for a general definition of what transhumanism stands for. *Transhumanism affirms the use of techniques to increase the likelihood of bringing about the posthuman.* It is this judgment which is most characteristic of transhumanists. However, transhumanist traditions differ with respect to their understanding of the posthuman or the most promising enhancement techniques. The posthuman can represent a new species which lies beyond the human species. In that case, the transhuman is another central concept, as it stands for a member of the human species who is in the process of becoming posthuman (see Bostrom 2005, 11). However, it is also possible that the posthuman represents a member of the human species who, however, has at least one quality that goes beyond the ones which current human beings can possess (see Bostrom 2009, 107-136). A further option is that the posthuman is not a biological entity, but exists in digital cyberspace (see More 2013, 7). In this case, the cyborg might be the most likely way of realizing a posthuman, as cybernetic organisms belong both to the organic as well as to the digital or mechanical realm of technology, which makes them a well suited intermediate entity between us today and a digital posthuman self. It is also an open question as to which techniques are most promising for bringing about the posthuman. The following enhancement procedures can be seen as central within various debates on this range of topics: 1. Genetic Enhancement (by selection or by modification); 2. Morphological Enhancement (e.g. plastic surgery); 3. Pharmacological Enhancement (e.g. Ritalin, Modafinil); 4. Cyborg Enhancement (e.g. deep brain stimulation; companies might already be working on a "brainstation" or an "I-brain"). Furthermore, it is also an open question which qualities are seen as most important for belonging to posthumanity. Some options are: 1. Super intelligence; 2. Strong memory; 3. Long health span; 4. A strong physiology due to strength, beauty or health; 5. Morality.

Given the various ways of conceptualizing the "posthuman" within transhumanism, it is important to distinguish two main strands of transhumanism concerning technologies of increasing the probability of bringing about the posthuman. In this context, it also needs to be pointed out that transhumanists do not solely rely on new technologies for realizing their goals. The emerging technologies are supposed to support and supplement the technologies we already have. Pharmaceutical products might be helpful for bringing about a specific state of consciousness. However, this does not mean that transhumanists reject traditional meditation techniques. In contrast, it can be the case that new techniques can support, supplement and enhance the effectiveness of traditional techniques. Hence, both options can be useful. Genetic enhancement by means of modification might be an important technique for increasing the likelihood of the coming about of the posthuman, but this does not mean that education is irrelevant. Both can be means for altering the genetic makeup of human beings (see Sorgner 2013a, 85-100). By means of these reflections, the first central line of human development towards the posthuman becomes clear. By means of genetic alterations a development towards the posthuman can occur, such that the posthuman either is a member of a new species or has at least one quality which goes beyond the ones held by current human beings. This does not mean that the posthuman is radically different from currently living human beings, but it can imply an understanding of the posthuman similar to the one upheld by posthumanists, and I will clarify their use of the term next. Hence, this understanding of human development can imply that the use of emerging technologies for promoting the alteration of human beings is not categorically different from the use of already known technologies. Human beings merely continue doing what they have always done, namely they have invented and used techniques for making their lives better or easier. Given this understanding, transhumanism is merely a particular affirmation of the use of technologies for promoting the alteration of human beings. However, in this case, transhumanism does not imply a radical break from traditional human habits. Transhumanism in this sense might merely be seen as a particular amplification of the use of techniques for goals which have been relevant in most cultures. However, there is also a second strong movement which belongs to transhumanism, namely the one which particularly stresses the posthuman as a cyberspace entity. In contrast to carbon-based transhumanism, silicon-based transhumanism particularly focuses on the technology of downloading ones personality to a computer, such that it can be multiplied, be reintegrated into a new organism or continue living in cyberspace. This procedure is being referred to as mind uploading or whole brain emulation. In contrast to carbon-based transhumanism, silicon-based transhumanism seems to start from a different anthropology. On the one hand, it seems to start from a naturalist anthropology, as it is assumed that by having a detailed brain scan a software model can be developed which can then be run again on a different hardware. On the other hand, this model seems to presuppose a dualist understanding of human beings, which separates the mind from the body such that the mind can be easily detached from the body. If both observations are correct, it can be questioned whether there is a non-self-contradictory way of formulating the related issues. I am not excluding the option that this is possible. Given that a functionalist philosophy of mind represents an appropriate description of the phenomena in question, it might be possible to consistently uphold a this-worldly anthropology and the option of "uploading" a mind (see More 2013, 7). It is a fascinating area of research, but more work is needed to clarify the central issues in question.[1] In any case, carbon-based transhumanism and its understanding of the posthuman seems more consistent concerning this issue and close to posthumanism in many respects, too.

Posthumanism

The concept of the posthuman also plays a central role in posthumanism. Yet, there is a conflict between the posthumanist and the transhumanist notion of a "posthuman". If the transhumanist's notion "posthuman" implies the membership in a new species, then the concept of the "posthuman", with which posthumanist's are being concerned, is different, as the notion of the posthuman in this case represents the attempt to put forward a new understanding of human beings whereby posthumanists have a special methodology and continental philosophical way of thinking for formulating this new anthropology (see Braidotti 2013; Hayles 1999). It is this specific aspect which provides the basis for formulating a basic definition of posthumanism: *Posthumanism represents the attempt to get rid of categorical dualities within any type of judgment, as it is being regarded as most plausible that thereby the complexity of the world is grasped best within propositional form.* This basic attitude has many implications. Concerning the notion of the posthuman it leads to the necessity to get rid of an anthropology which categorizes human beings as consisting of an immaterial soul and a material body. Consequently, posthumanists are putting forward a non-dualist account of human beings. As the concept of the human being in humanism implies the concept of the material body and the immaterial soul or mind, they suggest to refer to this new understanding of human beings as a posthuman one. Obviously, the attempt to transcend categorical dualities goes far beyond this specific point and touches the relationship between human beings and animals, that between human beings and digital and mechanical machines or that between men and women. However, the attempt to transcend categorical dualities represents only one aspect of posthumanism.

1 The political aspect of transhumanism is a central and much discussed one, but one which I am not tackling within this article on the traces of the beyond humanism discourses. An excellent survey of this topic can be found in the monograph *Citizen Cyborg* by James Hughes from 2004.

When it is said that posthumanism attempts to get rid of a dualist version of anthropology, which implies a material body and an immaterial soul, it implies that human beings "have always been posthuman" (Hayles 1999, 291). Given this understanding of the posthuman, it would not make any sense to ask for a period of time during which there has been a phylogenetic development from the human towards the posthuman. To have always been posthuman implies that human beings are part of gradual evolutionary processes which lead from common ancestors with today's living great apes towards the human who is living today. As posthumans, we have always been dependent on technologies and there is no clear cut categorical distinction between nature and culture, genetic and environmental influences or nature and technology. The posthumanist attempt to get rid of a dualist anthropology assumes that it is plausible that we understand ourselves as non-dualist entities. However, this has not been the case during the Enlightenment. Then, it was widely acknowledged that human beings possess a material body and an immaterial soul with Descartes and Kant being the leading philosophical representatives of such a self-understanding. To grasp ourselves as posthumans does not imply a phylogenetic development from the human towards the posthuman, but it does imply that concerning our own self-understanding we have become posthumans – a cultural move has taken place, as we used to understand ourselves as being constituted out of a material and an immaterial part, which is no longer valid today. During the Enlightenment, we understood ourselves as having a material body and an immaterial soul, but now we understand ourselves as non-dualist entities. This alteration concerning one's self-understanding has significant implications, in particular concerning many ethical and legal issues (see Sorgner 2013b; Sorgner 2010)

Another important posthumanist topic is the posthumanist conception of truth, as that what is being aimed for is not a truth concerning human beings in the sense of the correspondence theory of truth. As genealogically posthumanists are immediately connected to postmodern thinkers what posthumanists aim for is mere plausibility (see Sorgner 2013b, 135-144). Hence, it is being assumed that each judgment is an interpretation whereby an interpretation does not imply that it has to be false. All they are claiming is that each judgment can be false. As no theory has revealed itself as the only true one so far, however, we are not in a position yet, to distinguish between a true and a false interpretation, and it might be the case that we will never be in such a position. As long as no theory has revealed itself as the true one, the postmodernist's perspectivism is being seen as the most plausible epistemology, even though it cannot provide us with any knowledge in correspondence of the world. This does not mean that it is impossible to distinguish between plausible and implausible judgments. On the basis of contemporarily dominant paradigms, which change on the basis of the spirit of the times, foundations for distinguishing plausible from implausible judgments are given.

In Between Post- and Transhumanism: Metahumanism

From the short descriptions of post- and transhumanism it becomes clear already that both start from an anthropology which goes beyond a traditional humanist one, namely beyond one which relies on human beings as constituted of material and immaterial aspects. Hence, this issue is of central relevance for both movements and it is what both of them have in common. Nevertheless, a certain hostility between members of both movements is widespread and has to be acknowledged. The most important reasons for this hostility is connected to the following differences: 1. The use of language, style and methodology is radically different in both movements. Transhumanists use a linear way of thinking, employ technical words, and have a scientific methodology. Posthumanists, on the other hand, have a non-linear way of thinking, employ metaphorical words, and have a hermeneutic methodology. 2. The origin and genealogy of both movements is radically different. Transhumanists are embedded in the English language tradition which is closely related to Darwin's theory of evolution and Mill's utilitarianism. The intellectual founder of transhumanism, Julian Huxley, is a prime example for this insight. Posthumanists, on the other hand, are most closely related to the continental philosophical tradition, and thereby also literary theory and cultural studies, and a narrative and radically pluralistic approach to ethical issues.

However, the above reflections concerning the anthropologies show that both movements have more in common than they wish to acknowledge. Recently, an approach was established which is entitled metahumanism, which affirms weak versions of both trans- and posthumanism, and which attempts to bring these two discourses closer together, but at the same time represents an alternative to these approaches (see del Val/ Sorgner 2011, 1-4). It is entitled metahumanism because it lies beyond a dualist concept of humanism (*meta* can mean "beyond"), but also in between the movements of post- and transhumanism (*meta* can also mean "in between"). One of the suggestions of metahumanism was to introduce the notion of the metahuman as a way of referring to a this-worldly, non-dualist concept of the human to avoid the mix up with the term posthuman of transhumanists. In this way, the concepts of the trans- and the posthuman can be employed in the transhumanist sense, as a this-worldly approach implies the likelihood that human beings will eventually develop further into another species.

Without, going into too much detail concerning the historical developments of the various movements, as this has been done already by various scholars (see Pastourmatzi 2014; Tirosh-Samuelson 2014; Sorgner/ Grimm 2013), it is my goal here to provide a general map of the various movements beyond humanism. Consequently, I will put forward some general outlines concerning the relationship of these two movements to notions such as enlightenment, modernity, and postmodernity.

Modernity and Postmodernity

It is still a matter of debate which time period has been dominated by the humanist tradition. By clarifying the notion of humanism, the meanings of the various beyond humanism movements also get clarified further. Ihab Hassan pointed out the following in 1977: "We need to understand that five hundred years of humanism may be coming to an end" (1977, 843). According to Sloterdijk, humanism has dominated Western cultures since Stoic time (see Sloterdijk 2009, 13). Due to many dualist aspects which can be found in Stoic philosophy, it is clear that humanism has at least been dominant in Western cultures since Stoic times (see Sorgner 2010, 38-40). I disagree with Sloterdijk because there are several reasons for claiming that from Plato onwards humanism has been the leading cultural force in Western countries, e.g. the myth of Er from book 10 of Plato's *Republic* reveals strong dualist implications of Plato's philosophy. The three suggestions concerning the birth of humanism have significant philosophical implications, as there are various concepts of dualisms associated with these three types of humanism.

Hassan's concept of humanism: Given that the birth of humanism takes place with Descartes' philosophy, the dualism in question implies that human beings have an immaterial soul and a material body. Animals, plants and rocks, however, fall into the same category of belonging solely to the material world.

Sloterdijk's concept of humanism: Given that the birth of humanism is connected to the coming about of Stoic philosophies, the dualism affirmed by this movement is a different one, because animals are seen as in possession of a type of soul. However, the animal soul is different from the human soul in so far as only human beings, incl. slaves and women, have a rational soul. The rational soul enables human beings to speak and think. Animals according to Stoic philosophies do not possess these capacities.

Sorgner's concept of humanism: Even though, elements of dualist thinking can already be traced to Zoroastrianism, as this religion has already introduced a rigid reparation between good and devil, the central step towards the creation of humanism has taken place with the myth of Er in Plato's *Republic*. A significant difference between Plato's humanism and the humanism of Stoic philosopher's is that Stoic philosophers uphold that all human beings deserve equal consideration up to a certain degree due to their being rational whereas according to Plato's philosophy not all human beings are equally capable of using the rational part of their soul, as your capacities depend upon the type of soul you have – it can be either a golden, a silver or an iron soul. A further significant trace within the development of humanism is to be found in the birth of Ancient drama. There are several reasons why dualist thinking is represented well during the development of drama. Prior to the invention of drama, there was no distinction between actors and audience. Everyone was part of a Dionysian crowd. All participants were both performers as well as spectators and there was no structured location (the theatre) which separated one group from the other. Hence, with the birth process of the theatre, dualisms were introduced on various levels. Firstly, there was the duality between the Dionysian chorus and the protagonist or the protagonists. Secondly, there was the duality between the (male) actors (chorus plus protagonists) and the spectators. Thirdly, there was the locational, spatial separation of the actors from the audience by means of the theatre design. However, this short summary of some central elements which came along with the birth of Ancient drama are merely supposed to provide some initial hints concerning the question of duality and the arts. By structurally comparing a metaformance of Jaime del Val (see cover) with a performance of an Ancient Greek play, the relevance of dualist or non-dualist thinking for performing arts becomes even more explicit. By referring to the birth of Ancient drama and elements of Plato's philosophy, I was merely providing some reasons for the position that the birth of humanism has already taken place during Plato's lifetime.

No matter whether, Hassan, Sloterdijk or Sorgner is correct concerning the birth of humanism, many contemporary scholars and thinkers agree "that the crisis in humanism is happening everywhere" (Badmington 2000, 9), as Badmington correctly pointed out. Hence, the notions we have been referring to above, not only stand for cultural movements and a way of thinking, but also for a description of a time period, namely the time period which comes after humanism. In contrast to modernity and postmodernity, humanism has not been used frequently to refer to a certain time period. A more common kind of usage has been the one which relates humanism to a certain attitude and a kind of thinking about the world. In order to strengthen and clarify this usage of the concept humanism, it will be related to more common ways of referring to certain cultural periods like modernity or postmodernity. Thereby, I will be drawing on distinctions which have been suggested by Odo Marquard (see Marquard 1995, 92-

107), as his use of the concepts represents well a widespread, but not very plausible use of the notions in question.

According to him, today we are still living in modernity which is related to an affirmative way of thinking about progress (see Marquard 2000, 50) and which is still occurring (see Marquard 1989, 7). Modernity can by replaced by one of the following three kinds of thinking from his perspective: 1. A promodern variant of philosophy of history. Thinkers who uphold this approach often talk about the dark middle ages which are being substituted by modern times which are dominated by an affirmative view of progress. Marquard refers to Hegel as someone who represents this type of approach; 2. A "preteral" antimodern variant of the philosophy of history represents another option. It is characterized by the premise that a premodern epoch is regarded as cultural ideal whereas progress is seen as a decline. Novalis with respect to the middle ages, Winckelmann with respect to Ancient times and Rousseau with respect to a precultural nature are proponents of this approach. 3. Finally, there is the "futural" anti-modern approach to the philosophy of history (see Marquard 1995, 95-97). Again, enlightenment is interpreted as a decline, but in this case, a perfect future is expected. Marx proposed a specific version of this kind of approach. His ideal future society represents a classless society which is supposed to lie ahead of us as the goal of further developments.

Marquard's way of conceptualizing history is helpful, but does not seem comprehensive from my point of view. I do not think that either trans- or posthumanism fits into Marquard's suggested scheme. The same applies to postmodernism, and posthumanism is an outgrowth of postmodernism.

Postmodernists like Derrida, Foucault or Lyotard are neither pro-modern nor do they understand the enlightenment period as one of decline or put forward a goal which needs to be reached in the future. They do not even uphold the necessity of continuing the Enlightenment tradition of critiques. Concerning the developmental aspect, a certain kind of indifference can be analyzed in many of their philosophies. This is one reason for doubting that modernity can be reduced to an affirmative attitude towards progress, which had been suggested by Marquard. In the following passage, I will present a more complex way of thinking about modernity, such that the various ways of thinking beyond humanism can be integrated.

Marquard is certainly right in stressing the relevance of an affirmative attitude towards progress as a fundamental aspect of modernity, and by stressing this aspect, it also separates itself clearly from the middle ages. Duri
dle ages, Christianity believed to possess the one and only truth in
ence with the world. It is clear that and why progress was not a va
you are aware of the one and only unchanging truth, then any other

to be a move away from the truth. If culture in the middle ages saw itself as the manifestation of this truth, the cultural development away from this structure was clearly a descent and a development away from God, the truth and the good life. This development has begun with the introduction of the relevance of critiques. All the central insights which have been taken for granted during the middle ages started to be criticized during modern times. Such critiques occurred on several levels. Sloterdijk's *Critique of Cynical Reason* (1983) gives an excellent survey of some of the most important critical traditions during this period of time, e.g the critique of revelation whereby it was shown that biblical revelations cannot be justified by means of reason, the critique of religious illusion whereby it was hinted at the possibility that religious insights can be traced to the human fear of dealing with life issues, critique of metaphysics whereby it was explained that metaphysical questions can be raised but not answered, the critique of idealism whereby it was doubted that the political order was just or the critique of morality whereby the lustful monk, the aggressive cardinal and the corrupt pope were described in minute detail (see Sloterdijk 1987a, 23-47).

The examples mentioned provide us with some plausibility to hold that, besides progress, critique and reason are two further concepts which are closely connected to modernity. During modernity progress took place, as reason was used to criticize traditional absolutes. Many regard Descartes' *cogito ergo sum* as a starting point of modern times, because his skeptical method encloses all the central notions of modernity: The unified subject employs reason to criticize the boundaries of knowledge.

Not only in the realm of philosophy, central developments occurred, but also in the realm of the society, politics or the sciences. Both Nietzsche and Heidegger rightly pointed out that the importance of the sciences has increased during this period of times. Consequently, the various mortifications have occurred about which Freud was talking: Firstly, the Copernican mortification which brings about the realization that it is not the earth but the sun which is at the center of our solar system. Secondly, Darwin's theory of evolution, which implies that apes and human beings have common ancestors. The third mortification was brought about by Freud himself, and I will deal with it a bit later, as it represents a move away from modernity.

In the realm of politics, the aristocracies which embodied the divine order were gradually replaced by more liberal and democratic systems in which tolerance, autonomy and negative freedom play an important role. One's own freedom includes that one must not limit the freedom of others and not do harm to others. The strong and detailed concept of the good which was prescribed in the medieval political domain was gradually exchanged with a more pluralistic view of the good.

A related development can be analyzed within the arts. In modern times the development has occurred, which brought with it the separation of the people from the art world. As long as there used to be a unified realm of beliefs, which was commonly shared, it was possible for members of all levels of a community to relate to the arts. However, in the art world, the artists became more and more important, and the arts no longer had the obligation to serve a specific function, e.g. to praise god, to glorify the political order, to tell religious stories. From 1800 onwards, the artist, often referred to as the genius, was a specific subject who creates his works of art due to some inner necessity (see Sorgner/ Fürbeth 2010, 1-26).

Again, we can try to crystallize some central qualities of modernity. The belief in the value of progress was realized by means of reason. The belief in progress is closely connected to the notion of Enlightenment, too. Before the Enlightenment, truth was eternal and unchanging and accessible by means of reason. However, during the Enlightenment, the relevance of reason altered, and became more manifold whereby it developed the potential to undermine itself. The importance of reason was undermined by an increase of relevance of the sensual realm and all its empirical data, and the increase of the importance of the natural sciences and technologies. Both developments have been particularly strong in the English speaking world. On the other hand, reason was still important for grasping the truth and connected to the critical tradition (an aspect more closely related to the continental tradition). Descartes represents a paradigm case for this approach. Reason can be found in every human being, namely in the part of each human being which represents the unified subject. By drawing upon this aspect of reason, it was possible to criticize old prejudices, absolutist world views, and religious hierarchies. In this way, the importance of the metaphysical world decreased, and the importance of the sensual world increased, which again promoted the relevance of the sciences and technologies.

The medieval world sees all the absolutes and perfections in God. During modern times the element of subjectivity is being promoted whereby subjectivity is still connected to rationality, which again leads to a necessary internal tension. The rational subject employs his reason to criticize former judgments. Thus, progress takes place. As it is a movement initialized by the subject and in the interest of the subject, progress is connected to the belief in a betterment of the overall condition.

However, we have seen already that there is a potential tension which lies in the Enlightenment project and which necessarily had to bring about a self-undermining process. Process thinking was responsible for Darwin's realization of the theory of evolution. Taking processes and this-worldliness seriously leads to the process of applying this approach to knowledge and reason. If reason is merely a capacity which has been brought about by evolutionary processes, and something which is not identical in all human beings, we no longer have a reason for holding that reason provides us with the truth. Furthermore, we no longer have a unified reason which is our unchanging inner human nature. The initial realization process leads to the doubt concerning the concept of truth as correspondence to the world, and is represented best in Nietzsche's perspectivism. The second process implies the fragmentation of the former unified subject, and comes out clearly in Freud's psychoanalytical theory. Both insights are central notions connected to postmodernity.

As both notions play a significant role in Nietzsche's philosophy, it is no surprise that many philosophers regard him as the ancestor of postmodernity. Habermas (1990, 83-105), Vattimo (1988, 164), Sloterdijk (1987b, 55), Derrida and Foucault (see Robinson 1999, 34) agree on this issue. In particular, Nietzsche's perspectivism according to which each perspective is an interpretation is important for attributing to him this role (see Sorgner 2007). Most continental philosophers have worked on the basis of this insight. Only members of the Frankfurt school do not agree with Nietzsche in this context, as they still hold on to the unified rational subject. Besides them, continental philosophy is dominated by varieties of perspectival thinking, and hence postmodernity. The hermeneutic tradition can also be seen as closely related to postmodernity, which is also being recognized by Marquard (1981, 20). According to Rorty, truths are being expressed in sentences, and sentences are made by human beings (see Horster 1991, 88). According to Derrida all language is bound to be metaphorical which implies his doubt concerning the propositional knowledge of truth (see Robinson 1999, 38). Again it was Nietzsche who already put forward an explanation why language consists merely out of metaphors (see Nietzsche 1999 [1873], 879). Postmodernism is linked with the close connection between reason, language and the doubt concerning the truth. Reason is connected to the capacity of making propositional judgments. Propositional judgments consist of metaphors. How can propositional judgments ever be more than a set of metaphors?

Without there being a unified rational self, which provides us with the truth, the concept of the mind needs to be rethought, too. The mind is no longer something eternal and unchanging, but something which has come into existence on the basis of evolutionary processes. The human being who used to be unified due to it being connected to the unified rational entity, is no longer unified thus. Consequently, it becomes fragmented, and again it was Nietzsche who already stressed this insight (see Nietzsche 1999 [1884-1885], 650). It was dealt with in more scientific detail by Freud who is responsible for the third mortification which is related to the rational subject no longer being the master within his own house. Habermas in his article *The Entry into Postmodernity: Nietzsche as a Turning Point* refers to these two criteria which are being connected to postmodernity, e.g. the dissolution of the subject and the doubt concerning the possibility of grasping the truth (1990, 96-97). However, Habermas is critical concerning this development which gets upheld by Derrida, Foucault, and Bataille, and his referring to these thinkers as young conservatives is his way of expressing his disrespect. Of course, Habermas has reasons for this use of language, and Nussbaum states a clear example which supports potential consequences of this line of thought (1995, 64-65), e.g. the introduction of smallpox vaccination in India by Western scientists does not consider adequately the difference. This is an important issue to which I will return and which I will clarify further soon. In any case, I disagree with Habermas' usage of the concept "conservative", because traditionally it refers to the attempt to uphold established structures. As Foucault and friends attempt to move beyond modernity, but Habermas does not, it seems more plausible to refer to Habermas as a conservative thinker.

A further consequence of postmodern thinking is the increase of the concept of play. The language game of Wittgenstein's later philosophy can be seen as much of an expression of postmodernity, and the same applies to Feyerabend's "anything goes", Duchamps "readymades", John Cage's *4'33''*, DADAism or Warhol's attitude that everyone can be a star for 15 minutes. Everything becomes a game, if there is no ultimate criterion for superiority. Is this indeed the case? Is it not rather the case that postmodernity is itself self-contradictory, as it includes both perspectivism as well as the anthropological judgment that human beings are fragmented? Hence, it makes both an anthropological claim as well as an epistemological one, which seems self-contradictory. Maybe, it is not crucial for postmodernity to be self-contradictory, if nothing can count as an ultimate criterion for superiority?

Beyond Humanism Movements

Finally, we can deal with the various movements which attempt to transcend a type of humanism which encloses radically separate dualist categories. How do post- and transhumanism fit into this overall scheme of traces? Posthumanism affirms both perspectivism as well as a this-worldly, and hence fragmentary understanding of human beings. Hence, it becomes clear that posthumanist's are an immediate outgrowth of postmodernity, in particular postmoderns such as Deleuze and Foucault, but not postmoderns such as Levinas and Derrida. Someone like Derrida, even though he doubts the possibility of describing a truth propositionally, also upholds that truth can occur as an event which vanishes again, once one attempts to describe it propositionally (see Derrida 1991). Thereby, he does not affirm a type of immanentism, but is much more closely related to the history of negative theology and Jewish ethics. The main difference between posthumanists and postmoderns like Deleuze and Foucault might be that the element of this-worldliness is being stressed more intensely.

Transhumanism also affirms a this-worldly or rather naturalist understanding of human beings. However, it also affirms rationality and a type of truth. Thereby, transhumanism sees itself in the Enlightenment tradition (see More 2013, 10). Is this an appropriate and consistent way of thinking about itselves, given the reflections of the previous pages? If it is the case that rationality has had an evolutionary origin, e.g. the capacity of rationality came about for pragmatic reasons, it can be doubted that reason can actually provide us with the one and only truth in correspondence of this world? This does not mean that one has to abandon reason. However, it leads to the insight that the boundaries of reason need to be taken seriously: Reason is helpful due to pragmatic lines of thought, but not because it provides one with the truth in correspondence to the world. In any case, it needs to be pointed out that the concept of reason which modern thinkers like Descartes and Kant employed does not correspond to that of transhumanists. Descartes and Kant hold that human beings have an other-worldly rational part, and a this worldly material one. Transhumanists affirm a scientific, naturalist and this-worldly understanding of human beings, and hence cannot affirm a modern understanding of other-worldly rationality which used to be upheld by Descartes and Kant. This makes it clear that there is a clear gap between the Enlightenment and the transhumanist concepts of reason (see Hughes 2010, 622-640).

Does this mean that transhumanists have to give up their affirmative attitude towards reason? I think these reflections imply that the transhumanist's self-understanding of continuing the Enlightenment tradition ought to be revised. Transhumanists affirm reason, but a naturalized version of reason which implies a type of reason with much more limited capacities. The use of reason can still be seen as helpful but not because it provides us with a truth in correspondence to the world, but merely with a pragmatic concept of truth. Thereby, transhumanism is much closer to posthumanism than is commonly being acknowledged, in particular, if carbon-based transhumanism is taken into consideration.

Let us consider posthumanism a bit further, as the example Nussbaum is referring to is an issue worth considering in more detail. Western scientists introduced smallpox vaccination in India, and thereby destroyed the Indian cult of Sittala Devi, who is a goddess to whom people used to pray to be cured from smallpox. At a conference which Nussbaum attended, too, an elegant French anthropologist criticized this way of process, due to her affirming that there is no privileged point of view, which according to her has clearly and convincingly been shown by Foucault and Derrida. By acting thus, Western scientists did not consider adequately the difference, and treated the dominating local culture in a humiliating and colonial fashion, one could add further. After her speech, a participant asked her, whether it would not be better to live than to die. She responded that this point of view presupposes a Western essentialist concept of medicine which is founded on dualist opposites, and categorically separates living from dying. Once someone will have freed herself from this way of thinking, it will be possible to grasp the difference of the Indian tradition, the anthropologist claimed (see Nussbaum 1995, 64-65).

Due to these kinds of stories and examples, many transhumanists and other academic philosophers regard postmodern thinking as highly problematic, and doubt the value of entering into an intellectual discourse with it. In the case of the French anthropologist mentioned before, I can relate to this attitude. However, I also think that the way the French anthropologist applied postmodern thinking to this specific case implies a problematic way of applying postmodern attitudes. In other words, the problem is not connected to her basic way of thinking. She is right in so far as ultimate ontological questions are at issue; it is unclear whether a Western dualist or an Eastern non-dualist way of thinking about them is more appropriate. However, the case of smallpox vaccinations does not have anything to do with any ultimate truths about the world. It has to do with what works in this world. Given that it is the case, that smallpox vaccinations are helpful in most cases, whereas praying to Sittala Devi usually does not help patients, provides us with a reason for preferring Western medicine over the use of praying to a goddess, if one wishes not to have smallpox. However, by relying on what has proven to be reliable in most cases does not imply that it is better with respect to some ultimate truth. Progressing in this manner is merely better with respect to some pragmatic understanding of truth, and it seems sensible to act accordingly. It is the aspect of an application of postmodern and posthumanist ways of thinking to domains in which it is not helpful. And this is problematic for this tradition. In this respect, posthumanists can benefit a lot from transhumanists.

Conclusion

As I have tried to show in the previous passages there are elements in transhumanism, which can be of relevance for posthumanists as well as elements of posthumanism, which can be helpful for transhumanists. By promoting the exchanges between both traditions which are also related to different local cultures, e.g. in the case of transhumanists the Anglo-American scientific culture, and in the case of posthumanists the continental literary culture, it is possible to further a way of thinking which lies beyond humanism.

By progressing in this manner, metahumanist thinking is undertaken. Metahumanist thinking both lies beyond a dualist understanding of humanism as well as in between post- and transhumanism. The Greek word *meta* can mean both, "beyond" as well as "in between". Metahumanist thinking attempts to move beyond an understanding of the world which affirms categorical dualities like that between subject and object and matter and spirit. However, *meta* also moves in between post- and transhumanism by dealing with transhumanist and posthumanist challenges and by applying a hermeneutic version of philosophy, of a type of Vattimo's weak thinking, his *pensiero debole,* to contemporary challenges related to emerging technologies (see Sorgner 2013b, 135-144). Thereby, both the complexity of a Nietzschean and a hermeneutic philosophy are taken seriously as well as the complex and diversified discourses of analytic ethical exchanges. Metahumanism can be understood as affirming both a weak version of trans- as well as a weak version of posthumanism. At this point, the differences between strong and weak versions of both approaches need to be described:

Transhumanists affirm technologies in order to increase the likelihood of the coming about of posthumans. A strong version of transhumanism affirms that there is a moral but not a legal obligation to use specific enhancement techniques. The bioliberal Julian Savulescu who is not a transhumanist but closely associated with this movement represents well this perspective (see Savulescu 2001; Savulescu/ Kahane 2009). Another strong version of transhumanism holds that enhancement technologies necessarily promote the good life of all human beings and it is this insight which ought to be legally relevant. Aubrey de Grey can be seen as representative of this tradition (see de Grey 2007, 335-339). A weak version of transhumanism, on the other hand, might affirm that enhancement techniques increase the likelihood of many people leading good lives without this insight implying necessary legal or moral duties, but it does have consequences concerning moral and legal rights (see Sorgner 2013a, 2013b).

Posthumanists are concerned with non-dualist thinking and acting. A strong version of posthumanism assumes that human beings are merely gradually different from other natural beings, and it is this insight which ought to be legally obligatory. Peter Singer can be seen as defender of such a view (see Singer 2002, 2011). A weak version of posthumanism, on the other, might also affirm that human beings are merely gradually different from other natural beings, and this insight ought to be a legally legitimate perspective, i.e. it should not be legally impossible to think and act accordingly (see Sorgner 2013b).

Meta-, post- and transhumanism also reveal that Marquard's way of grasping modernity and the movements which can come after it, is far too limited. Postmodernism does not fit into Marquards's scheme, as it is indifferent concerning the concept of progress. Transhumanism seemingly fits into the first of Marquard's categories, because it demands a pro-modern attitude concerning progress. However, transhumanism is not pro-modern concerning their anthropology, as a modern anthropology implies a dualist concept of human beings with a material body and an immaterial soul (exemplified best by Descartes and Kant), which is not being upheld by most transhumanists. Therefore, it is problematic to classify transhumanists solely as pro-modern. They are pro-modern in one aspect (affirming progress), but anti-modern in another one (non-dualist anthropology). With respect to posthumanism the classification is even more problematic, as posthumanists are also indifferent concerning the concept of progress, which is one reason why they do not fit into Marquard's scheme. However, in a certain sense they would also acknowledge that it is better to live in a liberal and social democracy than it is to live in a medieval religious country dominated by the Pope. Would it be appropriate in that case that the political development from then to now is a kind of progress? In that case, they would affirm a certain kind of progress, but this would not apply to other kinds of progress, e.g. the insights of contemporary science do not necessarily count as progress in comparison to judgments made by Catholics. Concerning ultimate truths, it is unclear whether science, which many people affirm today, or Catholicism, which many people affirmed 1000 years ago, provides us with a better understanding. Hence, the question of a clear value judgment of the concept "progress" is rather difficult from a posthumanist point of view. An affirmative judgment can be defended as well as a depreciative one. Posthumanists affirm a non-dualist ontology, yet they could not exclude the possibility of Catholicism being true concerning truth as correspondence to the world, even though they regard this judgment as implausible. Yet, it seems clear that Marquard's above suggestions concerning the classification of philosophies of history are too limited. Still, they were helpful for our attempt of mapping the various movements beyond humanism. In any case, the questions concerning all the various issues related to the beyond humanism debates are so complex that there is a sufficient amount of challenges for many creative and clever thinkers to come. The present introduction is merely supposed to provide an initial stimulation for promoting the various exchanges within the beyond humanism discourses.

Bibliography

Badmington, N. (ed.) (2000): Posthumanism. New York: Palgrave.

Bostrom, N. (2005): A History of Transhumanist Thought. In: Journal of Evolution and Technology 14(1), 1-25.

Bostrom, N. (2009): Why I Want to be a Posthuman When I Grow Up. In: Gordijn, B./ Chadwick, R. (eds.): Medical Enhancement and Posthumanity. New York et al.: Springer, 107-136.

Braidotti, R. (2013): The Posthuman. Cambridge: Polity.

de Grey, A. (2007): Ending Aging: The Rejuvenation Breakthroughs That Could Reverse Aging in Our Lifetime. New York: St. Martin's Griffin.

del Val, J./ Sorgner, S.L. (2011): A Metahumanist Manifesto. In: The Agonist 4(2), 1-4.

Derrida, J. (1991): Gesetzeskraft: Der »mystische Grund der Autorität«. Frankfurt am Main: Suhrkamp.

Habermas, J. (1990): The Philosophical Discourse of Modernity: Twelve Lectures. Cambridge: Polity Press.

Hassan, I. (1977): Prometheus as Performer: Toward a Posthumanist Culture? In: The Georgia Review 31(4), 830-850.

Hayles, N.K. (1999): How We Became Posthuman: Virtual Bodies in Cybernetics, Literature, and Informatics. Chicago et al: The University of Chicago Press.

Horster, D. (1991): Rorty zur Einführung. Hamburg: Junius.

Hughes, J. (2004): Citizen Cyborg: Why Democratic Societies Must Respond to the Redesigned Human of the Future. Boulder: Westview Press.

Hughes, J. (2010): Contradictions from the Enlightenment Roots of Transhumanism. In: Journal of Medicine and Philosophy 35(6), 622-640.

Hughes, J. (2014): Politics. In: Ranisch, R./ Sorgner, S.L. (eds.): Post- and Transhumanism. An Introduction. Frankfurt am Main et al.: Peter Lang.

Marquard, O. (1981): Abschied vom Prinzipiellen: Philosophische Studien. Stuttgart: Reclam.

Marquard, O. (1989): Aesthetica und Anaesthetica: Philosophische Überlegungen. Paderborn: Ferdinand Schöningh.

Marquard, O. (1995): Glück im Unglück: Philosophische Überlegungen. München: Wilhelm Fink Verlag.

Marquard, O. (2000): Philosophie des Stattdessen: Studien. Stuttgart: Reclam.

More, M. (2013): The Philosophy of Transhumanism. In: More, M./ Vita-More, N. (eds.): The Transhumanist Reader: Classical and Contemporary Essays on the Science, Technology, and Philosophy of the Human Future. Chichester: Wiley-Blackwell, 3-17.

Nietzsche, F. (1999 [1873]) Ueber Wahrheit und Lüge im aussermoralischen Sinne. In: Colli, G./ Montinari, M. (eds.): Kritische Studienausgabe (Vol. 1). München et al.: Deutscher Taschenbuch Verlag & de Gruyter, 873-890.

Nietzsche, F. (1999 [1884-1885]) Nachlaß 1884-1885. In: Colli, G./ Montinari, M. (eds.): Kritische Studienausgabe (Vol. 11). München et al.: Deutscher Taschenbuch Verlag & de Gruyter.

Nussbaum, M. (1995): Human Capabilities, Female Human Beings. In: Nussbaum, M./ Glover, J. (eds.): Women, Culture and Development: A Study A Study of Human Capabilities. Oxford et al.: Oxford University Press 61-104.

Pastourmatzi, D. (2014): Science Fiction Literature. In: Ranisch, R./ Sorgner, S.L. (eds.): Post- and Transhumanism. An Introduction. Frankfurt am Main: Peter Lang.

Robinson, D.(1999): Nietzsche and Postmodernism. Cambridge: Icon Books.

Savulescu, J. (2001): Procreative Beneficence: Why We Should Select the Best Children. In: Bioethics 15 (5-6), 413-26.

Savulescu, J./ Kahane, G. (2009): The Moral Obligation to Create Children with the Best Chance of the Best Life. In: Bioethics 23(5), 274-90.

Singer, P. (2002): Animal Liberation. New York: Harper.

Singer, P. (2011): Practical Ethics. Cambridge: Cambridge University Press.

Sloterdijk, P. (1987a): Critique of Cynical Reason. Minneapolis et al.: University of Minnesota Press.

Sloterdijk, P. (1987b): Kopernikanische Mobilmachung und ptolemäische Abrüstung: Ästhetischer Versuch. Frankfurt am Main: Suhrkamp.

Sloterdijk, P. (2009): Rules for the Human Zoo: A Response to the Letter on Humanism. In: Environment and Planning D: Society and Space 27, 12-28.

Sorgner, S.L. (2007): Metaphysics without Truth: On the Importance of Consistency within Nietzsche's Philosophy. Milwaukee(WI): University of Marquette Press.

Sorgner, S.L. (2010): Menschenwürde nach Nietzsche: Die Geschichte eines Begriffs. Darmstadt: WBG.

Sorgner, S.L./ Fürbeth, O. (2010): Introduction. In: Sorgner, S.L./ Fürbeth, O. (eds.): Music in German Philosophy: An Introduction. Chicago et al.: University of Chicago Press, 1-26.

Sorgner, S.L. (2013a): Evolution, Education, and Genetic Enhancement. In: Sorgner, S.L./ Jovanovic, B.-R. (eds.): Evolution and the Future: Anthropology, Ethics, Religion. Frankfurt am Main et al.: Peter Lang, 85-100.

Sorgner, S.L. (2013b): Human Dignity 2.0. Beyond a Rigid Version of Anthropocentrism. In: Trans-Humanities 6(1), 135-159.

Sorgner, S.L./ Grimm, N. (2013): Introduction. Evolution Today. In: Sorgner, S.L./ Jovanovic, B.-R. (eds.): Evolution and the Future: Anthropology, Ethics, Religion. Frankfurt am Main et al.: Peter Lang, 9-20.

Tirosh-Samuelson, H. (2014): Religion. In: Ranisch, R./ Sorgner, S.L. (eds.): Post- and Transhumanism. An Introduction. Frankfurt am Main et al.: Peter Lang.

Vattimo, G. (1988): The End of Modernity: Nihilism and Hermeneutics in Post-Modern Culture. Cambridge: Polity Press.

Religion

Hava Tirosh-Samuelson

Clarification of Terms

The terms "posthumanism" and "transhumanism" are not well-defined, generating considerable confusion in the public debate about them. For clarity's sake I distinguish not only between posthumanism and transhumanism but also between three types of posthumanism: *philosophical posthumanism*, *cultural posthumanism*, and *technological posthumanism.* The chapter will expose some of the tensions and even contradictions between the various variants of post- and transhumanist discourses, and explain how religion functions in each case.

The terms posthumanism and transhumanism were coined in the mid-20th century. "*Posthumanism*" was used first in the Macy conferences on cybernetics from 1946-1953 with the invention of system theory which was searching for…

> "[…] a new theoretical model for biological, mechanical, and communicational processes that removed the human and *Homo sapiens* from any particularly privileged position in relation to matters of meaning, information, and cognition" (Wolfe 2010, xii).

The theorist Ihab Hassan (1977) was the first to use "posthumanism" in his call for the philosophical need to overcome the human race as well as humanism and his ideas inspired the most influential work of the cultural posthumanist, N. Katherine Hayles (1999), who focused on the genre of science fiction to assert that we have already become posthuman. Indeed, in *Shapers and Mechanics* (1979) the science fiction author, Bruce Sterling, labeled a future species as post-human and depicted its struggle with two sub-species. Science-fiction fantasies became a scientific reality in the work of computer scientist and artificial intelligence specialist Hans Moravec (1988) who speculated how the human species will be replaced by post-biological, intelligent robots.

By contrast, the term "*transhumanism*" was coined by the British evolutionary biologist, Julian Huxley, in 1957 to capture what he had earlier called "evolutionary humanism," or "scientific humanism." Huxley can be seen as the inspiration for a cultural and intellectual movement that calls for the gradual transition from (biological) humanism to (mechanical) posthumanism and the prefix "trans" in the term "transhumanism" is simply a shorthand for "transition." As an ideological movement, transhumanism advocates the application of science and technology to the amelioration of the human condition through genetic engineering, robotics, informatics, and nanotechnology. The convergence of these technologies and the advances in the life sciences, neuroscience, and medicine has been mobilized to facilitate the enhancement of human physical and mental characteristics, elimination of disease and pain, and radical extension of life expectancy. Because technological posthumanism is the inspiration for transhumanism, the two terms are often used interchangeably.

Philosophical and Cultural Posthumanisms

Philosophical and cultural posthumanisms need to be treated together because they belong to the postmodern philosophical and cultural critiques that spelled the end of humanism, namely, the end of "man-centered universe," or "the long held belief in the infallibility of human power and the arrogant belief in our superiority and uniqueness" (Pepperell 2003, 100). The atrocities of the 20th century – two world wars, the use of the atomic bomb on Hiroshima and Nagasaki, the industrialization of death in the Holocaust, and the ecological crisis – necessitated profound rethinking of the culture of modernity and its underlying humanistic assumptions. An entire range of assumptions which postmodernist thinkers labeled "the Enlightenment Project" came under attack: that Man is the measure of all things, that the individual subject is a being with a unique essence ("human nature") whose goal is self-realization, that human language accurately represents reality, that the human subject is the foundation of inherent political rights that demand political representation, and that the human species is superior to non-humans and can use natural resources solely for its own benefit. The postmodernist critiques exposed their theoretical shortcomings and harmful social results. Humanism was accused as the cause for the collapse of humanity and posthumanism (like postmodernism) was the attempt to rewrite the definition of being human in order to overcome the shortcomings of humanism.

Philosophical posthumanism consists of the philosophical critique of humanism (and the Enlightenment Project more broadly), whose assumptions are presented to be either naïve or self-contradictory. Because of its critical posture, philosophical posthumanism is also dubbed as "*anti-humanism*" (see Soper 1986). The two main examples of philosophical posthumanism are Jacques Derrida and Michel Foucault who declared the "end of Man," namely, the end of a certain conception of humanity which has prevailed in the Enlightenment Project.

In his reinterpretation of western philosophy from Plato to Heidegger, Derrida exposed the logocentrism that pervades the western philosophical tradition. The opening verse of the Gospel of John, "In the beginning was the Word [logos]" expresses the entire foundationalist outlook of Western thought, or what Derrida called "metaphysics of presence": the tendency to go back to origins, find centers, fix points of reference, certify truths, verify an author's intentions, or locate a text's core of meaning. The foundationalism of the western tradition, which expressed faith in God, the Self, Truth, and the Order of the Universe, and that privileged the singular and definitive over the multiple and indeterminate, all express logocentrism as well as a presumed metaphysical certainty as well as the assumption that representation is possible because words or images directly refer to pre-existent reality. Instead, Derrida advanced Deconstruction as a mode of reading texts that exposes the text's logic against itself by showing how the logic of its language can differ from and play against the logic of the author's stated claims (see Derrida 1976; 1982 [1968]). Deconstruction thus dismantles binary oppositions with their hierarchies of value while showing how a term both differs from and defers to the other term. Echoing Nietzsche, Derrida (1997) critiqued the conventional concept of truth; truth is no more than illusion.

Derrida is central to postmodern thought which informs cultural posthumanism, but it is Foucault's proclamation of the "death of Man" which signifies the direct assault on humanism that is prominent in cultural posthumanism. By "Man" Foucault referred to the philosophical anthropology of the 19th century that posited a self-contained, rational agent as the seat of inalienable human and political rights. For Foucault this concept appeared at a particular moment in history, that is, the French Revolution, and therefore it is possible to predict the demise of this conception. With the death of the human subject, so Foucault insisted, will perish as well the urge to classify, dominate, exclude and exploit that derives from the idea of Man and which has caused so much havoc in the modern age. In Foucault's genealogical archaeology, "Man" is no more than a creation of a unique set of historical contingencies, a consequence of certain relations of power, a figment of discourse. By "discourse" Foucault meant self-contained systems of thought, beliefs or social and political practices governed by internally accepted regulations and procedures. Medicine, politics, art, or sexuality are discourses with particular concerns and conventions of given periods. The crucial aspect of discourse is that is based on power relations, which Foucault exposed in his studies of hospitals, prisons, police and other institutions. Humanism, then, is no more than discourse that can and should be altered; one day humanism will pass away "like a face drawn in sand at the edge of the sea" (Foucault 1970 [1966], 387). For Foucault the repressive nature of humanism must be exposed and challenged, as he did in the analysis of the Western discourse on heterosexualty.

The anti-humanism of Derrida, Foucault and other postmodern thinkers inspired literary critics and scholars of cultural studies to subject western culture at large to close reading and criticism which would give rise to cultural posthumanism. Endorsing Foucault's call to engage in a "perpetual critique of ourselves," cultural posthumanists have insisted that humanism is not only a harmful dogma, but also that humanism is "replete with its own prejudices and universals" which are precisely the kind of "superstition" from which the Enlightenment called us to break free from. Under the influence of feminist theory, queer theory, postcolonial studies, and other trends in cultural studies, cultural posthumanisms uncovered the repressive implications of humanism for women, minorities, occupied and oppressed social groups and even animals (see Badmington 2000). This critique was not merely a list of complaints by groups that has been traditionally excluded or oppressed, but rather an attempt to reconsider what we have taken for granted about *Homo sapiens*, namely the boundaries between humans and "non-humans." Conceived as the Other, the "non-human" can be animals, machines, aliens, or monsters. Thus Elaine Graham (2002) studies Otherness as manifested in literary forms and draws on these images to reflect on the representation of the moral discourse about scientific and technological change.

The human body, which previously signified the difference between humans and non-humans, has been problematized and rendered ambiguous in the discourse of cultural posthumanism. The critique of traditional boundaries by cultural posthumanists is meant to bring humans to appreciate themselves as human animals who are not only part of the evolutionary history but also animals who are inherently…

> "[…] a prosthetic creature that has coevolved with various forms of technicity and materiality, forms that are fundamentally 'not-human' and yet have nevertheless made the human what it is" (Wolfe 2010, xxv).

No longer seen as a repository of the soul, the body is now viewed as the…

> "[…] interface between mind and experience […] and is narrated as a site of exploration and transfiguration, through which the interface with an electronically-based postmodern experience is inscribed" (Bukatman 2000, 98).

Cary Wolfe aptly summarizes cultural posthumanism as follows:

> "[P]osthumanism names a historical moment in which the decentering of the human by its imbrication in technical, medical, informatics, and economic networks is increasingly impossible to ignore, a historical development that points toward the necessity of new theoretical paradigms (but also thrust them on us), a new mode of thought that comes after the cultural repression and fantasies, the philosophical protocols and evasions, of humanism as a historical specific phenomenon (Wolfe 2010, xv-xvi).

One aspect of the reconfiguration of the human body is cyborgization, namely, the blurring the boundaries between humans and machines and the blurring the boundaries between humans and other animals. Articulated first by Donna Haraway's *Cyborg Manifesto* (1985) the figure of the Cyborg signifies the breaking of boundaries between nature and culture, organic and inorganic, human and animal and a new understanding of the human embodiment. Haraway intended her *Cyborg Manifesto* as a feminist project that wishes to reconstitute a new identity politics about gender norms, but her ideas were utilized by some posthumanists to advance the notion of "a post-gender world where being a cyborg is preferable to being a goddess" (Miah 2008, 78). Some use the cyborg to represent the complex relationship between humanity and technology; others develop narratives that explore the imaginative possibilities inspired by new technologies, and still other reflect theoretically about the relationship between humans and the nonhuman.

For the techno-utopians cyborgization is not merely a liberationist vision from the oppression of traditional hierarchies and dichotomies but a full-fledged vision of *human obsolescence*. Haraway herself, however, was not interested in a utopian techno-fantasy but in social-cultural reforms in the present.

The rethinking of human embodiment characteristic of cyborg discourse entered other cultural forms such as films, science fiction, performance and installation art, and horror genre. In all these cultural modalities, the human body is defamiliarized, depicted so as to inspire revulsion, or disengaged from its biological nature as the body is dissolved into electronic space and cybernetic existence. In the literary and artistic posthumanist discourse, "sexuality is a dispersed relations between bodies and things" (Halberstam/ Livingston 1995, 8), "post-familial bodies celebrate the end of His-and-her matching theories" (ibid., 10), and the biological link between sex and reproduction vanishes while the death of the human is celebrated.

The move away from biological embodiment into a new, posthuman configuration of embodiment, technology, and culture receives the most extensive expression in the work of the cultural posthumanist and feminist literary critic, N. Katherine Hayles. Deeply indebted to Haraway, Derrida, and Foucault as well as to information theory and cybernetics, her book, *How We Became Posthuman: Virtual Bodies in Cybernetics, Literature and Informatics* (1999) identified the salient characteristics of the posthumanist body: patterns of information are more essential to the state of being than any material instantiation; the embodiment in a biological substrate is seen as an accident of history rather than an inevitability of life; there is no immaterial soul and consciousness is an epiphenomenon; the body is nothing more than a prosthesis, and exchange this prosthesis for another is simply an extension of that relations; and a human being is capable of being seemingly articulated with intelligent machines. In the posthuman age there are no essential differences or absolute demarcations between bodily existence and computer simulation, cybernetic mechanism and biological organism, robot technology and human goals. Hayles "disembodiment through cybernetics reveals a lack of fixity to humanness that also diminishes the value of stable biological distinctions such as species categories" (Miah 2008, 80).

Postmodern anti-foundationalism and denial of the metaphysics of presence render traditional religious beliefs irrelevant to cultural posthumanism, although Derrida's own views on religion are quite subtle and complex. As an Algerian Jew who took his cultural heritage seriously, Derrida endorsed negative theology and reminded his readers that great religious traditions always call certainty and security into question. However, postmodern cultural posthumanists who lack Derrida's depth treat traditional religions as irrelevant to their critique of humanism.

The postmodern suspicion toward religion was deeply inspired by Nietzsche whose views on religion are anything but simple. Nietzsche was a son of a Lutheran minister and a theology student who was intimately familiar with the Bible and with Christian doctrine, but he broke with Christianity about 1870. Even though he continued to utilize biblical motifs, phrases, quotations, and allusions, he subjected all religions, and especially Christianity, to scathing historical critique which rendered invalid the mythical presuppositions of religion as well as the authority and credibility of Scriptures. No less devastating was Nietzsche's critique of Christian morality whose notions of sin and the afterlife Nietzsche declared to be entirely imaginary and psychological pernicious. Christianity he argued motivates its adherent to adopt somewhat paranoid and hostile attitudes toward their own behavior and to others and its insistence on absolute conformity to a single standard of human behavior results in self-denigration, vindictiveness toward others, escapism, and life denial (see Salaquarda 1996). Instead, Nietzsche called for appreciation each human situation for its particular uniqueness and acknowledging of the perspectives and the biases humans bring to the assessment of each situation.

Nietzsche's alternative to traditional religions in the form of immanent appreciation of this life in aesthetic terms, his perspectivalism and moral relativism are taken for granted in the literature generated by postmodern, cultural posthumanists. As influential is Nietzsche's famous pronouncement in *The Gay Science* (1882) that "God is dead" which is uttered by the Madman who speaks in the marketplace to the scientific atheists that gathered there. The Madman tells them: "We have killed him – you and I. All of us are his murderers." In *The Gay Science* Nietzsche offered a naturalistic and aesthetic vision for humanity in opposition to traditional religion: life's meaning is not to be found in the afterlife, but in this world that should be appreciated and celebrated in aesthetic terms. In his *Thus Spoke Zarathustra* (1883-1885), Nietzsche continued to educate his readers by showing them a new paradigm for the modern person – the Overman – who is "continually experimental, willing to risk all for the sake of the enhancement of humanity" (Magnus/ Higgins 1996, 40). The Overman stands in contrast to the "last man," the human type whose sole desire is personal comfort and happiness, a critique of the Enlightenment discourse on happiness by means of social reforms and technological progress. Nietzsche urged his readers to give up the dream of the afterlife; the body is the ground of all meaning and knowledge and the health and strength should be recognized and sought as virtuous (ibid., 41). Concomitantly, Nietzsche emphasized the importance of the will and the will's attempt to enhance its power. It is not clear whether the human "will to power" is to be understood as a psychological observation, an explanation of human conduct, or a metaphysical doctrine, but it is clear that Nietzsche's teaching about the "will to power" influenced Nazi war effort and their use of eugenics to rid humanity of undesirable traits of the weak and the inferior. Bodily self-enhancement by means of eugenics is the core project of technological posthumanism and transhumanism, although contemporary leaders are keen to dissociate themselves from any association with Nazi racial policies and enforced eugenics. Cultural posthumanists are not engaged in the project of biological self-enhancement, but their aesthetic discourse has no room for either traditional religions or even negative theology. The discourse of cultural studies is decidedly secular. Ironically, the discourse of technological posthumanism echoes religious motifs since its proponents posit man-made robots as god-like beings.

Technological Posthumanism and Transhumanism

Technological posthumanism envisions the emergence of a new phase in the evolution of the human species in which machines (especially super-intelligent machines) will not only augment human physical and mental capacity so as to eliminate current limitations, but will actually supersede the humans that have created them. For these techno-enthusiasts (see Minsky 1986, 2006; Moravec 1988, 1999; Kurzweil 1999, 2005), the posthuman Mechanical Age will come about after an irreversible turning point, the Singularity, will commence as a result of exponential, accelerated process of technological progress. Singularity is "a point of the graph of progress where explosive growth occurs in a blink of an eye" when machines "become sufficiently smart to start teaching themselves" (Geraci 2008, 5). When this happens, "the world will irrevocably shift from the biological to the mechanical" (ibid.) and the Mechanical Age will inaugurate the New Kingdom, the Virtual Kingdom. The transformation from the human to decision-making, super-intelligent machines will be gradual. At first, humans will upload their minds (the most salient aspect of their personalities) into supercomputers who will serve the material needs of humanity. Eventually the machines "will tire of caring for humanity and will decide to spread throughout the universe in the interest of discovering all the secrets of the cosmos" (ibid.). As Hans Moravec imagines it, machines will convert the entire universe into an "extended thinking entity" (Moravec 1988, 116). As the "Age of Robots" will be supplanted by the "Age of Mind," machines will create space for a "subtler world" (Moravec 1999, 163) in which computations alone remain. In the Virtual Kingdom the "Mind Fire" will render earthly life meaningless, ultimately swallowed by cyberspace (see ibid., 167). This is the ultimate *telos* of the transformation and transfiguration of the human to the posthuman.

If technological posthumanism sets the *goals* of the process, transhumanism engages the process that will realize those goals. Transhumanism is an intellectual and cultural movement that promotes the desirability and feasibility of the futuristic, posthuman techno-scientific scenario. In the transhuman age, so it is claimed, enhanced humans will live longer, happier, and presumably more virtuous life because they will be engineered to become "better humans." While still recognizably human, the augmented humans (or transhumans) will prepare the road for the self-destruction of the human species, because these enhanced humans will voluntarily upload their minds into the machines that will eventually supplant them. In the transition from the human to the posthuman, the enhanced transhuman will usher the way for the Virtual Kingdom, in which humans will be irrevocably transformed. The planned disappearance of embodied human is viewed as a blessing and constitutes the hope for humanity, since human biological embodiment is regarded as a burden and a curse. It is precisely because humans take charge of the evolutionary process through engineering that humans will be able to liberate themselves from their limitations. This is the core of the transhumanist vision (see Young 2005). The project of creating faster, stronger, and smarter human beings is not just an idle fantasy, but an expensive program that siphons off precious resources from other projects for the betterment of the human condition.

The relationship between philosophical and cultural posthumanism, on the one hand, and technological posthumanism and transhumanism, is thus filled with ironies. What the cultural posthumanists muse about in fiction and art, the techno-posthumanists actually attempt to actualize through science and technology. But the very progress that the postmodernist literary theorists have critiqued, because of its flawed metaphysics and harmful social consequences, the techno-enthusiasts celebrate. We can go further to say that whereas cultural posthumanists are critical of the Enlightenment Project, the techno-scientists *perpetuate and even intensify* the assumptions of the Enlightenment Project.

The tension between these two communities is also evident in regard to religion. Although technological posthumanism is ostensibly secular it is in fact rife with religious motifs. Indeed, the techno-futuristic scenario envisions mechanical creativity itself as salvation of humanity, since it will destroy that which is most problematic about the biologically evolved human body. Human reason itself has created artificial intelligence, but the very product of human rationality – the robot – will do what biological life cannot do. There is little communication between the (postmodern) literary-philosophical-cultural posthumanists and the (largely modern) techno-scientific community, but they both seek the same end result: *the self-destruction of the embodied human.*

The Religious Roots of Transhumanism

How does religion function in technological posthumanism and transhumanism? The leading transhumanist philosopher, Nick Bostrom, presents transhumanism as extension of secular humanism (see Bostrom 2005), but a closer examination of transhumanism shows a much more complicated story. Even without tracing the transhumanist vision back to ancient religious myths such as the Sumerian Gilgamesh myth or the Greek Icarus myth, it is important to note that Julian Huxley who coined the term "transhumanism" considered it as "religion without revelation." This was the title of his short treatise (see Huxley 1927) which functions as a foundational text of the transhumanist project. Huxley saw himself as a "midwife" who would deliver into the world a "new ideology" or a "new system of ideas appropriate to man's new situation" (Tirosh-Samuelson 2012, 56-64). Originally he titled this "new ideology" "evolutionary humanism" and considered it "an attitude of mind" that would address the crisis of humanity by bridging science and the arts and by using science to build a better world. Like all English intellectuals at the end of the Victorian age, Huxley saw all biological phenomena in the context of evolutionary theory and from childhood cultivated love of nature, especially during the time he spent at the countryside home of his paternal grandfather, Thomas Henry Huxley, the man who did most to popularize and disseminate Darwinism. The elder Huxley, who coined the term "agnosticism," clearly rejected Christian tenets, but he was also a deeply religious man who believed that science and religion are "twin sisters" that were interdependent; the conflict was not between science and religion but between science and questionable theology.

Unlike his grandfather, Julian Huxley would seek to establish relationship between science (i.e., evolutionary theory) and ethics, but his desire to present a unified picture of the human being's place in nature was related to the pantheistic proclivities of his mother, Julia, a deeply spiritual person who developed her own brand of pantheism that eventually contributed to Julian's view of nature as a cosmic unity. Indeed, in his first published work in 1912, *The Individual in the Animal Kingdom*, Julian's exercise in philosophical biology was written under the influence of Henri Bergson's *Creative Evolution* (1907) and it understood the emergence of the human mind as a distinctive phase of the evolutionary process, moving from biology to culture. According to Huxley's evolutionary humanism, the destiny of humanity is to understand human nature and to actualize the possibilities of development inherent in it. The human mind inspires the march of progress in nature and "the source of all truth, beauty, morality, and purpose is to be found in human nature" (Huxley 1934, 7). Highlighting human evolving nature, Huxley urged his readers to "utilize available knowledge in giving guidance and encouragement for the continuing adventure of human development." This is the core belief of the transhumanist program.

Huxley encouraged all people to take control of the evolutionary process in order to attain the human ideal in this life. As human-controlled evolution transhumanism was articulated by a person who understood his mission and vision in religious terms, albeit pantheistic rather than theistic. Huxley's evolutionary humanism was a statement of a secularist faith for a world that had to come to terms with the facts of evolution and was decidedly articulated in ethical and aesthetic terms. While Huxley opposed supernatural explanations, he deeply appreciated the mystery of existence and had no qualms using ethical and religious concepts such as "destiny" and "the sacred" to articulate his vision of and for humanity.

Huxley's unified cosmic vision that privileges the human mind is remarkably similar to that of Pierre Teilhard de Chardin, the Jesuit paleontologist for whom progressive evolution led to the "noösphere" (namely a sphere of mind as opposed to or rather superimposed on the biosphere or sphere of life) and later to the collective consciousness of the Omega Point (see Steinhart 2008). For Huxley, the task of humanity is to actualize the immense potential of the human mind and take control of the evolutionary process itself. For this reason Huxley was an ardent supporter of the eugenics movement, long after eugenics was a discredited. During the 1930s and 1940s, he wrote prolifically about eugenic topics and from 1959 to 1964 he served as the President of the Eugenics Society.

Huxley's "religion without revelation" had much in common with yet another modern, utopian program – Communism. Indeed a main inspiration for the transhumanist movement comes from two friends of Julian Huxley: J. S. B. Haldane (1892-1964) and J. D. Bernal (1901-1971), both of whom were members of the Communist Party of Greater Britain (see Tirosh-Samuelson 2012, 64-78). Haldane was deeply interested in bettering human life by employing science and technology since human progress moves the species to transcend its biological limitations. Although Haldane rebelled against traditional mores in Victorian England, his faith in biological engineering and his futuristic speculations about human-machine interface had a quasi-religious quality. After his disillusionment with Communism in the mid-1950s he was drawn to Hinduism, and became committed to international peace initiatives. Bernal, who remained a Communist to the end of his life, expressed faith in science that could be described as secularized religious devotion: only through science (the new secularized religion) can humanity overcome the enemies of the rational soul. Bernal concerned himself with long term perspectives of the human species and contemplated the future transformation of the human form. He too supported the eugenics movement and envisioned the emergence of the mechanical man as a "break in organic evolution." Like Huxley, Bernal saw the "new man" as the logical outcome of the immense, still largely unrealized possibilities of the human brain and his youthful scientific fantasy predicted many of the technological developments of the second half of the 20th century: computers, information technology, and artificial intelligence.

Transhumanism as a New Religious Movement

Whereas the British "prophets" of transhumanism were highly literate men who were at home in the humanities and the arts, the contemporary transhumanist community is dominated by engineers and computer scientists who lack the humanistic imagination their British antecedents received in England's elite schools. Furthermore, whereas the early visionaries of transhumanism believed in the responsibility of the state for the welfare of human beings, the contemporary community is divided between *libertarians* and the *liberal democrats*. The former group highlights the freedom of the individual to choose technological enhancement, regardless of its impact on the collective social good or questions of justice. The latter group believes that by means of technology it will be possible to generate virtuous human beings who will function responsibly as citizens in a democratic, technologically driven society (see Hughes 2004). But whether they are libertarians or liberal democrats, both groups do not shy away from using governmental funding if it helps them to attain the transhumanist agenda.

Since Huxley envisioned transhumanism as a "religion without revelation," should we define transhumanism today as a religion? Most transhumanists will answer this question in the negative because they consider their enterprise an extension of the secular Enlightenment project. As a result, many transhumanists speak dismissively about traditional religions, especially Christianity and ridicule persons of faith as "weak-minded" because of their ignorance of contemporary science and technology (see Campbell/ Walker 2005, ii-iv). However, it is important to note that transhumanism shares many elements with traditional religions: the pursuit of perfection and the focus on human improvement; the concern for the betterment of society by eliminating social ills such as poverty, sickness, and suffering; the progressive understanding of human history that sees the future as necessarily better than the past, the preoccupation with transcendence. Transhumanism also shares with western monotheistic religions a strong eschatological impulse, but it speculates about the eschatological end of the world as a goal that can be accomplished by human efforts alone. Indeed, the main difference between traditional religions and transhumanism concerns the "methods of transcendence" (Hopkins 2005, 22): whereas traditional believers look to prayer, ritual, meditation, and moral discipline, the proponents of transhumanism mobilize technology. Hopkins suggests that "transhumanism could be seen as *religious*, if not a *religion*" (ibid., 20).

Defining religion is by no means easy, but most scholars of religious studies agree that religions share at least some of the following characteristics: the beliefs in supernatural beings; a distinction between the sacred and the profane, rituals; a moral code; religious feelings and experiences; prayer and communication with gods; a comprehensive worldview, a life-style based on that worldview and a social group that promotes that life style (see Alles 2005). Even when religions claim to reveal truths that transcend time and space, religions are always products of socio-cultural activities that reflect historical conditions. How to assess the religiosity of a given society, or conversely, its secularity, has become quite complicated in recent years. On the one hand, societies that have considered themselves secular (e.g., most European countries, Canada, Australia, and New Zealand), have witnessed the return the religion to the public discourse, after a long period during which religion was relegated to the private sphere. On the other hand, religious societies (e.g., the United States) have witnessed the revival of a very militant form of atheism (see Hitchens 2007). This paradoxical moment has been labeled by Jürgen Habermas and others as "post-secular:" whereas the public influence and relevance of religion has increased, the secularist certainty that religion will disappear worldwide in the course of modernization is losing ground. However, today it is not traditional religions that are growing in numbers, but rather New Religious Movements that express certain displeasure with traditional religions and offer a different kind of religiosity to their adherents.

New Religious Movements share some of the features of traditional religions but they are also distinct from them. According to Amarasingam (2008), new religious movements...

> "[…] are concerned with meeting the needs of individual members […] lay claim to some esoteric knowledge that has been lost or repressed or newly discovered […] offer their believers some kind of ecstatic or transfiguring experience that is more direct than that provided by traditional modes of religious life […] display no systematic orientation to a broader society and are usually loosely organized […] always almost center on charismatic leader and face disintegration when the leader dies or is discredited" (Amarasingam 2008, 2).

These features are exhibited by the transhumanist movement as well, especially the more futuristic aspect of transhumanism that speculates about cyber-immortality as the necessary phase toward the posthumanist goal. Indeed Amarasingam argues that futurology should be viewed as new religious movement because it has "charismatic leaders, authoritative texts, mystique, and a fairly complete vision of salvation" (ibid., 13). Yet futurology, which has a distinctive narrative of salvation, will have to compete with other new religious movements in the market-place of ideas. Ironically, the success of futurology is to be found in the fact that (presumably secular) science has an aura of the sacred in contemporary culture.

While most adherents of transhumanism define themselves in secular terms, there are some who are willing to acknowledge the compatibility between established religions and transhumanism, or even call upon the transhumanist community to regard transhumanism as a religion and develop religious transhumanism with its symbolic language and rituals. For example, James Hughes who admits that "transhumanists see themselves as part of the Enlightenment humanist tradition, most are atheist and many feel that one cannot be a theist transhumanist," (Hughes 2007, 5) also pleads with his fellow transhumanists to enter a dialogue with members of faith communities because…

> "[…] pursing a future world community that makes safe human enhancement universally accessible requires a broad, diverse coalition including both secular humanists and people of faith sympathetic with transhumanism" (Hughes 2007, 7).

Out of this dialogue, a new, syncretistic "trans-spirtuality" will emerge "in which enhancement technologies are selectively incorporated by groups in all religious traditions" (ibid.). Hughes counters some of the critique leveled against transhumanism by religious thinkers especially from the Christian Right, on the one hand, while highlighting the positive attitudes toward the transhumanist technological project by liberal Christian theologians, on the other hand. He also correctly notes that Eastern religious traditions such as Buddhism and Shintoism are much open to the transhumanist project, both in terms of human enhancement and in terms of non-dualistic metaphysics.

What will "trans-spirituality" look like is explored by Michael LaTorra, a proponent of transhumanism who is similarly open to Eastern spiritual traditions. LaTorra admits that transhumanists "are practical, scientifically-oriented, rational beings who seek to enhance themselves and bring about benefits for others who voluntarily accept them". In this regard, transhumanists are already fulfilling one of the vows of Mahayana Buddhism "to bring about abundant good for – all beings" (LaTorra 2005, 50). To fellow atheist and agnostic transhumanists, LaTorra notes that spiritual practices (e.g., meditation and prayer) are engaged without any religious component whatsoever. LaTorra proposes a scientifically-based transhumanist spirituality that will utilize the advances of psychology and neuroscience, without recourse to any myth or religious dogma. Because of human scientific understanding of how and why spiritual practices are beneficial to humans, these mechanisms "can be monitored, manipulated, and managed benevolently as a living art" (ibid., 52). Unlike traditional religions, the trans-spiritual project will eschew proselytism and will not engage in theological and metaphysical disputes, but it could enter into dialogue "with people of religious and spiritual orientation who wish to better understand the phenomena associated with those pursuits" (ibid.).

Going beyond Hughes and LaTorra, Gregory Jordan (2005) makes a passionate plea for seeing transhumanism as a religion and for developing a transhumanist religiosity. According to Jordan, …

> "[…] transhumanism serves some of the 'functions' of religion, with regard to providing sense of direction and purpose and providing something greater than the present condition" (Jordan 2005, 58).

While transhumanist does not use the theistic concept of God, it does…

> "[…] imply the possibility of 'godlike' beings […] [who are] 'supernatural' in the sense of attaining the fullest imaginable powers possible in nature, far beyond what humans are presently capable" (Jordan 2005, 58).

Jordan also imputes to transhumanism, "symbolic representations of shared meaning in the form of transhumanist art, which includes symbols, vocabulary, images, songs, film and science fiction literature." Transhumanism also exhibits a "sense of awe associated with the scientific worldview and the contemplation of nature," and its "all-encompassing scientific epistemology combined with theories of sufficient provisional explanatory powers, may soon give rise to a comprehensive worldview" (ibid., 59-60). Jordan maintains that the similarities between transhumanism and traditional religions can be accounted for by "commonalities in fundamental human ambitions, desires, and longing" (ibid.). According to Jordan transhumanist religiosity, however, will be different from traditional religions because it will lack any form of dogmatism, and the transhumanist belief in the "'possibility and desirability' of developing advanced technologies 'to improve the human condition'" is quite different from "fideistic certitude" (ibid., 62). Jordan concludes that "even if transhumanism is not perceived as a religion, it could easily be analyzed as one" (ibid., 65). Moreover, it will be beneficial for transhumanism to be viewed as a religion since religions provide a context for the consideration of meaning, value and the purpose. If and when Singularity occurs, the transhumanist religion will be in its infancy but transhumanist religion will displace traditional religions and will become "what we know" and "how we live" (ibid., 69).

Religious Traditions Engage Transhumanism

The initial responses of established religious traditions to the transhumanist project of human enhancement have been quite varied, although advocates of transhumanism often fail to appreciate this complexity. For example, William Sims Bainbridge a sociologist of religions and a techno-enthusiast has created the impression that transhumanism and established religions are necessarily in conflict with each other. He conducted initial social scientific research of 435 individuals which reached the following conclusion: those who hold traditional religious beliefs tend to be more critical of the transhumanist project of human enhancement (see Bainbridge 2005). Bainbridge also asserts that religious people may be more likely than other people to reject various forms of technological transcendence and he accentuates the potential conflict between religions and transhumanism because he sees them as competitors in the market place of eternal life, so to speak. For Bainbridge, traditional religions are threatened by transhumanism and therefore they can be predicted to try to suppress transhumanism. Since Bainbridge endorses and promotes technological-based immortality, he predicts that it "will put religions largely out of business, and [therefore] religious fundamentalists would condemns activities in these directions" (ibid., 3). Particularly protective of the transhumanist notion of cyber-immortality, Bainbridge speculates about the immoral scenario in which "mob of fanatic will break into personality archives to erase their content" (ibid.). He regards this as a form of murder, an "infocide," "because it kills people in their pure form" and against such dark forces, he presents transhumanism as a religion for the *galactic civilization* and calls us to exercise our imagination so that the current virtual world "could evolve into extrasolar homes for posthuman beings" (ibid., 5). Bainbridge's willingness to extend moral status to bits of information (that is, to uploaded mind-files) lies at the heart of the debate between transhumanists and their religious opponents. In this regard the transhumanists share much with the cultural posthumanists who accord moral status to non-humans, especially animals. But Bainbridge's portrayal of transhumanism and its opposition i borne by the facts generated by social research about the movement.

It is true that in the early debates about genetic engineering, stem-cell research, assisted reproductive technologies, and human cloning, some of the most critical voices came from members of faith communities who challenged the new technologies as assault on human nature and a challenge to human dignity (see Kass 2002; Song 1997; Waters 2001). However, this initial criticism by no means captures the entire story of religious engagement with techno-science. First, some members of the World Transhumanist Association define themselves as religious believers or are members of traditional religious communities (see Hughes 2007). Second, while it is true that religious critics of the technological project view it as a form of hubris, there are also many areas of confluence and overlap between the transhumanist project and traditional religious social concerns for the improvement of the human condition (see Garner 2005). Third, there are some religious traditions that are quite open to the transhumanist technological project even though they do not accept transhumanist futuristic vision.

Judaism is a case in point. The main forms of modern Judaism (Orthodox, Conservative, Reform and Reconstructionist) are very open to biotechnology, especially reproductive technology (including human cloning) because it helps alleviate human suffering (see Zoloth 2011). Orthodox jurists, for example, evaluate each and every new technology not in terms of its impact on the society at large, but in terms of its permissibility within the principles and reasoning procedures of Jewish law. So long as a certain technology does not entail transgression of Jewish legal strictures, it is discretionary and permissible. The rationale for this pro-biotechnology stance is found in the rabbinic portrayal of the human being as God's "partner in the work of creation." Orthodox authorities reason that to be a "partner of God" means that humans have an obligation to improve and ameliorate what God has created because "God left it for human beings to complete the world" as Rabbi Abraham Steinberg put it (Wahrman 2002, 72). The project of human amelioration is thus divinely sanctioned because human beings are obligated to interfere in nature in order to improve the world. Conservative Jewish theologians also accept this principle but emphasize the commandment to heal the sick and prevent or alleviate suffering (see Dorff 1998) as the way for human beings to fulfill the obligation to be a partner in God's creation. Although Jewish religious endorsement of biotechnology is [illegible]ite remarkable (see Sherwin 2004), it does not mean that Judaism endorses the [illegible]ook of the transhumanist project and its relentless individualism [illegible]sh-Samuelson 2012). The utopian and eschatological im[illegible]elves in other forms.

[illegible] human beings are partners of God has also been advocated [illegible] theologians. Philip Hefner, a leading Lutheran theologian, [illegible]man as "created co-creator" in order to "help us to interpret human nature theologically" (Hefner 2009, 169). Hefner elaborates the meaning of this concept in the context of Christian reflections on the "doctrines of creation, creation in the image of God (which introduces the meaning of Jesus Christ), sin and grace, and the final fulfillment or consummation" (ibid.) and argues that "we are created to push the envelope, to envision the possibilities of the creation's future, because we are rooted in the energies of God who has sourced a creation that is defined by envelop pushing" (ibid., 172). For Hefner, then, the transhumanist challenge "constitutes a numinous moment, in which we are engaged in the holy" (ibid.). To be created in the image of God means to be creative, since God is creativity, a view shared by many other Christian theologians. According to Hefner the transhumanist project of technological enhancement has religious significance because the transhumanist imagination itself is an aspect of human nature, the way humans have been created by God. In a similar vein, a fellow Lutheran theologian, Ted Peters, also considers technology not external to humans but very much part of human nature (see Peters 2003), even though Peters is quite critical of the transhumanist materialism, especially the reduction of mind to the brain and understanding of human personhood as disembodied and non-relational (see Peters 2005).

Support for the technological enhancement is found also in Orthodox Christianity. The Greek Orthodox theologian Nikolai Fedorovich Fedorov (1829-1903) envisioned the ultimate end of salvation as deification (*theosis*) – "a radical transfiguration of the whole person, body and soul, and the whole cosmos" (Clay 2012, 158). As Eugene Clay explains, Fedorov contended that all humans should unite in the common cause of raising the dead and regulating the universe through scientific means and he called for the enhancing of the human body in many ways that anticipated the transhumanist project by a century. Like the transhumanists, he believed that human beings are in large measure responsible for their own destiny and that they can fulfill the role that God has assigned for them: "to become a part of a single family [...] to triumph over death [...] [and] to become the governors of the universe" (ibid., 169-170). Fedorov inspired several leading Russian scientists who were at the helm of the Russian space exploration (ibid., 160) and not surprisingly the declaration of the Russian Transhumanist Association founded in 2003 has adopted Fedorov's view (ibid., 157). Even Ray Kurzweil shares Fedorov's vision of the universal resurrection of the dead, when he speculated how technology could be used to resurrect his own father (ibid., 173).

Indeed, a close reading of Ray Kurzweil's vision of the Singularity exposes the degree to which he too views it as *theosis*. Singularity is indeed a religious event. The religiosity of Kurzweil's understanding of Singularity has been noted by several scholars (see Geraci 2008, 2010, 2012; Zimmerman 2008, 2009).

Robert Geraci highlights the degree to which "several pioneers in robotics and AI speak the language of apocalypticism" (Geraci 2008, 2). Like ancient Jewish and Christian apocalypticists, Kurzweil and his cohorts have a strong alienation from the imperfect state of humans and a desire to radically break with it and inaugurate the New Age. Geraci exposes the parallels between "popular science AI and ancient apocalypticism" but without ignoring their differences: whereas in ancient apocalypticism, God has final victory over the forces of evil, in Apocalyptic AI "evolution operates to guarantee the victory of intelligent computation over the forces of ignorance and inefficiency" (ibid., 10). A different interpretation is offered by Michael Zimmerman who explains how much Kurzweil is indebted to Hegel's secularization of Christian motifs. Zimmerman explains:

> "[…] Hegel depicted humankind as the instrument through which absolute *Geist* (spirit) achieves total self-consciousness. Jesus Christ was the man who became God, as much as the God who became man. Similarly, leading post- and transhumanist, Ray Kurzweil revises the customary conception of God to accommodate the possibility that humans are taking part in a process by which post-human beings (*creatures*, according to traditional theism) will attain powers equivalent to those usually attributed to God" (Zimmerman 2008, 348).

Zimmerman concludes that "the God-like post-human amounts to a creature that has become divine, and that has thereby attained the status of cosmic Logos" (ibid., 363), a notion that cannot be reconciled with traditional Christian beliefs. For this reason, perhaps Bainbridge is right to speak about transhumanism as a "heresy" (see Bainbridge 2005).

Interestingly, the fastest growing religion today is the Church of Latter Day Saints, which some Christians do regard as a "heresy." Mormonism exhibits the most positive attitude toward transhumanism and the Mormon Transhumanist Association (2007) was the first religious affiliate of the World Transhumanist Association. The Mormon Transhumanist Association endorses the vision of a "neohuman future that will evolve as time goes on." This future will consist of highly advanced intellectual capabilities; a physical body immune to disease and aging; an ability to commune complex thoughts and emotions instantaneously; expanded sensory inputs that enable higher awareness of even distant environs; superhuman strength and agility; perfect control of individual desires, moods and mental states; and increased capacity to experience joy, love, pleasure and other emotions. Going beyond physical enhancement, Mormons endorse the transhumanist project on theological grounds since they believe in the principle of *theosis*, the concept of eternal progress of humans, and the concept of a progressing God. Mormons see mortal existence as but a preparation for the work that will continue after death, and they hold that individuals will take with them into the next life the knowledge and intelligence that they have garnered during their earthly life. According to Lincoln Canon, the President of the Mormon Transhumanist Association, Mormonism is in fact "the most transhumanist religion" because Mormon beliefs "parallel the transhumanists' common expectation that we will someday be capable of engineering intelligence and worlds" (Cannon/ Goertzel 2011). However, the good works in this world that Mormons consider necessary for eternal life consist of service to others and massive investment in education; while transhumanists talk about the benefit of technology to humanity, they have yet to translate their ideology into social action or education.

Conclusion: Post- and Transhumanism and the Post-Secular Moment

This essay argues that term "posthumanism" is used to mean quite different things in postmodernist philosophical and literary discourse, on the one hand, and in the techno-scientific discourse on the other hand. As a philosophical term, posthumanism denotes the decentering of the human and the attempt to reconfigure the relationship between humans and animals and between humans and machines. The critique by postmodernist cultural posthumanists reflects suspicion toward traditional western ideologies, religions, and philosophies and a denial of the ideology of progress. The "dark side" of many technological innovations is exposed even though cultural posthumanists use technology in the making of postmodern, posthumanist art. By contrast, the technological interpretation of "posthumanism" is committed to modernist ideology of progress by means of science and technology and envisions an eschatological end in which only minds and their computational activity remains, constituting immortality. While there is little actual communication between the two communities who imagine the posthuman phase, both communities share a negative view of human biological embodiment and seek to transcend it.

Transhumanism is the program of human enhancement that is supposed to generate the newly designed human through genetic engineering and other technologies in order to reach the ideal posthuman state. The essay emphasizes Julian Huxley's original vision of transhumanism as "religion without revelation," the willingness of some transhumanists to see transhumanism as religious, and conversely, the openness of some religious traditions toward human enhancement on religious grounds. Although most transhumanists define themselves as secularists and some of the critics of the transhumanists project are members of religious communities, there is no necessary conflict between transhumanism and traditional religions. Given the place of religion in the public sphere today, it may even be beneficial for transhumanism to define itself as a religion and to openly compete in the market of religious ideas. Such competition might compel the advocates of transhumanism to articulate their ideas with greater depth. Whether or not transhumanist will emerge as the religion of the future remains to be seen, but it is clear that transhumanism cannot identify itself naively as a "secular" movement.

A close examination of the religious dimensions of technology (see Noble 1997) and hybridization of religious and secular motifs in the post-secular moment shows how "transhumanism extends in a secularized idiom a form of transcendent religiosity that has deep roots within the Western Christian tradition" (Cady 2012, 100). Future research into transhumanism could explore how the transhumanist quasi-religious imagination of the eschatological future generates technological innovations and how these innovations shape the quality of human life in the present.[1]

Bibliography

Alles, G.D. (2005): Religion [further considerations]. In: Jones, L. (ed.): Encyclopedia of Religion. Detroit: Macmillan Reference, 7701-7706.

Amarasingam, A. (2008): Transcending Technology: Looking at Futurology as a New Religious Movement. In: Journal of Contemporary Religion 23(1), 1-16.

Badmington, N. (ed.) (2000): Posthumanism. New York: Palgrave.

Bainbridge, W.S. (1982): Religions for a Galactic Civilization. In: Emme, E.M. (ed.): Science Fiction and Space Futures. San Diego: American Astronautical Society, 187-201.

Bainbridge, W.S. (2005): The Transhumanist Heresy. In: Journal of Evolution and Technology 14(2), 1-10.

Bainbridge, W.S. (2007): Trajectories to the Heavens. In: The Journal of Personal Cyberconsciousness 2(3). http://www.terasemjournals.org/PCJournal/PC0203/wb1.html (accessed July 6, 2013).

Bostrom, N. (2005): A History of Transhumanist Thought. In: Journal of Evolution and Technology 14(1), 1-25.

Bukatman, S. (2000): Postcard from the Posthuman Solar System. In: Badminigton, N (ed.): Posthumanism, New York: Palgrave, 98-111.

Cady, L.E. (2012): Religion and the Technowonderland of Transhumanism. In: Tirosh-Samuelson, H./ Mossman, K.L. (eds.): Building Better Humans? Refocusing the Debate on Transhumanism, Frankfurt am Main: Peter Lang, 83-104.

1 A slightly different version of this article was published as *Transhumanism as a Secularist Faith* in Zygon: Journal of Religion & Science 47(4), 710-734. I am very grateful to the editor of the journal for granting permission to reproduce material from this publication.

Campbell H./ Walker, M. (2005): Religion and Transhumanism: Introducing a Conversation. In: Journal of Evolution and Technology 14(2), i-xv.

Cannon, L./ Goertzel, B. (2011): Mormonism: The Most Transhumanist Religion? In: H+ Magazine. http://hplusmagazine.com/2011/05/09/mormonism-the-most-transhumanist-religion/ (accessed July 6, 2013).

Clay, E. (2012): Transhumanism and the Orthodox Christian Tradition. In: Tirosh-Samuelson, H./ Mossman, K.L. (eds.): Building Better Humans? Refocusing the Debate on Transhumanism, Frankfurt am Main: Peter Lang, 157-180.

Derrida, J. (1976): Of Grammatology. Baltimore: Johns Hopkins University Press.

Derrida, J. (1982 [1968]): The End of Man. In: Derrida, J.: Margins of Philosophy. Chicago: University Press of Chicago, 109-136.

Derrida, J. (1997): Deconstruction in a Nutshell: A Conversation with Jacques Derrida (Edited and with a Commentary by J. D. Captuo). New York: Fordham University Press.

Dorff, E. (1998): Matters of Life and Death: A Jewish Approach to Modern Medical Ethics. Philadelphia: Jewish Publication Society.

Foucault, M. (1970 [1966]): The Order of Things: An Archaeology of the Human Sciences. New York: Random House.

Garner, S. (2005): Transhumanism and Christian Social Concern. In: Journal of Evolution and Technology 14(2), 29-43.

Garreau, J. (2004): Radical Evolution: The Promise and Peril of Enhancing Our Minds, Our Bodies – and What it Means to Be Human. New York: Doubleday.

Geraci, R.M. (2008). Apocalyptic AI: Religion and the Promise of Artificial Intelligence. In: Journal of American Academy of Religion 76(1), 138-166.

Geraci, R.M. (2010). Apocalyptic AI: Visions of Heaven in Robotics, Artificial Intelligence, and Virtual Reality. New York: Oxford University Press.

Geraci, R.M. (2012): Cyborgs, Robots, and Eternal Avatars: Transhumanist Salvation at the Interface of Brains and Machines. In: Haag, J./ Peterson, G.R./ Spezio, M.L. (eds.): The Routledge Companion to Religion and Science. London et al.: Routledge, 578-590.

Graham, E.L. (2002): Representations of the Post/Human: Monsters, Aliens and Others in Popular Culture. New Brunswick(NJ): Rutgers University Press.

Halberstam, J./ Livingston, I. (1995): Posthuman Bodies. Bloomington: Indiana University Press.

Haraway, D. (1985): A Cyborg Manifesto: Science, Technology, and Socialist Feminism in the Late Twentieth Century. In: Socialist Review 80, 65-108.

Hefner, Ph. (1993): The Human Factor: Evolution, Culture and Religion. Minneapolis: Fortress Press.

Hefner, Ph. (2009): The Animal that Aspires to be an Angel. In: Dialog: A Journal of Theology 48(2), 158-167.

Herzfeld, N. (2012): Human-Directed Evolution: A Christian Perspective. In: Haag, J./ Peterson, G.R./ Spezio, M.L. (eds.): The Routledge Companion to Religion and Science. London et al.: Routledge, 591-601.

Hitchens, Ch. (ed.) (2007): The Portable Atheist: Essential Readings for the Nonbeliever. Philadelphia: De Capo Press.

Hopkins, P.D. (2005): Transcending the Animal: How Transhumanism and Religion Are and Are Not Alike. In: Journal of Evolution and Technology 14(2), 13-28.

Hughes, J. (2004): Citizen Cyborg: Why Democratic Societies Must Respond to the Redesigned Human of the Future. Boulder: Westview Press.

Hughes, J. (2007): The Compatibility of Religious and Transhumanist Views of Metaphysics, Suffering, Virtue and the Transcendence in an Enhanced Future. In: The Global Spiral 8(2).

Huxley, J. (1927): Religion without Revelation. London: E. Benn.

Huxley, J. (1934): If I Were a Dictator. London: Methuen.

Jordan, G. (2006): Apologia for Transhumanist Religion. In: Journal of Evolution and Technology 15(1), 55-72.

Kass, L.R. (2002): Life, Liberty, and the Defense of Dignity: The Challenge for Bioethics. San Francisco: Encounter.

Kurzweil, R. (1999): The Age of Spiritual Machines: When Computers Exceed Human Intelligence. New York: Viking.

Kurzweil, R. (2005): The Singularity is Near: When Humans Transcend Biology. New York: Penguin Books.

LaTorra, M. (2005): Trans-Spirit: Religion, Spirituality and Transhumanism. Journal of Evolution and Technology 14(2), 41-55.

Magnus, B./ Higgins, K.M. (1996): Nietzsche's Work and Their Themes. In: Magnus, B./ Higgins, K.M. (eds.): The Cambridge Companion to Nietzsche. Cambridge: Cambridge University Press, 21-70.

Miah, A. (2008) A Critical History of Posthumanism. In: Gordijn B./ Chadwick, R.F. (eds.): Medical Enhancement and Posthumanity. Dordrecht: Springer, 71-94.

Minsky, M. (1986): The Society of Mind. New York: Simon & Schuster.

Minsky, M. (2006): The Emotion Machine: Commonsense Thinking, Artificial Intelligence, and the Future of the Human Mind. New York et al.: Simon & Schuster.

Moravec, H. (1988): Mind Children: The Future of Robot and Human Intelligence. Cambridge(MA): Harvard University Press.

Moravec, H. (1999): Robot: Mere Machine to Transcendent Mind. New York: Oxford University Press.

Mormon Transhumanist Association (2007): Mormon Transhumanist Association. http://transfigurism.org/ (accessed July 6, 2013).

Noble, D. (1997): The Religion of Technology: The Divinity of Man and the Spirit of Invention. New York: A.A. Knopf.

Pepperell, R. (2003): The Post-Human Condition. Bristol et al.: Intellect.

Peters, T. (2003): Science, Theology, and Ethics. Aldershot et al.: Ashgate.

Peters, T. (2005): The Soul of Trans-Humanism. In: Dialog: A Journal of Theology 44(4), 381-95.

Salaquarda, J. (1996): Nietzsche and the Judaeo-Christian tradition. In: Magnus, B./ Higgins, K.M. (eds.): The Cambridge Companion to Nietzsche. Cambridge: Cambridge University Press, 90-118.

Samuelson, N./ Tirosh-Samuelson, H. (2012): Jewish Perspectives on Transhumanism. In: Tirosh-Samuelson, H./ Mossman, K.L. (eds.): Building Better Humans? Refocusing the Debate on Transhumanism, Frankfurt am Main: Peter Lang, 105-132.

Sherwin, B. (2004): Golems Among Us: How a Jewish Legend Can Help Us Navigate the Biotech Century. Chicago: Ivan R. Dee.

Song, R. (2002): Human Genetics: Fabricating the Future. London: Darton Longman & Todd.

Soper, K. (1986): Humanism and Anti-Humanism. LaSalle(IL): Open Court.

Steinhart, E. (2008): Teilhard de Chardin and Transhumanism. In: Journal of Evolution and Technology 20, 1-22.

Tirosh-Samuelson, H. (2009): Jewish Philosophy, Human Dignity, and the New Genetics. In: Sutton, S.D. (ed.): Biotechnology, Our Future as Human Beings and Citizens. Albany(NY): State University of New York Press, 81-122.

Tirosh-Samuelson, H. (2012): Science and Human Betterment: Three British Prophets of Transhumanism. In: Tirosh-Samuelson, H./ Mossman, K.L. (eds.): Building Better Humans? Refocusing the Debate on Transhumanism, Frankfurt am Main: Peter Lang, 55-82.

Wahrman, M.Z. (2002): Brave New Judaism: When Science and Scripture Collide. Hanover(NH) et al.: University Press of New England for Brandeis University Press.

Waters, B. (2001): Reproductive Technology: Towards a Theology of Procreative Stewardship. Cleveland: Pilgrim Press.

Waters, B. (2006): From Human to Posthuman: Christian Theology and Technology in a Postmodern World. Williston(VT): Ashgate.

Wolfe, C. (2010): What is Posthumanism? Minneapolis et al.: University of Minnesota Press.

Young, S. (2005): Designer Evolution: A Transhumanist Manifesto. Amherst(NY): Prometheus Books.

Zimmerman, M. (2008): The Singularity: A Crucial Phase in Divine Self-Actualization? In: Cosmos and History: Journal of Natural and Social Philosophy 4(1-2), 347-370.

Zimmerman, M. (2009): Religious Motifs in Technological Posthumanism. In: Western Humanities Review (3), 67-83.

Zoloth, L. (2011): Justice in the Margins of the Land: Jewish Responses to the Challenges of Biotechnology. In: Haag, J.W. / Peterson, G.R./ Spezio, M.L. (eds.): The Routledge Companion of Religion and Science. London et al.: Routledge, 476-483.

Prometheus
Performer or Transformer?

Trijsje Franssen

In an article called *Prometheus as Performer: Toward a Posthumanist Culture* (1977) the literary theorist Ihab Hassan was one of the first to use the word "posthumanism". As the title suggests, the mythological figure of Prometheus is used to signal the emergence of a posthumanist culture. Interestingly, not only Hassan referred to Prometheus to make his point, but so did many posthumanists after him, and quite a few transhumanists use the myth as well to support their arguments. By focusing on these references in the following I will try to clarify some of the important differences between the two movements. I will start with a description of the myth and will then analyze a selection of key posthumanist and transhumanist texts.[1]

The Myth

There are many versions of the myth of Prometheus, of which one of the best known is *Prometheus Bound* by Aeschylus (5/6th century BC). After the older generation of deities had been conquered in the Clash of the Titans, Zeus threw all of them, including his father Kronos, in the dark hole of Tartaros, the lowest depths of the underworld. Only one of them, Prometheus, was saved because he had helped Zeus to win the war by means of his cunning and advice. Soon, however, Zeus turned out to be a merciless tyrant. When he conceived a plan to wipe out the whole human race, Prometheus took pity on them. He stole fire for them from heaven, gave them wisdom and taught them all kinds of techniques and arts – from mathematics to reading and the art of prophecy. However, when Zeus found out, Prometheus was severely punished. Zeus chained the immortal god to a rock, where a vulture would eat his liver. Every night it would regenerate so that his torture could be repeated the next day, until many centuries later Hercules should free him.

Hesiod's earlier version of the myth,[2] tells how Zeus also punished mankind by sending them Pandora, the first woman. She carried the famous box that spread out evil, misery and disaster over the human race. Later, in Plato's *Protagoras* (4th century BC), Prometheus is described as taking part in the creation of mankind. He and his not-so-clever brother Epimetheus were put in charge by

---

1 Since there are many different understandings of both concepts, I don't claim to present an exhaustive explanation of either of them.

2 In his *Theogony* and *Works and Days* (8th century BC).

the gods to assign to all the mortal races their defining attributes. Epimetheus, however, used up all the qualities on the animals, so that no powers were left when he came to man: "the human race was naked, unshod, unbedded, and unarmed" (Plato 1997, 757). To compensate for his brother's fault, Prometheus decided to give them fire, knowledge, and other civilizing arts which, again, he stole from the gods. Plato's story does not mention Pandora or the rock, but merely that later Prometheus was charged with theft. The humans started worshipping the gods, because "they alone among the animals had a share of the divine dispensation" (ibid.). First, however, "[t]hey were being destroyed by wild beasts because they were weaker in every way" (ibid.). Only after Zeus sent them the art of politics, justice and shame, they were able to establish order, found cities, and bonds of friendship.

Posthumanism

The Prometheus myth is used in Hassan's paper, in which an emergent, posthumanist culture is announced. Explaining how we should understand the term, he writes:

> "We need first to understand that the human form [...] may be changing radically, and thus must be re-visioned. We need to understand that five hundred years of humanism may be coming to an end, as humanism transforms itself into something that we must helplessly call posthumanism" (Hassan 1977, 212).

Hassan observes the dissolution of classical humanist dichotomies – such as subject/object, man/machine, or science/culture – its idea of the human and its strong anthropocentrism. The culture is characterized by "[c]onvergences and divergences, conjunctions and disjunctions." On the one hand, there's fragmentation: "Our planet continually splinters, breaks according to ideology, religion, [...] sex, and age" (ibid., 203). On the other hand, it sees traditional distinctions blurring, such as those between "the One and the Many," "the Universal and the Concrete" (ibid., 207). Prometheus mirrors this culture because of his (and the myth's) ambiguity: on the one hand, he is a hubristic trickster, a thief, on the other hand a hero, a savior. Moreover, by means of his cunning, courage and theft he helped to create the human being, and to *transform* him into a smarter, better, more civilized being.

> "Prometheus is himself the figure of a flawed consciousness struggling to transcend [...] divisions [...]. [W]ith regard to posthumanism itself, the most relevant aspect of the Promethean dialectic concerns Imagination and Science, Myth and Technology, Earth and Sky" (Hassan 1977, 207).

Prometheus crosses boundaries between the human and the divine and makes mankind overcome its limits by means of art and technology. This is relevant since, as Hassan shows, in contemporary culture many divisions are dissolving. There is creative imagination involved in science – in man's expansion into the Galaxy for instance – while technology is incorporated into the arts – in photography for instance, or electronic music. The concept of the human as such, and the dichotomy subject-object should also be reconsidered, for it is questionable whether we, having developed things such as space travel and organ transplantation, could still be said to be the same species. "Will artificial intelligences supersede the human brain […]? We do not know. But this we do know: artificial intelligences […] help to transform the image of man, the concept of the human" (ibid., 214). The boundaries between man and machine, in short, between human and non-human, are blurring as well, and changing continuously.

> "Prometheus is our performer. He performs Space and Time; he performs Desire. He suffers. We are ourselves that performance […]. We are the pain or play of the human, which will not remain human. […] Everything changes, and nothing, not even Death, can tire" (Hassan 1977, 217).

Because of his ambiguity, his boundary-crossing and his help to enable humanity overcome its own limits and evolve, for Hassan Prometheus exemplifies a posthumanist culture in which humanism's binaries are dissolving and its idea of the human and its anthropocentrism are challenged.

The philosopher Jacques Derrida uses the image of the Titan in his work *The Animal That Therefore I Am* (2008).[3] As the title suggests already, it deals with what Derrida calls "the question of the animal" (Derrida 2008, 8). Reflecting on the shame he feels at the moment when he is "caught naked, in silence, by the gaze of an animal" (ibid., 3) – his cat, namely – Derrida starts questioning the concept of nudity. It is generally assumed, he says, that what distinguishes animals from humans is that they are naked without being aware of it. Only humans decided to dress themselves because they are ashamed of their nudity, and thereby "nudity" as such reveals itself as inherently human – namely as something opposed to being dressed. One could say the animal *isn't* naked: it doesn't have knowledge of its own nudity, feel shame, or dress itself, and therefore it isn't naked. Nudity thus draws a boundary between human and animal – just like shame, and clothing. Like so many words and statements made about animals – their alleged inability to speak, to reason, to address us – "nudity" assigns to the animal the place of "the absolute other". That is, man defines himself in contrast with the animal. The gaze of the cat, however, makes Derrida realize it is *look-*

3 The text arose from a lengthy address given by Derrida at a conference in Cerisy, (France) in 1997 and was published earlier in the journal *Critical Inquiry* (2002).

ing at him, *seeing* him, perhaps even *addressing* him, which would invalidate our assumptions about the animal's inabilities. The gaze thus deconstructs its place as the "wholly other", leading Derrida to wonder who he is, and question his humanity and subjectivity.

The establishment of the animal as "wholly other" already starts in the Genesis, when God told man to name the animals, to "have authority […] over all the wild beasts […] that crawl upon the earth!" (ibid.).

> "[I]n the Genesis tale as much as in the myth of Prometheus (let's remember the *Protagoras* and the moment when Prometheus steals fire […], in order to make up for the forgetfulness or tardiness of Epimetheus, who had perfectly equipped all breeds of animal but left 'man naked [gymnon],' without shoes, covering, or arms), it is paradoxically on the basis of a fault or failing in man that the latter will be made a subject who is master of nature and of the animal. From within the pit of that lack […], man installs or claims in a single stroke *his property* […] and his *superiority* over what is called animal life" (Derrida 2008, 20).

The myth of Prometheus – Plato's version, that is – is, like the Genesis, a classic story about the origin of humanity. It appoints to the human a central place in the world, a position as proprietor of arts and technology and as "master of nature", which also implies his superiority over animals. However, Derrida argues, this supposed mastery is based first, on a *fault* – Epimetheus' failure to save some powers for the mortals; and second, on a *lack* – man's nakedness and original lack of abilities.[4] By stressing a different aspect of the Prometheus myth than "usual", Derrida shows how unfounded this supposed superiority is. Although elaborated rather differently than Hassan, again the myth thus provides a means to present posthumanist ideas, to deconstruct anthropocentrism and humanist dichotomies such as human/animal and subject/object.

In *A Cautious Prometheus? A Few Steps Toward a Philosophy of Design* (2008), the sociologist and philosopher Bruno Latour also criticizes humanism with the help of the image of the mythological god. He investigates the word "design", which used to have a limited significance as the "form" or "shape" of an object, as one side of the form/function or material/aesthetic dichotomy. However, its meaning has grown to "comprehend more elements of what a thing is" and "is applicable to ever larger assemblages of production. […] [T]he typically modernist divide between materiality on the one hand and design on the other is slowly being dissolved away" (Latour 2008, 2). While he analyzes the concept's connotations, Prometheus emerges. "Design", Latour argues, implies a certain humility and modesty since it is not "foundational".

---

4 In the Genesis the "fault" and "lack" are (respectively) the original sin and man's initial nudity.

> "It seems to me that to say you plan to design something, does not carry the same risk of hubris as saying one is going to build something. [...] A second and perhaps more important implication of design is an attentiveness to *details* that is completely lacking in the heroic, Promethean, hubristic dream of action. [...] [T]hings are no longer 'made' or 'fabricated', but rather carefully 'designed' [...]; it is as though we had to imagine Prometheus stealing fire from heaven in a cautious way!" (Latour 2008, 3-4).

Apart from humility and attention to details, "design" also has a semiotic, a remedial, and a moral dimension. It adds something to be interpreted to (what was originally) the "object": "matter is absorbed into meaning." Further, to design means to "redesign". There is always already a basis on which is worked: "[t]o design is never to create *ex nihilo*". Finally, since something can be designed "well" or "badly" the concept shows that normativity is inherent to design: "it is as if materiality and morality were finally coalescing" (ibid., 5).

Thus for Latour, Prometheus symbolizes hubris, mastery, rebellion, and creation (from scratch). Although he doesn't consider the myth to be ambiguous, it does provide a means to both signal (like Hassan) and call for (like Derrida) conceptual and practical change. "Humanists are concerned only about humans; the rest, for them, is mere materiality or cold objectivity" (Latour 2008, 10). It is this humanist – or "modernist" – view that Prometheus represents. Calling for a "precautionary Prometheus", Latour asks to overcome humanist anthropocentrism and binaries such as form/function, fact/value, objective/subjective and human/nonhuman. Mere deconstruction, however, won't do, since these divides never really existed in the first place: objects and subjects have always been integrated, just like the "natural" and the "artificial". "What I am pressing for is a means for drawing *things* together – gods, non humans and mortals included" (ibid., 13). "Things", in Latour's vocabulary, thus include objects as much as subjects, and artifacts as much as humans. This is what we need to recognize "if we are to adequately represent the conflicting natures of all the things that are to be designed" (ibid.).

Although not all three would literally call themselves "posthumanists", in view of the way they criticize humanism the thinkers treated so far do hold posthumanist ideas – visible in the references to Prometheus.

Transhumanism

Transhumanism is a movement of people who argue that we should try to "enhance" the human being in every possible way, especially with new technologies such as genetic engineering, cloning, or nanotechnology. A variety of arguments is used: enhancement is inevitable, a logical new step in humanity's evolution, and/or a moral duty. It will cure disease, reduce inequality, make us mentally stronger, more intelligent, and happier. According to some in the end it will even generate a *posthuman* species. Which, as leading transhumanist Nick Bostrom explains, we should understand as a "possible type of human mode of being – if I am right, an exceedingly worthwhile type" (2009, 135).

Several transhumanists – or pro-enhancement thinkers[5] – appeal to the Promethean image in order to articulate their point of view. In his book *Redesigning Humans* (2003), biophysicist Gregory Stock confidently announces that we are "on the cusp of profound biological change" (Stock 2003, 1). Given emerging technologies such as cloning and genetic modification it is only a matter of time before we will be able "to seize control of our evolutionary future" (ibid., 2). Whether we like it or not, he argues, the trend has been set and further developments are inevitable. Some of us *are* already enhancing themselves by means of, for instance, "performance enhancement" – drugs – in sports or aesthetic surgery. Of course we should be careful with the new technologies, but, Stock claims, no serious scientist will start playing around with human genes until such interventions can be safely carried out. So "why all the fuss, then?" (ibid., 12). To try to stop the developments is unrealistic and simply impossible. Rather, we should think about how to minimize the risks and maximize the benefits, be brave and face the unknown dangers that accompany all radical new developments.

> "Some imagine we will see the perils, come to our senses, and turn away from such possibilities. But when we imagine Prometheus stealing fire from the gods, we are not incredulous or shocked by his act. It is too characteristically human. To forego the powerful technologies [...] would be as out of character for humanity as it would be to use them without concern for the dangers they pose" (Stock 2003, 2).

In other words: Prometheus sought adventure, faced danger, and crossed boundaries, which led to civilization and technological progress. This, Stock seems to say, is exactly what we should do as well. Or better: what we *will* do, for it is *too characteristically human.* A *true* human is like Prometheus: he takes control, acquires knowledge and develops technologies in order to improve. Enhancement is only natural, and therefore inevitable.

It seems like Stock rather supports than opposes humanism. First, his argument is very anthropocentric. All reasoning is done exclusively from a human perspective, championing his control and mastery without any attention for animals for example, or "things" in Latour's sense. Moreover, behind his claims lies a particular idea of what human nature is in the first place: a Promethean being that naturally faces danger, transcends his borders, and looks for infinite

5 Not all people who endorse these views call themselves "transhumanists".

improvement. Second, he shows a firm belief in science and technological development which reveals a very humanist emphasis on – and faith in – reason, knowledge, and progress. Third, an assertion stating that we will "seize control of our evolutionary future", shows how many humanist dichotomies are still at work. The (human) subject manipulates the object; science takes control over nature; and the mind engineers the body – which is nothing but an instrument. We should exclusively focus on rationality and cast aside emotions such as anxiety.

Pretty much all of transhumanism's standard assumptions and statements are gathered in the *Designer Evolution: A Transhumanist Manifesto* (2006) by transhumanist Simon Young. He defines it as "the belief in overcoming human limitations through reason, science and technology" (Young 2006, 15). To conquer the greatest "tragedies" of life – man's biological limitations and death – is not a mere wish, but our destiny. Humans, Young explains, are by nature imbued with the innate "Will to Evolve": "the instinctive drive [...] to expand [his] abilities in pursuit of ever-increasing survivability and well-being" (ibid., 39). Therefore, a so-called "designer evolution" is inevitable: "Humanity will take evolution out of the hands of butterfingered nature into its own transhuman hands" (ibid., 38).

The "Will to Evolve" is symbolized by Prometheus, who represents "the innate human drive to increase knowledge and abilities, even at the expense of present pains" (ibid.) – the drive, that is, to progress, improve, *enhance.*[6] Young recognizes that a future of "self-design" is not without risks. However, to reject the "Prometheus Drive" will lead to decline, for "that which ceases to grow, begins to decay" (ibid., 39). It would mean to remain forever in the power of our limitations and keep on suffering from disease and death. Therefore, Young pleads:

> "Let us be the *New Prometheans*. Let us unite in our commitment to boldly go where none have gone before in search of the knowledge by which to transcend the limitations of the human condition. Let us cast aside cowardice and seize the torch of Prometheus with both hands" (Young 2006, 40).

Again, Prometheus thus symbolizes courage, mastery and transcendence of limits in order to gain knowledge, develop techniques and improve the human being. And again, all humans have a Promethean nature, since we all possess the "Will to Evolve", the drive to progress. More explicit than in Stock's case is the element of "creation": humanity will not merely take control of its species but – like Prometheus – *create*, *design* it, literally taking "evolution [...] into its own

6 Young explains later that the *Will* consists of two drives: the *Prometheus* and *Orpheus Drives*, or the *Will to Grow* and the *Will to Love* respectively.

transhuman hands". Further, Young's moral urge is stronger than Stock's. Not only is this "designer evolution" inevitable, but we *have to* fight nature by all means for otherwise misery and decay will be our fate.

But in general Young argues just like Stock in a very humanist, anthropocentric way and employs a specific idea of human nature. With respect to his belief in science he even literally mentions humanism. "To boldly go where none have gone before" is a reference to Star Trek, and Young emphasizes how the series' philosophy "is the essence of humanism: the belief in the ongoing progress of the species through reason, science, and technology" (ibid., 39). By invoking the Star Trek ambition and explaining it the way he does, he explicitly affirms the humanist character of his faith in science. Obviously, Young's arguments in general also imply several humanist dichotomies, with science, reason and the human mind on the one hand; and nature, emotions and the body on the other.

Various transhumanists thus employ the myth to encourage enhancement and celebrate the infinite possibilities that contemporary technology can offer humanity – all based on a rather humanist perspective.[7] Interestingly, the figure of Prometheus is also used to argue the exact opposite from the transhumanists. In this paper I do not have the space to discuss all such views and analyze them in any detail, but I would like to briefly mention two thinkers.

Decades before the so-called "enhancement debate" starts, the philosopher Günther Anders (2010 [1956]) criticizes the technology-driven society and its effects on humanity. He argues that contemporary humans feel that artifices have taken over their position of the most perfect, unique and superior being. It fills them with what Anders calls *Promethean shame* (*Prometheische Scham*) – "shame for the 'shamefully' high quality" of the things they fabricated themselves.[8] They consider it their duty to overcome their inferiority, their contingency, their *nature*, and attain the perfection of the artifice. One could say Anders already saw enhancement coming – and perhaps even the posthuman – and lamented the sad wish of man to become one with the machine.

Today, the political philosopher Michael Sandel – "bioconservative" according to his pro-enhancement opponents – passionately argues against genetic en-

7 Although they would probably not call themselves transhumanists, similar pro-enhancement statements are made by the philosophers Ronald Dworkin and Donrich Jordaan. Both speaking in the context of genetic engineering, the former tells us that "[p]laying God is indeed playing with fire. But that is what we mortals have done since Prometheus, the patron saint of dangerous discoveries" (2000, 446); and the latter warns us to "[b]eware the day when we betray our promethean heritage" (2009, 590).

8 "'*Prometheische Scham*' […] die '*Scham vor der ›beschämend‹ hohen Qualität der selbstgemachten Dinge*'" (Anders 2010 [1956]), 23).

gineering and other forms of enhancement. The problem is that "they represent a kind of hyperagency – a Promethean aspiration to remake nature, including human nature, to serve our purposes and satisfy our desires" (Sandel 2007, 26-27). Such a Promethean drive to mastery will destroy our appreciation of what he calls the "giftedness of life", our natural talents and gifts. A certain anthropocentrism and some humanist dichotomies are still also at work in Sandel's thinking, yet obviously in order to sustain an entirely different argument than the transhumanists. In contrast with them, both Anders and Sandel deplore the Promethean urge to cross our boundaries and transform ourselves, for instead of enhancing it is humiliating us and will perhaps even destroy our very nature.

Conclusion

The transhumanists discussed clearly endorse a *humanist* rather than a posthumanist view: their ideas are anthropocentric, they have an unshakeable belief in science and technology and rely on some of the most basic dichotomies which are challenged so ardently by many posthumanists.

Of course, there are some differences between transhumanism and humanism as well. For a start, enhancement by means of technology and drugs is rather distinct from the Renaissance focus on education (although this difference is vehemently denied by many transhumanists). Further, transhumanism's faith in science and evolution must lead them to recognize that technically humanity is merely one of many species, which forces them to adjust the original humanist view of man's unassailable superiority. Finally, the "posthuman" is obviously a creature that moves beyond the human in a way. The creation of a being consisting of both organic and electronic or mechanical parts would, for instance, indeed synthesize man and machine, radically changing the traditional idea of what it means to be human.

The latter is probably one of the most important reasons why posthumanism and transhumanism are often used interchangeably. Both movements pay a lot of attention to emerging technologies and the way these affect (the concept of) the human in particular. The image of a posthuman being who is not 100% organic anymore, arises rather often in both cases and, as said, is an example of the way in which transhumanism, just like posthumanism, challenges the dichotomy man/machine. However, for transhumanists this is only in order to enhance the human, not to equalize man and machine. And as we saw, many other binaries are still prospering in transhumanist theories. Of the two movements, only posthumanism seems to truly aim to move beyond humanism. Clearly we are dealing with two rather different philosophies: a *post-humanist* and *posthuman-*

ist one. So each time Prometheus enters the stage in this context, we should ask ourselves: is he a *Post-humanist* Performer, or a *Posthuman-ist* Transformer?

Bibliography

Anders, G. (2010 [1956]): Die Antiquiertheit des Menschen (Vol. 1): Über die Seele im Zeitalter der zweiten industriellen Revolution. München: C.H. Beck.

Bostrom, N. (2009): Why I Want to Be a Posthuman When I Grow Up. In: Gordijn, B./ Chadwick, R. (eds.): Medical Enhancement and Posthumanity. Dordrecht: Springer, 107-137.

Derrida, J. (2008): The Animal That Therefore I Am. New York: Fordham University Press.

Dworkin, R. (2000): Sovereign Virtue: The Theory and Practice of Equality. Cambridge(MA) et al.: Harvard University Press.

Hassan, I. (1977): Prometheus as Performer: Toward a Posthumanist Culture? In: Benamou, M./ Caramello, C. (eds.): Performance in Postmodern Culture. Madison(WI): Coda Press, 201-217.

Jordaan, D. (2009): Antipromethean Fallacies: A Critique of Fukuyama's Bioethics. In: Biotechnology Law Report 28(5), 577-590.

Latour, B. (2008): A Cautious Prometheus? A Few Steps Toward a Philosophy of Design (with Special Attention to Peter Sloterdijk). http://www.bruno-latour.fr/node/69 (accessed May 3, 2013).

Plato (1997): Protagoras. In: Complete Works (Edited by J.M. Copper). Cambridge et al.: Hackett Publishing.

Sandel, M. (2007): The Case Against Perfection: Ethics in the Age of Genetic Engineering. Cambridge(MA) et al.: Belknap Press of Harvard University Press.

Stock, G. (2003): Redesigning Humans. London: Profile Books.

Young, S. (2006): Designer Evolution: A Transhumanist Manifesto. New York: Prometheus Books.

Nietzsche

Yunus Tuncel

Since his death in 1900 Nietzsche's influence on culture and thought has proliferated, as this influence has spread over many diverse interpretations of his works. Thinkers, writers, artists, and ideologues found a wealth of ideas there with which they can engage for their own needs and purposes. While writers like Gide, Shaw, Hesse, Musil, and Mann contributed to the rise of Nietzsche's posthumous fame, painters and musicians like Kandinsky and Strauss found a source of inspiration in Nietzsche's Dionysian philosophy. The scope of diversity of Nietzsche interpretations became acute in 1930s and 40s when thinkers like Heidegger and Bataille found a worthy philosopher in Nietzsche, while the Nazi ideologues tried to appropriate Nietzsche for their own political agenda. The post-war era, on the other hand, saw different Nietzsches, Nietzsches that were responding to the needs of a cultural transformation. Nietzsche's call for a new type of human being, his critique of European morality and humanism, his announcement of the death of God echoed in many different circles and movements. Two of these movements are transhumanism and posthumanism (see Woodward 2011, 185-208); the former aims to seek the continuation and acceleration of the evolution of intelligent life beyond its currently human form by means of science and technology, while the latter is an attempt to critique the foundational assumptions of Western thought and culture and its outdated conceptions of human nature and to go beyond them. In this essay I will explore some of the issues and debates that connect Nietzsche to these movements, while pointing out to their divergences. As I split my essay into two parts accordingly, I will address the following topics: power, the will to power, perspectivism, rationality, the status of animals, the new type of human being, the overhuman, Renaissance, Enlightenment, and evolution. At least two things must be kept in mind: first, there are many different ideas that make up these movements some of which cohere and some do not. This essay will not address the issue of coherence within these movements, but rather orient itself towards some of their prominent aspects. Second, there are many philosophers or philosophical movements that have inspired these movements. I will not address all of these schools, but only those that are pertinent to the scope of this introductory essay.

1. Nietzsche as Ancestor of Posthumanism

One can find Nietzschean traces in recent philosophical currents that inform posthumanism. In what follows below, these traces will be surveyed in four areas: power, perspectivism, human-animal relationship, and the posthuman conception of human being. Nietzsche's radical ideas on power have been interpreted in a variety of ways. Heidegger's emphasis on the will to power as a metaphysical principle in Nietzsche did not detract later thinkers like Deleuze and Foucault from seeing insights in Nietzsche's philosophy of power. Nietzsche's perspectivism opened new horizons and debates regarding questions of interpretation and theories of knowledge. Moreover, Nietzsche's critique of human being as constructed by the highest values of Europe up to the nineteenth century and all the related cultural phenomena provoked later thinkers to re-think the place of human being in the universe (in relation to animals and other beings) and to search for new conceptions, new "subjectivities," and new technologies of the self. Below is a survey of some of these new trends in posthumanism.

1.1 The Will to Power Ontology

Nietzsche inaugurates a new way of thinking about power, as he dislodges the question of power from a representational theory that treats power[1] as a thing, as static, as political in the limited sense, and as detached from its affects and its context. While understanding power in its multiple aspects, as power of creation and Dionysian power, Nietzsche unearths the power of instincts or the body in general and the power of unconscious forces. Moreover, Nietzsche sees the pervasiveness of power relations, albeit often unconscious, considers them to be multiplistic, conceives of different matrices of power relations (vertical and horizontal, for instance), and is the first thinker to expose the workings of *active* and *reactive*[2] forms of power (with degrees of separation between them). Both Deleuze and Foucault incorporate many of Nietzsche's ideas on power into their conception of bio-power.

Inspired by Spinoza and acknowledging with Nietzsche that the hour of the body has come, Deleuze expands on the notions of active and reactive forces, quantity and quality of forces, and presents his own reading of the will to power. Reactive forces are inferior forces and have to do with the "mechanical and utilitarian accommodations" (Deleuze 1983, 41)[3] and, as such, are within the easy

1 Nietzsche's ideas on power are spread throughout his works. Although Nietzsche uses the term in his early works, the turning point can be located in his works from late 1870s when he reflects on power dynamics in *Daybreak* (1982 [1881]) and coins the terms "feeling of power" and "will to power".

2 Nietzsche uses these two terms in *On the Genealogy of Morals* I (1969 [1887]), to refer to specific forms of force; they can also, respectively, be applied to forms of power.

3 In one scoop Deleuze took an agonistic position against three schools of philosophy: mechanistic, utilitarian, and consciousness or subjectivity. In *On the Genealogy of Mor-*

grasp of consciousness, whereas active forces are spontaneous, aggressive, expansive, and form-giving forces that give new interpretations and directions (see Nietzsche 1969 [1887] II, 12) and often remain unconscious. After working out an understanding of active and reactive forces, Deleuze moves on to quantity and quality of forces; here he emphasizes the singularity of each force, "the irreducible element of quantity," and affirms the role of chance in the relation of forces. "By affirming chance we affirm the relation of *all* forces. And, of course, we affirm all of chance all at once in the thought of the eternal return" (Deleuze 1983, 44).[4] All forces return singularly and cannot be reduced to an identity; such reduction is what reactive forces attempt to do. Not only quantum cannot be thought of in the abstract for Deleuze, but quantum cannot be reduced to quality since the latter has to do with relation of forces. Deleuze wraps up many issues when he next discusses the will to power, which he considers to be the genealogical element of force, both differential and genetic:

> "The will to power is the element from which derive both the quantitative difference of related forces and the quality that devolves into each force in this relation" (Deleuze 1983, 50).

On the one hand, the will to power is an immanent force among other forces (it is a force that wills, that has a direction and an impact); on other other hand, it is a force that gathers all forces together in its own context. Being singular and different, it relates to that which is singular and different. In this way, Deleuze ties the will to power to the issues of "active and reactive" and "quantity and quality". Quantity determines the domination of forces, whereas quality is a reflection of their being active or reactive. Finally, it is through the will to power that a force prevails over other forces, and there is will to power in active forces as much as in reactive forces.

Deleuze's Nietzsche-inspired theses about power, namely that power is immanent, pervasive, and relational, are shared by Foucault who takes these ideas and creates a power analytics for his critique of institutions in their historical context. The best example for this application is *Discipline & Punish.* We cannot follow through this application closely here, but two things can be said regarding what Foucault owes Nietzsche on power: first, the relationship between power, knowledge, and truth is amply shown in Nietzsche's works. The second one has to do with the *productive* aspect of power. For this issue, one needs to understand how and why power, in any of its form, is creative or *affective*. Fou-

---

als I (1969 [1887]) Nietzsche presents his initial ideas on reactivity as he defines ressentiment. Reaction, revenge, and ressentiment form a trinity for Nietzsche, as these three form the unconscious of the morality of good and evil.

4 Chance must be related to the spontaneity of the active forces.

cault's model of power as productive resonates with many of Nietzsche's ideas. Additionally, the five points that Foucault makes on power in the first volume of *The History of Sexuality* (1990, 94-96) can all be found in some form or another in Nietzsche's writings: the first point has to do with the fluidity of power and power relations. The second one shows power's immanence (from Spinoza). The third one starts with a thesis that does not agree with Nietzsche, "Power comes from below [...];" for Nietzsche power comes from all directions. But the gist of this point lies in the multiplistic aspect of power relations (as opposed to binarisms). Fourth, power relations are both intentional and nonsubjective; in other words, there are individual and collective dimensions to power relations. Finally, resistance is an integral aspect of power relations. It must be added here that Foucault took off with these ideas and applied them concretely to specific institutional practices and power relations. In this regard, his contribution to philosophy of power is invaluable. One can only study the way he diagnoses the automatic functioning of power in the Panopticon, a power analysis, which Nietzsche could not have made, but which would not have been possible without Nietzsche (see Foucault 1995, 201; Part 3).

In conclusion, we can establish a connection between Nietzsche's philosophy of power and posthumanistic reflections on power, as in Deleuze, Foucault and others, in the areas of immanence of power, forms of power as *reactive* and *active*, power as affect, the problems of disciplinary power, and how power relations are constituted in relation to bodies of knowledge and regimes of truth within their own historical context. Insofar as posthumanism is a new attempt to re-define what the human being is and his/her relation to other beings, it is bound to examine the question of power in its depths; Nietzsche presents many ideas and insights in this direction.

1.2 Rationality and Perspectivism

A central theme that runs throughout Nietzsche's works is his critique of Western rationality, which he traces back to the Socratic Greeks. Nietzsche not only exposes the historical conditions out of which this rationality emerged in ancient Greece, as in *The Birth of Tragedy* (1967 [1872]) where he takes Socratic rationality[5] to task, but also shows its genealogical workings at the linguistic, psy-

5 *The Birth of Tragedy* (1967 [1872]) can be read as a specific study on the interaction between a specific mode of thought, that is, Socratic rationality, and different forces of culture such as art, myth and poetry at the macro-level of ancient Greece and the micro-level of its cultural formation, i.e. theater, within the context of 5th century BC. Here Nietzsche shows the dangers of an excessively rational culture as he diagnoses the hypertrophy of logical instincts.

chic, and somatic levels. In other words, rationality and its related subphenomena operate with assumptions at these levels; for instance, the forgetting of the origin of concepts in metaphors, the priority of consciousness over the unconscious, and denial of the body and the bodily forces. Nietzsche, as a physician of culture, undertakes the task of uncovering these layers hitherto unfathomed. While destroying eternal truths and their grounding, ultimately God and all those values symbolized by and brought together under this name, Nietzsche shows the nontenability of foundationalism as construed by Western thought. The will to truth brought us here, as he says in Part I of *Beyond Good and Evil* (1966 [1886]), while the problem does not rest entirely with truth, but also with error: "The will to truth which will still tempt us to many a venture [...] what questions has this will to truth not laid before us!" (Nietzsche 1992, 199)

While undermining rationality within the context of highest values since the Greeks, Nietzsche builds alternative ways of thinking one of which is perspectivism; namely that there are multiple truths, multiple interpretations of existence that are true to their holders and without perspectival interpretations there would be no life at all (see Nietzsche 1966 [1886], II, 34). While much of Nietzsche's theory of perspectivism is based on his ideas on truth, we must not oversee the difficulties it opens up for thought, as Nehamas observes in *Nietzsche: Life as Literature*:

> "[...] if the view that there are only interpretations is itself only an interpretation, and therefore possibly wrong, it may seem to follow that not every view is after all an interpretation and that Nietzsche's position undermines itself" (Nehamas 1985, 2).

However, if Nietzsche's many ideas on truth and power relations are kept in mind, some of the difficulties are removed, at least at the level of ideas. In *Metaphysics without Truth*, Sorgner discusses perspectivism and truth in Nietzsche. Regarding truth, he makes distinctions among a variety of notions of truth (see Sorgner 2007, 88): Nietzsche's truth, each interpretation being a "truth", "our truth", and finally "the truth" which is the sum-total of all possible perspectives (and which cannot be known). As Sorgner observes, for Nietzsche there is no "the truth;" therefore, Nietzsche does not accept the correspondence theory of truth. What we have are many "truths" that are individual perspectives. Sorgner reiterates a question often posed against Nietzsche: If there is no "the truth," then why believe in what Nietzsche says? Sorgner rightly observes that some perspectives are superior to others; one might also add that this may be so within the context of a particular set of highest values, and this brings up the question of hierarchy. Nietzsche must have believed that his perspective was higher than others so that it can be taken into account, so that his works are read and they have the power of persuasion. We can conclude by stating that Nietzsche's critique of Western rationality, his projection for a new pathos of truth, and his perspectivism, paved the way for posthumanism in its quest for a different conception of being in the world that is beyond good and evil.

1.3 Relationship between Humans and Animals

Another important Nietzsche inspired theme in posthumanism is the question of animal and human-animal relationship. All throughout Nietzsche's writings the human being is decentered, loses his status as a privileged being, which stems from superiority due to his rationality (the pride of the intellect). Nietzsche's diagnosis culminates in the conception of human being as "sick animal", who suffers from "bad conscience" that has to do with the denial of the animal human, the regression of animal instincts in the Occidental world-order (see Nietzsche 1969 [1887], II). The lowering of the status of the animal that is rooted in Western rationalism and monotheisms is related to, at least, these following phenomena according to Nietzsche: the underestimation of the Dionysian; the forgetfulness of forgetting (while animals represent forgetting); the susceptibility to pain (and concomitantly to cruelty); the symbolic absence of "animal wisdom" (as in the animals in *Thus Spoke Zarathustra*); the repression of animal instincts, the rise of bad consience, and the creation of an ideal out of these (namely ascetic idealism); and related to this last one is the denial of the body in its many dimensions. Recent scholarship has dealt with this question of animality in Nietzsche. I will discuss some of the central issues that Sorgner (2010a) and Lemm (2009) deal with in their books; while the former addresses this question in relation to human dignity and the latter in relation to questions of culture vs. civilization.

By taking Aphorism 115 of *The Gay Science* (1974 [1882]) as a framework where Nietzsche presents four errors, Sorgner expounds on each of them. Third error concerns the "false rank and file of animal and nature" (Sorgner 2010a, 183-193). This point addresses the question of Nietzsche's new hierarchy of beings, as it de-centers the non-agonistic human hegemony of the world conceived by previous thinkers. Not only Nietzsche does not assign a special place to the human being in the world, but he has also developed a new type of human being. On the one hand, human being is a type of animal (up to now, under the old regime, a "sick animal"); here Sorgner discusses Nietzsche's theory of evolution as he sees no gradual development but rather new forms appearing in leaps and detects an affinity between Nietzsche and Darwin. On the other hand, Nietzsche discerns a plethora of qualities in human being from insane, unhappy, unfortunate, artificial and interesting to cruel, brave, crafty, and sick, all of which can be said to be as important as being rational. Sorgner concludes this section by reiterating two important points: first, human-animal relationship is a complex one; this complexity has fallen into oblivion in the morality of good and evil, and its assignment of the animal to a lesser degree of being is highly problematic. Second, human being is not superior to animal, but is rather bound to an evolutionary process and can be seen as a transition to the overhuman. The overhuman has a different relationship to animality, which could not have been conceived prior to Nietzsche.

On the other hand, Lemm focuses on animality in relation to culture-making and the civilizing process. According to her, culture stands for cultivation, freedom from moralization, and counter-memory, while civilization is understood as taming and breeding, morality of repression, and memory. These two different types of forces are in perpetual conflict that plays itself out in the antagonism between human life and animal life. Civilization is "[…] directed against the animality of the human being" (Lemm 2009, 11), whereas culture is the liberation of the animal human. This distinction, which is supported by passages from Nietzsche's works, provides a sound framework for the book from which many questions can be posed on the animality of the human and its status. Another important theme of Lemm's book is how Nietzsche de-centers the human as he retrieves animality or the animal human, which is also the project of culture. The de-centering of the human is a theme that runs from Nietzsche's earliest philosophical writings to the latest. The opening paragraph of *On Truth and Lie in an Extra-Moral Sense* (1976 [1873]), for instance, presents a *humbled* picture of the human, not in relation to animals but in relation to the whole universe. On the other hand, Lemm presents many examples to illustrate how the Nietzschean culture-project works regarding the "promising animal". Animals lead Zarathustra[6] toward the overhuman, as they embody the wisdom that he needs to overcome himself.

Finally, indirectly or directly influenced by Nietzsche's vision, posthumanism does not accept the classical paradigm that considers human beings to be superior to animals due to the former's rationality. In addition, posthumanism acknowledges the animal in the human or, better said, the animal-human. As Sorgner and Lemm argue, we are symbiotically connected to all other beings of this world, to animals first and for most, insofar as we are their most recent direct descendants in the evolutionary process.

---

6 Many different kinds of animals appear in *Thus Spoke Zarathustra* (1954 [1883-1885]), making it a rich text in animal symbolism. It is not the goal of Nietzsche's Animal Philosophy to explore this symbolism, but rather animality in Nietzsche in general and its many dimensions. For animal symbolism in *Thus Spoke Zarathustra* see Acampora/Acampora (eds.) 2004.

1.4 The Posthuman, the Cyborg, and Nietzsche's New Type of Human

Nietzsche's critique of humanism, which one finds throughout his works in different forms sparked many debates on what the human being is. This critique can be summed up in several propositions: First, human being does not have a privileged position in the universe, a privilege that was accorded due to reason; Nietzsche presents this position in his early essays (see Nietzsche 1976 [1873]; 1979). Second, human being is not an isolated entity removed from his/her surroundings or environment, but is rather Dionysically connected; Nietzsche presents his notion of the Dionysian more specifically in *The Birth of Tragedy* (1967 [1872]) and *Twilight of Idols* (1954 [1889]). Third, human being is a bridge to higher/highest types, gathered together in and symbolized by the overhuman. Finally, "God is dead" means that human being, understood so far as a specific type of human being under God, is also dead. Although Nietzsche does not have much to say on machines, cyborgs, artificial intelligence, and cybernetics, we can observe some parallels between his critique of dualistic (man vs. nature) models and the posthumanistic conception of human being. Below I will explore Hayles' ideas on the posthuman in relation to those of Nietzsche.

> "What is the posthuman? Think of it as a point of view characterized by the following assumptions [...] First, the posthuman view privileges informational pattern over material instantiation, so that embodiment in a biological substrate is seen as an accident of history rather than an inevitability of life" (Hayles 1999, 2).

For Nietzsche, embodiment (individuation, or coming to be) does not follow an already pre-determined pattern, a rigid causality, but rather operates within a field of forces ruled by chance.

> "Second, the posthuman view considers consciousness, regarded as the seat of human identity in the Western tradition long before Descartes thought he was a mind thinking, as an epiphenomenon, as an evolutionary upstart trying to claim that it is the whole show when in actuality it is only a minor sideshow" (Hayles 1999, 2-3).

Many of Nietzsche's notes reveal why and how consciousness is a "minor sideshow," a late development, only a surface phenomenon in relation to unconscious forces;[7] these insights are closely related to his critique of subjectivity and dualism in philosophy.

> "Third, the posthuman view thinks of the body as the original prosthesis we all learn to manipulate, so that extending or replacing the body with other prostheses be-

---

7 See, for instance, in *The Gay Science* (1974 [1882], I, 11), and many notes from *The Will to Power* (1968, III, I). Nietzsche was influenced by Schopenhauer who is the first major thinker to show the priority of the unconscious over the conscious. Schopenhauer's and Nietzsche's ideas played a crucial role in the philosophical aspect of psychoanalysis.

comes a continuation of a process that began before we were born" (Hayles 1999, 3).

Here one must assume the evolution of the body and consider its archaic layers. Nietzsche often discusses these archaic layers, especially when he genealogically dissects the human civilization (see Nietzsche 1969 [1887], II). In relation to this point, Hayles also argues throughout her book that human being is an embodied being.

> "The body is the net result of thousands of years of sedimented evolutionary history, and it is naïve to think that this history does not affect human behaviors at every level of thought and action" (Hayles 1999, 284).

Although Nietzsche does not present a linear development of human history, there are *evolutionary* forces that make up the unconscious history of humanity.

> "Fourth, and most important, by these and other means, the posthuman view configures human being so that it can be seamlessly articulated with intelligent machines. In the posthuman, there are no essential differences or absolute demarcations between bodily existence and computer simulation, cybernetic mechanism and biological organism, robot teleology and human goals" (Hayles 1999, 3).

Although Nietzsche does not speak of robots, intelligent machines, and cyborgs, we can speculate as to what he may say on the subject. Since Nietzsche is opposed to binary conception of the universe and to a mechanical universe (passive objects as opposed to an active intellect that runs it according to a deterministic pattern), it can be tentatively suggested that his ideas would support artificial intelligence where matter is infused with intelligence through a human agency – I say tentatively because Nietzsche would clearly take a critical stance towards logocentricity and subjectivity that may underlie artificial intelligence. To oppose an anthropomorphic vision of the world that separates *techne* from being, Ansell-Pearson emphasises symbiosis as the underlying process of life and human life and sees in it a challenge and an "urgency of adopting a rizomatic praxis" (Ansell-Pearson 1997, 182). What is at stake, according to Ansell-Pearson, is not technogenesis but rather *bio-technogenesis*.

Finally for Hayles, "the posthuman subject is an amalgam, a collection of heterogeneous components, a material-informational entity whose boundaries undergo continuous construction and reconstruction" (Hayles 1999, 3). All the qualities mentioned here that define the posthuman, the multiplicity, the fusion of matter/spirit, and the process of re-creation, are in agreement with Nietzsche's basic ideas. But the posthuman and the cyborg cannot be identified, according to Hayles, since human beings have different bodily experiences as part of their evolutionary process. As clearly demonstrated above, many posthumanistic trends, such as opposition to binarism, critique of paradigms of consciousness, and acceptance of an evolutionary process, can be detected in Nietzsche's writings, albeit in different forms. I do not, however, think that Nietzsche would espouse artificial intelligence insofar as it is grounded in the values of morality of good and evil.

2. Nietzsche as Ancestor of Transhumanism

Bostrom, a leading figure of transhumanism, rejects Nietzsche as an ancestor of transhumanism:

> "It might be thought that the German philosopher Friedrich Nietzsche (1844-1900) would have been a major inspiration for transhumanism [...]. What Nietzsche had in mind, however, was not technological transformation but rather a kind of soaring personal growth and cultural refinement in exceptional individuals (who he thought would have to overcome the life-sapping 'slave-morality' of Christianity). Despite some surface-level similarities with the Nietzschean vision, transhumanism – with its Enlightenment roots, its emphasis on individual liberties, and its humanistic concern for the welfare of all humans (and other sentient beings) – probably has as much or more in common with Nietzsche's contemporary J.S. Mill, the English liberal thinker and utilitarian" (Bostrom 2005, 4).

Insofar as transhumanism has affinity to liberalism and utilitarianism, Bostrom is right; Nietzsche's persistent attacks on liberalism and utilitarianism are proof for that. Liberalism promotes an egalitarian vision for human society, effacing the difference between the strong and the weak, the high and the low, within the human soul and among human beings. Nietzsche exposes this effacement as the revenge of the weak, the mob, against the strong. Utilitarianism establishes its goal as the maximization of happiness for the many and calls for elimination of pain and suffering. For Nietzsche, utilitarianism is short-sighted, its conception of good stems from "slave morality" as he presents it in *On the Genealogy of Morals* (1969 [1887], I),[8] and suffering, understood in any sense, is a necessary ingredient for becoming strong; the central question for Nietzsche is not whether we can eliminate suffering or not, but rather what human beings, individually and collectively, do with their sufferings. Despite this divergence, there are transhumanistic trends that have affinity to Nietzsche. In contrast to Bostrom, Max More (2010), for instance, claims that Nietzsche strongly influenced transhumanist thinkers. Below is a brief survey of Nietzsche's relationship to trans-

8 Although Nietzsche does not mention Mill by name, the first four sections of this essay is a polemic against utilitarianism.

humanism in three divisions: the overhuman, the Renaissance and Enlightenment ideals, and self-overcoming and work-in-progress.[9]

2.1 The Übermensch[10] and the Posthuman and the Transhuman of Transhumanists

We can start by presenting some of the common elements between Nietzsche and transhumanists, as discussed by Sorgner (2009). First, both transhumanists and Nietzsche hold a dynamic view of nature and values. "Transhumanists view human nature as a work-in-progress," Bostrom says (2001). Second, both Nietzsche and transhumanists are post-Godly and diverge significantly from the traditional Christian view of the world. Another similarity resides in the way they conceive of power and how power is not static and homogeneized, but rather is malleable, dynamic, and diffusive. Each power constellation, and hence each human being, according to Nietzsche, has a different perspective of the world.

Furthermore, each individual's experience of power depends on who someone is and which history someone has had, each individual human being has a unique exercise of power and consequently a unique conception "of what their own perfection would consist in" (Bostrom 2001). Transhumanists and Nietzsche agree in this regard, as Sorgner rightly points out (see Sorgner 2009, 35). Nietzsche himself has an insightful, fully developed and complex conception of power, and the states which he identifies with the highest feeling of power are immediately connected to the classical ideal (see Sorgner 2007, 53-58). A similar concept of the good seems to be upheld by many transhumanists, as Bostrom stresses the following:

> "Transhumanism imports from secular humanism the ideal of the fully-developed and well-rounded personality. We can't all be renaissance geniuses, but we can strive to constantly refine ourselves and to broaden our intellectual horizons" (Bostrom 2001).

After exploring Nietzsche's overhuman and higher humans from an evolutionary standpoint, Sorgner points to the possibility of the birth of an overhuman when the conditions are ripe, including the existence of many higher human beings. He then makes an evolutionary analysis:

---

9 Central articles of the ongoing debate are accessible at the webpage of the Institute for Ethics and Emerging Technologies (see IEET 2012).

10 Although the main body of Nietzsche's teaching of the overhuman is in *Thus Spoke Zarathustra* (1954 [1883-1885]), the concept is used in different forms before this work and can be traced back to Nietzsche's understanding of ancient Greece and its heroic/agonistic culture and types, as I argue in my essay (see Tuncel 2009).

> "The overhuman has a significantly different potential from that of higher humans. So far no overhuman has existed, but the normal capacities of an overhuman are beyond the capacities even of a higher human. Like every species, the species of the overhuman has limits, but their limits are different from the limits of the human species. The overhuman comes about via an evolutionary step which originates from the group of higher humans. Nietzsche does not exclude the possibility that technological means bring about the evolutionary step. His comments concerning the conditions for the evolutionary step toward the overhuman are rather vague in general, but in this respect his attitude is similar to that of transhumanists" (Sorgner 2009, 38).

Regarding the evolutionary aspect of the overhuman, Sorgner finds Esfandiary's ideas on the transhuman closer to Nietzsche than those of Bostrom. Based on his discussion of Bostrom's and Esfandiary's ideas, Sorgner concludes…

> "[…] that Nietzsche and the transhumanists share many aspects in their general anthropologies and their values, but Nietzsche's concept of the overhuman does not correspond to the concept of the posthuman of all transhumanists. However, there are transhumanists whose concept of the posthuman bears many significant similarities to that of Nietzsche's overhuman" (Sorgner 2009, 38-39).

A similar observation about Nietzsche's uneasy relationship to transhumanism is made by Zimmermann when he writes:

> "Some variants of transhumanism, then, are motivated – at least on the surface – by such humanistic ideals as decreasing human suffering and increasing the prospects for widespread human happiness. Such goals are shared by the utilitarian modern, whom Nietzsche called contemptuously 'the last man.' Most transhumanists, however, propose an additional goal that resonates far more with Nietzsche's thought. Transhuman beings are often envisioned as having not only greater intelligence, but also the increased aesthetic, moral, athletic, and experiential capacities necessary for *superior individuals*. Techno-posthumans go even further: they want to bring forth god-like immortals, capable of undertaking projects far beyond the capacity of even the most advanced transhuman, such as making the whole universe self-conscious" (Zimmermann 2011).

As Zimmermann suggests, Nietzsche's critical distance to utilitarianism is clear, which one can detect in many of his texts; the second point, on the other hand, cannot be accepted *prime facie*. The enhancement of capacities is necessary, but not sufficient for Nietzsche's overhumanly types. In order to assess this point, one needs to consider the many different aspects of self-overcoming in *Thus Spoke Zarathustra* (1954 [1883-1885]) both in Zarathustra's teachings of the overhuman and in his exemplary journey. Here we may see a significant divergence between Nietzsche's *value* based conception of self-overcoming and the transhumanist conception of technology-based enhancement.

2.2 The Importance of the Renaissance Ideal for Transhumanists and Nietzsche

What was crucial in the Renaissance for Nietzsche? It was a new beginning, an epoch-making, a turn to this-worldly life after the medieval other-worldliness, investment in artistic creations and creation of new works based on ancient models. On the other hand, for the transhumanists the Renaissance meant human progress under the guidance of scientific rationality. The Hegelian model of a teleological conception of history – the model of progress is based on this conception – was already undermined by Nietzsche in his second *Untimely Meditation* (1983 [1876]) where he presents different ways of relating to the past and exposes the problems of overestimation of the historical:

> "[…] there is a degree of sleeplessness, of rumination, of the historical sense, which is harmful and ultimately fatal to the living thing, whether this living thing be a man or a people or a culture" (Nietzsche 1983 [1876], 62).

According to this account, the late-comer is not necessarily higher; here Nietzsche remains loyal to his ancient Greeks and their teachings. Moreover, the linear conception of time as a primary paradigm would later be replaced by the eternal return, a radical conception of time. Although Nietzsche and the transhumanists may share the ideal of this-worldly creation, there is a stark difference regarding the idea of progress and the privileged role given to sciences and technology in it. Let's now examine some of Bostrom's ideas in relation to Nietzsche's world-view.

In his assesment of the Renaissance and discussion of Pico, Bostrom highlights its concern for self-creation of the individual:

> "Renaissance humanism encouraged people to rely on their own observations and their own judgment rather than to defer in every matter to religious authorities […]. A landmark of the period is Giovanni Pico della Mirandola's *Oration on the Dignity of Man* (1486), which proclaims that man does not have a readymade form and is responsible for shaping himself" (Bostrom 2005, 2).

Nietzsche would be in agreement with this spirit of self-creation. There is, however, always a cultural context for individual self-creation, and, if we push the discussion further and place the terms like "people", "observation" and "judgment" under a genealogical microscope, we will find disagreements between Nietzsche, Pico, and Bostrom. Bostrom then proceeds to discussing the Age of Enlightenment and states that "transhumanism has roots in rational humanism [which] emphasizes empirical science and critical reason – rather than revelation and religious authority – as ways of learning about the natural world and our place within it, and of providing a grounding for morality" (ibid., 4). Here Bostrom's version of transhumanism is further removed from Nietzsche's vision. For Nietzsche, modern scientific rationality is a problem to be overcome;

for Bostrom it is the main source of progress and the transhumanistic agenda. Many of the points Nietzsche raises against rationality apply to modern scientific rationality, but two of them stand out as uniquely applicable; namely, scientific objectivity[11] and consciousness (the problem of subjectivity). For Nietzsche, scientific objectivity is only a scheme of interpretation, while consciousness remains only on the surface of an ocean of unconsciousness. In conclusion, although Nietzsche and the transhumanists are inspired by the same ideal, the ideal of Renaissance, they do so for different reasons and they have different interpretations of this ideal. Their interpretations diverge radically, as transhumanism embraces modern scientific project *in toto*, while Nietzsche offers its critique and exposes its fundamental problems.

2.3 Nietzsche's Self-Overcoming and Human Beings as Work-in-progress

Both transhumanists and Nietzsche hold a dynamic view of nature and values. "Transhumanists view human nature as a work-in-progress," as Bostrom (2001) says. Nietzsche too has a dynamic view of life and human life; this view finds its expression in his idea of overcoming and overhuman as the highest (but not a final) type of human being. Nietzsche's emphasis on the process of creation is already evident in his first book, *The Birth of Tragedy* (1967 [1872]), where he opposes, via Lessing, the (Socratic) possession of truth against truthfulness, which has to do with the search for truth. The creator is more interested in the process of unveiling[12] than the unveiled. Similarly, in his early writings on the Greek culture of contest, Nietzsche places more weight on the process of competition, on the large picture, than the end-result of competition; therefore, *agon* (assembly, gathering) becomes more important than *athlios* (prize of victory). In agreement with his earlier thoughts, in his later works too, as in *Thus Spoke Zarathustra* (1954 [1883-1885]), Nietzsche regards human being to be a bridge and not a goal, a dangerous crossing, a rope stretched over an abyss. His conception of the overhuman is a heightened version of these ideas, which is the highest point of self-creation based on affirmation of life and love of the earth. The hightest point, however, is said only figuratively; for, in Nietzsche, there is no highest point, there is no final stop in self-creation except in death for an individual human being.

---

11 On this topic one may find many ideas in Part 6 of *Beyond Good and Evil* (1966 [1886]), especially in Aphorism 207 where Nietzsche shows how modern objective spirit is dangerously overstated and dissects the type that reflects this spirit.

12 "Whenever the truth is uncovered, the artist will always cling with rapt gaze to what still remains covering even after such uncovering; but the theoretical man enjoys and finds satisfaction in the discarded covering […]" (Nietzsche 1967 [1872], Sec.15).

It is for this reason that Sorgner argues against Hibbard who claims that "the overhuman has no need for improvement, having achieved satisfaction with life" (Hibbard 2010, 10). Not only there is no textual evidence for this in Nietzsche, but it goes against the basic aspect of the overhuman. Sorgner rightly questions Hibbard, when he states:

> "Why should overhumans have no need for improvement? I think Hibbard makes this one-sided judgment, because he focuses on the claim that overhumans can get into a situation where they can say *Yes* to one moment, and thereby they manage to affirm the eternal recurrence of everything. However, being able to affirm one moment does not mean that overhumans have achieved satisfaction in life. Satisfaction is not something overhumans aim for" (Sorgner 2010b, 12).

What the overhuman has is *amor fati*, love of what is, the past, what has already been attained, but this *love* should not be confused with satisfaction that carries the connotation of complacency. Sorgner then concludes:

> "They wish to be creative, to permanently [and perpetually] overcome themselves, and to reach higher creative goals. Even if they managed to say *Yes* to one moment, there is no reason why they should stop willing to overcome themselves" (Sorgner 2010b, 12).

Epilogue

Transhumanism and posthumanism present a new conception of human being, a conception that has affinity to post-modern theories, cybernetics, and recent technologies (electronic, computer, genetic enhancement et al.); these are developments only of the last sixty years or so. Nietzsche, however, says very little about technology although he lived in the first century of the industrial revolution. He rather critiques the overestimation of scientific rationality that underlies technology. This is not to say that Nietzsche was opposed to sciences or would be opposed to all or any kind of technology. As Sorgner rightly says, "Indeed, Nietzsche's respect for the various sciences is immense" (ibid., 3). I would go further than him and suggest that Nietzsche calls for a different "scientific" (*wissenschaftliche*) experience (what he calls "gay science") and a different constellation of forces of culture. As for technology, Nietzsche would be critical of a technological being in the world insofar as this being becomes complacent, uncreative, and non-Dionysian because of the use or abuse of technology. On the other hand, he would support technology that helps humans strive for the overhuman, as Sorgner observes: "it seems plausible to hold that Nietzsche would also have been positive about technological means for realizing the overhuman" (Sorgner 2010b, 7). The question of technology, as Heidegger suggests in his lecture on the topic, has become a crucial question of our times. We can confront this question as we study its role in human enhancement and explore the kind of force technology constitutes with other forces and the kinds of affects it leaves on human beings. To that end, Nietzsche has many ideas and insights to offer.[13]

Bibliography

Acampora, C.D./ Acampora, R.R. (eds.) (2004): A Nietzschean Bestiary: Becoming Animal Beyond Docile and Brutal. Lanham(MD) et al.: Rowman & Littlefield.

Ansell-Pearson, K. (1997): Viroid Life: Perspectives on Nietzsche and the Transhuman Condition. London: Routledge.

Ansell-Pearson, K. (2011): The Future is Superhuman: Nietzsche's Gift. In: The Agonist: A Nietzsche Circle Journal 4(2).

Babich, B. (2011): On the "All-too-Human" Dream of Transhumanism. In: The Agonist: A Nietzsche Circle Journal 4(2).

Bostrom, N. (2001): Transhumanist Values. http://www.nickbostrom.com/tra/values.html (accessed July 6, 2013).

Bostrom, N. (2005): A History of Transhumanist Thought. In: Journal of Evolution and Technology 14(1), 1-25.

Deleuze, G. (1983): Nietzsche and Philosophy. New York: Columbia University Press.

Esfandiary, F.M. (1973): Up-Wingers: A Futurist Manifesto. New York: John Day Co.

FM-2030 (1989): Are you a Transhuman? Monitoring and Stimulating your Personal Rate of Growth in a Rapidly Changing World. New York: Warner Books.

Foucault, M (1990): History of Sexuality. New York: Vintage Books.

Foucault, M (1995): Discipline and Punish: The Birth of the Prison. New York: Vintage Books.

Hayles, N.K. (1999): How We Became Posthuman: Virtual Bodies in Cybernetics, Literature, and Informatics. Chicago: University of Chicago Press.

Hibbard, B. (2010): Nietzsche's Overhuman is an Ideal Whereas Posthumans Will be Real. In: Journal of Evolution and Technology 21(1), 9-12

IEET (2012): Was Nietzsche a Transhumanist? In: Institute for Ethics and Emerging Technologies. http://ieet.org/index.php/IEET/more/pellissier20120423 (accessed July 6, 2013).

Lemm, V. (2009): Nietzsche's Animal Philosophy. New York: Fordham University Press

Loeb, P.S. (2011): Nietzsche's Transhumanism. In: The Agonist: A Nietzsche Circle Journal 4(2).

Mill, J.S. (2002): Utilitarianism. Indianapolis: Hackett Publishing Co.

More, M. (2010): The Overhuman in the Transhuman. In: Journal of Evolution and Technology 21(1).

Nehamas, A. (1985): Nietzsche: Life as Literature. Cambridge: Harvard University Press.

13 In a recent special issue of the Nietzsche journal The Agonist leading Nietzsche scholars added further insights concerning this range of topics (see, e.g., Ansell-Pearson 2011; Babich 2011; Loeb 2011; Sorgner 2011).

Nietzsche, F. (1954 [1883-1885]): Thus Spoke Zarathustra. In: The Portable Nietzsche (Edited and Translated by W. Kaufmann). New York: The Viking Press.

Nietzsche, F. (1954 [1889]): Twilight of Idols. In: The Portable Nietzsche (Edited and Translated by W. Kaufmann). New York: The Viking Press.

Nietzsche, F. (1966 [1886]): Beyond Good and Evil (Translated by W. Kaufmann). New York: Random House.

Nietzsche, F. (1967 [1872]): The Birth of Tragedy (Translated by W. Kaufmann). New York: Vintage Books.

Nietzsche, F. (1968): The Will to Power (Translated by W. Kaufmann/ R.J. Hollingdale). New York: Vintage Books.

Nietzsche, F. (1969 [1887]): On the Genealogy of Morals (Translated by W. Kaufmann/ R.J. Hollingdale). New York: Vintage Books.

Nietzsche, F. (1974 [1882]): The Gay Science (Translated by W. Kaufmann). New York: Vintage Books.

Nietzsche, F. (1976 [1873]): On Truth and Lie in an Extra-Moral Sense. In: The Portable Nietzsche (Edited and Translated by W. Kaufmann). New York: The Viking Press.

Nietzsche, F (1979): Philosophy and Truth: Selections from Nietzsche's Notebooks of the Early 1870's (Translated by D. Breazeale). Atlantic Highlands(NJ): Humanities Press.

Nietzsche, F. (1982 [1881]): Daybreak: Thoughts on the Prejudices of Morality (Translated by R. J. Hollingdale). Cambridge: Cambridge University Press.

Nietzsche, F. (1983 [1876]): On the Uses and Disadvantages of History for Life. In: Nietzsche, F.: Untimely Meditations (Translated by R.J. Hollingdale). Cambridge: Cambridge University Press.

Nietzsche, F (1992): Basic Writings of Nietzsche (Edited and Translated by W. Kaufmann) New York: The Modern Library.

Pico della Mirandola, G. (1996): Oration on the Dignity of Man. Washington: Regnery Gateway.

Sorgner, S.L. (2007): Metaphysics without Truth: On the Importance of Consistency within Nietzsche's Philosophy. Milwaukee: Marquette University Press.

Sorgner, S.L. (2009): Nietzsche, the Overhuman, and Transhumanism. In: Journal of Evolution and Technology 21(1), 29-42.

Sorgner, S.L. (2010a): Menschenwürde nach Nietzsche: Die Geschichte eines Begriffs. Darmstadt: Wissenschaftliche Buchgesellschaft.

Sorgner, S.L. (2010b): Beyond Humanism: Reflections on Trans- and Posthumanism. In: Journal of Evolution and Technology 21(2), 1-19.

Sorgner, S.L. (2011): Zarathustra 2.0 and Beyond: Further Remarks on the Complex Relationship between Nietzsche and Transhumanism. In: The Agonist: A Nietzsche Circle Journal 4(2).

Spinoza, Benedict (2005): Ethics. New York et al.: Penguin Classics.

Tuncel, Y. (2009): Agon Symbolism in Nietzsche. In: Nikephoros 22(8), 145-185.

Woodward, A. (2011): Understanding Nietzscheanism. Durham: Acumen.

Zimmermann, M. (2011): Last Man or Overman? Transhuman Appropriations of a Nietzschean Theme. In: Integral Post. http://integrallife.com/integral-post/last-man-or-overman/ (accessed July 6, 2013).

Utopia

Michael Hauskeller

Progress has often been driven by utopian dreams of a better world. This better world is always one that allows people's lives to be, in some important (albeit varying) respect, better than they normally are at the time when, and the place where, the dream is dreamt. That imagined world, which compares favorably with the here and now, can be in the past (the Golden Age, Paradise Lost), in the future (Heaven and a New Earth, Paradise Regained, and secularized versions thereof), and even in the present (mythical places like the Isles of the Blessed or Avalon, but also real places such as America – the "land of the blessed" – for European emigrants in the early 1900s or Communist Russia in the 1930s). Utopian dreams fulfill an important function. They serve as a reminder that the world doesn't *have* to be as it is: that there are other possible worlds that we could live in – worlds in which nobody is poor and where everyone has enough to eat, worlds in which people are not being oppressed and each can say what they please, where everyone counts for one and no one for more than one; worlds perhaps where we don't have to work so hard and where there is more enjoyment, where being alive is an unimpaired pleasure, where there is no suffering, disease, or death, where we are powerful and no longer have to fear anything or anyone. Utopian dreams like these have no doubt stimulated social, scientific and technological progress. However, they have also led to terror and humanitarian disaster when concerted attempts to make the dream come true failed miserably. Unfortunately, some worlds turn out to be less desirable than they appeared to be in our dreams, and some dreams get compromised by the means thought necessary to realize them. Others are repugnant in their own right, like the utopian dream of a world in which, say, the Aryan Race reigns supreme. Clearly not all dreams are worth dreaming, and not all survive their implementation into the real world undamaged. The challenge is to know in advance what will happen if we endeavor to turn utopia into reality.

Utopian thinking can be found both in transhumanism and in posthumanism (or, as Miah 2008 calls them, *philosophical* posthumanism and *cultural* posthumanism, largely because transhumanism is mostly advocated by philosophers, whereas posthumanism is more the domain of cultural theorists). Transhumanism is without doubt a philosophy with strong utopian tendencies, both in motivation and in outlook (see for a more detailed discussion Hauskeller 2012). It is a practice-oriented, increasingly influential philosophical-political movement whose proponents and allies frequently and quite openly declare themselves to be motivated by a desire to create a better world or make this world "a better place" (see e.g. Harris 2007, 3; Bostrom 2011; UK Transhumanist Association

2011). Transhumanists believe that the best chance we have to make this world a better place is through the use of already existing or soon to be developed human enhancement technologies. By gradually improving human capability we will eventually change into beings far superior to any human that has ever lived and hence can be seen, in this respect, as "posthuman". It is commonly assumed that posthumans will lead lives and have experiences that are on the one hand unimaginable, but are on the other far superior to, i.e. much better than, anything we can experience now. When transhumanists describe the posthuman future that allegedly awaits us, they often indulge in fantasies that borrow their imagery from religious hymns and ancient myths. Nick Bostrom, transhumanism's most prolific academic proponent, is particularly apt at painting our posthuman future in the most glorious colors. We are being promised nothing less than "lives wonderful beyond imagination" (Bostrom 2011). In his *Letter from Utopia* (2010), in which one of those fortunate posthumans of the future addresses us merely humans, we are reminded of those few and all-too-short precious moments in which we experience life at its best, only to be told that those moments are nothing compared to the bliss permanently experienced by the posthuman:

> "And yet, what you had in your best moment is not close to what I have now – a beckoning scintilla at most. If the distance between base and apex for you is eight kilometers, then to reach my dwelling requires a million light-year ascent. The altitude is outside moon and planets and all the stars your eyes can see. Beyond dreams. Beyond imagination" (Bostrom 2010, 3).

Posthumans will no longer be cursed with ageing bodies, and will no longer have to die; they will know and understand things that are entirely beyond our reach now; and above all, they will have lots and lots of pleasurable experiences:

> "Pleasure! A few grains of this magic ingredient are dearer than a king's treasure, and we have it aplenty here in Utopia. It pervades into everything we do and everything we experience. We sprinkle it in our tea" (Bostrom 2010, 5).

The letter ends with an urgent call to bring the posthuman into existence and is signed by "your possible future self".

There is nothing very unusual about the utopian outlook that Bostrom endorses so unabashedly. On the contrary, it is rather common and apparently shared by many who see humanity's salvation in emerging and converging technologies and technological growth in general. The authors of the 2002 landmark report *Converging Technologies for Improving Human Performance*, commissioned by the U.S. National Science Foundation and Department of Commerce, seriously expect that through the convergence of nanotechnology, biotechnology, information technology and cognitive science we will soon be able to solve all the world's problems. Technological progress will result in "world peace" and "evolution to a higher level of compassion and accomplishment" (Roco/ Bainbridge [eds.] 2003, 6). More importantly, it will also lead to "a golden age of prosperity" (ibid., 291) and "economic wealth on a scale hitherto unimaginable" (ibid., 293). Economic wealth is here clearly seen as both necessary and sufficient for permanent human happiness, where the latter, in well-tried utilitarian fashion, is equated with unlimited access to, and enjoyment of, pleasurable experiences. This essentially materialistic and hedonistic understanding of human progress is reminiscent of the medieval legend of the Land of Cockaigne, where supposedly "no one suffers shortages/ the walls are made of sausages" and "lovely women and girls may be taken to bed/ without the encumbrance of having to wed" (Pleij 2001, 33; 39). Transhumanists occasionally betray similar sentiments and ideals. David Pearce for instance, who in 1998, with Nick Bostrom and a few others, drafted the *Transhumanist Declaration* (the founding document of the World Transhumanist Association), advocates a form of negative Utilitarianism that sees as the ultimate goal of all human action the abolition of all suffering. In his internet manifesto *The Hedonistic Imperative* he predicts that over "the next thousand years or so, the biological substrates of suffering will be eradicated completely" and that consequently the "states of mind of our descendants [...] will share at least one common feature: a sublime and all-pervasive happiness" (Pearce 1995, 0.1.). What awaits us (or rather our posthuman descendents) is nothing short of a "naturalisation of heaven", where we...

> "[...] will have the chance to enjoy modes of experience we primitives cruelly lack. For on offer are sights more majestically beautiful, music more deeply soul-stirring, sex more exquisitely erotic, mystical epiphanies more awe-inspiring, and love more profoundly intense than anything we can now properly comprehend" (Pearce 1995, 0.4.).

By and large, all transhumanists are optimists regarding the future of humanity (see Berthoud 2007, 295). They look forward to what lies ahead of us, and embrace without much hesitation the technologies that are supposed to lead us there. They tend to believe that everything will be for the best, and that the best is what we will get if we are only courageous enough to wholeheartedly commit ourselves to scientific and technological progress. Transhumanists do not doubt that humans are special, that reason sets us apart from the rest of nature, and that we all carry the potential in us to ascend the heavens and to be (or live) like Gods – very much in accordance with the very modern human self-understanding that Pico della Mirandola laid down in his *Oration on the Dignity of Man* (1985 [1486]), which can be seen as the foundation charter of Renaissance humanism. For Pico humans were by nature free to invent themselves, and not confined by any natural boundaries: "Thou art the molder and maker of thyself, thou mayest sculpt thyself into whatever shape thou dost prefer" (Pico della Mirandola 1985 [1486], 4). As humans we are naturally disposed to change and to progress to higher spheres. It is in our very essence to transgress boundaries, to go ever further on our way to perfection and godliness. This belief is also at the core of transhumanism. Scratch a transhumanist and you will find a humanist underneath.

In contrast, despite being rather a diverse lot, (cultural) posthumanists are normally decidedly anti-humanist – or "posthuman*ist*" (Wolfe 2010, xv) – and hence also deeply suspicious of transhumanist aspirations to create better, even more glorious humans by means of technology. Posthumanists generally refuse to see humans as a "superior species in the natural order" (Miah 2008, 72), ontologically distinct from animals on the one hand, and machines on the other. They insist that the boundaries between the human and the non-human are rather fluent and in fact have always been so: it is just that this fact has become more pronounced and thus more obvious through recent technological advances. This makes the posthuman that posthumanists talk about an altogether different entity from the posthuman of the transhumanists. In contrast to the latter, the posthumanist posthuman is not an entity of an imagined future, but an entity that already exists. For the posthumanist we are already posthuman (see Hayles 1999) and in a certain sense have always been so. The human (as something essentially different from other entities) has never existed. As Halberstam and Livingston in their seminal collection of articles on "posthuman bodies", echoing Donna Haraway's "we are cyborgs" (1985, 191) programmatically declare: "You're not human until you're posthuman. You were never human." (Halberstam/ Livingston [eds.] 1995, 8) Thus "the human" is merely an ideological construct, a myth, and ultimately a lie, because the phrase suggests that there is an essential distinction between the human and the non-human, while in fact there isn't. Any appearance of an ontological difference between humans and machines on the one side, and humans and animals on the other, is merely a discursive practice that…

> "[…] functions to domesticate and hierarchize difference within the human (whether according to race, class, gender) and to absolutize difference between the human and the nonhuman" (Halberstam/ Livingston [eds.] 1995, 10).

It is the ideology of the human that posthumanists seek to uncover and to attack. The political goal is to rupture and exceed traditional cultural "narratives" of the human and to "destabilize the ontological hygiene of Western modernity" (Graham 2002, 16) in order to overcome historic divisions between class, race and gender. For this reason, posthumanists are equally opposed to so-called "bioconservative" critics of radical human enhancement such as Francis Fukuyama, Michael Sandel, or Leon Kass, and to transhumanist enhancement enthusiasts. From a posthumanist perspective both parties commit the same basic mistake: that, although they may have different ideas about what it means to be human, they both believe in the existence of the human, and in the value of being one. Transhumanists welcome and endorse the new technologies because they seem to provide new, far-ranging possibilities for human progress. Posthumanists often do the same, but for other reasons. The increasing incorporation of modern technology into our lives and bodies is a fact that we have to deal with, and whether we like it or not, it is to be welcomed to the extent that it confuses boundaries (e.g. between human and non-human, male and female, physical and non-physical) and forces (or at least allows) us to review and revise the way we are used to look at the world.

> "The dichotomies between mind and body, animal and human, organism and machine, public and private, nature and culture, men and women, primitive and civilized are all in question ideologically" (Haraway 1985, 205).

There is, of course, a utopian dimension to the posthumanist critique of humanist and transhumanist progressivism and utopianism, which was initially acknowledged by Donna Haraway in her early *Manifesto*:

> "This chapter […] is an effort to contribute to socialist-feminist culture and theory in a post-modernist, nonnaturalist mode and in the utopian tradition of imagining a world without gender" (Haraway 1985, 193).

20 years later, however, she expressed discomfort with her own utopian interpretation of posthumanism. In an interview with Nicholas Gane she revokes her earlier remark: "It's not a utopian dream but an on-the-ground working project. I have trouble with the way people go for a utopian post-gender world" (Gane/ Haraway 2006, 137). Clearly part of Haraway's discomfort with being seen as trying to launch some kind of utopian project stems from her distaste for the goals of transhumanism: "I can't believe the blissed-out techno-idiocy of people who talk about downloading human consciousness onto a chip" (ibid., 146). Yet she still acknowledges the importance of utopian thinking for the purpose of critiquing (and possibly changing) established practices:

> "I suppose there is a kind of fantastic hope that runs through a manifesto. There's some kind of without warrant insistence that the fantasy of an elsewhere is not escapism but it's a powerful tool" (Gane/ Haraway 2006, 152).

It is obvious that Haraway does not share the enthusiasm that
ists seem to feel for the ongoing technification of the life wor
mits that it is something of a "nightmare" (Gane/ Haraway
wise, Katherine Hayles, in her influential book *How We Be*

(1999, 1), speaks of the "nightmare" of a downloaded consciousness, and contrasts it with a "dream" of her own:

> "If my nightmare is a culture inhabited by posthumans who regard their bodies as fashion accessories rather than the ground of being, my dream is a version of the posthuman that embraces the possibilities of information technologies without being seduced by fantasies of unlimited power and disembodied immortality, that recognizes and celebrates finitude as a condition of human being" (Hayles 1999, 5).

Other posthumanists express a similarly ambivalent attitude. Thus David Wills (2008), while embracing what he calls the "technological turn" and claiming that the "human thing" has never been "simply human", but is and has always been in its very essence a "technological thing" (Wills 2008, 3), argues that, precisely because we always already have technology in our backs, we can and should resist a "technology that defines itself as straight-forward, as straight and forward, straight-ahead linear advance, the totally concentrated confidence and pure technological fiat of an unwavering lift-off" and "reserve the right to *hold back*, not to presume that every technology is an advance" (ibid., 6). According to Wills, control and mastery are an illusion, never to be fully accomplished because technology has us rather than the other way around. In the same vein, though not always for the same reasons, other posthumanists such as Elaine Graham also scorn what they see as transhumanists' "technocratic futurism" (Graham 2002, 155) and "libertarian philosophy" (ibid., 159).

However, despite the widespread posthumanist opposition to transhumanist techno-utopianism, the desired and recommended dissolution of all confining boundaries is clearly itself a utopian idea, whether those boundaries are conceived as physical boundaries (as in transhumanism) or rather conceptual, i.e., social and political boundaries (as in posthumanism). At the heart of posthumanism is clearly a liberationist ideal: the hoped-for redistribution of difference and identity is ultimately a redistribution of power. Haraway and those who have been following in her footsteps urge us to see the confusion of boundaries that our use of modern technologies forces upon us not as a threat, but rather as an opportunity to develop resistance to domination:

> "[…] certain dualisms have been persistent in Western traditions; they have all been systemic to the logics and practices of domination of women, people of color, nature, workers, animals – in short, domination of all constituted as others, whose task is to mirror the self" (Haraway 1985, 219).

Instead of bemoaning the increasing technification of our life world and resigning ourselves to the role of victims, we are asked to use it in order to undermine existing structures of domination. Again, we are told to be brave in the face of developments and to see them as an opportunity rather than a threat. However, while transhumanists tell us not to be afraid of letting go of the familiar but defective human and paving the way for the unfamiliar, but vastly improved posthuman, posthumanists ask us not to be afraid of "permanently partial identities and contradictory standpoints" (Haraway 1985, 194) and to suppress and firmly reject the perhaps all-too-human desire for clear demarcations. This requires an appreciation of disorder and illogic, and a repudiation of (normative conceptualizations of) health, purity and stability (see Halberstam/ Livingston [eds.] 1995, 13). Katherine Hayles makes it clear that "the posthuman" is just as much a construct as "the human". It is not a real entity that is meant to replace the human at some point in the future, but rather a certain point of view, a new way of looking at things and at ourselves:

> "Whether or not interventions have been made on the body, new models of subjectivity emerging from such fields as cognitive science and artificial life imply that even a biologically unaltered *Homo sapiens* counts as posthuman" (Hayles 1999, 4).

Whether we are human or posthuman thus entirely depends on our own self-understanding: "People become posthuman because they think they are posthuman" (ibid., 6). Along the same lines, Elaine Graham (2002) analyzes the different "representational practices" that create the differing worlds of the human and the posthuman. Technology changes things, but the really important changes, according to posthumanists, are ultimately in the head. Haraway's "Cyborg" was a metaphor for a changed, or changing, perspective. And so is "the posthuman" for many cultural theorists. For transhumanists on the other hand, the posthuman is the radically enhanced, virtually omnipotent human of the future.

Haraway famously concluded her *Manifesto* with the statement that she'd rather be a cyborg than a goddess. These words signify alternative utopias. What distinguishes posthumanists from transhumanists is this: while posthumanists would rather be cyborgs than goddesses or gods, transhumanists wish to be both, but if they had to choose, they would much rather be gods.

Bibliography

Berthoud, G. (2007): The Techno-Utopia of 'Human Performance Enhancement'. In: Sitter-Liver, B. (ed.): Utopie heute I. Fribourg et al.: Academic Press.

Bostrom, N. (2010): Letter from Utopia. http://www.nickbostrom.com/utopia.pdf (accessed June 15, 2011).

Bostrom, N. (2011): Nick Bostrom's Home Page. http://research.lifeboat.com/bostrom.htm (accessed June 15, 2011).

Gane, N./ Haraway, D. (2006): When We Have Never Been Human, What Is to Be Done? Interview with Donna Haraway. In: Theory, Culture & Society 23(7-8), 135-158.

Graham, E.L. (2002): Representations of the Post/Human. New Brunswick: Rutgers University Press.

Halberstam, J./ Livingston, I. (eds.) (1995): Posthuman Bodies. Bloomington et al: Indiana University Press.

Haraway, D. (1985): A Manifesto for Cyborgs. Science, Technology, and Socialist Feminism in the 1980s. In: Nicholson, L. (ed.) (1990): Feminism/Postmodernism. New York et al.: Routledge, 190-233.

Harris, J. (2007): Enhancing Evolution. Princeton et al.: Princeton University Press.

Hauskeller, M. (2012): Reinventing Cockaigne. Utopian Themes in Transhumanist Thought. In: Hastings Center Report 42(2), 39-47.

Hayles, N.K. (1999): How We Became Posthuman. Chicago et al.: The University of Chicago Press.

Miah, A. (2008): A Critical History of Posthumanism. In: Gordijn, B./ Chadwick, R. (eds.): Medical Enhancement and Posthumanity. New York: Springer, 71-94.

Pearce, D. (1995): The Hedonistic Imperative. http://www.hedweb.com (accessed June 15, 2011).

Pico della Mirandola (1985 [1486]): On the Dignity of Man, On Being and the One, Heptaplus. New York et al.: Macmillan.

Pleij, H. (2001): Dreaming of Cockaigne: Medieval Fantasies of the Perfect Life. New York: Columbia University Press.

Roco, M.C./ Bainbridge, W.S. (eds.) (2003): Converging Technologies for Improving Human Performance: Nanotechnology, Biotechnology, Information Technology and Cognitive Science. Dordrecht: Kluver Academic Publishers.

UK Transhumanist Association (2011): UK Transhumanist Association Home Page. http://www.uktranshumanistassociation.org (accessed June 15, 2011).

Wills, D. (2008): Dorsality: Thinking Back through Technology and Politics. Minneapolis: University of Minnesota Press.

Wolfe, C. (2010): What is Posthumanism? Minneapolis et al.: University of Minnesota Press.

Brave New World

Curtis D. Carbonell

This article emerged out of previous research on the idea that bioluddites misuse Aldous Huxley's twentieth century, dystopian novel *Brave New World* (2007 [1932])[1] as a scare tactic (see my article, *Misreading Brave New World,* forthcoming). While this inflammatory approach of some bioluddites such as Francis Fukuyama and Leon Kass[2] is echoed in the popular use of the phrase "brave new world" for any new techno-social formation with possible ominous outcomes, Huxley's *Brave New World* is best read as a literary science fiction novel that critiques an imagined future utopia he calls the World State, as well as reflects Huxley's fears of his mid-twentieth century present. Moreover, a more helpful way to approach *Brave New World* runs counter to a salient feature often mentioned by readers: that there is something prophetic about the novel. Granted, Huxley foresaw a variety of interesting social phenomena from artificial development to rising acceptance of pharmaceuticals to the lowering of sexual mores; but one need not focus on how right the novel is about the present to see its value.

The award winning science fiction novelist Ursula K. Le Guin writes in an introduction to her seminal novel *The Left Hand of Darkness* that "science fiction is not predictive; it is descriptive" (2000, xii). Moving from the predictive/extrapolative to the descriptive allows us to view *Brave New World* through other lenses besides those preferred by bioconservatives. This reorients *Brave New World* for us and helps us understand that Huxley's novel is about the fears of a mid 20th century author, even as its readers consume it today. Of course, since *Brave New World* is often praised at getting so much of the future right, from its recognition that drugs would be used to affect many aspects of human emotion and mood, to the rise of genetic engineering, to the rise of promiscuousness in modern society, we often see it as predictive. But Le Guin reminds us see that science fiction is just fiction. As she notes, it is written by artists who tell lies that tell the truth. And the literary impact of *Brave New World* is humbly addressed by Huxley in his preface when he writes "its defects as a work of art are considerable" (xli), but the most "serious defect in the story" is that John "the Savage is offered only two alternatives, an insane life in utopia, or the life of a primitive in an Indian village" (xlii). Both the satirized future of an ultra-technical society with transhumans like Mustapha Mond in charge is a problem,

---

1 All inline citations will be taken from Huxley (2004).

2 See Kass (2002, 313); Fukuyama (2002, 256); Fukuyama (2004); see also Agar (2004).

but so is leaving the world in a primitive state. This is the ultimate, ironic insight of the novel.

In this article's brief examination of only one aspect of the novel, the biotech world of the World State in relation to current transhumanist and posthumanist discourse, we should remember that the problems of technoscience gone wrong represent an insane world for Huxley. However, the World State, and its fully organized society, is only part of the problem in the novel – but the area in which bioluddites solely (and wrongly) focus. We should not forget that the non-technical and primitive world of John the Savage is just as problematic as the fully organized World State (see below).[3] The question, for this article, though, focuses on answering how does Huxley's science fiction utopian critique work today within the discourses of post- and transhumanism?

First, it should be noted that *Brave New World* is not a posthuman novel. The privileged Alpha characters like Bernard Marx, Helmholtz Watson, Lenina Crowne, and Alpha Double Plus World Controllers like Mustapha Mond are not posthuman.[4] They are problematic transhumans. In particular, some, but not all of the Alpha enhancements should be read as negative: for example, the World State's most privileged and enhanced individuals have lost passion, a key ingredient of being human, in their conditioning toward the perfect, stable citizen. We see this referenced in two key later chapters in which World Controller Mustapha Mond justifies society's totally controlled and organized society. He says, "The greatest care is taken to prevent you from loving anyone too much" (209). As Mustapha has argued, truth and beauty are suspect, as are art, science and religion in this world in which motherhood, viviparous birth, and the family (and even history) have been superseded through technical means.

---

3 The novel *Island* (1962) is Huxley's solution, a novel that should be read in tandem with Brave New World, as should the last chapter of *Brave New World Revisited* (1958). In both, Huxley provides his solution: a particular humanist cocktail of science, philosophy, and religion, mixed up in such a way to create, Huxley would argue, the free individual. In *Island*, he presents a picture of the alternative he left out of *Brave New World* in which technology is harnessed for human needs and spirituality is the focus of ones life. In this way he redefines a mechanistic/materialist modernity to make it sane. And in *Brave New World Revisited*, Huxley fears "the completely organized society, the scientific caste system, the abolition of free will by methodological conditioning, the servitude made acceptable by regular doses of chemically induced happiness" (1958, 1). Both texts, ultimately, highlight Huxley's primary theme that spiritual freedom, above all else, is seminal for humanity.

4 For a helpful anthology that examines the current state of transhumanist discourse, see Hansell/ Grassie (eds.) (2011). Also, for a broader account of the prior ideas that led to transhumanism, see Alexander (2004).

Thus, in many ways the novel should be read today as not just a utopian critique (i.e., dystopia), but a transhumanist critique. It takes the values (see below) of positive technological enhancement of human beings and represents what is missing in its success. Moreover, the novel is ultimately an indictment of the world of human frailty that so seeks improvement it will sacrifice human freedom. For example, later in the novel when Mond is justifying the World State's worldview, the dominant voice of resistance, John the Savage states, "Alright, I'm claiming the right to be unhappy" (212). Such is the cost of human freedom that the World State refuses to pay. Moreover, the novel wonders at other costs, such as getting what we want in comfortable lives full of free sex and euphoric drug use. In the end it is the cost of the successful application of (what would later be called) transhumanist techniques that Huxley challenges.

In this examination of how *Brave New World* is a transhumanist critique, the novel should be viewed as a novel before it is looked at as a social warning. *Brave New World* has had a varied reception from its beginning in which it was widely panned as a novel. In literary critic Harold Bloom's analysis (2004), he provides an early quote from the *New Statesman* and *Nation* that provide a cogent and still relevant critique of the novel, as a novel. "The fact is Mr. Huxley does not really care for the story – the idea alone excites him." The reviewer whom Bloom quotes then levels the critique that Huxley turned an essay into a novel (2004, 13) – something Huxley would agree with.[5] Bloom, rightly, sees this as the main literary fault in the work.

Where *Brave New World* fails as a novel is in its mostly flat characterization of its primary characters (Bernard, Lenina, and John). While minor transformations occur, each of these characters is represented with little psychological depth. Bernard Marx is the outsider, damaged, and marginalized by the other perfected Alphas. In his quest for Lenina Crowne he uses John the Savage to further his own popularity, then crumbles and betrays his friends in the end. And, more importantly, John's primary transformation of believing in an idealized brave new world like the one mentioned by Miranda in her speech in Shakespeare's *The Tempest* turns to horror when he realizes the truth of the World State. Of course, Huxley ominously leaves us with the image of the once hopeful John the Savage's dangling feet, his body hanging under an arch, swinging to and fro. But these transformations feel secondary to the other world-building elements in the novel, from the Bokanovsky process to the representation of dying in a retirement home to the soma use. Bloom ultimately writes that,

---

5 In his essay *Tomorrow, Tomorrow, and Tomorrow* he calls Brave New World a "fictional essay of Utopianism" (see Huxley 1956).

for him, now the novel "scarcely sustains reading" (2010, 1) and claims it is "threadbare" (2004, 7) when it's considered strictly as a novel.[6]

Moreover, Bloom notes that *Brave New World* is a quintessential two cultures novel (see Snow 1969, 107). It blends the sciences and literature in a way that is expected from someone with Huxley's heritage; the fact Huxley's last book *Literature and Science* (1963) addresses this very topic lends weight to the notion. Bloom's two culture's observation should be no surprise because Huxley was the descendent of Charles Darwin's bulldog, Thomas Henry Huxley (Aldous Huxley's grandfather) and T. H. Huxley's sparring partner in the humanities Matthew Arnold, to whom Huxley was related on his mother's side. Biographer Nicholas Murphy writes, Huxley…

> "[…] was thus a kind of conduit or link between the world of high Victorian liberal intellectualism and the world of the twentieth century, whose course those ardent, progressively-minded meliorists could not have predicted" (Murphy 2009, 7).

This recognition of his pedigree and its surrounding two culture's debate that began between Arnold and T. H. Huxley, later to be refought by C. P. Snow and F. R. Leavis,[7] then to emerge in the more recent science wars (see Parsons 2003; Segerstrêale 2000), was paralleled by a broader intellectual debate between materialist and vitalist/idealist thinking in science and culture. Murray writes that Huxley's last work, *Literature and Science*, …

> "[…] addressed itself to the 'two cultures' debate, pouring scorn equally on C.P. Snow's *The Two Cultures* with its 'bland scientism' and F.R. Leavis's 'violent and ill-mannered' Richmond lecture, which had replied to Snow" (Murphy 2009, 41).

Furthermore, Robert Firchow sees both J. B. Haldane and Bertrand Russell's humanist ideas as influential on Huxley. "Again, the age-old battle was joined: was man matter or was he idea, or was he a mixture of both" (1975, 310)? Huxley, like Haldane and Russell, was keenly aware of the social and cultural results of the rise of Science Triumphant and feared a denuded world it might be making in which key humanist categories, like the free individual, were in jeopardy. At stake was the spiritual well-being of humanity in a world increasingly defined by the rational, instrumental pursuit of science and society. Technology, of

---

6 However, he does notice its relevance in the era of genetic engineering but (oddly) thinks the science-fiction genre of cyberpunk has "nothing to match Huxley's outrageous inventions" (Bloom 2004, 7). A quick look through cyberpunk's foundational text, *Neuromancer* (Gibson 1985), offers some outrageous inventions from the matrix to simstim to all the transhuman technologies – like Molly's razor nails to her mirror shades – that make Huxley's technical inventions in the novel quaint in comparison.

7 For more information on the argument Snow makes and the challenge by F. R. Leavis, see Leavis/ Yudkin (1963); Snow/ Collini (1993).

course, is the lever that moves this new world. And to technology's affect on human beings the novel lends its most keen insight.

What we should not forget in our examination of reading *Brave New World* within transhumanist discourse is that, first, it is a novel and, second, it is a science fiction novel. At the time of its publication, contemporary "science fiction" had moved beyond the science romances of H. G. Wells and the *voyages extraordinaires* of Jules Verne that were then most fully being articulated in American pulp magazines (see Seed [ed.] 2005). Huxley's literary critique that challenged utopian fictions such as Wells's *Men Like Gods* (1923) has little to do with Hugo Gernsback's notion of scientifiction, which used story telling as a didactic way to educate a public increasingly affected by technology or with John W. Campbell's editorial practice of centralizing stories within scientific contexts. But by imagining a future society in which science radically affects human beings, *Brave New World* constructs its idea in a similar space as those written by Science Fiction Golden Age heroes like Issac Asimov and Robert A. Heinlein, as well as the later New Wave writers (such as J. G. Ballard and Ursula K. Le Guin).

It is in this regard that the novel helps us refract its mid-twentieth century themes into new current transhumanist discourse. One key voice, the philosopher of science, Nick Bostrom, is highly influential in mapping the terrain of transhumanist thought. In particular, in *In Defense of Posthuman Dignity* (2005) Bostrom challenges bioconservative Leon Kass' argument that technically mastering our human nature to the point we change it will lead to full dehumanization. Of course, Kass uses *Brave New World* as an example of what could happen if all goes wrong, as if Huxley's novel is truly predictive in its representation of a totally organized society formed, from the ground up, by Taylorized and Fordist principles applied to human society. Bostrom provides his own reading of the novel and notes, regarding the characters, "yet posthumans they are not" (2005, 206). Huxley's characters aren't so changed they have crossed a threshold and become something outside the range of *Homo sapiens*. However, Bostrom recognizes that the characters in the novel are emotionally and physically altered to manipulate the potential of the individual in a rigid caste system, a notion that runs counter to the transhumanist project that would use technology to create individual flourishing. Bostrom's position helps because he argues that *Brave New World* is actually a warning against letting technoscience work toward the debasement of the human being.

While unraveling the nuanced differences in definition between the labels posthumanism and transhumanism would require its own careful consideration, my brief article operates under the assumption that the broader concept of antihumanism is less helpful for understanding *Brave New World* than what, today, we are calling transhumanism. Antihumanism, broadly construed, comprises a variety of alternatives to traditional Western humanism (see Davies 1997). The human has a few favorite sons and daughters who have come under attack since Modernity disenchanted the West. We have Hamlet and his will-negating nausea. Milton's triumphant but doomed Satan. Nietzsche's prophetic Zarathustra who claims man is something that must be overcome. And even a trace of the human left by Foucault's in the famous ending of *The Order of Things* (1970) where he writes that man will be erased like a face drawn in the sand at the edge of the sea. The idea of "man," what we now call the human, has been rethought in many different discourses within the humanities. And while there is plenty in *Brave New World* that demonstrates a crumbling of traditional humanist values from the atrophied freedom of thought in which the World State's citizens are conditioned to love specific elements within their caste to the hobbled freedom of the active individual who knows only the happiness of soma and sex, of work and play, a less articulated (but very helpful) filter through which to wash the novel's conceptual structures and literary elements is transhumanism.

Moreover, it is necessary to think in terms of how *Brave New World* refracts a posthumanism discourse informed by antihumanism. The cultural critic Theodore Adorno, who, along with Max Horkheimer, provided a famous critique of the Enlightenment Project's failure to save us from dehumanizing capitalism (see Horkheimer/ Adorno 1995), also wrote about the problems of (according to Adorno) a pernicious type of dehumanization: Americanization. In *Prisms* Adorno writes, "Huxley's *Brave New World* is a manifestation of this panic, or rather, its rationalization" (1981, 98). Adorno is critiquing the way of life the new émigré to America face. In particular it is the dehumanizing process of Americanization that he sees as a threat, primarily to humanistic concerns being flattened by plastic concerns and one that informs Huxley's novel. Of course, the key element for the émigré to the New World was survival, but, for Adorno, the embracing of this new form of culture industry finalizes a process of blinding one to one's true and authentic self. It is this sort of dehumanization that creates an antihumanism for Adorno, although this is in no way a technologically created posthumanism. Of course, his critique of *Brave New World* sees the horror in mass production applied to biology, as Huxley put it – in essence, the conditioning of human beings via the mechanisms of a scientifically organized society. What we see through Adorno's reading is that *Brave New World* is a novel representing, in its transhumanist reversals, discrete examples of post- and antihumanism.

And, of course, as a key note in the great chorus of literature of the Modern Crisis, as Adorno would have us see, *Brave New World* is not alone. From Kafka's imagined horrors so explicitly seen in – to take one example – the short story *In the Penal Colony*, in which the crimes of prisoners are inscribed into their flesh by a machine, to the entire swath of existential literature from Camus to DeLillo that describes humanity in an absurd world dominated by a soulless Modernity, to more contemporary literature like Michel Houellebecq's (2000) *Les Particules Élémentaires* (also known as *The Elementary Particles* and *Atomised*) in which sex and reproduction are problematized much as Huxley's problematized viviparous birth and soma use. These dystopian representations are not only the disenchantment of a working humanist self from itself, but of the mechanisms of a rationalized, bureaucratic science as the culprit. And this differs from the current version of hyperhumanist discourse, transhumanism, in that it pushes in the opposite direction: away from enhancing and refining core human categories into eliding them under unseen but real cultural pressures.

Finally, my reading of *Brave New World* takes transhumanism to mean the transformation of human beings via advanced technology – or as James Hughes claims, "Transhumanism is the idea that humans can use reason to transcend the limitations of the human condition" (2004, 156). Moreover, Julian Huxley, Aldous's brother, coined the term to explain how humanity can transcend itself and society through a humanized science and technology (1957). I follow these very general definitions with one provided in the *Transhumanist Declaration* that defines the term as a process that views humans as already "profoundly affected by science and technology" (Humanity+ 2011) and one that embraces this change in allowing humanity's potential to emerge. There are other aspects to this definition, of course, e.g., the recognition of existential risks and the steps to avoid them, as well as the (controversial) recognition that other forms of sentience will emerge and that these need to be afforded rights. My use of this standard definition allows me to read *Brave New World* not just as a satire of American commercialism or a parody of Behaviorist psychology or a critique of utopian fiction, but as a novel that challenges the potential dangers inherent in the biotech revolution, while also admitting the need for advances.

If we look closely at the types of humans in the novel, we see that with the rigid caste system Huxley creates for the World State, as opposed to the "natural" individuals who live in primitive villages, only the highest caste, the Alphas, exhibit the types of enhancements we would consider transhuman. They are genetically developed to be superior individuals in intelligence and health, while the other castes, in decreasing order, share less enhanced mental capabilities. In fact, the very bottom caste, the Epsilons, are nothing more than brutes designed for menial labor and, thus, have been purposely stunted (the very opposite of the transhumanist project). In particular, the transhumanist elements in the novel can be clearly seen in the first two chapters, both of which function as introductions to the world Huxley's novel represents. The story of Bernard

Marx's challenge to the promiscuity and emotional vacuity of the World State emerges in his quest for pneumatic Lenina Crowne and his encounter with Shakespeare reading John the Savage. The story shifts from Bernard's dissatisfaction with his life as a defective Alpha to John's hope to see the ideal world of his mother, to the final horror at what that world really is. The human drama that leads to Bernard's exile, Lenina's rejection, and John's suicide all serves a purpose for Huxley: to reinforce a theme that the scientifically organized society leads to a loss of human freedom.

The first two chapters setup this complex world in which the characters find themselves. Chapter One begins with a picture of artificial development, the Director of Haterchies and Conditioning leading a group of hopeful students through the facility where incubators are at work in the "modern fertilizing process" (3). Here we learn how the bulk of citizens in the World State are developed. The castes are rigidly constructed for specific purposes. The Gammas, Deltas, and Epsilons undergo the Bokanovsky process to streamline their development – up to ninety-six buds from one embryo. The result is "Progress" and "Social Stability." "The principle of mass production at last applied to biology" (5). The basest and most inhuman result is a stunted person whose jobs it is to do the most mindless labor – and to love it. Later, when Bernard takes a lift to the roof of a building he meets "a small simian creature, dressed in the black tunic of an Epsilon-Minus Semi-Moron" (50). This clone's only joy is the hope of seeing the "roof," a word he exclaims over and over again, until Bernard exits and the Epsilon returns "into the droning twilight of the well, the twilight of his own habitual stupor" (51).

Examples like this demonstrate how Huxley actually satirizes through reversals the future hopes of current transhumanists. Where optimists like Bostrom sees transhumanism "evaluating the opportunities for enhancing the human condition and the human organism opened up by the advancement of technology" (Bostrom 2003, 493), Huxley's novel sees loss of freedom through the ultimate insult: the manipulation of the biological development process to create machine-like persons fit for specific jobs and places in society. While the most dehumanized example is with the Epsilon lift operator, the most horrific occurs in Chapter Two in the Infant Nurseries and Neo-Pavlonian Conditioning Rooms. In a sadistic but effective process in conditioning, books and roses are used to make infants hate reading and nature. A row on the floor alternates bowls of roses with bowls of books "opened invitingly each at some gaily-colored image of beast or fish or bird" (16). The tiny Delta caste infants crawl forward to touch the rose petals and to look at the pictures in the books. A frightening alarm sounds first, followed by a mild shock. The intent of the World State controllers is to make these young Alphas "safe from books and botany" (17). Such a result is Huxley's fear that intellectual learning and a love of the natural world will be lost in a Taylorized and Fordist future. Here the humanist longings of the novel are evident in what is being eradicated in the bulk of the World State's workers.

Moreover, other key categories of the traditional human experience are challenged. Motherhood and viviparous birth are considered smut. Also, sex is communal so that individual love and passion don't emerge and challenge social stability – "everyone belongs to everyone else" (34). To make this effective, the bromide "history is bunk" (29) becomes a mantra because it is the history of human individuality (and passion), and all the negativity that comes with it, that must be eradicated. To facilitate this process whereby human impulses are muted, the drug soma is introduced; its function is to raise "a quite impenetrable wall between the actual universe and their minds" (67). This tool gives the World State's citizens a type of faux freedom "to have the most wonderful time" (79) – again for the novel, the satirical elements highlight what is lost through the implementation. This primary critical aspect of the novel, the "transhumanist" techniques of biotech on its citizenry, clearly runs counter to the hopes founds in documents like the *Transhumanist Declaration* or, to take one individual thinker's text, Bostrom's *In Defense of Posthuman Dignity*.

In the end, *Brave New World* is more than just a warning about the negative effects of the scientifically organized society. It also reminds us that life prior to modern science is short and brutish and certainly something to be remedied. And when viewed through the lenses of current hopeful, transhumanist discourse, *Brave New World* becomes humorless satire that uses exaggeration to great effect. It's most powerful result is in showing what happens when our enhancements do just what they are intended to do. The notion of humanistic freedom is up for grabs. And Huxley wants a humanized science to create a humanized society. *Brave New World*, his most popular comment, offers no solution. But its warnings should not be read as encouraging a lack of will. It should be read as encouraging a humanistic use of science and technology in our battle with our own frailties.

Bibliography

Adorno, T.W. (1981): Prisms. Cambridge(MA): MIT Press.

Agar, N. (2004): Liberal Eugenics - In Defence of Human Enhancement. Malden(MA), Blackwell.

Alexander, B. (2004): Rapture: A Raucous Tour Of Cloning, Transhumanism, and the New Era of Immortality (Kindle Edition). New York: Basic Books.

Bloom, H. (2004): Aldous Huxley's Brave New World. Broomall(PA): Chelsea House.

Bloom, H. (ed.) (2010): Aldous Huxley: New Edition (Bloom's Modern Critical Views). New York: Infobase Publishing.
Bostrom, N. (2003). Human Genetic Enhancements: A Transhumanist Perspective. In: Journal of Value Inquiry 37(4), 493-506.
Bostrom, N. (2005): In Defence of Posthuman Dignity. In: Bioethics 19(3), 202-214.
Davies, T (1997): Humanism. London et al.: Routledge.
Firchow, P. (1975): Science and Conscience in Huxley's Brave New World. In: Contemporary Literature 16(3), 301-316.
Foucault, M. (1970): The Order of Things: An Archaeology of the Human Sciences. London: Tavistock Publications.
Fukuyama, F. (2002): Our Posthuman Future: Consequences of the Biotechnology Revolution. New York: Farrar Straus & Giroux.
Fukuyama, F. (2004): Transhumanism. In: Foreign Policy 144, 42-43.
Gibson, W. (1985): Neuromancer. London: V. Gollancz.
Hansell, G.R./ Grassie, W. (eds.) (2011): H±: Transhumanism and Its Critics. Philadelphia: Metanexus.
Horkheimer, M./ Adorno, T.W. (1995): Dialectic of Enlightenment. New York: Continuum.
Houellebecq, M. (2000): Atomised. London: Heinemann.
Hughes, J. (2004): Citizen Cyborg: Why Democratic Societies Must Respond to the Redesigned Human of the Future. Boulder(CO): Westview Press.
Humanity+ (2011): Transhumanist Declaration. http://humanityplus.org/philosophy/transhumanist-declaration/ (accessed June 4, 2011).
Huxley, A. (1956): Tomorrow and Tomorrow and Tomorrow and Other Essays. New York: Harper.
Huxley, A. (1958): Brave New World Revisited. New York: Harper & Row.
Huxley, A. (1962): Island: A Novel. New York: Harper.
Huxley, A. (1963): Literature and Science. New York: Harper & Row.
Huxley, A. (2004): Brave New World (New Edition). London: Vintage.
Huxley, A. (2007 [1932]): Brave New World. London: Vintage.
Huxley, J. (1957): New Bottles for New Wine: Essays. London: Chatto & Windus.
Kass, L. (2002): Life, Liberty and the Defense of Dignity: The Challenge for Bioethics. San Francisco: Encounter Books.
Le Guin, U.K. (2000): The Left Hand of Darkness. New York: Ace Books.
Leavis, F.R./ Yudkin, M. (1963): Two Cultures? The Significance of C. P. Snow. New York: Pantheon Books.
Murray, N. (2003): Aldous Huxley: A Biography. New York: Thomas Dunne Books.
Parsons, K. (ed.) (2003): The Science Wars: Debating Scientific Knowledge and Technology. Amherst(NY): Prometheus Books.
Seed, D. (ed.) (2005): A Companion to Science Fiction. Malden(MA): Blackwell.
Segerstrêale, U.C.O. (2000): Beyond the Science Wars: The Missing Discourse About Science and Society. Albany: State University of New York Press.
Snow, C.P. (1969): The Two Cultures; and, A Second Look: An Expanded Version of 'The Two Cultures and the Scientific Revolution'. London: Cambridge University Press.
Snow, C.P./ Collini, S. (1993): The Two Cultures. Cambridge: Cambridge University Press.
Wells, H.G. (1923): Men Like Gods. London et al.: Cassell.

Life Extension
Eternal Debates on Immortality

Sascha Dickel & Andreas Frewer

From the epic of Gilgamesh to the tale of the fountain of youth, the quest for immortality and eternal healthy life has been a recurring theme in human history. The kings and adventurers in these mythic tales don't accept the inevitability of aging and dying. Instead they travel far into the unknown to pluck the forbidden fruit of immortality. In contrast to religious concepts of immortality found in monotheistic traditions, immortality in these stories is not something *given* by a higher power, but something that must be actively *taken*. The notion that immortality can be achieved by applied reason and a bit of bravery has accompanied humanity from the first recordings of history to the modern age. But so far none of the visions of eternal life has changed the reality that all humans must die (see Cortese 2013; Höhn 2004; Stoff 2004; Knell/ Weber 2009; Frewer 2010; Hilt et al. 2010).

With the dawn of modern science utopias of immortality by *technological* means became popular and replaced the myths of the past (see Gordijn 2004). Since the 1980s *life extension* has become a common term for recent technological approaches to immortality (see Pearson/ Shaw 1982). The goal of life extension is to slow down or even reverse the processes of aging in order to extend the maximum human lifespan. The (mostly speculative) methods of life extension typically do not promise literary immortality, meaning that they typically do not aspire a state where dying would become impossible altogether. It is rather the aim of these technological approaches to transform the human body in such ways that death would only occur by severe accidents or by voluntary choice (see Freitas 2004).

Today the concept of technological life extension is strongly associated with the intellectual and social movement of transhumanism. In this article we will first present some of the most popular transhumanist approaches to life extension. Thereafter we will reconstruct the transhumanist discourse on life extension as a variant of modern utopianism. Finally our article will confront the discourse on life extension with a posthumanist perspective on immortality.

1. Suggested Methods of Life Extension in Transhumanist Thought

If someone would ever write the history of transhumanism and life extension it would be appropriate to bring the suggested methods of life extension into a chronological order. But for the purpose of this paper it is more suitable to order the transhumanist visions of technological immortality depending on their speculativeness, i.e. how much their hopes rest on future technologies that have not been invented yet and how much their underlying assumption are outside the realm of "normal science". The term normal science should not be confused with sound science. It rather refers to a routinized practice of a scientific field which is usually not put into question from the insiders of the field. None of the following concepts of life extension are considered as established and uncontested parts of aging research (gerontology) and are sometimes even regarded as pseudoscientific. Also the proponents of these ideas typically position *themselves* as outsiders of their respective fields – though not as exponents of pseudoscientific alternatives but rather as agents of possible paradigm shifts (see Kuhn 1976).

1.1. Strategies for Engineered Negligible Senescence

It is typical for transhumanists to treat aging as a disease like any other. Joao Pedro de Magalhães considers aging as "a sexually transmitted terminal disease that can be defined as a number of time-dependent changes in the body that lead to discomfort, pain, and eventually death" (de Magalhães 2004, 48). Few transhumanists have delved so deeply into the physical causes of this "disease" as Audrey de Grey. He thinks that an…

> "[…] anti-aging medicine worthy of the name does not yet exist and seems certain not to exist for at least 15-20 years. By 'worthy of the name' I mean interventions that can reliably restore someone exhibiting age-related dysfunction to the physiological and cognitive robustness that they enjoyed in early adulthood" (de Grey 2004b, 31).

De Grey regrets that there are already products on the market which are labelled "anti-aging" but have no considerable effect on the aging process. At the same time he suggests that "real" anti-aging research does not receive the attention and funding it deserves. Ten years ago de Grey coined the term "Strategies for Engineered Negligible Senescence" (SENS) as an umbrella term for a range of biomedical therapies with the ultimate purpose of postponing age-related effects. In his writings de Grey identified seven categories of "damage" that constitute aging: (1) cell loss, (2) oncogenic nuclear mutations and epimutations, (3) death-resistant cells, (4) mitochondrial mutations, (5) intracellular junk, (6) extracellular junk and (7) random extracellular cross-linking. He also proposed specific biomedical treatments for each of these damages that aim to cure aging at the molecular level (see de Grey 2004a; SENS Foundation 2012a). De Grey suggests that the necessary precursor technologies for these treatments have already been developed. Therefore the first "immortals" may already live among us (see de Grey 2004b; Miller/ Wilsdon 2006).

De Grey is a controversial figure in the field of aging research. Although de Grey perceives himself as "integrated into the mainstream of gerontology" and asserts that he is "considered an intellectual equal of the leading people in the field" (de Grey as cited in Miller/ Wilsdon 2006, 53), his theories are still not supported by the gerontology community at large. Furthermore, research on the basis of SENS has not received the amount of funding that de Grey hoped for. In response to this de Grey founded the SENS Foundation to promote the development of "rejuvenation biotechnologies" and to gather a notable group of scientists who support his vision (see SENS Foundation 2012b).

1.2. Nanomedicine

Aubrey de Grey perceives the human body as a very complex machine and therefore approaches the problem of aging "from an 'engineering' point of view" (SENS Foundation 2012c). In this regard the concept of nanomedicine, proposed by Robert A. Freitas, is based on very similar assumptions. Nanomedicine in general refers to the application of nanotechnology for "the preservation and improvement of human health" (Freitas 2004, 77). Freitas' approach, however, is quite specific. In his works he theorizes about medical machines which would be only a few micrometers in size. These "nanorobots" should be introduced into the body in large amounts in order to detect and repair all kinds of damages. Present technology is not able to produce those nanorobots, but Freitas believes that in the years to come science will make the creation of "molecular assemblers" possible: desktop sized nanotechnological factories with the ability to position matter with molecular control (see Freitas 1999). The concept of nanorobots rests on an early paradigm of nanotechnology that dates from the writings of Richard Feynman (1959) and Eric Drexler (1986). This paradigm is no longer accepted by the majority of nanoscientists (see Rip/ van Amerom 2010). However, visions of molecular manufacturing are still part of the field and also influence the public discourse on nanotechnology.

1.3. Mind Uploading

In contrast to visions of "real" immortality, concepts of life extension can only promise "accident-limited healthspans" (Freitas 2004, 77). To reduce the risk of those accidents transhumanists speculate about the possibility to transfer the human mind to a computer. This process is called mind uploading or "whole brain emulation" (see Bostrom/ Sandberg 2008). Transhumanist engineers and philosophers have thought about different methods to reach this goal:

> "One way of doing this might be by first scanning the synaptic structure of a particular brain and then implementing the same computations in an electronic medium. A brain scan of sufficient resolution could be produced by disassembling the brain atom for atom by means of nanotechnology. Other approaches, such as analyzing pieces of the brain slice by slice in an electron microscope with automatic image processing have also been proposed" (Humanity+ 2012).

According to transhumanists the original consciousness as well as the personal identity could be completely maintained. In digital form, the mind should be freed from the frailty of the human body. Furthermore, after the human mind is essentially transformed into a piece of software, it should be fairly easy to create copies and backups.

The concept of mind uploading rests on some variant of functionalism, which assumes "that the mind is based on the functional relations between physical elements and not on those elements themselves" (Hauskeller 2012, 189). Although functionalism is a legitimate position in the philosophy of mind, visions of mind uploading are typically restricted to transhumanist circles and works of science fiction. Even outspoken advocates of mind uploading think that it will take at least several decades until this radical technological vision will be possible. They hope for bio- and nanotechnology to work as "bridges" to a future where mind uploading finally becomes a reality. These bridges should allow us to "live long enough to live forever" (Kurzweil/ Grossman 2004).

1.4. Cryonics

But maybe even these bridges will arrive too late. All proponents of life extension share the fear that their desired breakthroughs might arrive just *after* they have died. Confronted with this discomforting prospect some place their hope in the work of cryonics organizations like Alcor Life Extension Foundation.[1] In the words of Alcor:

> "Cryonics is an effort to save lives by using temperatures so cold that a person beyond help by today's medicine might be preserved for decades or centuries until a future medical technology can restore that person to full health. Cryonics sounds like science fiction, but is based on modern science. It's an experiment in the most literal sense of the word. The question you have to ask yourself is this: would you

1 Alcor is not the only cryonics organization around. There are (a few) other organizations that offer a cryonic preservation service or promise to take care of transporting clients who have recently died (see Cryonics Institute 2012).

> rather be in the experimental group, or the control group?" (Alcor Life Extension Foundation 2012a).

Currently Alcor has 976 clients and 113 "patients" – corpses of dead people in cryonic tanks (see Alcor Life Extension Foundation 2012b). As a client of Alcor, you invest in a kind of life insurance that should guarantee that you will end up in a cryonic tank after you have died, in the hope that you will be brought back to life by advanced technologies at some point in the future.

The idea of cryonics was presented to the public by Robert Ettinger in the 1960s (see Ettinger 1964; 1989). Early pioneers of cryonics like Ettinger had no clear idea about the nature of future technologies that might bring the dead back to life. With the emergence of visions of nanotechnology and mind uploading advocates of cryonics started to build their hopes on the development of these technologies. As a matter of fact one of the most important intellectual fathers of nanotechnology, Eric Drexler, regarded cryonics as a "door to the future" that would allow us to experience the coming age of nanotechnological wonders (see Drexler 1986).

Most people in the scientific community consider cryonics a prime example of fringe science, as even transhumanists such as Bostrom are ready to admit (see Bostrom 2005a, 10). But several transhumanists have nevertheless signed a cryonics contract or have said that they will do so in the near future. They consider this a rational decision, because, according to Bostrom, …

> "[…] even a 5% or 10% chance of success could make an Alcor contract a rational option for people who can afford it and who place a great value on their continued personal existence" (Bostrom 2001).

2. Technological Life Extension: A Modern Utopia

The transhumanist quest for life extension, with a particular focus on the extension of the healthspan, is only the latest incarnation of the idea that technology will someday allow us to conquer death.[2] However, no technology has so far

2 Take for example the Russian intellectual milieu at the turn of the 20th century: In this pre-revolutionary environment the dream of a scientific quest to find a technological equivalent to the fountain of youth was shared by many influential intellectuals. Among them were Konstantin Tsiolkovsky (known as a pioneer of rocket science) and Alexander Bogdanov (considered as one of the founders of Soviet science fiction). Bogdanov even founded an experimental scientific institution to promote his fight against aging – the Institute for Hematology and Blood Transfusions. He also conducted experiments on himself. One of those trials cost him his life (when he took blood of a student suffering from malaria and tuberculosis), which turned him into a tragic figure in the history of immortality research (see Groys/ Hagemeister 2005).

fulfilled the promise of life extension. Even the increased life expectancy after the industrial revolution is not the result of an technological intervention into the aging process but rather the outcome of general improvements in public health (see Gordijn 2004, 149). This poses a problem for the credibility of every new proposal to fight aging and dying. Since the ideas of those scientists who pursue that goal are totally in contrast to historical experience, they are always viewed with skepticism or are outright ridiculed.

2.1. The Discourse of Technological Immortality

Confronted with this problem scientists who believe in technological possibilities to end aging seem to use the same kind of frames and arguments over and over – whatever their preferred technological method might be: The reason for the inevitability of death in human history is not viewed as an *eternal* truth but rather a *historical* one. It is suggested that *so far* humanity lacked the right instruments to conquer death, but that *now* our progress in science and technology will *soon* provide us with the adequate tools to fight aging and dying. If we act *now* and put enough effort into the respective research we might harvest the fruit of eternal life *just in time* – during *our lifetime*. This kind of discourse transforms death from a certain event, which *will happen*, regardless of whether we might hope otherwise, into a *risk* that can be avoided – a *possible* future, but no unavoidable fate without alternative (see Dickel 2011).

The transhumanist writings on life extension technologies reproduce this fundamental discourse structure: In a popular fable of transhumanist philosopher Nick Bostrom, death is perceived as a "dragon-tyrant" that rules humanity. For the most time of human history we lacked the tools to confront this monster, *but now* we might finally possess the weapons to fight the spectrum of death. We just haven't tried hard enough yet (see Bostrom 2005b). It is easy to see that Bostroms writing reproduces the structure of former discourses on technological immortality. This observation does not imply that transhumanists like Bostrom are *wrong* – since the history of technology shows us that technology can *indeed* turn former impossibilities into possibilities (see Kaminski 2010). The burden of proof, however, must be carried by the transhumanist advocates of life extension technologies.

2.2. Never-Ending Individual Options

For transhumanism life extension is no goal like any other. One might even claim that life extension is the overall goal of transhumanism itself. Admittedly not all transhumanist visions are concerned with life extension but focus on other forms of human enhancement (e.g. the improvement of cognitive capacities). However, it is difficult to deny that a considerable amount of transhumanist writing is dedicated to the topic technological immortality. The reason for this becomes obvious if the evaluative core of transhumanist thinking is explored. The core value of transhumanism is the extension of the space of possibilities beyond the restrictions that are given by human biology (see Bostrom 2003). This explains why life extension might well be the *most prominent* goal of transhumanism. From the perspective of an individual human being, the space of possibilities is reduced to zero when it dies. Death can therefore be seen as the greatest enemy of the core value of transhumanism.

In its dedication to extend the space of possibilities and transgress boundaries transhumanism is a deeply modernist discourse. The aim to unlock options in order to improve a perceived status quo is one of the defining features of classical modern utopianism (see Dickel 2011).[3] The unique feature of transhumanism as a recent variant of modern utopianism is its strong focus on the individual human body whose limitations should be overcome to unlock options that nature denies us. But this also constitutes no breach with modern thinking. It is rather in line with modernity's celebration of the subject – which has only increased with the recent trend of individualization in late modern societies (see Beck/ Beck-Gernsheim 2002).

Therefore transhumanist visions of life extension could be regarded as a radicalization of the promises of modernity. Transhumanists strongly believe in never ending progress: They believe in the possibility of a world where nanotechnology, biotechnology, augmented and simulated reality, artificial intelligence, and the colonization of space will transform culture and society in unprecedented ways – and *they* (as individuals) want to experience this "brave new world" of the future (and give other individuals the opportunity to experience it also). On the one hand this emphasis of a "new world" distinguishes transhumanism from former visions of physical immortality that just promised more of the same. On the other hand this new world of tomorrow is still regarded as part of mundane reality (and not seen as a some kind otherworld). This distinguishes transhumanism from typical religious hopes of an afterlife.

3 The narrative of never ending progress is as important for the constitution of modernity as its various structural features like the rationalization, acceleration or the domestication of nature, because these structural features are legitimized through utopias of progress. Therefore modernity itself can be understood as a culture that is programmed to increase possibilities (see Nassehi 1994; Rosa 2003).

2.3. Critical Perspectives

As transhumanist ideas gained prominence in the last decade the idea of technological immortality has become a subject of critique. Criticism of life extension typically comes in two forms. Either the *feasibility* of technological life extension is denied or the *desirability* of a radical longer life is put into question. The task of critics of the first kind is very easy – the just need to point out that all former visions of immortality turned out to be illusionary. It is far more difficult to criticize visions of techno-immortality from a normative point of view – exactly because life extension is in line with dominant narratives of modernity. Classical types of criticism that condemn the quest for immortality as unnatural, as hubris, as a violation of god's rule, or simply as presumptuous, position themselves against the cultural matrix of modern life, because modernity itself calls for a constant transgression of boundaries. A society that favors never-ending improvement finds it difficult to acknowledge absolute limits such as death. In this situation critics of life extension that aim to stay within the cultural framework of modernity try to counter visions of life extension with other modern narratives. They point out that pursuing the goal of life extension would create problems of social justice, that it would accelerate a global ecological breakdown, or that it might produce radically risk averse and conservative subjects. However, this kind of criticism invites advocates of techno-immortality to suggest technological solutions for these "side effects" of life extension.[4]

This doesn't mean that a *modern critique* of life extension is futile. But critics must reflect that their criticism can also be *productive* for the discourse of life extension itself, because this kind of critique "feeds" the discourse with positions for further arguments and counter arguments. As a form of modern technological utopianism the discourse on life extension is independent of the success of specific technologies. The history of this discourse shows that it always creates *new technological visions* if expectations in *former technologies* are disappointed (see Dickel 2011).

But even if the discourse on techno-immortality seems to be "eternal" we have also shown that it so far stayed on the fringe of science. But what might happen if actual technologies of radical life extension are developed? It would be ignorant to definitely exclude this possibility, because we know that technology indeed has the power to extend the space of possibilities (see Kaminski 2010). Today we can talk to people thousands of miles away, we have learned to

4 For an overview of the debate see Knell/ Weber (2009) and Hilt et al. (2010); furthermore with regard to other aspects of immortality and eternal fame see Williams (1973) and Thiele-Dohrmann (2000).

cross the oceans and to fly, our weapons can destroy thousands of lives within a blink of an eye – who is to say that we cannot live forever?

3. Posthuman Immortals

However, if humans would live forever, would they still be humans? The classical answer of transhumanism to this question is "yes". This answer dates back to Julian Huxley, who provided one of the earliest definitions of transhumanism. He defined it as…

> "[…] man remaining man, but transcending himself, by realizing new possibilities of and for his human nature. 'I believe in transhumanism'. Once there are enough people who can truly say that, the human species will be on the threshold of a new kind of existence, as different from ours as ours is from that of Pekin man. It will at last be consciously fulfilling its real destiny" (Huxley 1957, 17).

Most transhumanists would still agree with Huxley that the goal of their aspirations is *human enhancement*. In this perspective life extension, like all kinds of technological interventions in human nature endorsed by transhumanists, is viewed as a mere extension of human possibilities.

In critical posthumanist thinking this assumption is put into question. Critical posthumanism – as a variant of postmodern thinking – problematizes the cultural framework of modernity itself (see Miah 2009). Critical posthumanist like Haraway (1991) and Hayles (1999) emphasize that with the arrival of industrial civilization in general and recent advancements in information technology in particular the idea of a coherent human subject can no longer be maintained. They suggest that even in our current technoscientific culture, we can no longer speak of human subjects independent of their technology. Therefore the modernist narrative of humanism does no longer reflect our current condition.[5] The writings of critical posthumanists share a latent skeptical view on emerging technologies, which Andy Miah relates to Heidegger's philosophy of technology:

> "Often considered to be a pessimistic view on technology, Heidegger's concern was that technology is perpetually an assault on nature since it always involves its alteration through destruction. This struggle over how technology corrupts nature is visible in contemporary notions of posthumanism" (Miah 2009, 85).

Even if we don't perceive technology as a force of *destruction*, it is hard to deny that technology is a force of *transformation* – of nature and culture alike. If the

---

5 An even more radical position comes from Bruno Latour who claims that modernity was always an illusion – and that "we have never been modern" (see Latour 1993).

status of present human subjects is problematic, it is even more problematic to assume that transhumanism's immortals could be considered as immortal *humans*. Although transhumanists use the term "posthuman" for uploaded minds or persons transformed by nanotechnology (see Humanity+ 2012) they, nevertheless, often implicitly, assume some form of continuity in this transfer to posthumanity. Otherwise the whole concept of life extension as an extension of *our lives* would fall apart. In non-transhumanist visions of physical immortality this might be unproblematic, because those visions can assume that (except death) all other aspects of the human condition will just stay the same. But in the narratives of transhumanism the bodies and minds of the future will be transformed by technology. Immortality is the very result of this transformation.[6]

If visions of the future found in transhumanism incorporate the critical perspective of posthumanism (and vice versa) the result is a "speculative posthumanism" (see Roden 2010). Speculative posthumanism is concerned with the possible "emergence of an incommensurate *posthuman alterity*" (ibid., 29). From the perspective of speculative posthumanism the hope that "we" might become immortals could be futile – even if we would believe in the futuristic visions of transhumanism. Future technologies would rather turn us into posthuman beings with minds and experiences that are totally alien to us. These posthumans could still have memories of their former human lives, but these memories might mean nothing more to them than a half remembered dream.

Bibliography

Alcor Life Extension Foundation (2012a): What is Cryonics? http://www.alcor.org/AboutCryonics/index.html (accessed December 15, 2012).

Alcor Life Extension Foundation (2012b): Alcor Membership Statistics. http://www.alcor.org/AboutAlcor/membershipstats.html (accessed December 15, 2012).

Beck, U./ Beck-Gernsheim, E. (2002): Individualization: Institutionalized individualism and its Social and Political Consequences. London: Sage.

Bostrom, N. (2001): What is Transhumanism? http://www.nickbostrom.com/old/transhumanism.html (accessed December 15, 2012).

Bostrom, N. (2003): Transhumanist Values. In: Review of Contemporary Philosophy 4(1-2), 87-101.

Bostrom, N. (2005a): A History of Transhumanist Thought. In: Journal of Evolution and Technology 14(1).

6 Also the environment of the expected immortals will be totally different from the world as we know it. It is not necessary to believe in a specific vision of the future (like molecular manufacturing). We just need to compare our world to the early 20th century and assume (like transhumanists usually do) that technological change is exponential, to get an idea of the possible otherness of the early 22th century.

Bostrom, N. (2005b): The Fable of the Dragon-Tyrant. In: Journal of Medical Ethics 31(5), 273-277.
Bostrom, N./ Sandberg, A. (2008): Whole Brain Emulation: A Roadmap (Technical Report. 3). Oxford: Future of Humanity Institute. http://www.philosophy.ox.ac.uk/__data/assets/pdf_file/0019/3853/brain-emulation-roadmap-report.pdf (accessed December 15, 2012).
Cortese, F. (2013) Longevitize! Essays on the Science, Philosophy & Politics of Longevity. Center for Transhumanity.
Cryonics Institute (2012): Comparing Procedures and Policies. http://cryonics.org/comparisons.html (accessed December 15, 2012).
de Grey, A. (ed.) (2004a): Strategies for Engineered Negligible Senescence: Why Genuine Control of Aging May Be Forseeable. New York: Academy of Sciences.
de Grey, A. (2004b): The War on Aging. Speculations on Some Future Chapters in the Never-Ending Story of Human Life Extension. In: Immortality Institute (ed.): The Scientific Conquest of Death: Essays on Infinite Lifespans. Buenos Aires: Libros en Red, 29-45.
de Magalhães, J.P. (2004): The Dream of the Elixir Vitae. In: Immortality Institute (ed.): The Scientific Conquest of Death: Essays on Infinite Lifespans. Buenos Aires: Libros en Red, 47-62.
Dickel, S (2011): Enhancement-Utopien: Soziologische Studien zur Konstruktion des Neuen Menschen. Baden-Baden: Nomos.
Drexler, K.E. (1986): Engines of Creation: The Coming Era of Nanotechnology. New York: Anchor Books.
Ettinger, R.C.W. (1964): The Prospect of Immortality. Garden City(NY): Doubleday.
Ettinger, R.C.W. (1989): Man into Superman. New York: St. Martin's Press.
Feynman, R.P. (1959): There's Plenty of Room at the Bottom. http://www.zyvex.com/nanotech/feynman.html (accessed December 15, 2012).
Freitas, R.A. (1999): Nanomedicine: Basic Capabilities. Austin(TX): Landes Bioscience.
Freitas, R.A (2004): Nanomedicine. The Quest for Accident-Limited Healthspans. In: Immortality Institute (ed.): The Scientific Conquest of Death: Essays on Infinite Lifespans. Buenos Aires: Libros en Red, 77–91.
Frewer, A. (2010): Endlichkeit als Kränkung, Unsterblichkeit als Heilungswunsch? In: Hilt, A./ Jordan, I./ Frewer, A. (eds.): Endlichkeit, Medizin und Unsterblichkeit: Geschichte – Theorie – Ethik. Stuttgart: Steiner, 323-326.
Fukuyama, F. (2004): Transhumanism. In: Foreign Policy 124, 42-44.
Fukuyama, F. (2006): The End of History and the Last Man: With a New Afterword. New York et al.: Free Press.
Gordijn, B. (2004): Medizinische Utopien: Eine ethische Betrachtung. Göttingen: Vandenhoeck & Ruprecht.
Groys, B./ Hagemeister, M. (eds.) (2005): Die neue Menschheit: Biopolitische Utopien in Russland zu Beginn des 20. Jahrhunderts. Frankfurt am Main: Suhrkamp.
Haraway, D. (1991): A Cyborg Manifesto. In: Haraway, D. (ed.): Simians, Cyborgs, and Women: The Reinvention of Nature. New York: Routledge, 149-181.
Hauskeller, M. (2012): My Brain, My Mind, and I. Some Philosophical Assumptions of Mind-Uploading. In: International Journal of Machine Consciousness 4(1), 187-200.
Hayles, N.K. (1999): How We Became Posthuman: Virtual Bodies in Cybernetics, Literature, and Informatics. Chicago: University of Chicago Press.

Hilt, A./ Jordan, I./ Frewer, A. (eds.) (2010): Endlichkeit, Medizin und Unsterblichkeit: Geschichte – Theorie – Ethik. Stuttgart: Steiner.

Höhn, H.-J. (ed.) (2004): Welt ohne Tod: Hoffnung oder Schreckensvision? Göttingen: Wallstein.

Humanity+ (2012): Transhumanist FAQ. http://humanityplus.org/philosophy/transhumanist-faq/ (accessed December 15, 2012).

Huxley, J. (1957): Transhumanism. In: Huxley, J.: New Bottles for New Wine. London: Chatto & Windus, 13-17.

Kaminski, A. (2010): Technik als Erwartung: Grundzüge einer allgemeinen Technikphilosophie. Bielefeld: transcript.

Knell, S./ Weber, M. (eds.) (2009): Länger leben? Philosophische und biowissenschaftliche Perspektiven. Frankfurt am Main: Suhrkamp.

Krüger, O. (2004): Virtualität und Unsterblichkeit: Die Visionen des Posthumanismus. Freiburg im Breisgau: Rombach.

Kuhn, T.S. (1976): Die Struktur wissenschaftlicher Revolutionen. Frankfurt am Main: Suhrkamp.

Kurzweil, R. (1999): The Age of Spiritual Machines: When Computers Exceed Human Intelligence. Viking: New York.

Kurzweil, R./ Grossman, T. (2004): Fantastic Voyage: Live Long Enough to Live Forever. Emmaus(PA): Rodale Press.

Latour, B. (1993): We Have Never Been Modern. Cambridge(MA): Harvard University Press.

McNamee, M./ Edwards, S. (2006): Transhumanism, Medical Technology and Slippery Slopes. In: Journal of Medical Ethics 32(9), 513-518.

Miah, A. (2009) A Critical History of Posthumanism. In: Gordijn B./ Chadwick, R.F. (eds.): Medical Enhancement and Posthumanity. Heidelberg: Springer, 71-94.

Miller, P./ Wilsdon, J. (2006): The Man Who Wants to Live Forever. In: Miller P./ Wilsdon, J. (eds.): Better Humans? The Politics of Human Enhancement and Life Extension. London: Demos, 51-58.

Nassehi, A. (1994): No Time for Utopia: The Absence of Utopian Contents in Modern Concepts of Time. In: Time & Society 3(1), 47-78.

Pearson, D./ Shaw, S. (1982): Life extension: A Practical Scientific Approach. New York: Warner Books.

Rip, A./ van Amerom, M. (2010): Emerging de facto Agendas Around Nanotechnology. Two Cases full of Contingencies, Lock-outs, and Lock-ins. In: Kaiser, M. et al. (eds.): Governing Future Technologies: Nanotechnology and the Rise of an Assessment Regime. Dordrecht et al.: Springer, 131-155.

Roden, D. (2010): Deconstruction and Excision in Philosophical Posthumanism. In: Journal of Evolution and Technology 21(1), 27-36.

Rosa, H. (2003): Social Acceleration: Ethical and Political Consequences of a Desynchronized High-Speed Society. In: Constellations 10(1), 3-33.

SENS Foundation (2012a): Research Themes. http://www.sens.org/sens-research/research-themes (accessed December 15, 2012).

SENS Foundation (2012b): Research Advisory Board. http://www.sens.org/sens-research/advisory-board (accessed December 15, 2012).

SENS Foundation (2012c): What is SENS? http://sens.org/sens-research/what-is-sens (accessed December 15, 2012).

Stoff, H. (2004): Ewige Jugend: Konzepte der Verjüngung vom späten 19. Jahrhundert bis ins Dritte Reich. Köln et al.: Böhlau.

Thiele-Dohrmann, K. (2000): Ruhm und Unsterblichkeit. Weimar: H. Böhlaus Nachfolger.

Williams, B. (1973): The Makropulos Case: Reflections on the Tedium of Immortality. In: Williams, B.: Problems of the Self: Philosophical Papers 1956-1972. Cambridge et al.: Cambridge University Press, 82-100.

Politics

James Hughes

The "liberalism" of the United States and the "liberalism" of Europe are both descendents of eighteenth century Enlightenment thought. Both kinds of liberalism share some ideas in common, while being diametrically opposed on others. Similarly, "transhumanism" and "posthumanism" are used for different purposes in different communities, with some overlaps, but often with divergent values. Transhumanism expressses the ancient human aspiration to be wiser, longer lived, and to transcend the limitations of the human body, joined with the Enlightenment's faith in science, reason and individual freedom (see Hughes 2004; Bostrom 2005). Transhumanism is "the Enlightenment on steroids" (see Hughes 2009). Posthumanism is a loosely connected set of topics for academic study, and a conflicting set of intellectual positions that are sometimes critical of Enlightenment values. Both share a concern with how to create a liberatory future as technology transforms the body, and their radically different discourses and analytical frameworks complement one another in ways that deserve a deeper dialogue.

Becoming Posthuman

The term transhumanism has several antecedents. One is Julian Huxley coinage in his 1957 *New Bottles for New Wine* where he wrote:

> "The human species can, if it wishes, transcend itself [...]. We need a name for this new belief. Perhaps *transhumanism* will serve: man remaining man, but transcending himself, by realizing new possibilities of and for his human nature" (Huxley 1957, 17).

Huxley's conception of transhumanism focused on education, however, and did not yet embrace the more radical prospects of human genetic enhancement being promoted by his proto-transhumanist friend J. B. S. Haldane (1924), or the bio-utopianism being condemned by his brother Aldous Huxley (1932) in *Brave New World.*

It would not be until the 1970s that futurists would begin to seriously use the term "transhuman" to refer to the technological transcendence of the human condition. In the 1972 *Man into Superman* the cryonics pioneer Robert Ettinger proposed radical modifications of human physiology and a transition to "transhumanity." In the 1970s the futurist FM-2030 (nee F. M. Esfandiary) began using "transhuman" to refer to people whose worldviews and use of technology made them transitional to post-humanity. In his 1989 book *Are You Transhuman?* FM-2030 says transhumans…

> "[…] are the earliest manifestations of new evolutionary beings. They are like those earliest hominids who many millions of years ago came down from the trees and began to look around […]. Many of them are not even aware of their bridging role in evolution" (FM-2030 1989).

Like the cultural posthumanists, this use of the term transhuman is more descriptive: the transhuman period of history is the transition from upright ape to posthuman, a transition that began with the use of fire, clothing and language.

Transhumanism as an ideological term however can be dated to Max More's 1990 essay *Transhumanism: Toward a Futurist Philosophy*. More and his Extropian movement grew out of a fertile mix of techno-futurist utopianism and libertarian politics in Southern California which exploded onto the internet with email and the Web. The Extropians defined transhumanism as…

> "[…] a class of philosophies that seek to guide us towards a posthuman condition. Transhumanism shares many elements of humanism, including a respect for reason and science, a commitment to progress, and a valuing of human (or transhuman) existence in this life rather than in some supernatural 'afterlife'. Transhumanism differs from humanism in recognizing and anticipating the radical alterations in the nature and possibilities of our lives resulting from various sciences and technologies such as neuroscience and neuropharmacology, life extension, nanotechnology, artificial ultraintelligence, and space habitation, combined with a rational philosophy and value system" (More 1990).

In 1997 European transhumanists organized the World Transhumanist Association (now known as Humanity+), and, under the guidance of philosopher and co-founder Nick Bostrom, wrote the *Transhumanist Declaration* and the 30,000 word *Transhumanist Frequently Asked Questions* document (see Bostrom et al. 1998-2003). These remain canonical definitions of the transhumanist worldview today, although the movement has since developed many subsects and flavors (see Bostrom 2005).

Although transhumanists are insistent that there is no clear demarcation between the human and the posthuman, they often employ the term "posthuman" to describe their intended goal. The 1998 version of Max More's *Extropian Principles* says "We advocate using science to accelerate our move from human to a transhuman or posthuman condition." The *Transhumanist Declaration* (1998 version) says: "Transhumanism advocates the well- being of all sentience (whether in artificial intellects, humans, posthumans, or non-human animals)." But transhumanists rejected adopting "posthumanism" as the label for their movement on the grounds that this would imply a mysanthropic rejection of the human instead of a desire to provide each human the opportunity to choose their own forms of enhancement. It would also imply a false clarity about the boundaries between the human, transhuman and posthuman, boundaries that transhumanists are more interested in blurring than reifying.

By contrast the ideas that developed into academic posthumanism in the 1990s have their roots in the postmodernist and critical theory of the 1980s. One landmark posthumanist essay was Donna Haraway's 1985 *A Manifesto for Cyborgs: Science, Technology and Socialist Feminism in the 1980s.* At the time socialist-feminists were crossing swords with liberal feminists on one hand, and gender-essentialist radical feminists on the other. For Haraway the cyborg was a revolutionary icon because it represented the utopian imagination about radically transformed society that the liberal feminists abjured, while transgressing the false essentialist dualisms of the radical feminists. Embracing the revolutionary cyborg meant transgressing the boundaries of humanity, of nature and machine, of male and female, and accepting the fluidity of a cybernetic information society and the self-determined identity construction it requires. Haraway concludes "I would rather be a cyborg than goddess." Although its opaque, academic postmodernist style has meant that few transhumanists have read Haraway's essay it certainly pointed in a transhumanist direction.

For cyborgologists like Chris Gray, posthumanism emerges out of an investigation of the effects of technology on the body because this illumination reveals the limits of the humanist worldview in understanding our present cultural moment, and in shaping a liberatory future. For Gray posthumanism…

> "[…] might recoup the best parts of humanism by showing that posthumanism is both a social construction of what it means to be human in the present as well as the technological construction of a new type of techno-bio-body in the near future through cyborgization" (Gray 2002, 15).

The subsequent evolution of academic "cyborgology" (see Gray 1995) into posthumanism, and Haraway's own development of her argument, led to most cyborg writers adopting a much more critical stance toward the technologically-impacted body. While transhumanists distinguish between the descriptive "transhuman era" and ideological advocacy of "transhumanism," some cyborgologists and posthumanists use the "posthuman" to denote a cultural condition or set of anthropological interests instead of an ideology promoting the option of humans becoming posthuman. For Best and Kellner…

> "[…] the 'posthuman' means not the literal end of humanity, nor the dramatic mutations in the human body brought on by various technologies. Rather it signifies the end of certain misguided ways of conceiving human identity and the nature of human relations to the social and natural environments, other species, and technology" (Best/ Kellner 2001, 271).

These writers are interested in rejecting the alleged faults of humanism, not in heralding the advent of humans so technologically enhanced that they are post-human. For instance for Halberstam and Livingstone (1995), in their *Posthuman Bodies*, the body becomes posthuman because it is shaped by "power and pleasure, virtuality and reality, sex and its consequences" (Halberstam/ Livingstone 1995, 3), which presumably marks the invention of body art, perfume and cosmetics as the moment we became posthuman.

The most influential articulator of this approach to cultural posthumanism has been Katherine Hayles and her 1999 book *How We Became Posthuman*. Hayles sees the posthuman condition as one in which the mind and body are translated into information. The most radical version of this project is the effort to record and upload minds into machines, as proposed by transhumanists, a project that she is skeptical of. But for Hayles equating the mind with information is a much broader cultural phenomenon with largely welcome political effects.

Transhumanism and Humanism's Critics

Both transhumanism and posthumanism argue for a move beyond humanist anthropocentric ethics, but often towards opposite ends. Transhumanists see the idea of "humanness" as chimerical, shorthand for a supernatural "soul," and that this empty idea cannot be the basis for moral status. Moral status should instead be based on sentience and self-aware personhood, characteristics which may also be found in non-human animals, machines and post-humans (see Hughes 2004). Transhumanists follow Renaissance humanism and the Enlightenment in focusing on the central importance of mental traits that were formerly, but wrongly, presumed to be distinctively human. For posthumanists like Hayles (1999) this transhumanist championing of personhood is simply the most extreme version of the central assumption of the cybernetic, posthuman era: that mind is an information pattern that is only accidentally embodied in human flesh, and which can be found in other media or transferred to machines.

Other posthumanists have, however, seen posthumanism as precisely an argument against the Enlightenment's valorization of human reason and agency, which they see as the root of our alienation from animals and nature. For Neil Badmington (2000; 2003) posthumanism is the practice of criticizing "humanist discourses" (Badmington 2003, 22). Pepperell (2005, 171) argues that posthumanism is the "end of [...] that long-held belief in the infallibility of human power and the arrogant belief in our superiority and uniqueness." In her work on human-animal relationships Haraway (1989; 1997; 2003) criticizes the way that humanism and science construct the human-animal relationship, ignoring or projecting characteristics onto animals in fulfilment of our narrative of supremacy (see Weisberg 2009).

Posthumanists are also suspicious of animal rights and other rights projects because they identify the project of universal rights as a pernicious effort by the Enlightenment to suppress diversity and difference, a form of neo-colonialism. For these writers…

> "[…] the ethical community is a community of people that adopts and amends laws that ensure the voices of the marginalized others will be heard, not to protect an exclusionary vision of human nature" (Benko 2005, 16).

Of course it is puzzling to assert that one is rejecting the Enlightenment by embracing "multiplicity and difference" (see Best/ Kellner 2001, 197) when it was precisely the Enlightenment thinkers who championed the value of tolerance, the marketplace of ideas, and the freedom for all to investigate and pursue their own life ways. When they argue against the Enlightenment in this way posthumanists are actually another group of Enlightenment partisans, part of the long internal churn of the contradictions of the Enlightenment tradition, where Enlightenment scepticism or respect for difference undermines other Enlightenment values and concepts such as ethical universalism, the self or progress.

Cary Wolfe is clearer than most that posthumanism is the Enlightenment eating its own tail. Wolfe argues that his posthumanism is a *humanist* critique of the humanist "autonomous liberal subject." Wolfe rejects the transhumanist attempt to transcend anthropocentrism by identifying the "autonomous liberal subject" outside of humanity; according to Wolfe the transhumanist idea of personhood is still profoundly anthropocentric. In his 2003 *Animal Rites* Wolfe embraces Peter Singer's project of a non-anthropocentric ethics, while rejecting the human/animal distinctions and human-derived moral codes that he thinks still are implicit in the "species discourse" of the animal rights project. In his 2010 *What is Posthumanism?* Wolfe argues that animal rights and disability rights "reproduce the very kind of normative subjectivity – a specific concept of the human – that grounds discrimination against nonhuman animals and the disabled in the first place" (Wolfe 2010, xvii). For Wolfe, "posthumanism is the opposite of transhumanism, […] posthumanism in my sense […] opposes the fantasies of disembodiment and autonomy, inherited from humanism itself" (Wolfe 2010, xv).

The posthumanists are absolutely correct in pointing to the inescapably human origins of ideas of moral status and citizenship that transhumanists hope to use to create a transhuman future in which all individuals, whether uplifted ape, sentient robot or posthuman cyborg, have equal rights. Few transhumanists have considered the complexities of a transhuman society. Will the uplifted ape have to give up poo-slinging, or would that be bio-cultural imperialism? Will the Borg get one vote or ten thousand? Will uploaded and multiply copied cyber-people all own a piece of their brain parent's property? Transhumanists are still constrained by Enlightenment's continuous, discrete, autonomous self, a self that never existed and whose illusion will be swept away by future neurotechnologies. But then posthumanists are no less constrained by Enlightenment concepts and values, they are just more focused on the contradictions.

Robert Pepperell (2000; 2003) has done the best job of making the deconstruction of the illusion of an individual self the center of his posthumanism. For Pepperell, drawing on both Buddhist psychology and Clark and Chalmers' (1998) paper on the extended mind, the posthumanist condition is defined by the growing realization that human minds are continuous with both nature and machines, that mind does not happen in the brain but in a larger system that includes nature, other people and now machines (see Pepperell 2005a). Now that so many people in the developed world have constant access to electronic calendars and rolodexes, and every question can be put to the global brain through Google, we feel lobotomized when we lose access to our "exocortex." For Pepperell the embrace of the posthuman condition can be liberating and enriching.

> "The disavowal of the unique and distinct human proposed here need not lead to the abstracted, dislocated existence touted by some posthumanists, but to a human implicated in a wider corporeal-technological realm. It will be a being that, if it ceases to be human at all, will not be abandoned as a redundant shell, but implicated so widely in its extended eco-technological environment that it can no longer be demarcated. After all, the machines are really human, and through our mechanically embodied existence we may yet find salvation from the limits of bounded experience and the means to a fully extended life" (Pepperell 2005a, 37).

Unfortunately most posthumanists, including Pepperell who went so far as to author a *Posthumanist Manifesto* (2005b), offer no coherent proposal for the values, laws and social practices that *should* govern such a future. If we need to transcend the humanist focus on subjectivity does that mean that slapping a mosquito or a rock should be punished the same as killing a human? Should contracts be enforced or criminals punished if there are no continuous subjects? Is taking away someone's internet access as much a violation of their rights as tying them to a chair? Posthumanists ask deeper questions, but it is only practical biopolitical activists like the transhumanists who are committed to answering them.

One notable exception has been Chris Hables Gray's 2002 *Cyborg Citizen*. In this work Gray attempted to flesh out what the political implications of a cyborg or posthuman society will be, and he proposed ten constitutional amendments as a "Cyborg Bill of Rights" which included:

> "Freedom of Consciousness. […] Individuals shall retain all rights to modify their consciousness through psychopharmological, medical, genetic, spiritual and other practices in so far as they do not threaten the fundamental rights of other individuals and citizens and if they do so at their own risk and expense. […]
>
> Right to Life. […] Individuals shall retain all rights to modify their bodies, at their own risk and expense, through psychopharmological, medical, genetic, spiritual and other practices in so far as they do not threaten the fundamental rights of other individuals and citizens. […]
>
> Freedom of Family, Sexuality and Gender. Citizens and individuals have the right to determine their own sexual and gender orientations, at their own risk and expense, including matrimonial and other forms of alliance. Congress shall make no law arbitrarily restricting the definition of the family, of marriage, or of parenthood based on religious or other subjective criteria" (Gray 2002, 27-29).

In other words, the posthuman cyborg rights agenda for Gray is the same reaffirmation and radicalization of liberal individualism's body autonomy, cognitive liberty and reproductive rights that is championed by transhumanists, while it is simultaneously championed, deconstructed and condemned by the posthumanist writers.

Transhumanism's programmatic clarity and posthumanism's normative diffidence makes the comparison one of apples to oranges. Transhumanism is one end of an ideological axis, with bioconservatives at the other end. But posthumanism is not a coherent position in normative politics; posthumanists are not even clear amongst themselves what they are "post" of, much less what they are for.

Transhumanist Politics

While transhumanists have more normative consensus than the posthumanists, they are not in agreement about very much beyond their core commitments to non-anthropocentric personhood, techno-optimism and individual liberty. Transhumanists generally agree that the development of life extension and cognitive enhancement therapies should be pursued and that individuals should be able to choose to use them. They agree that individuals should be able to use reproductive technologies to have children, and to choose those children's characteristics. But they radically disagree about whether these enabling technologies should be developed with state funding, or whether they should be subject to safety regulations, or made universally available through public health systems. In other words, transhumanists have inherited all the arguments about the value and meaning of liberty, equality and solidarity that divided their Enlightenment forebears.

On the one hand, the Lockean tradition has framed individual liberty as one in which free individuals are entitled to self ownership, the fruits of their labor, and to enter into contracts free from coercion. The extropian anarcho-capitalists, inspired by contemporary anarchist theorists such as David Friedman (1973) and Robert Nozick (1973), have argued that democracy and the state are intrinsically conservative towards the kinds of radical experimentation, personal and social, that they want to pursue. In the last twenty years the extropian flavor of transhumanism has found ready allies in libertarian political circles, such as at *Reason* magazine. *Reason's* science writer Ronald Bailey (2005) has been one of the key articulators of the libertarian transhumanist policy agenda, opposing any and all regulatory restrictions on enhancement technologies. This libertarian strain has also been disproportionately influential because of its appeal to affluent Silicon Valley millionaires and billionaires, most prominently Peter Thiel. Thiel co-founded Paypal, and runs a hedge fund called Clarium Capital. He is a financial backer for a number of conservative and libertarian causes and groups, such as the conservative thinktank the Hoover Institution and the libertarian Republican candidate Ron Paul, and has written for the need to be free of democracy (see Thiel 2009). He also is the major philanthropic backer of a number of transhumanist-dominated groups, including the Singularity Institute for Artificial Intelligence, the anti-aging Methusaleh Foundation and the Seasteading Institute.

The Seasteading Institute is headed by the transhumanist Patri Friedman, the grandson of the libertarian Milton Friedman and son of anarcho-capitalist David Friedman. The Seasteaders are generally inspired by the idea of a colonies of high-tech anarcho-capitalists freed from the constraints of democratic statism, like the CEOs who form the utopian colony at the conclusion of Ayn Rand's 1957 novel *Atlas Shrugged*. In his 2009 essay *The Education of a Libertarian* Thiel explains that multi-million dollar underwriting of seasteading and other technological ventures is driven by his pessimism about the control of statism.

> "Because there are no truly free places left in our world, I suspect that the mode for escape must involve some sort of new and hitherto untried process that leads us to some undiscovered country; and for this reason I have focused my efforts on new technologies that may create a new space for freedom" (Thiel 2009).

The majority of transhumanists worldwide, however, do not appear to be economic conservatives. In a series of surveys of the global membership of the World Transhumanist Association conducted in 2003, 2005 and 2007 transhumanists on the left significantly out-numbered transhumanists on the right (Hughes 2003; 2005; 2008).

Which of these best describes your political views?

	2003	2005	2007
Left	36%	39%	47%
Technoprogressive	--	--	16%
Libertarian socialist	7%	7%	7%
Progressive	6%	7%	4%
Democratic socialist	4%	6%	5%
Social democrat	5%	5%	4%
Green	4%	4%	4%
US-style liberal	4%	4%	3%
Left anarchist	2%	3%	2%
Radical	2%	1%	<0.5%
Communist	1%	1%	1%
Libertarian	22%	22%	20%
Libertarian	11%	10%	10%
European Liberal	6%	7%	5%
Anarcho-capitalist	4%	2%	2%
Randian/Objectivist	1%	2%	1%
Minarchist	1%	1%	1%
Other	17%	16%	14%
Upwinger/advocate of future political system	8%	10%	7%
Other	9%	7%	7%
Not political	15%	12%	11%
Moderate	7%	8%	7%
Conservative	4%	3%	2%
Christian Democrat	1%	<0.5%	<0.5%
Conservative	2%	2%	1%
Far right	1%	<0.5%	<0.5%

As the table above suggests, the term "technoprogressive," associated with the Institute for Ethics and Emerging Technologies (IEET), has acquired some currency since the mid-2000s as a label for left-leaning transhumanists. Technoprogressives can be seen as the heirs of Enlightenment thinkers such as Condorcet and Diderot, and of political movements such as Fabian and Marxian socialism, in combining techno-optimism with radical egalitarianism.

However the coiner of the term "technoprogressivism," the postmodernist writer Dale Carrico (2006), also illustrates some of the tensions between the posthumanist intellectual milieu and transhumanism. When he first began promoting the term Carrico saw technoprogressivism as the application of progressive politics to questions of technoscience. Although a founding scholar at transhumanist-dominated IEET, he attempted to play the role of critical supporter. The principals of the IEET were at the time engaged in factional disputes with libertarians over the direction of the World Transhumanist Association. By 2008, however, Carrico had decided that the effort by left transhumanists to concretize technoprogressivism as a political program was antithetical to his intentions. Like his fellow posthumanists he believed the drafting of any political program to be intrinsically authoritarian.

> "[...] technoprogressivisms will never properly crystallize into a tribal designation, an identity movement, a political party machine, a subcultural movement, an army marching in lockstep toward 'the future,' or any such thing. The future is not a place or a 'goal': futurity is the political condition of plurality, democracy, freedom and it is open, unpredictable, collective, promising, unforgivable or it is nothing at all, whatever it calls itself. Democratic and progressive movements are inherently anti-monolithicizing, inherently pluralizing" (Carrico 2007b).

In 2008 Carrico broke with the IEET and launched a trenchant critique of any transhumanist agenda, left or right, as intrinsically reactionary, an attempt to use fantasies of "superlative technologies" to distract from actual political struggles. Carrico summarized his arguments about the reactionary role of transhumanism and "superlative futurology" as:

> "One: To be hyperbolically unrealistic and sensationalist in ways that derange urgently necessary public deliberation about technoscience issues,
>
> Two: To exacerbate irrational fears and fantasies about agency typically activated in any case by discussions of technology, especially dreams of omnipotence and nightmares of impotence,
>
> Three: To lend themselves to parochial moralizing social forms and identity-based political models that tend to be psychologically harmful and dangerously anti-democratizing,
>
> Four: To facilitate elitist, alarmist, escapist, reductionist attitudes and rhetoric especially well suited to incumbent interests and anti-democratic politics, whatever the professed politics of those who advocate them, and
>
> Five: To represent in their Superlative extremity a clarifying and symptomatic expression of the basic irrationality and authoritarianism of prevailing discourses of 'Global Development' and 'Technoscientific Progress' in an era of neoliberal and neoconservative politics" (Carrico 2007a).

In other words, transhumanism distracts from real politics, suggesting that technoutopia can be achieved without political struggle, and scaring people about imaginary threats like nanogoo and super robots when they should be worried about automation making everyone unemployed.

By 2009 the old extropians and their new libertarian friends in Silicon Valley, centered in Thiel-backed organizations, mobilized to replace the left-leaning leaders of the World Transhumanist Association with more sympathetic people like Max More, Patri Friedman and the libertarian writer Sonia Arrison. Peter Thiel began to raise monies for the new Humanity+, along with other transhumanist charities, and the Humanity+ leaders became deeply involved in Ray Kurzweil's six week seminars for techno-utopian entrepeneurs, the Singularity University, a project backed by dozens of corporate sponsors. As the world economy lurched from crisis to crisis, and unemployment, austerity and counter-hegemonic protests like Occupy Wall Street spread around the world, the transhumanist leadership were increasingly focused on how to ensure that future god-like AI rulers would bestow manna instead of destruction. While the global transhumanist base presumably has moved even farther to the Left, the hegemonic control of transhumanist discourse by wealthy Californian libertarians has fulfilled Carrico's worst fears. As I outlined in my 2004 agenda for a left transhumanism, *Citizen Cyborg,* the only way to break the hegemonic control of the bioutopian imagination by the privileged is to build alliances with other progressive movements, such as struggles for health care access, internet freedom, drug decriminalization, and reproductive, disability, and great ape rights. One of those arenas for progressive political alliance building, the struggle for freedom from the gender binary, is also a ripe opportunity for deepening the dialogue between transhumanists and posthumanists.

Post-Genderism: An Opportunity for Posthumanist/Transhumanist Dialogue

Transgender people and sexual minorities have been disproportionately attracted to transhumanism because of its advocacy of the right to control and modify one's own body. But transhumanists, dominated by 18-40 year old men with engineering and natural science backgrounds, have given surprisingly little attention to the effects of human enhancement technologies on pleasure, sexuality and gender. Some notable exceptions are the transhumanist theorists Martine Rothblatt, George Dvorsky and myself, James Hughes, inventor and transhumanist author Ray Kurzweil, and the transhumanist artist Natasha Vita-More.

Martine Rothblatt was born Martin, and transitioned in 1993 after pioneering treaties governing communication satellites and helping to start Sirius Satellite Radio. Trained as an attorney, she wrote *The Apartheid of Sex* in 1995, which argued that all laws that encoded gender difference should be re-written. After starting a biotechnology company, and earning a PhD in medical ethics from the University of London in 2001, Dr. Rothblatt became a central transhumanist philanthropist and thinker. Her Terasem foundation provides grants to numerous transhumanist causes, and sponsors its own transhumanist research programs, journals, conferences and film-making. Dr. Rothblatt has made the connection between her gender radicalism and her transhumanism more explicit in her 2011 *From Transgender to Transhuman: A Manifesto on the Freedom of Form*.

The transhumanist inventor Ray Kurzweil has asserted that one of his life goals is the instantiation of his inner female chanteuse persona, Ramona. He has performed through a virtual reality Ramona avatar at conferences, and the plot of Kurzweil's 2010 film *The Singularity is Near* focuses on Ramona's struggle for recognition as a legal person. A long married father of two, Kurzweil says that his interest in cross-gender experience is about expanding the boundaries of human experience.

> "Women are more interesting than men [...] and if it's more interesting to be with a woman, it is probably more interesting to be a woman [...]. I don't necessarily only want to be Ramona. It's not necessarily about gender confusion, it's just about freedom to express yourself" (Kurzweil as cited in Wolf 2008).

Natasha Vita-More, wife of the founder of extropianism Max More and the current Chair of Humanity+, has written several pieces on posthuman sex/gender, arguing that the...

> "[...] new sexual landscapes will bring about different types of sexuality, different types of genders. In the future, we may still want to perform the traditional types of sex – meaning rubbing mucus membranes against one another – or we may want to participate in the reconstituted and reconfigured gender roles and sexuality that will radically change us. We may do away with our bodily nerves, but keep some sensations, the ones for pleasure of perhaps some for pain to remind us not to do something. Yet, eventually we will begin to shuttle more and more parts of ourselves as we become post-biological [...]. The possibility is that we might have as many genders as colors in the rainbow or as many types of genitalia as patterns of flowers" (Vita-More 1997).

In 2008 transhumanist George Dvorsky and I wrote our mini-manifesto *Postgenderism: Beyond the Gender Binary* which argued that the biology of gender was a constraint on full human flourishing.

> "Postgenderists [...] foresee the elimination of involuntary biological and psychological gendering in the human species through the application of neurotechnology, biotechnology and reproductive technologies [...]. Assisted reproduction will make it possible for individuals of any sex to reproduce in any combinations they choose, with or without 'mothers' and 'fathers,' and artificial wombs will make biological wombs unnecessary for reproduction. Greater biological fluidity and psychological androgyny will allow future persons to explore both masculine and feminine aspects of personality. Postgenderists do not call for the end of all gender traits, or universal androgyny, but rather that those traits become a matter of choice. Bodies and personalities in our postgender future will no longer be constrained and circumscribed by gendered traits, but enriched by their use in the palette of diverse self-expression" (Dvorsky/ Hughes 2008, 1).

But these thinkers are the exceptions. Given the importance of the topic far too few transhumanists have speculated on how everything from sexual desire, to sexual preference, to the gender binary will or should dissolve as we gain control over our brains and bodies. The central role that homosexuality, pornography and gender play in contemporary politics make clear that the transition to a post-gender society will be one of the most profound and contentious aspects of the transhuman project.

Posthumanists, on the other hand, have been very engaged in the (de-) construction of the sex/gender system. From Donna Haraway's embrace of the gender-transgressive cyborg, to Anne Balsamo's (1995) *Technologies of the Gendered Body*, to investigations of the gendering of posthumans in collections like Giffney and Hird's 2008 *Gendering the Non/Human,* posthumanists have pointed out how our imagination about the future is still shaped by our now irrelevant mammalian biology and the cultural edifice we have built on it.

The posthumanists have attempted to break down sex/gender at the level of ideology, or at best at how some uses of technology blur gender, but have not advanced the kind of materialist postgender program advanced by Kurzweil, Rothblatt, Vita-More, Dvorsky and myself, that there should be a conscious use of technologies to free us from the gendered body and brain. A dialogue between posthumanists and transhumanists over how far the "free" use of technology can go in liberating us from the constraints of gender illustrates how the two communities can complement one another.

Conclusion

In the end, transhumanism and posthumanism are distinguished by the work they are trying to do. Transhumanists want to create a future in which every individual can use science and technology to free themselves from the constraints of nature and fulfill their own concepts of the good life. Posthumanists are attempting to show how our concepts of the body, nature, happiness, freedom and fulfilment are socially constructed, so that we are pushed to a deeper questioning about the future that we create. The transhumanist project grounds the posthumanists in applied biopolitics defending our bodies, brains and reproduction from counter-Enlightenment. Posthumanists are the sceptical intellectuals teasing apart the ways that the revolutionary project needs to question its own categories and agendas so that the revolution will be truly liberatory. By engaging with one another the two communities have much to gain.

Bibliography

Badmington, N. (ed.) (2000): Posthumanism: London: Palgrave.

Badmington, N. (2003): Theorizing Posthumanism. In: Cultural Critique 53, 11-27.

Bailey, R. (2005): Liberation Biology: The Scientific and Moral Case for the Biotech Revolution. Lexington(KY): Prometheus Books.

Balsamo, A. (1995): Technologies of the Gendered Body. Durham(NC): Duke University Press.

Benko, S. (2005): Ethics, Technology, and Posthuman Communities. In: The Philosophy of Technology 6(1), 1-22.

Best, D./ Kellner, S. (2001): The Postmodern Adventure: Science, Technology and Cultural Studies at the Third Millenium. New York: Guilford Press.

Bostrom, N. et al. (1998): The Transhumanist Declaration. In: Humanity+. http://humanityplus.org/learn/transhumanist-declaration/ (accessed July 14, 2013).

Bostrom, N. et al. (1998-2003): The Transhumanist Frequently Asked Questions. In: Humanity+. http://humanityplus.org/learn/transhumanist-faq/ (accessed July 14, 2013).

Bostrom N. (2005): A History of Transhumanist Thought. In: Journal of Evolution and Technology 14(1), 1-25.

Carrico, D. (2006): Technoprogressivism: Beyond Technophilia and Technophobia. http://ieet.org/index.php/IEET/more/carrico20060812/ (accessed July 14, 2013).

Carrico, D. (2007a): The Superlative Summary. In: Amor Mundi. http://amormundi.blogspot.com/2007/10/superlative-summary.html (accessed July 14, 2013).

Carrico, D. (2007b) Amor Mundi and Technoprogressive Advocacy. In: Amor Mundi. http://amormundi.blogspot.com/2007/11/amor-mundi-and-technoprogressive.html (accessed July 14, 2013).

Carrico, D. (2009): Condensed Critique of Transhumanism. In: Amor Mundi. http://amormundi.blogspot.com/2009/01/condensed-critique-of-transhumanism.html (accessed July 14, 2013).

Clark, A./ Chalmers, D. (1998): The Extended Mind. In: Analysis 58(1), 7-19.

Dvorsky, G./ Hughes, J. (2008): Postgenderism: Beyond the Gender Binary (IEET White Paper, 3). Hartford(CT): Institute for Ethics and Emerging Technologies. http://ieet.org/archive/IEET-03-PostGender.pdf (accessed July 14, 2013).

Ettinger, R.C.W. (1972): Man into Superman: The Startling Potential of Human Evolution – And how to be Part of It. New York: St. Martin's Press.

FM-2030 (1989): Are you a Transhuman? Monitoring and Stimulating your Personal Rate of Growth in a Rapidly Changing World. New York: Warner Books.

Friedman, D. (1973): Machinery of Freedom: Guide to a Radical Capitalism. New York: Harper.

Giffney, N./ Hird, M.J. (2008): Queering the Non/Human. Burlington(VT): Ashgate Publishing Company.

Gray, C.H. (2002): Cyborg Citizen: Politics in the Posthuman Age. London: Routledge.

Gray, C.H./ Mentor, S./ Figueroa-Sarriera, H.J. (1995): Cyborgology: Constructing the Knowledge of Cybernetic Organisms. In: Gray, C.H. (ed.): The Cyborg Handbook. New York: Routledge.

Halberstam, J./ Livingston, I. (1995): Posthuman Bodies. Bloomington: Indiana University Press.

Haldane, J.B.S. (1924): Daedalus; or, Science and the Future. London: Kegan Paul & Co.

Haraway, D. (1985): A Manifesto for Cyborgs: Science, Technology and Socialist Feminism in the 1980s. In: Socialist Review 80, 65-107.

Haraway, D. (1989): Primate Visions: Gender, Race, and Nature in the World of Modern Science. New York: Routledge.

Haraway, D. (1997): Modest_Witness @ Second_Millennium. FemaleMan©_ Meets_ OncoMouse™: Feminism and Technoscience. New York: Routledge.

Haraway, D. (2003): The Companion Species Manifesto: Dogs, People, and Significant Otherness. Chicago: Prickly Paradigm Press.

Hayles, N.K. (1999): How We Became Posthuman: Virtual Bodies in Cybernetics, Literature, and Informatics. Chicago: University of Chicago Press.

Hughes, J. (2003): Report on the 2003 Interests and Beliefs Survey of the Members of the World Transhumanist Association. In: World Transhumanist Association. http://ieet.org/archive/WTASurvey03Report.pdf (accessed September 15, 2013).

Hughes, J. (2004): Citizen Cyborg: Why Democratic Societies Must Respond to the Redesigned Human of the Future. Boulder: Westview Press.

Hughes, J. (2005): Report on the 2005 Interests and Beliefs Survey of the Members of the World Transhumanist Association. In: World Transhumanist Association. http://www.transhumanism.org/resources/survey2005.pdf (accessed July 14, 2013).

Hughes, J. (2008): Report on the 2007 Interests and Beliefs Survey of the Members of the World Transhumanist Association. In: World Transhumanist Association. http://www.transhumanism.org/resources/WTASurvey2007.pdf (accessed July 14, 2013).

Hughes, J. (2009): Transhumanist Politics, 1700 to the Near Future. In: *Re-Public.* http://ieet.org/index.php/IEET/more/hughes20090409/ (accessed July 14, 2013).

Huxley, A. (1932): Brave New World. London: Chatto & Windus.

Huxley, J. (1927): Religion without Revelation. London: E. Benn.

Huxley, J. (1957): New Bottles for New Wine. Chatto & Windus: London.

Miah, A. (2008): A Critical History of Posthumanism. In: Gordijn B./ Chadwick, R.F. (eds.): Medical Enhancement and Posthumanity. Dordrecht: Springer, 71-94.

More, M. (1990): Transhumanism: Toward a Futurist Philosophy. In: Extropy 6, 6-11.

Nozick, R. (1973): Anarchy, State and Utopia. New York: Basic Books.

Pepperell, R. (2000): The Posthuman Conception of Consciousness: A 10-point Guide. http://robertpepperell.com/papers/The%20Posthuman%20Conception.pdf (accessed July 14, 2013).

Pepperell, R. (2003): The Posthuman Condition: Consciousness Beyond the Brain. Bristol: Intellect.

Pepperell, R. (2005a): Posthumans and Extended Experience. In: Journal of Evolution and Technology 14(1), 27-41. http://jetpress.org/volume14/pepperell.html (accessed July 14, 2013).

Pepperell, R. (2005b): The Posthuman Manifesto. In: Kritikos 2. http://intertheory.org/pepperell.htm (accessed July 14, 2013).

Rand, A. (1957): Atlas Shrugged. New York: Random House.

Rothblatt, M. (1995): The Apartheid of Sex: A Manifesto on the Freedom of Gender. New York: Crown Publishers.

Rothblatt, M. (2011): From Transgender to Transhuman: A Manifesto on the Freedom of Form.

Thiel, P. (2009): The Education of a Libertarian. In: Cato Unbound. http://www.cato-unbound.org/2009/04/13/peter-thiel/the-education-of-a-libertarian/ (accessed July 14, 2013).

Vita-More, N. (1997): Future of Sexuality (EXTRO 3 Conference). http://www.natasha.cc/sex.htm (accessed July 14, 2013).

Weisberg, Z. (2009): The Broken Promises of Monsters: Haraway, Animals and the Humanist Legacy. In: Journal for Critical Animal Studies 7(2), 21-61.

Wolf, G. (2008): Futurist Ray Kurzweil Pulls Out All the Stops (and Pills) to Live to Witness the Singularity. In: Wired 16(4). http://www.wired.com/medtech/drugs/magazine/16-04/ff_kurzweil?currentPage=all (accessed July 14, 2013).

Wolfe, C. (2003): Animal Rites: American Culture, the Discourse of Species, and Posthumanist Theory. Chicago: University of Chicago Press.

Wolfe, C. (2010): What is Posthumanism? Minneapolis: University of Minnesota Press.

Morality

Robert Ranisch

There is no comprehensive transhumanist morality or moral theory.[1] It is still possible to identify common moral claims concerning right or wrong action, what is of value and what constitutes a good or virtuous character. Without a doubt, transhumanism as a techno-optimistic political and cultural movement is distinguished by a specific set of normative assumptions, and transhumanist organizations dedicate themselves to moral questions.[2] Nevertheless, transhumanism comes in many forms, representing a wide spectrum of moral and political orientations.

The question concerning morality of posthumanism[3] is even more intricate. Because posthumanism is often associated with postmodernism, which is known for "the celebration of the 'demise of the ethical'" and the "substitution of aesthetics for ethics" (Bauman 1993, 2), some posthumanists eventually reject "morality", which they identify with a universalist, categorical and norm-based system that has its origin in (allegedly) false beliefs about humans' rationality, subjectivity, and autonomous agency. Nevertheless, posthumanism, just like every form of moral criticism, is not free from moral judgments. Often these do not however form a coherent code of conduct but present themselves as critique of a specific morality.

This chapter critically examines essential moral topics in transhumanism. The first sections will discuss the relation between transhumanism and the so-called bioliberal positions, as well as provide a review of bioconservative's criticism of transhumanism. By identifying ten major claims of transhumanist morality, a particular tension between individual freedom and perfectionism will be pointed out. In the next chapter a brief overview on posthumanist's engagement

---

1 "Morality" and "ethics" is sometimes used interchangeable. While there is no common definition in academic literature, some authors distinguish ethics from morality. Often it is said that morality is the subject of ethics, i.e. of moral philosophy. Sometimes "morality" is used to describe questions of what we owe to other people while "ethics" refers to questions of a good life. These terminological questions are beyond the scope of this article. Throughout this article I shall refer to "morality" rather than to "ethics" to discuss evaluative questions in a broad sense, i.e. questions of right actions and a good life.

2 On their webpage Humanity+ states its mission as "the ethical use of technology to expand human capacities", which, in fact, repeats the slogan of its precursor, the World Transhumanist Association (WTA). One of the most famous transhumanist platforms, the Institute for Ethics and Emerging Technologies (IEET), carries the label "ethics" in its name as well.

3 For the conceptual differences between "transhumanism" and "posthumanism", see the introduction to this volume.

with transhumanism follows. After a short review of current debates on moral enhancement, i.e., the augmentation of moral capacities by means of technology, the questions of moral status enhancement will be discussed. Addressing these questions is crucial for investigating into transhumanist morality, because it makes explicit what transhumanists believe to matter morally. Discussing transhumanist's struggle with moral status enhancement will finally lead to some concluding remarks concerning posthumanists' contribution to the controversies about transhumanism.

Transhumanism and the Bioliberals

Not all authors that share transhumanist ideas regard themselves as transhumanists. In bioethics, for instance, we find numerous theorists supporting human enhancement just like the transhumanists. Authors such as John Harris, Julian Savulescu, Nicholas Agar or Allen Buchanan, just to name a few, can loosely be described as *bioliberals*.[4] The distinguishing mark of bioliberalism is its claim for liberty and (state) neutrality concerning the use of enhancement technologies. As long as no third party is harmed, people should be free to use these technologies as means to realize their own ideal of the good life. Moreover, just like transhumanists, many bioliberal thinkers believe that we do something good by augmenting the human cognitive, physical, or mental capacities. Discussing the question of transhumanist morality, we shall include these bioliberal positions.

There are, however, two differences between transhumanism and bioliberalism that are worth considering in particular because the differences rise from their distinct moral assumptions. One concerns their attitude towards (state) neutrality, and the other, the desirability of posthumanity.

First, while transhumanists often defend some ideal of human perfection, bioliberals are more neutral concerning this question. Transhumanists advocate the desirability to enhance human beings by means of technology and typically defend a certain objective standard on how to enhance human beings. Not only should individuals be allowed to use enhancement technology, but also, "it could be good for most human beings to become posthuman" (Bostrom 2008, 135). Compared to this, bioliberals primarily defend human liberty, something

4 The liberal aspect of bio-liberalisms may be seen in its commitment to a specific form of (state) neutrality. Following Dworkin, liberalism supposes that "government must be neutral on what might be called the question of the good life [...]" and "political decisions must be, so far as is possible, independent of any particular concept of the good life" (Dworkin 2002 [1978], 67).

manifested in their claim to neutrality concerning different forms of life. People should "lead the life that they believe is best for themselves" (Savulescu 2007, 526), and the question, whether or how to use enhancement technologies, should be based on their free choice and their individual concept of the good life. As Agar puts it, bioliberals…

> "[…] do not present themselves as marketing any particular view of human excellence. Rather they defend institutions that allow individuals to make their own choices about how to live" (Agar 2007, 14).

Bioliberals' commitment to state neutrality, however, is compatible with the suggestion that, from a moral point of view, it would be better to enhance human capacities.

Second, most transhumanists explicitly affirm the possibility to overcome human biological nature in a radical way. To realize transhumanist visions "ideally, everybody should have the opportunity to become posthuman" (Bostrom 2005b, 10). By the same token, technology is not yet developed, and admittedly, "there is no manner by which any human can become a posthuman" (Humanity+ n.d.) at the moment. As a consequence, everything transhumanists can hope for is that people are willing to submit themselves to the transhumanist "social experiment" (see Walker 2011), which makes them part of an evolutionary chain that may eventually lead to posthumanity.

By contrast, achieving posthumanity is not the aim of bioliberals. While a few bioliberals embrace such possibility (see Savulescu 2009), this should rather be seen as a side effect of human enhancement. Even though "there is nothing wrong" that we may end up in posthumanity, "becoming transhumans is not the agenda" (Harris 2007, 39). The bioliberal focus is not a broad-scale attempt to overcome the humankind in the long run. Rather, it concerns itself with individuals and their desire to benefit from enhancement technologies for themselves and their offspring.

This perspective also makes plausible why some bioliberals openly reject transhumanism. Nicholas Agar for instance, a champion of liberal eugenics (see Agar 2004), opposes the prospects of posthumanity. By defending a species-relativist view about values, he insists radical enhancement "alienates us from experiences that give meaning to our lives" (Agar 2010, 179). While moderate enhancement might be desirable and does not prevent human beings to relate to themselves, their offspring, and fellow citizens, posthumanity threatens our common values und will eventually cause the loss of our humanity.

Transhumanism versus Bioconservatism

While Agar rejects transhumanism, he still defends the enhancement project as such. He also makes clear that his critique must not be mistaken for a number of positions that tend to reject the enhancement project altogether. Such positions are often labeled as *bioconservative* and are frequently perceived as opposition to transhumanism. The clash of transhumanists and bioconservatives is not so much a dispute about the general possibilities of achieving posthumanity or about the technological aspects of such enterprise. At stake are evaluative and moral questions concerning the desirability of (radical) human enhancement.

Bioconservatives maintain, that in order to deal with posthumanity, we must not be politically neutral about such questions. When the prospects of radical human enhancement induce a moral vertigo, as Michael Sandel puts it, people in liberal societies…

> "[…] reach first for the language of autonomy, fairness, and individual rights. But this part of our moral vocabulary does not equip us to address the hardest questions posed by cloning, designer children, and genetic engineering" (Sandel 2007, 9).

There is a consensus among bioconservatives that bioliberals are incapable of addressing the problem of human enhancement in the right way. Autonomy is not the most important concern for the ethics of enhancement. In order to deal with emerging technologies, we rather need "to confront questions largely lost from view in the modern world". Questions about "the moral status of nature" (ibid.), the human good, and the merits of certain life forms and aspects, such as authenticity, need to be considered.

Several attempts have been made to reject the transhumanist project altogether. There are comprehensive criticisms from leading bioconservatives – above all Leon R. Kass – in the US President's Council on Bioethics report *Beyond Therapy* (see PCBE 2003). Most famously, Francis Fukuyama argues that transhumanism is the world's most dangerous idea (see Fukuyama 2004). George J. Annas' prediction that advances in genetic technologies will most likely cause a "genetic genocide," and his call for a "human species protection" expresses similar concerns (see Annas 2005). While these arguments are expressed in the language of equality, Annas, Fukuyama (2002), as well as Kass (2003) primarily fear that the use of enhancement technologies will eventually cause the loss of essential human qualities, and thus, threaten human rights or dignity.

Calling for the moralization of human nature and a post-metaphysical concept of the good life, Jürgen Habermas (2003) certainly shares some assumptions with the bioconservatives. His critique on enhancement technologies primarily targets liberal eugenics, and Habermas' main worry is that genetic interventions "undermine the essentially symmetric relations between free and equal human beings" (ibid., 23). Addressing the same issue of planned reproduction, Sandel (2007) is worried about the drive of mastery that he sees central for the human enhancement project. This, however, may distort the relation between parents and their (genetically engineered) offspring as well as solidarity in society.

Morality of Transhumanism

It has been argued by transhumanists that there is no coherent moral doctrine in their own camp. Furthermore, some authors maintain that there is a greater disagreement among transhumanists about moral assumptions than about metaphysical or epistemological matters (see More 2013, 6). Nevertheless, concerning moral theory and moral claims, there is at least some convergence among transhumanists.

Most transhumanists broadly defend a consequentialist theory of morality. According to this, the rightness of actions depends on the goodness of consequences. Thus, most transhumanists are indifferent concerning the means of enhancement as long as the outcome is good. Hence, there is no decisive moral difference between therapy and enhancement, or between improving people with biotechnologies or by means of education (see Agar 1998; Sorgner 2013a). Furthermore, transhumanist's consequentialism scrutinizes the distinction between actions and omissions. If safe enhancement technologies were available, failing to improve future generations' "capacities is to wrong them, just as it would be to harm them" (Savulescu 2007, 529; see Harris 2007).

There is also a moral conviction that is shared by literally all transhumanists: transcending human's biological limitations is desirable. This normative thesis rests on an empirical assumption about the possibility to radically enhance human beings. Apart from this general aspect that distinguishes transhumanist morality, the subsequent section identifies ten further moral claims that most transhumanists embrace. While these topics are not presented in a hierarchical order, they show a continuum from liberal to perfectionist ideas in transhumanism. Furthermore, this continuum displays a peculiar tension in transhumanist morality, which will be discussed briefly in the following chapter.

(Morphological) Freedom

For transhumanists (and bioliberals), individual freedom is considered as being one of the most important, if not the most important, value. Freedom or liberty is frequently sketched negatively, that is, as the absence of constraint or compulsion. This involves a strong case against paternalism when it comes to questions of choosing a certain plan of life. Individuals should be free to decide for themselves how to live and institutions should be designed in a way to guarantee neutrality between different forms of life. Sometimes individual freedom is perceived in a more demanding sense, embracing conditions that enable individuals to realize their ideal of a good life.

Closely related to transhumanists' defense of individual freedom is their call for *morphological freedom*. It has been argued that liberal rights, such as freedom of speech, should be extended by "the right to modify oneself according to one's desire" (Sandberg 2013, 56). Thus, people should be free to use enhancement technologies to alter their biological traits and eventually transform themselves into transhumans.

The strong emphasis on (morphological) freedom, which is frequently brought forward to argue for the permissibility of enhancement technologies, has neglected implications. For instance, if people have the right to modify themselves by means of biotechnologies, they also have the right to refrain from the transhumanist project. Hence, "it is crucial that no single solution be imposed on everyone", but rather that "individuals get to consult their own consciences as to what is right for themselves" (Bostrom 2005a, 206). Consequently, morphological freedom should embrace protection of those who do not wish to use enhancement technologies, too. This may also include measures to compensate for possible competitive disadvantages people may have compared to their biotechnologically augmented fellow citizens.

Harm-Principle

While morphological freedom must not be limited in cases where well-informed people use enhancement technological, which may even cause side-effects, transhumanists believe that freedom must be limited only if harm is caused to third parties. This idea echoes a line of argument from the liberal tradition and is often associated with J. S. Mill's *harm principle*. According to this, the…

> "[…] only purpose for which power can be rightfully exercised over any member of a civilized community, against his will, is to prevent harm to others. His own good, either physical or moral, is not sufficient warrant" (Mill 1977 [1859], 223).

Morphological freedom and the harm principle generate a strong case in favor of human enhancement. It is often argued that an informed decision to use technology to transform one's own biology must not be limited if no third party is harmed.

There are many diverging views about the nature of harm that must have been caused in order to legitimize constraints on individual freedom. While some transhumanists believe that only a direct impact on other people's freedom or well-being justifies constraints, it is sometimes assumed that resulting inequalities, unfairness, or structural effects might be sufficient to impose constraints on freedom. As a consequence of this, some transhumanists reject enhancement technologies if the mere purpose is to improve position relative to others. They defend enhancements as *absolute goods* rather than *positional goods*, because "they are good for people, not because they confer advantages on some but not on others" (Harris 2007, 29).

Reproductive Freedom

While transhumanists believe that people should decide whether and how to use enhancement technologies, they also argue that (future) parents should be free to enhance their offspring. This idea is frequently expressed in language of *reproductive freedom* or *procreative liberty*: "a right [of people] to control their own role in procreation unless the state has compelling reasons for denying them that control" (Dworkin 1993, 148). Not only should reproducers be free to decide whether, how often, with whom and when to procreate, but they should also be free to choose what kind of children to have (see Buchanan et al. 2001, 204-213; Agar 2004). This encompasses the right to use means of reproductive technologies to determine children's genetic traits.

Like morphological freedom, reproductive freedom has certain limits. It ought to be constrained in cases where reproductive decisions clearly cause harm to offspring. More controversially, it is often argued that parents should only be allowed to use genetic interventions to promote *general-purpose means*. These are means that promote human capacities "useful and valuable in carrying out nearly any plan of life or set of aims that humans typically have" (Buchanan et al. 2000, 167). These capacities would not restrict or even determine children's ways of life and thus it would guarantee their *right to an open future*.

Promoting Well-being and Reducing Suffering

Apart from their focus on morphological freedom and avoidance of harm, transhumanists often make a much stronger, positive moral claim: we should promote people's well-being. While there are diverging views of what constitutes well-being or a good life, there is a consensus that normative reasons speak in favor of a clever use of technologies for this purpose. While transhumanists sometimes promise good life in a distant posthuman future, bioliberals are more concerned with short-time effects of enhancement technologies. Yet, the idea of promoting happiness for all people is central for both and shows their humanist roots.

Sometimes, it is not only stated that we should promote well-being, but we should also reduce suffering. Such an idea, which is also known from the (negative-) utilitarian tradition, has been brought forward by WTA co-founder David Pearce in *The Hedonistic Imperative.* This transhumanist manifesto defends an admittedly "ambitious, implausible, but technically feasible" plan "to eradicate the biological substrates of suffering" and guarantee a "sublime and all-pervasive happiness" (Pearce n.d.).

Rejecting Anthropocentrism

In their aspiration to reduce suffering and promote well-being, transhumanists do not only focus on human beings, but also defend an inclusive pathocentric or welfarist account of morality. In contrast to humanist's anthropocentric scope transhumanists …

> "[…] advocate the well-being of all sentience, including humans, non-human animals, and any future artificial intellects, modified life forms, or other intelligences to which technological and scientific advance may give rise." (Humanity+ 2013, 54)

Human beings are not the only beings that matter. Nonhuman beings may also belong to our moral community: they can be carriers of rights and even hold personhood status.

Transhumanists' attitude towards anthropocentrism, however, is ambiguous. On the one hand, they are willing to grant full moral status or personhood to some sentient beings other than humans (e.g. Hughes 2004). Transhumanists consider the possibility of artificial intelligence and interspecies hybrids as indication that no clear line can be drawn between human beings, nonhuman beings, and possible artificial life forms that could justify discrimination in moral status. Furthermore, the transhumanist ambition to create superior life forms, which are "unambiguously human by our current standards" (Humanity+ n.d.), suggests, that it might not even be human beings who ultimately matter. If posthuman life forms are greatly superior, we might even "have reason to save or create such vastly superior lives, rather than continue the human line" (Savulescu 2009, 244).

On the other hand, it seems equally true that transhumanists still privilege humanity above animality (see Fuller 2013, 41). Even though there might be no reason to preserve the human condition in its current form, most transhumanists are eager that posthumanity emerges out of humanity. In the end it remains an open question why it should be *our* descendants who continue the human line. Regardless of transhumanist's skeptical attitude towards anthropocentrism, to a great extent the posthuman realm is imagined as an extension of the human realm of values (see, e.g., Bostrom 2005b).

Rejecting the Wisdom of Nature

While some transhumanists see a certain wisdom in nature, which makes it possible to "identify promising human enhancements and to evaluate the risk-benefit ratio" (Bostrom/ Sandberg 2009, 408), the idea that human biological nature is of inherent value is widely rejected (see, e.g., Buchanan 2011, 115-141). As a matter of fact, transhumanists repeatedly try to debunk faith in the value of human nature as prejudice (see Savulescu 2009) or irrational bias (see Bostrom/ Ord 2006). They argue that our nature is nothing more than "a half-baked beginning that we can learn to remold in desirable ways" (Bostrom 2005b, 4). Even more, not only is human nature open to modification, but there is also the imperative to improve human nature. The reason for this is that human biological nature – shaped by blind evolutionary forces – is not equipped to serve (post)human needs and achieve (post)human goods.

Transhumanists not only maintain that there is no intrinsic value in human nature in its current form, but they also argue against bioconservative's belief in the very existence of some essential human characteristic. Nevertheless, it has rightly been pointed out that transhumanists implicitly advocate normative concepts of human nature, too (see Hauskeller 2009). By maintaining that perpetual self-overcoming is an essential human characteristic, not only do they suggest a controversial idea of human nature, but they also believe to find the ground for their techno-progressive aspirations in some common human core features.

Progressivism

Transhumanists share the belief in the ongoing and accelerating progress of science and technology. Such progressivism shows transhumanist's Enlightenment roots (see Hughes 2010) and can be found in most varieties of transhumanism. Bostrom (2005b) sees progress as the basic condition for the entire transhumanist project and ideas such as the singularity hypothesis fundamentally rest on a peculiar model of exponential technological progress (see Kurzweil 2005). Most clearly, progressivism can be found in Max More's *Principles of Extropy* (2003) where "perpetual progress" is the number one principle. His early sketch of the transhumanist philosophy calls for "progress without end" where life and "intelligence must never stagnate" (More 1996).

While there is much to argue about such a concept and the rhetoric of progress from a theoretical point of view (see, e.g., Verdoux 2009), progressivism also has a moral dimension. For instance, belief in exponential growth eventually implies a "claim about the history of technology" and may show up as a "blunt tool in the effort to render an otherwise remote and speculative future as something that demands our immediate attention" (Nordmann 2007, 36). Often mere possible futures and speculations about emerging technologies determine transhumanist agenda. These speculations are frequently employed to support normative claims for today's policies, e.g., when questions about the distribution of scarce resources arise. In addition, progressivism may lead to a future-oriented paternalism, as present generations pretend to know what is good for future generations (ibid., 40).

Obligation to Support Science

The hope for ongoing progress does not come from nothing. For this reason, it is essential for transhumanists to support science and technology. In order to radically change the human condition, appropriate technologies need to be developed. This is not only necessary to increase the benefits for future (post)humanity but also to reduce existential risks that threaten life (see Humanity+ 2013). Without a doubt, technological progress is a basic condition for transhumanism and it is required to take a "proactive approach to technology policy" (Bostrom 2005b, 4) rather than a precautionary approach. This amounts to the protection of rights for free research as well as investment in research.

The call for supporting science sometimes comes in more radical forms. John Harris, for instances, argues that it is not only the moral imperative to fund and undertake scientific research, but there is also a "clear moral obligation to participate" in some form of medical research to benefit humankind. This obligation, he argues, is "not confined to purely therapeutic research" but also involves "research into human enhancement" (Harris 2007, 192).

Perfectionism

So far it has been suggested that transhumanists approach the question of human enhancement from a subjectivist perspective. Their claim for neutrality concerning the good life as well as their defense of morphological freedom eventually suggests that people should be free to use or refrain from enhancement technologies. This analysis of the transhumanist morality, however, is not sufficient. As a matter of fact, transhumanists often value certain forms of life over others and even have a positive account of human perfection.

First of all, it becomes clear that transhumanists "favor future people being posthuman rather than human". Compared to humanity, posthumanity is considered to be of superior value and transhumanists maintain that people have reasons to explore this "hitherto inaccessible realms of value" (Bostrom 2005b, 9). Despite of their liberal commitment and subjectivist rhetoric concerning questions of values, some transhumanists advocate objective accounts of human perfection. They believe in the intrinsic superiority of certain values and privilege specific (intellectual, creative etc.) human capacities over others (see Hauskeller 2009). It has been pointed out that bioliberals implicitly endorse perfectionist ideals of an autonomous individual (see Roduit et al. 2013). As for Savulescu (2001), he even advocates specific (genetic) traits to be desirable for future persons. Some transhumanist visions of human enhancements resemble a Renaissance-ideal, aiming at a well-rounded person, having intellectual, artistic, and physical traits (see, e.g., Bostrom 2008). Sorgner, then again, brings forward a pluralistic account of human perfection (see Sorgner 2013b).

Obligation to Enhance

From the ideal of human perfection, it becomes clear that transhumanists do not only consider human enhancement as being permissible but believe that "enhancements [are] obviously good for us" (Harris 2007, 35). Some bioliberals argue that we "clearly have moral reasons, perhaps amounting to an obligation" (ibid.) to engage in the enhancement project, and transhumanists maintain that "becoming posthuman is imperative" (Walker 2011, 95).

The obligation to enhance does not only concern existing, autonomous individuals. It is sometimes argued that there is also an obligation to enhance offspring. Most famously, Julian Savulescu defends a principle called *procreative beneficence.* According to this principle, future parents have a moral obligation to genetically select the best offspring. Savulescu and others maintain that…

> "couples (or single reproducers) should select the child, of the possible children they could have, who is expected to have the best life, or at least as good a life as the others, based on the relevant, available information" (Savulescu 2001, 415).

Procreative beneficence has invoked heavy criticism, and several commentators pointed out that it bears similarities to "old" eugenics (see, e.g., Bennett 2009). Nevertheless, it should be recognized that the proposed obligation to enhance is *not* a legal obligation. While Savulescu argues that moral reasons may justify an obligation to enhance our children, on the legal level, he maintains morphological and reproductive freedom. While it might be wrong not to enhance from a moral perspective, this statement is compatible with the "enjoyment of a right to autonomy" on a legal level. This encompasses the right to "make procreative choices which foreseeably and avoidably result in less than the best child" (Savulescu/ Kahane 2009, 268). From the fact that something is morally wrong or suboptimal, it does not follow that it should be legally prohibited or punished.

Transhumanist Morality: Between Neutrality and Perfectionism

It becomes clear that the above-mentioned aspects of transhumanist morality bear some tensions. In particular, the tension between the emphasis of individual liberty and the aspiration to bring about posthumanity has concerned a number of authors. Even some transhumanists such as James Hughes warn that faith in posthumanity may, in the end, legitimize technocratic authoritarianism to realize transhumanist visions (see Hughes 2010). Other critics are harsher: it has been pointed out that the tension between transhumanist libertarianism and perfectionism may eventually have consequences similar to those of authoritarian eugenics (see Sparrow 2011).

No wonder, transhumanists are cautious to distance themselves from authoritarian policies such as eugenics, which they consider to be "entirely contrary to the tolerant humanistic and scientific tenets of transhumanism" (Humanity+ n.d.).[5] As a matter of fact, despite some transhumanists who flirt with the advantages of antidemocratic systems (see Persson/ Savulescu 2012, 86-90; Bostrom 2006), there is little evidence that mainstream transhumanism intends some form of technocratic authoritarianism. Still, transhumanists have to face a major difficulty: making plausible how, on a theoretical level, their commitment to liberty is compatible with the imperative to become posthuman. On a practical level, they need to ensure that their project will not bring in a coercive eugenics "through the back door".[6]

---

5 There are many reasons to doubt that transhumanism has nothing to do with eugenics. Prominent references and ancestor of transhumanism such as Julian Huxley (who coined the term "transhumanism") or J. S. B. Haldane (the WTA named an award after him) can be seen as a direct link from 20th century eugenics to contemporary transhumanism (see Bashford 2013). Of course, everything depends and what is meant by "eugenics". Transhumanists, however, are particularly anxious of getting associated with Nazi eugenics and have little interest in dealing with their own cultural history.

6 In this regard, the results of a recent survey by the Institute of Ethics & Emerging Technologies (IEET) are disturbing (see Hughes 2013). The IEET webpage asked their transhumanist community: "When there are safe cures for these conditions should parents be legally obliged to provide them for their children?" Respondents (>500) were alarmingly happy to introduce legal obligations for parents to fix their kids' near-sightedness (67%), propensity to obesity (66%) or attention deficit disorder (58%).

Posthumanism: A Critical Take on the Transhumanist Project

Post-World War II antihumanism and critical theory certainly had something to contribute to the ongoing debates on liberal eugenics (see Seubold 2001). After all, their critique is fostered by the experience of the horrors of the 20th century, which witnessed the failures of humanism, rationality, and morality. Habermas, who perceives transhumanists as a "handful of freaked-out intellectuals" defending an "all-too-familiar […] German ideology" (2003, 22), still echoes this tradition.

In recent years, an increasing amount of posthumanist literature has considered the relationship between humanity and technology. Authors such as Peter Sloterdijk spelled out the implications of transhumanist technologies for our perception of humanism. Sloterdijk is frequently misinterpreted as the champion of human enhancement, even though he has little in common with the mainstream transhumanists. He rather suggests a critique on humanism out of human engagement with technology. At the same time, he is very critical of transhumanist ideas that he would describe as "primitive biologisms with helpless humanisms and theologisms […] without a trace of insight into evolutionary conditions of anthropogenesis" (Sloterdijk 2001, 221). Yet, Sloterdijk is far away from rejecting technology as such. If there is a humankind, he maintains, this is because technology made the human evolve from the pre-human.

> "Hence, nothing unfamiliar happens to humans when they expose themselves to further creation and manipulation. They do nothing perverse or against their 'nature' when they change themselves autotechnologically" (Sloterdijk 2001, 225).

In his notorious response to Heidegger's *Letter on 'Humanism'* entitled *Rules for the Human Park* (2009 [1999]), Sloterdijk proposes an unconventional reinterpretation of the history of humanism in the advent of the transhuman age. This attempt is motivated by advances in biotechnologies and the necessity for regulations that will…

> "[…] retroactively alter the meaning of the old humanism, for it will be made explicit, and codified, that humanity is not just the friendship of man with man, but that man has become the higher power for man" (Sloterdijk 2009, 24).

Sloterdijk's analysis stems from a particular interpretation of Western history. He sees humanism as a history of taming human beings by means of proper "reading" (*Lesen*). Even more, not only did humanism involve the taming of humans, but also the breeding of humans.[7] People "domesticated themselves and

---

7 Sloterdijk's interpretation of humanism gains some plausibility from the German etymology of his central concepts. In German language it is a short way from *lesen* ("to read") to *auslesen* ("to select"). Furthermore, *Erziehung* ("rearing" or "education"),

have committed themselves to a breeding program aimed at a pet-like accommodation." That is also the "great unthinkable" insight that Nietzsche's Zarathustra reveals, from which "humanism from antiquity to the present has averted its eyes". Human beings have been a product "of intimate constraints of breeding, taming, and raising," which for the most time has been an invisible project, a "breeding without breeder" (ibid., 22-23). Sloterdijk, however, diagnoses a shift in our biotechnological age. Facing new possibilities such as embryo selection, he insists:

> "It is characteristic of our technological and anthropotechnological age that people fall more and more into the active, or agent, side of selection, even without having sought out the role of selectors willingly [...]. As soon as an area of knowledge has developed, people begin to look bad if they still [...] allow higher power, whether it is the gods, chance, or other people, to act in their stead [...]" (Sloterdijk 2009, 23-24; translation modified[8]).

Sloterdijk concludes that it will become necessary to seize actively our role as selectors and prepare a "codex of anthropotechnology" (ibid., 24). Although Sloterdijk does not make any suggestions about this codex and *Rules for the Human Park* can hardly be read as a celebration of posthumanity, it has frequently been interpreted as a transhumanist manifesto. The most famous instance of this misinterpretation is Jürgen Habermas' (2003) criticism on liberal eugenics, which could be seen as an attack against Sloterdijk. This criticism does not do justice to the fact that Sloterdijk is much more concerned with developing a posthumanist (post)anthropology than defending some form of transhumanism (see Herbrechter 2013, 165-168).

Bruno Latour (2009) is certainly right in pointing out that Habermas fails to recognize the posthumanistic thesis in Sloterdijk. He is not only far from "post human dreams of cyborgs" but also from the "humanists' limited view of what humans are". Whereas Sloterdijk does raise the question how humans could be "designed", this bears only superficial similarities with the "old phantasm of eugenic manipulation." "Yes, humans have to be artificially made and remade," Latour agrees with Sloterdijk, "but everything depends on what you mean by artificial and even more deeply by what you mean by 'making'." Sloterdijk's "philosophy of design" (ibid., 8) offers an alternative account of humanization

---

which Sloterdijk sees as central for the taiming of humans, is etymologically linked to *Zucht* ("breed") and *züchten* ("to breed").

8 The English translation of this central passage is misleading. It states: "people *willingly* fall more and more into the active, or agent side of selection" (Sloterdijk 2009, 23; emphasis added). The German text rather stresses that this actually did not happen willingly: "ohne daß sie sich willentlich in die Rolle des Selektors gedrängt haben müßten" (Sloterdijk 2001, 328).

that scrutinizes that "deeply rooted categorical distinctions between the subjective and the objective, the grown and the made" (Habermas 2003, 71), which Habermas sees essential for our self-understanding as autonomous subjects.

Sloterdijk's rejection of techno-utopianism as well as his denial of a fixed human nature bears similarities to other posthumanistic analyses. In her seminal work on posthumanism, N. Katherine Hayles (1999) already identified major flaws in transhumanist fantasies of mind uploading. Recently, she directly engaged with transhumanism and expressed criticism on its individualistic and neoliberal assumptions (see Hayles 2011). Hayles shows little sympathy for the bioconservative's attempt to moralize human nature and, at the same time, finds transhumanism too ideologically fraught. While the transhumanist rhetoric is deeply individualistic, she sees a "conspicuous absence of considering socioeconomic dynamics beyond the individual" (ibid., 217). All forms of transhumanism "perform decontextualizing moves that over-simplify the situation and carry into the new millennium some of the most questionable aspects of capitalist ideology" (ibid., 215).

Contrasting transhumanism and posthumanism, we get the following impression: Both recognize human coevolution with technology and reject the belief in human nature as a moral constraint on human auto-evolution. The transhumanist call for technological enhancement aims at liberating human beings from human biological limitations. Compared to this, posthumanists want to liberate human beings from these dominant ideologies that foster transhumanist visions. Nevertheless, posthumanist's engagement with the moral challenges of posthumanity is ambiguously vague. They rarely offer any positive account of how to deal with emerging biotechnologies, but rather express doubt that all problems can be solved with technological enhancement. Sloterdijk as well as Hayles see the transhuman future coming, but they are silent about how the "(post)human park" should be governed and what moral codex is necessary to maintain it.

Moral Bio-Enhancement: Better Acting Trough Chemistry

Sloterdijk upholds that humanism has always been a commitment to save human beings from barbarism (see Sloterdijk 2009, 15). While it is certainly true that humanism embraces some form of moral education, Sloterdijk's provocation lies in his claim that this enterprise did not only involve cultivating forces but also taming and breeding forces. Even though his playful interpretation of humanism as a breeding program is controversial, in some way, it anticipated current trends in transhumanism. As a matter of fact, the issue of moral perfection recently entered technophile discourses and possibilities of moral enhancement caused a vigorous debate (see, e.g., Douglas 2008; Persson/ Savulescu 2012). Some bioliberals even argue that we should rather aim at getting morally better than anything else, because our (potentially dangerous) research needs to be accompanied by the moral enhancement of humanity (see Persson/ Savulescu 2008).

While transhumanists show their humanist roots in addressing such questions of moral perfection, their approach radically differs from traditional moral education. Moral goodness is not only associated with proper cultivation, a right way of practical reasoning of a fully developed, virtuous person, but also with right human biology. Immoral behavior is deemed to be a question of anatomy (e.g. damage to the prefrontal cortex), hormones (e.g. lack of Oxytocin), and genetics (e.g. abnormality in MAOA). Naturalization of morality is no new phenomena and has a tradition in philosophy (e.g. Nietzsche) as well as in science (e.g. Delgado). However, genetics, neuroscience of ethics, and social psychology brought new momentum to debates on moral enhancement. If science can explain where and how moral decisions are made, so the theory goes, we might be able to directly influence human behavior for the better. Pharmaceutics, neural implants, or even "breeding forces" such as genetic selection (see Faust 2008), should complete traditional moral education by means of *moral bioenhancement*. At the core of this debate, we find the belief that…

> "[…] the current predicament of humankind is so serious that it is imperative that scientific research explore every possibility of developing effective means of moral bioenhancement" (Persson/ Savulescu 2012, 2).

This is necessary because human's biological and psychological nature is ill equipped to deal with the most serious and pressing problems of the 21st century. Our common-sense morality may have worked for a long period of our evolutionary history. But today we have to tackle global problems such as the climate change and the weapons of mass destruction, which make possible for a small number of criminals to cause great harm to the whole of humanity. Our moral shortcomings prevent us from addressing these challenges adequately. Moral bioenhancement might be the key for the survival of (post)humanity (see Persson/ Savulescu 2012).

The theoretical assumptions and practical implications of moral bioenhancement have been strongly challenged, even from the bioliberal camp (see Harris 2011). The utopian character of this debate has been pointed out; after all, we are far away from having the "morality pill"[9] developed. Moral bioenhance-

9 Typically three substances are discussed in debates on psychopharmacological moral enhancement: SSRIs such as citalopram, the hormone oxytocin and beta blockers like

ment might not even be a challenge for scientific development but rather points to fundamental conceptual and philosophical questions: What, after all, could it mean to enhance "morality" biotechnologically? Even if it were possible to influence human behavior in a desirable way, it remains an open question what this has to do with moral agency. Apart from these philosophical questions, additional serious social and political worries still remain: How does one establish the practice of moral bioenhancement without introducing a coercive system? Who should decide what counts as moral enhancement? What would it do to the legal, political, and moral statuses of the ordinary people, if we lived in a society where some people are distinguished by their moral superiority?

Moral Status Enhancement and the Fear of Post-Persons

The last questions point towards a concern related to moral enhancement: the question of *moral status enhancement*. The very idea of transhumanism is to improve human's cognitive, physical, or moral capacities so radically that we regard these enhanced beings as other than human. It might be argued, then, that these trans- or posthuman beings "may even be able to attain higher levels of […] excellence than any of us humans" (Bostrom 2005a, 210). Would this superiority not only justify a higher degree of excellence but also a higher moral status than ours and thus guarantee more moral rights compared to the unenhanced persons? If human beings having equal moral status were the ground for personhood, would moral status enhancement bring about *post-persons*, i.e., beings with a moral status higher than personhood? Such conclusion resembles the bioconservative fears that, if superior beings emerge, we should worry that they are legitimate to wear boots and spurs while we have saddles on our back (see Fukuyama 2002, 10).

Most transhumanists reject this conclusion. Bostrom and some bioliberals such as Harris argue that no "enhancement however dramatic […] implies lesser (or greater) moral, political, or ethical status, worth, or value" (Harris 2007, 86). It is certainly possible and even likely that the future posthuman beings would have a higher degree of intellectual, artistic, or even moral excellence. And yet, this fact has little bearing on our common concept of moral status that is the basis for equal moral rights, dignity, or personhood. Buchanan (2011, 209-241) has brought forward an argument for the conceptual impossibility of post-persons. He finds it difficult to perceive how enhancement technologies could bring about beings with a moral status higher than that of a person. Moral status

---

propranolol. While recent studies show certain influence on human attitude, behavior and motivation, no serious findings supports the idea of a "morality pill".

as well as personhood, he argues, are threshold concepts, "not a matter of relative superiority" but "a matter of sufficiency" (ibid., 224). All beings above a certain limit – be it human, nonhuman, or posthuman – count as persons and thus they have equal moral status.

Buchanan's argument supports the widespread belief that all persons have equal moral status. Still, it can be doubted that the possible impact of radical enhancement on the question of moral status is unproblematic for transhumanists. In recent discussions, the conceptual possibility of post-personhood has been embraced by a number of authors. Agar (2012) provides an inductive argument for a moral status that is higher than personhood. The fact that we already distinguish moral statuses of inanimate objects, sentient beings and, persons, makes a superior status plausible. DeGrazia (2012) supports this view. He argues that Buchanan's model is perfectly compatible with acknowledging that there could also be a second (higher) threshold corresponding to a higher moral status than that of a person. Both, Agar and DeGrazia are aware of the consequences: if post-persons are brought into existence, their moral status justifies that "their needs should take precedence over our own" (Agar 2012, 5), and they may legitimately "regard us […] as resources for their use" (DeGrazia 2012, 138). These are not good prospects for transhumanists.

From this alarming outlook both authors draw different conclusions: Agar argues that we should refrain from creating such post-persons. For DeGrazia, the discussion of post-personhood rather indicates that there is something fundamentally wrong with our established moral categories. He eventually drops the very idea of levels of moral statuses and proposes an "interests model of moral status." According to this model, all sentient beings have a moral status. This implies that "no morally important difference between persons and animals – or between post-persons and persons – amounts to a difference in moral status." Even though "differences in interests, capacities and circumstances" (DeGrazia 2012, 139) could justify certain differences in treatment of these beings, this does not indicate a hierarchy in moral status.

Posthumanist Criticism on Human Exceptionalism

The discussion of moral status enhancement brings about an interesting dialectic: facing the possibility of human progress up to a point where the biotechnologically-enhanced, superior beings may come about raises new fears of how to protect human uniqueness and supremacy. This attempt eventually leads back to the question why human beings actually have been the privileged being in the first place. DeGrazia's discussion of this topic is indicative to this dialectic. The consideration of the question of post-personhood leads him to reject moral anthropocentrism. He ultimately defends an inclusive account of morality, which encompasses persons as well as sentient animals. Such a view bears close resemblance to posthumanism that points to the fundamental flaws in the moral framework of humanism. At this point, transhumanism meets posthumanism and gets in line with environmentalism, animal rights theory, and many others criticisms of human exceptionalism.

In moral philosophy, the critique of anthropocentrism is primarily associated with the contemporary utilitarian tradition rather than with the postmodern theory. The best know work is Peter Singer's *Animal Liberation* (1975) where he popularized the concept of *speciesism* that stands for "a prejudice or attitude of bias in favor of the interests of members of one's own species and against those of members of other species" (Singer 2002 [1975], 6). In his analysis of Singer's critique on anthropocentrism, Sorgner (2013b) recently brought forward a posthumanist approach concerning moral status, personhood, and dignity. Like posthumanists such as Hayles (1999), Sorgner challenges established boundaries between human and non-human beings as well as bodily existences and virtual simulations. Unlike Hayles, he defends a naturalistic version of posthumanism with a genuine moral concern. According to Sorgner, not only are there merely gradual differences between human beings and other living beings, but also merely gradual differences between them and cybernetic organisms. Without a dualistic metaphysics, a categorical special status of human beings cannot be maintained. He eventually suggests a plurality of moral statuses and different types of persons, ranging from self-conscious nonhuman animals to sentient unborn humans. By dissociating the concept of personhood from that of dignity, Sorgner, nevertheless, still attributes dignity to the born human beings exclusively.

Singer's critique on moral anthropocentrism has sometimes been associated with posthumanism (see Fuller 2013). Cary Wolfe, however, who sees "the problem of anthropocentrism and speciesism" (Wolfe 2010, xix) as the key focus of posthumanism, has doubts concerning Singer's attempt. Wolfe is not only critical of Singer's naturalism but also argues that his rejection of anthropocentrism "ends up reinforcing the very same humanism" that posthumanism wants to overcome. Singer, and the same criticism applies to DeGrazia, does recognize nonhuman animals *not* because they are different from human beings but only because they are an "inferior versions of ourselves". Hence, Singer reproduces the "ethical humanism that was the problem from the outset simply […] on another level" (Wolfe 2003, 192).

Recently, a considerable amount of posthumanist literature has scrutinized human exceptionalism by refusing the humanist dichotomies and boundaries between the human and the nonhuman. Apart from being critical with the humanistic narrative of "the human," the reasons for rejecting anthropocentrism differ and the umbrella-term "posthumanism" hardly does justice to capture this plurality. Also, some posthumanist critique on anthropocentrism is not motivated by genuine moral concerns alone but also calls the dominant Western ideologies into question. This, however, can have profound social and political implications (see, e.g., Braidotti 2013). The posthumanist's debunking of the established ontological and epistemological beliefs eventually has straightforward implications for concepts such as gender, species, (dis)ability, or nature, which are central for Western moral codes.[10]

Concluding Remarks

The aim of this paper was to introduce norms and values that underlie the transhumanist project. While it has been argued that there is no coherent transhumanist morality, it was possible to identify claims that are shared by some transhumanists and bioliberals. One of the most significant findings was a particular tension within transhumanism that is rooted in its emphasis on individual liberty and praise of perfectionism. The controversies about moral enhancement as well as moral status enhancement have been analyzed.

The article did not discuss posthumanist morality in greater length. This was partly due to the plurality of posthumanist philosophies, but also because of postmodernist's denial of the traditional concept of morality. It has been argued, however, that the posthumanist criticism has straightforward normative implications. Furthermore, it also showed how the posthumanist critique could contribute to current controversies about transhumanism.

First, regarding the general desirability of human enhancement. The analysis showed that some bioconservatives reject transhumanism especially because they fear a technological violation of human nature. While it became clear that some posthumanists share a skeptical attitude towards transhumanist's techno-optimism, their skepticism does not come from the desire to moralize human nature. Posthumanism rather aims at overcoming established distinctions such as natural/artificial, grown/made, or human/machine. Much clearer than anyone else, their analysis of human's engagement with technology as well as with animality helps to overcome the humanist categories and may eventually set the stage for a more nuanced debate about the morality of human enhancement technologies.

10 See, in particular, the contributions in this volume by James Hughes and Francesca Ferrando.

Second, it has been argued that the transhumanist rejection of anthropocentrism is ambiguous. While posthumanism radically questions the established narratives and rejects human exceptionalism, transhumanism still rests on a humanistic framework with its belief in rationality and progress. Even though transhumanists are willing to abandon exclusive morality and grant moral status to nonhuman and posthuman life forms, "the human" remains the measure for all things. Nonhuman life forms are recognized as moral patients if they resemble human characteristics. Animals matter insofar as they are inferior humans, and posthumans are imagined as augmented beings, equipped with specific characteristics that have always been essential for human pride. The transhumanist dedication to humanism is the reason why the possibility of post-personhood could leave them perplexed. Associating moral status to humanistic values confirms a hierarchy between the human and the posthuman, which brings difficulties for egalitarian aspiration. The posthumanist's radical non-anthropocentrism, which celebrates the difference rather than the normative force of the universal, may be seen as an attractive alternative to humanist's order of rank. While this option is not readily available for the transhumanists as long as they uphold the credibility of their own humanistic framework, a future dialog between both movements might be promising.[11]

Bibliography

Agar, N. (1998): Liberal Eugenics. In: Public Affairs Quarterly 12(2), 137-155.

Agar, N. (2004): Liberal Eugenics: In Defence of Human Enhancement. Malden(MA): Blackwell.

Agar, N. (2007): Whereto Transhumanism? The Literature Reaches a Critical Mass. In: Hastings Center Report 37(3), 12-17.

Agar, N. (2010): Humanity's End: Why We Should Reject Radical Enhancement. Cambridge(MA) et al.: MIT Press.

Agar, N. (2012): Why is it Possible to Enhance Moral Status and Why Doing so is Wrong? In: Journal of Medical Ethics (Online First).

Annas, G.J. (2005): American Bioethics: Crossing Human Rights and Health Law Boundaries. Oxford et al.: Oxford University Press.

Bashford, A. (2013): Julian Huxley's Transhumanism. In: Turda, M. (ed.): Crafting Humans: From Genesis to Eugenics and Beyond. Göttingen et al.: V&R Unipress & National Taiwan University Press, 153-67.

Bauman, Z. (1993): Postmodern Ethics. Malden(MA) et al.: Blackwell.

---

11 I owe a special thanks to Paul D. K. Kim for his support with the late draft of this article. Simon Ledder, Marcus Rockoff, and Lisa Schöttl provided helpful comments on earlier drafts of this article.

Bennett, R. (2009): The Fallacy of the Principle of Procreative Beneficence. In: Bioethics 23(5), 265-273.

Buchanan, A. et al. (2000): From Chance to Choice: Genetics & Justice. Cambridge et al.: Cambridge University Press.

Buchanan, A. (2011): Beyond Humanity? The Ethics of Biomedical Enhancement. Oxford et al.: Oxford University Press.

Bostrom, N. (2005a): In Defence of Posthuman Dignity. In: Bioethics 19(3), 202-214.

Bostrom, N. (2005b): Transhumanist Values. In: Journal of Philosophical Research 30 (Issue Supplement - Ethical Issues for the Twenty-First Century), 3-14.

Bostrom, N. (2006): What is a Singleton? In: Linguistic and Philosophical Investigations 5(2), 48-54.

Bostrom, N. (2008): Why I Want to be a Posthuman When I Grow Up. In: Gordijn B./ Chadwick, R.F. (eds.): Medical Enhancement and Posthumanity. Dordrecht: Springer, 107-136.

Bostrom, N./ Ord, R. (2006): The Reversal Test: Eliminating Status Quo Bias in Applied Ethics. In: Ethics 116(4), 656-79.

Bostrom, N./ Sandberg, A. (2009): The Wisdom of Nature: An Evolutionary Heuristic for Human Enhancement. In: Savulescu J./ Bostrom N. (eds.): Human Enhancement. Oxford: Oxford University Press, 375-416.

Braidotti, R. (2013): The Posthuman. Cambridge: Polity Press.

DeGrazia, D. (2012): Genetic Enhancement, Post-Persons and Moral Status: A Reply to Buchanan. In: Journal of Medical Ethics 38(3), 135-139.

Douglas, T. (2008): Moral Enhancement. In: Journal of Applied Philosophy 25(3), 228-245.

Dworkin, R. (1993): Life's Dominion: An Argument About Abortion, Euthanasia, and Individual Freedom. New York: Alfred A. Knopf.

Dworkin, R. (2002 [1978]): Liberalism. In: Smith, G.W. (ed.): Liberalism: Critical Concepts in Political Theory. London: Routledge, 57-80.

Faust, H.S. (2008): Should We Select for Genetic Moral Enhancement? A Thought Experiment Using the MoralKinder (MK+) Haplotype. In: Theoretical Medicine and Bioethics 29(6), 397-416.

Fukuyama, F. (2002): Our Posthuman Future: Consequences of the Biotechnology Revolution. New York: Farrar Straus & Giroux

Fukuyama, F. (2004): Transhumanism. In: Foreign Policy 144, 42-43.

Fuller, S. (2013): Preparing for Life in Humanity 2.0. Basingstoke: Palgrave Macmillan.

Habermas, J. (2003): The Future of Human Nature. Cambridge: Polity Press.

Harris, J. (2007): Enhancing Evolution: The Ethical Case for Making Better People. Princeton et al.: Princeton University Press.

Harris, J. (2011): Moral Enhancement and Freedom. In: Bioethics 25(2), 102-111.

Hauskeller, M. (2009): Prometheus Unbound: Transhumanist Arguments from (Human) Nature. In: Ethical Perspectives 16(1), 3-20.

Herbrechter, S. (2013): Posthumanism: A Critical Analysis. London et al.: Bloomsbury.

Hughes, J. (2004): Citizen Cyborg: Why Democratic Societies Must Respond to the Redesigned Human of the Future. Boulder: Westview Press.

Hughes, J. (2010): Contradictions from the Enlightenment Roots of Transhumanism. In: Journal of Medicine and Philosophy 35(6), 622-640.

Hughes, J. (2013): Parental Autonomy versus the Rights of Children to Enablement. In: IEET. http://ieet.org/index.php/IEET/more/hughes20130726 (accessed January 2, 2014).
Hayles, N.K. (1999): How We Became Posthuman: Virtual Bodies in Cybernetics, Literature, and Informatics. Chicago et al.: The University of Chicago Press.
Hayles, N.K. (2011): Wrestling with Transhumanism. In: Hansell, G.R./ Grassie, W. (eds.): H±: Transhumanism and Its Critics. Philadelphia: Metanexus Institute, 215-226.
Humanity+ (n.d.): Transhumanist FAQ: 3.0. http://humanityplus.org/philosophy/transhumanist-faq/ (accessed December 3, 2013).
Humanity+ (2013): Transhumanist Declaration (2012). In: More, M./ Vita-More, N.: The Transhumanist Reader: Classical and Contemporary Essays on the Science, Technology, and Philosophy of the Human Future. Chichester: Wiley-Blackwell, 54-55.
Kass, L.R. (2003): Life, Liberty, and the Defense of Dignity: The Challenge for Bioethics. San Francisco: Encounter Books.
Kurzweil, R. (2005): The Singularity is Near. New York: Viking Books
Latour, B. (2008): A Cautious Prometheus? A Few Steps Towards a Philosophy of Design (With Special Attention to Peter Sloterdijk). In: Glynne, J./ Hackne, F./ Minto, V. (eds): Networks of Design: Proceedings of the 2008 Annual International Conference of the Design History Society (UK). Boca Raton(FL): Universal Publishers, 2-11.
Mill, J.S. (1977 [1859]): On Liberty. In: Robson, J.M. (ed.): The Collected Works of John Stuart Mill (Vol. XVIII – Essays on Politics and Society). Toronto et al.: Toronto University Press, 213-310.
More, M. (1996): Transhumanism: Towards a Futurist Philosophy http://www.maxmore.com/transhum.htm (accessed May 4, 2013).
More, M. (2003): Principles of Extropy: Version 3.11. In: Extropy Institute. http://www.extropy.org/principles.htm (accessed October 15, 2013).
More, M. (2013): The Philosophy of Transhumanism. In: More, M./ Vita-More, N. (eds.): The Transhumanist Reader: Classical and Contemporary Essays on the Science, Technology, and Philosophy of the Human Future. Chichester: Wiley-Blackwell, 3-17.
Nordmann, A. (2007): If and Then: A Critique of Speculative NanoEthics. In: Nanoethics 1(1), 31-46.
PCBE (2003): Beyond Therapy: Biotechnology and the Pursuit of Happiness. A Report of The President's Council on Bioethics. http://bioethics.georgetown.edu/pcbe/reports/beyondtherapy/index.html (accessed December 4, 2013).
Pearce, D. (n.d.): The Hedonistic Imperative. http://www.hedweb.com/ (accessed December 3, 2013).
Persson, I./ Savulescu, J. (2008): The Perils of Cognitive Enhancement and the Urgent Imperative to Enhance the Moral Character of Humanity. In: Journal of Applied Philosophy 25(3), 162-177.
Persson, I./ Savulescu, J. (2012): Unfit for the Future: The Need for Moral Enhancement. Oxford: Oxford University Press.
Roduit, J.A.R./ Baumann, H./ Heilinger, J.-C. (2013): Human Enhancement and Perfection. In: Journal of Medical Ethics 39(10), 647-650.
Sandberg, A. (2013): Morphological Freedom: Why We Not Just Want It, but Need It. In: More, M./ Vita-More, N. (eds.): The Transhumanist Reader: Classical and Contemporary

Essays on the Science, Technology, and Philosophy of the Human Future. Chichester: Wiley-Blackwell, 56-64.

Sandel, M. (2007): The Case Against Perfection: Ethics in the Age of Genetic Engineering. Cambridge(MA) et al.: Belknap Press of Harvard University Press.

Savulescu, J. (2001): Procreative Beneficence: Why We Should Select the Best Children. In: Bioethics 15 (5-6), 413-26.

Savulescu, J. (2007): Genetic Interventions and the Ethics of Enhancement of Human Beings. In: Steinbock, B. (ed.): The Oxford Handbook of Bioethics. Oxford et al.: Oxford University Press, 516–35.

Savulescu, J. (2009): The Human Prejudice and the Moral Status of Enhanced Beings: What Do We Owe the Gods? In: Savulescu J./ Bostrom N. (eds.): Human Enhancement. Oxford: Oxford University Press, 211-47.

Savulescu, J./ Kahane, G. (2009): The Moral Obligation to Create Children with the Best Chance of the Best Life. In: Bioethics 23(5), 274-90.

Seubold, G. (2001): Die Freiheit vom Menschen: Die philosophische Humanismusdebatte der Nachkriegszeit. Alfter et al.: DenkMal Verlag.

Singer, P. (2002 [1975]): Animal Liberation. New York: HarperCollins Publishers.

Sloterdijk, P. (2001): Nicht gerettet: Versuche nach Heidegger. Frankfurt a. M.: Suhrkamp.

Sloterdijk, P. (2009 [1999]): Rules for the Human Zoo: A Response to the Letter on Humanism. In: Environment and Planning D: Society and Space 27, 12-28.

Sorgner, S.L. (2010): Beyond Humanism: Reflections on Trans- and Posthumanism. In: Journal of Evolution and Technology 21(2), 1-19.

Sorgner, S.L (2013a): Evolution, Education, and Genetic Enhancement. In: Sorgner, S.L./ Jovanovic, B.-R. (eds.): Evolution and the Future: Anthropology, Ethics, Religion. Frankfurt am Main et al.: Peter Lang, 85-100.

Sorgner, S.L. (2013b): Human Dignity 2.0: Beyond a Rigid Version of Anthropocentrism. In: Trans-Humanities 6(1), 135-159.

Sparrow, R. (2011): A Not-So-New Eugenics: Harris and Savulescu on Human Enhancement. In: Hastings Center Report 41(1), 32-42.

Verdoux, P. (2009): Transhumanism, Progress and the Future. In: Journal of Evolution & Technology 20(2), 49-69.

Walker, M. (2011): Ship of Fools: Why Transhumanism Is the Best Bet to Prevent the Extinction of Civilization. In: Hansell, G.R./ Grassie, W. (eds.): H±: Transhumanism and Its Critics. Philadelphia: Metanexus Institute, 94-111.

Wolfe, C. (2003): Animal Rites: American Culture, the Discourse of Species, and Posthumanist Theory. Chicago & London: Chicago University Press.

Wolfe, C. (2010): What is Posthumanism? Minneapolis et al.: University of Minnesota Press.

Ontology

Thomas D. Philbeck

Long after the pessimistic determinism of the mid-twentieth century, it appears that sophisticated electronic technologies have found their way into almost all the societies on earth, even where basic infrastructure, agriculture, and medicine are still lacking. Images of tribesmen from various continents employing mobile phones while otherwise equipped only with rudimentary tools are evidence of the extent of this technosocial diffusion. Furthermore, technology is not only spreading to the far corners of the world, it is transforming us. It is changing our understanding of ourselves and challenging the ontological models and the foundational claims that we rely upon to define being human. Over the last two decades, the terms "transhumanism" and "posthumanism" have been gaining currency in academics and popular culture, inspiring dozens of texts and energizing a mood of reflective engagement with the changing character of the human condition. Traditional modes of social engagement and interaction are fading and are being replaced by technological modes of mediation. The internet and mobile networks, together with increasingly portable non-dedicated devices like mobile phones, tablets, and laptops, are transforming how people, and entire societies, interoperate.

Though announced repeatedly over the last half-century, the gravity of this last point is being felt all over the world, reflected in the daily news and almost every other facet of life. Technological determinism may still rear its head from time to time, mostly for sensational purposes, but the practical understanding is that the technologies are not the issue in and of themselves. It is the way that they change who and how we are within our world that matters to us. Far from an instrumental version of determinism, where technologies are void of any ethical characteristics, the contemporary practical view eschews unproductive talk about the metaphysical nature of technologies, and understands that technologies do indeed exert a social influence and that this influence must be managed (see Feenberg 1999). Nuclear power entails living in a world of increased threat and having to be worried about the consequences. Making one's life available on Facebook means having to live with a reduced expectation of privacy, personally and legally. Algorithms define our identities to corporations, make decisions for us at work and at home, and predictively return personalized forms of information we search for using electronic resources on the internet. Technologies construct our environments, recommend actions for us, redefine our political structures and personal networks, facilitate social movements, deliver responses to questions that we seek, and have enhanced our ability to contain and access knowledge. For good or ill, integrating this technological complexity into the quotidian means realizing two important lessons about the changing nature of what it means to be 'human'[1]: 1) Processes that were once biological and neurological can be, and have been, outsourced to devices and 2) some of those processes and results that we co-opt as part of being human are not attainable through biological and neurological processes. Technologies mediate us, even to ourselves, make us possible, and extend our potentialities, in our present state.

Transhumanism and posthumanism both address this continuing trend in techno-human integration. Though these monikers may often be transposed or conflated in non-academic settings, it is quite important to understand their differences. Both discourses fundamentally claim that technologies are being employed in a way that is transforming the foundational characteristics of being human, but they focus upon very different aspects of this process. In the end, they are quite different from, if not incompatible with, each other. This article will discuss the approaches of both movements, specifically their ontological frameworks, in order to establish a basis of comparison for the general claims associated with each of them in the public sphere. First, we will consider the claims of both transhumanism and posthumanism, as exhibited by major figures within these movements. Following this, we will examine each movement's perspective toward techno-human integration in order to demonstrate how these areas of concern reflect an implicit ontological framework. Next, we will detail the ontological frameworks of transhumanism and posthumanism in relation to the dominant ontological framework of Western humanism. Doing so will help to clearly illustrate the areas where the two discourses diverge and conflict with each other, and establish them as definitively separate areas of study regarding the development of techno-human relations and integration.

Definitions and Differences

A major issue with this area of study is the confusion surrounding the terminology. Transhumanism and posthumanism both posit "posthumans", and their definitions of these posthumans are at times commensurate and at other times divergent. In addition, there are two types of posthumanism. That is to say, there are two posthumanist discourses, though popular use of the term generally reflects only one of these. For the sake of clarity, a short explanation of terms should help the reader distinguish between them and understand their usage in this article.

1 In this paper, the term 'human', enclosed in single quotes, is meant to interrupt the reader and reinforce recognition of the term as a construct that relies on a foundational set of ontological assumptions.

Transhumanism refers to the use of science and technology to extend human opportunities and potential by transforming the human being so that its capacities and abilities are able to overcome any number of natural human limitations such as aging, death, suffering, intellectual capacity, moral shortcomings and so forth. This extension of human capacities takes place through the integration of technology and could be a simple as medical supplements or prosthetics, or as complex (and imaginative) as expanding the mind's abilities and lifespan by transitioning it into a quantum computer. The key feature here is that transhumanism, from an ontological perspective, wishes to preserve and extend capacities and characteristics that we associate with our contemporary understanding of the word 'human'. The direct goal is not to overcome being a human per se, but to guide the evolution of the human via technological mediation for specific purposes such as moral beneficence or superior DNA configuration (see Bostrom 2003). Confusingly, transhumanists often refer to this new form of human as "posthuman", even though this delineation is made primarily on physiological rather than on philosophical grounds.

The "posthuman" in posthumanism, on the other hand, refers to a state of being that is beyond our understanding from a humanist philosophical paradigm. It delineates an entity that defines and understands itself differently than through the contemporary notion of 'human' because of technology's impact on basic human characteristics. For example, a transhumanist posthuman might be something like a super smart child that has been enhanced genetically and neurologically with computer implants. A posthumanist posthuman might be something like the alien Q from the Star Trek series – an individual so advanced, or with such a fundamentally different understanding of the universe, that basic human concerns over things like ethics are incomprehensible to it. Again, these posthumans may be completely different entities, or perhaps the enhanced child will understand herself so differently that she may represent both forms of posthuman in one form. It is quite easy to see why these two discourses can be conflated. The key difference to remember is that posthumanism is rather different than transhumanism in that posthumanism focuses upon the ontological framework through which humans understand themselves in addition to the transformation of human beings through continuous techno-social integration.

Beginning with this last point, we can make a distinction between the two types of posthumanist discourse. The first places posthumanism within the history of philosophy and critical theory. In this sense, posthumanism is a rejection of both scientific realism and social realism, and prefers a tandem approach to the development of representation and knowledge (see Jones 1996). Conceived this way, as beyond post-structuralist critique, posthumanism is situated as a challenge to the entire dualist ontological framework of Enlightenment humanism that, in most western societies, still grounds the majority of social and legal definitions of the human being. This posthumanist discourse is actively seeking an ontological framework that is beyond the metaphysical subject-object dualism of traditional humanistic selfhood. In addition, it is fundamentally philosophical and, like many recent sociological models, incorporates complex forms of interaction, influence, and agency into its model of the human being. The difference is that while sociological models might focus on memes or group influences, posthumanism is concerned specifically with the influence of technology's integration into human identity (see Hayles 1999).

The second form of posthumanist discourse is what often causes the confusion with transhumanism. This form of posthumanism discusses what some academics and popular science figures imagine will occur if human beings, using bio-technical processes, evolve completely beyond their current state, leading to an entirely new assemblage of material composition and agency. One example would be occupying the structure of a computer or replacing an entire body including the brain with prostheses, functionally rendering one a cyborg, psychologically and physically. This second form acknowledges that it is possible through a process of accretion for one set of humans to become dislocated from others much in the way speciation occurs in the natural world. In an abbreviated manner, it is much easier to distinguish between the two if one considers transhumanism as discussing superhumans, who might possess absolutized versions of what we consider contemporary virtues, and considers posthumanism to refer to mutants, who either no longer understand themselves as classically 'human' or who understand the 'human' completely differently. To quote *Gattaca*, transhumans would still be us, but the best of us. Posthumans, on the other hand, would be something beyond our grasp. This latter point is of key concern for their ontological models. In other words, if transhumanism realizes the future it foresees, the implicit expectation is that we would still be coherent to ourselves within our current ontological framework, even though transhumanists know this cannot be the case. On the other hand, if posthumanism succeeds in overcoming the dualistic humanist paradigm, we will become something other than we are, and notions of responsibility, justice, and selfhood will have to be rethought from the ground up.

Transhumanism and Posthumanism

The notion of the 'human' as a coherent, rational, responsible, immaterial moral subject and agent has dominated our self-understanding since the eighteenth century. The physical world and its influence have been ignored in the makeup of the individual until the last half-century. Artifacts and the natural world have remained "outside" the psychological self. The self has continued to be conceived, for popular understanding, as a Cartesian mind floating in an immaterial abyss. This model at the beginning of the Enlightenment humanist notion of selfhood carried forward an ancient dualist perspective, and built the 'human' upon this bifurcated ground. Yet even at the beginning of this modern construction, technology played a fundamental role in the development of Cartesian notions of selfhood. Don Ihde (2004, 364-366) points out in his *Merleau-Ponty and Epistemology Engines*, that the notion of the subject and object as metaphors for the self and world were themselves explicitly connected to the technological attributes of the camera obscura. The dualism of Enlightenment humanism took its most famous division from a technological example and used it to constitute being 'human'.

Transhumanism embraces both this dualism and the Enlightenment project of rational "progress" that was born historically alongside it. One can see the outline of transhumanism taking shape in the nineteenth century industrial social orientation toward nature that usurped its province and incorporated it technologically into social projects. Historical accounts, such as Thomas Hughes' *Human Built World* (2004), detail the redemptive value of technology in society's reframing of a post-industrial revolution world. It is through the hope that technology will improve humanity that transhumanism recognizes its roots in the desire for human "progress". Still holding to this position, the explicit message of bioethicists like Julian Savulescu and John Harris, is that not only can we be better, but we should be better (see Harris 2007). Transhumanists and extropians[2] like Nick Bostrom and Max More concur. Transhumanists see improvement as a primary goal, and this prescribed improvement is not limited to health or intellectual acuity. Moral improvement is also argued for as a duty and an obligation (see Persson/ Savulescu 2008). Such an explicit invocation of moral authority and cultural dominance rests, once again, on the back of the metaphysics of a vestigial worldview that led to the problems of colonialism that most societies seek not to repeat. That such moral goals could be reached solely through the injection of technologies into society highlights transhumanism's optimistic vision of technology's illimitable powers.

For examples of transhumanism's ontology at work, take a look at the phenomena that are so widely present and talked about in the modern media, such as the possibility of building bigger and better prosthetics that will outstrip the functionality of our organic limbs, or the ability to alter and augment our sight through the use of sophisticated eyewear or perhaps an embedded computer chip

2 Extropianism is usually considered an extreme form of transhumanism that contains political elements in addition to the desire for human enhancement.

in our brains. Transhumanism accepts large ontological structures such as "mind" and "body" and then focuses on how to extend these categories. Transhumanism seeks to create humans differently in terms of physical construction, i.e. super sight, bionic power, extreme longevity or even superior ethical demeanor via superintelligence. But transhumanism does not actually attack or challenge the philosophical problems that emerge from dualist metaphysical foundations that presuppose a mind-body split as an acceptable ontological structure to begin with. Take, for instance, the case of mind uploading into computers. The idea that the mind is a separable entity from the material brain is a presupposition required to perform such a theoretical operation. To assume that a person with prosthetic limbs is still the same person, and that the limbs are extensions of that person, is quite different from seeing a person with prosthetics limbs as a different 'human' being than before, wherein the prosthetics have influence in the conceptual construction of that person's being, identity, and agency. Also, in terms of modern genetic research, it is clear that some advocates assume that we can make humans objectively better by choosing and extending "good" attributes of behavior such as compliance, and extinguishing "bad" attributes such as aggressiveness (see Persson/ Savulescu 2013). Codifying these descriptive characteristics as actual ontological categories, whether they be physical or behavioral, shows that transhumanists are reaffirming the ontological structures that were developed during the Enlightenment (and before) and want to extend them in the name of progress.

In contrast to transhumanism's desire to appropriate technology for the goals of humanism's long standing ontological framework, posthumanism approaches the phenomenon of technology with a much different posture. Posthumanism asserts that the missing ingredient in Enlightenment humanism's recipe for the 'human' is technology itself. The claim is that the 'human' is not separable from technology. In other words, the constitution of the human is a technological constitution. A clear example of this constitution is the archaeological classification of human history through the presence of artifacts. It is only through the presence of such technological engagement with the world that we recognize ourselves, or our ancient ancestors. Posthumanism's stance is directly in opposition to transhumanism on this point. Instead of assuming an already defined human for whom technology can function, posthumanism attempts to critique the concept of the 'human' and its taken-for-granted constitution. For posthumanism, technology must become part of the first principles that constitute the 'human', meaning that the immaterial subject and material world can no longer be fundamentally distinct.

For posthumanism to be successful, technology must be understood to be the behavioral way through which we constitute our being. If this can be achieved, posthumanism will have fulfilled its goals and dismantled a dualistic ontology that has been a part of human self-understanding for as long as there has been record. Unfortunately, it is not that easily done. Humanist dualism explains the phenomenon of feeling like a coherent "self" in an incomplete, tautological and yet paradoxically satisfying way. We feel like individual rational subjects and thus we rarely question the premise. Thus it should be no surprise that many transhumanists unwittingly uphold its structure. Though to be fair, as we shall see in the next section, ontological frameworks are tricky, and posthumanism does not have a particularly satisfying replacement.

Ontological Frameworks

As previously noted, transhumanism piggybacks humanism's dualist ontology. This framework is both simple and yet very difficult to pry apart due to its phenomenological coherence. Since we feel like agents in control of a body, our experience (compounded with our explanation of it) tells us that our agency is derived from a discrete self that inhabits the body. This is the Cartesian mind example. The ontological framework is quite direct. Like the Platonic system before it, there are both material and immaterial dimensions. The immaterial dimension is aligned with the internal characteristics of being such as thinking, agency, and the notion of self as a subject. The material dimension of the framework is aligned with the external aspects of being such as the senses, technology, and the world as an object. The immaterial characteristics that accompany the 'human' being such as intelligence and morality are the ultimate target of transhumanists, yet, ironically, they target them via material means such as DNA augmentation and bionic enhancement. Thus transhumanists both affirm and betray the dualist framework. They hope to extend the ontological categories that are part of the immaterial constitution of the internal moral agent, and at the same time they demonstrate that they realize that this immaterial realm is dependent upon, and not separate from, the external material world.

Quite visibly, transhumanism is problematic in terms of a coherent ontological foundation. Nevertheless, technology studies have covered some ground toward newer frameworks. One notable example comes from Don Ihde in the field of post-phenomenology. Ihde's 1990 text, *Technology and the Lifeworld* develops a set of ontological constellations, which he calls hermeneutic technics for various human technology relations. He first breaks away from humanist ontology by separating technology from the world, so that self, technology, and world must form different types of relationships in order to produce meaning. The first type of relationship, embodiment relations, collapses technology into the self, so that the self is realized through technology over against the world. Ihde's classic example here is a pair of eyeglasses, which rearrange the world for the self. The second type of relationship, hermeneutic relations, collapses technology into the world, so that the world is constituted through technology over against the self. Ihde's example here is a nuclear reactor's instruments. One must assume the world to be as the instruments indicate. In both cases, the technologies mediate the world, sometimes as part of the self, sometimes as part of the world. A third type of relationship, alterity relations, focuses on technology as an intermediary into dimensions incapable of representation in their natural state to human senses. False color images of heat maps or recalibrated audio for the spectrum beyond human hearing are some examples.

Though Ihde has spent his career in technology studies and has a popular voice in contemporary technoscience studies, he has not weighed in too heavily in transhumanist and posthumanist discourse. Nevertheless, through Ihde's insightful deconstruction of technology's mediating role, transhumanism's ontological naivety is skillfully exposed, and the challenge for posthumanism is clearly delineated. Agency, selfhood, and the world shift with each technology encountered or employed, transforming the ontological constellation dynamically and often. The static dualism of humanism is no longer satisfactory even though it feels good. Yet, Ihde's new constellations are not intended as a replaccment for the classic ontological model. Posthumanism must find a way to describe and deploy a new model that can account for what Bruno Latour (1993) calls "a parliament of things", and to date has not done so. In addition, Latour and Callon, in their Actor Network Theory, recognize that agency is grounded in the very ontological framework that constitutes the 'human'. That is to say, up until this point in time, agency has been articulated from a humanist framework. We now see that technology and the material world encroach upon that ground regularly and often, and a newer framework must be articulated that will consider constellations of varieties of objects, including people, and then assess agency and selfhood based on dynamic constellation composition. Doing this, however, will change the meaning of the 'human', and once again decenter our ontological position.

The most difficult challenge for posthumanist accounts is exactly how to articulate this matrix of agency. It does not matter that this idea is attractive or that we seem to intuit a relationship of sorts with artifacts. The question remains, how much agency is given to whom or what? While transhumanism might be alright with using humanist subject-object dichotomies to discuss the subject's employment of the technology for her own purposes, the posthumanist paradigm would envision a more distributed sense of agency across the objects involved, of which the human person is one object among others. In either case, the foundations of agency are complicated by suggesting that either mere things can have human-like agency or that humans are fully commensurable with or reducible to material objects. The phenomenological experience of being a person plays havoc with this attempt to navigate the waters of material agency, and it is difficult to consider notions of responsibility being granted to objects, since it would seemingly detract from the responsibility we assign to human agents. The anthropological view that equates humans with artifacts in order to describe a network of relations only works so long as we are regarding the system from a third person perspective. The moment we change perspectives and describe the same system from a first-person point-of-view, the self reappears as a source of motivation and a unique producer of initial causes via will, and posthumanism has not yet succeeded in articulating an ontological model in spite of ourselves.

The more sophisticated or numerous the technologies, the more sophisticated the possibilities of interaction and the potentialities for selfhood. Consequently, transhumanists and posthumanists recognize that what it means to be human is in large part determined by the possibilities that the material world of artifacts affords. But here lies the rub and the difficulty with the larger problem that transhumanism and posthumanism have yet to answer. While some see human beings as problem solving mind machines that incorporate the world, or as biotechnological matrices (see Clark 2004), they do not necessarily discuss wherein lies the agency of the problem-solving constellation. It may seem obvious that it is the human that has the agency, but how can a human have the only agency if the very make-up of her mind is comprised of objects that show that the "line between biological self and technological world was, in fact, never very firm" (ibid., 8)? Even if the lion's share of agency is given to the human object in this biotechnological matrix, there must be some agency allocated for the material objects that exert enough influence to change the conditions and opportunities available, and thus the very way in which the person is capable of realizing herself within that matrix. After all, techné, as both artifactual and symbolic production, exists as the condition for our capacity to conceive of ourselves and perhaps even to think, in general.

Conclusion

Both transhumanism and posthumanism address the continuing techno-social integration and its effect on society. Neither, however, has a firm grasp on the new ontology that is developing before our eyes due to our continuingly deepening integration with technology. Transhumanism relies on outdated notions from a crumbling humanist paradigm, and posthumanism has yet to figure out what a new paradigm might look like. But either way, there is something attractive and enticing about these discourses that seem to narrow the gap between our things and us. It registers something we already recognize, always already engaged as we are, in a world of objects that form the content of our social lives. Our technologies are the conditions of our existence. They and we determine each other, shape each other and are responsible for each other. We cannot be 'human' without them. We are, in the words of archaeologist Timothy Taylor (2010), artificial apes. We are perhaps the only animals on earth that would die without technology. Despite deep ontological differences, transhumanists and posthumanists would agree that, in the words of Andy Clark, we are "thinking and reasoning systems distributed across brain, body and world" and "we need to understand that the very ideas of minds and persons are not limited to the biological skin-bag" (Clark 2004, 32-33).

Bibliography

Aristotle (1934): Nicomachean Ethics (Translated by H. Rackham). Cambridge(MA): Harvard University Press.

Bijker, W.E./ Hughes, T.P./ Pinch, T.J. (eds.) (1987): The Social Construction of Technological Systems: New Directions in the Sociology and History of Technology. Cambridge(MA) et al.: MIT Press.

Borgmann, A. (1984): Technology and the Character of Contemporary Life: A Philosophical Inquiry. Chicago et al.: University of Chicago Press.

Bostrom, N. (2003): Human Genetic Enhancements: A Transhumanist Perspective. In: Journal of Value Inquiry 37(4), 493-506.

Clark, A. (2003): Natural-Born Cyborgs: Why Minds and Technologies are Made to Merge. New York: Oxford University Press.

Dennett, D. (1987): The Intentional Stance. Cambridge(MA): MIT Press.

Ellul, J. (1970): The Technological Society (With an Introduction by R.K. Merton). New York: Vintage Books.

Feenberg, A. (1999): Questioning Technology. New York: Routledge.

Hale, B. (2009): Technology, the Environment and the Moral Considerability of Artefacts. In: Olsen, J.L.B./ Selinger, E./ Riis, S. (eds.): New Waves in the Technology of Philosophy. New York: Palgrave Macmillan.

Harris, J. (2007): Enhancing Evolution. Princeton: Princeton University Press.

Hayles, K.N. (1999): How We Became Posthuman. Chicago: University of Chicago Press.

Heidegger, M. (1977): The Question Concerning Technology and Other Essays. New York: Harper & Row.

Heidegger, M. (1995): The Fundamental Concepts of Metaphysics: World, Finitude, Solitude. Bloomington(IN): Indiana University Press.

Hughes, T.P. (2004): Human-Built World: How to Think About Technology and Culture. Chicago et al.: University of Chicago Press.

Ihde, D. (1990): Technology and the Lifeworld: From Garden to Earth. Bloomington: Indiana University Press.

Ihde, D. (2004): Merleau-Ponty and Epistemology Engines. In: Human Studies 27, 361-376.
Ihde, D. (2010): Heidegger's Technologies: Postphenomenological Perspectives. New York: Fordham University Press.
Jones, M.P. (1996): Posthuman Agency: Between Theoretical Traditions. In: Sociology Theory 14(3), 290-309.
Kuhn, T.S. (1996): The Structure of Scientific Revolutions. Chicago et al.: University of Chicago Press.
Latour, B. (1993): We Have Never Been Modern. Cambridge(MA): Harvard University Press.
Latour, B. (1999): Pandora's Hope: Essays On The Reality of Science Studies. Cambridge(MA) et al.: Harvard University Press.
Latour, B. (2002): Morality and Technology: The End of the Means. In: Theory, Culture & Society 19(5/6), 247-260.
Latour, B. (2005): Reassembling the Social: An Introduction to Actor-Network-Theory. Oxford: Oxford University Press.
Merleau-Ponty, M (2005): Phenomenology of Perception. London: Routledge.
Mitcham, C.A. (1969): From Sociology to Philosophy: On the Nature of Criticisms of the Technological Society. University of Colorado.
Nietzsche, F. (2001). The Gay Science: With a Prelude in German Rhymes and an Appendix of Songs. Cambridge: Cambridge University Press.
Persson, I./ Savulescu, J. (2008): The Perils of Cognitive Enhancement and the Urgent Imperative to Enhance the Moral Character of Humanity. In: Journal of Applied Philosophy 25(3), 162-177.
Persson, I./ Savulescu, J. (2012): Unfit for the Future: The Need for Moral Enhancement. Oxford: Oxford University Press.
Pickering, A. (1995): The Mangle of Practice: Time, Agency, and Science. Chicago et al.: University of Chicago Press.
Taylor, T. (2010): The Artificial Ape: How Technology Changed the Course of Human Evolution. New York: Palgrave MacMillan.
Winner, L. (2005): Resistance is Futile: The Posthuman Condition in Its Advocates. In: Baillie, H./ Casey, T. (eds.): Is Human Nature Osolete? Cambrige(MA): MIT Press, 385-411.

Nature

Martin G. Weiss

The term "nature", deriving from the Latin *nasci* – meaning "becoming", "be born" – which for its part is derived from the Greek verb *phyein* having the same meaning, had from its first appearance in pre-Socratic writings on two different, but intertwined, meanings: a) the phenomena of the physical world opposed to humans and human creations (*techne*), and b) the inherent characteristic feature of something, its essence (*ousia*).

Aristotle characterizes "natural things" (*physei on*) as things which have the principle of movement in themselves (keep in mind that Aristotle's concept of motion includes local movement as well as becoming and dying), whereas artifacts, i.e. products of human craftsmanship (*techne*) have the principle of their movement, i.e. their becoming, in the human craftsman.

Whereas for the longest time the difference between what was natural – i.e. becoming, growing and dying by its own – and what was artificial – i.e. the product of human activity (culture) – was unquestionable, the advent of modern technology made it increasingly difficult to identify truly natural objects, not yet intertwined with some kind of human action. Nowadays, where even the global climate is manmade there seems to be left no genuine nature at all.

The problem to distinguish nature form culture becomes actually more difficult when it comes to human nature, as in this context the question arises in which way the nature of the human being – i.e. its biological material, the way it is organized and the laws reigning its development – is related to the essence of a human being, the second meaning of human nature.

In the context of posthumanism and transhumanism the notions "nature" and "human nature" are crucial, as posthumanism and transhumanism challenge both meanings of nature, i.e. "biology" as well as "essence", by questioning the relation between human nature in the sense of essence and human nature in the sense of the biology of the human being. Is human nature (its biology) a normative boundary, which one has to preserve in order not to harm human dignity? Or is the will to transform the nature of humans (their biology) a genuine expression of the very essence of human being and therefore of their constitutive freedom, which again is the fundament of human dignity?

Whereas posthumanism in challenging the nature/culture dichotomy tends towards culturalism – seeing in the notion of a given biological nature of the human being a product of culture –, transhumanism embraces a more naturalistic view, insofar as the transhumanist movement considers the human being primarily to be an animal, although an animal which has the power to manipulate its biological features. Both posthumanism and transhumanism share the Aristotelian definition of human being as rational animal. But whereas for posthumanism the biology of human being is a cultural concept – and therefor a product of human rationality –, according to transhumanism human rationality is foremost the product of biology.

Nature and Posthumanism or Heidegger and Agamben on Human Being and the Animal

In his notorious paper *Regeln für den Menschenpark* Peter Sloterdijk compares Martin Heidegger – one of the most influential posthumanists – with an angry Angel who, armed with swords, tries to keep human beings and animals separated in the desperate attempt to prevent every ontological contamination between what is human and what is not-human (see Sloterdijk 1999, 25).

The classical anthropological model expressed most famously in Aristotle's definition of human being as *zoon logon echon* identifies the human *telos* with the emancipation of human being from his biological nature. Being human means not to be an animal anymore. In this model humanity, identified with rationality, emerges from biology, and is conceived as some sort of human surplus added at one point of the natural evolution of the great apes from which *Homo sapiens* descends.

It is widely known that Heidegger rejects this form of "modular anthropology" which conceives human being as build up of two layers, the one being basal animality, the other genuine human rationality. Heidegger had two reasons to reject this classical anthropological model: he rejected it, because from an ontological point of view this model is unable to conceive humanity from within itself. In fact, according to the layer-model, humanity is only an added value to the basic animality human being shares with every other creature. If we start from the outside, so to speak, in order to understand what it means to be human, looking firstly at bare life and biology and only secondly at ourselves, we will never be able to grasp human being as human being, because according to Heidegger humanity cannot be grasped as a kind of spiritual addition to a biological substratum. For Heidegger, the classical anthropological model starting from the biological nature of human being will never reach neither the true "essence" of human being, nor the "essence of nature", as it has adopted from the beginning several preliminary decisions concerning the nature of human being and the nature of nature, which make it impossible to conceive human being as human being and nature as nature. According to Heidegger the classical anthropological model reduces nature to mere mechanical biology and human being to a strange compound of material biology and spiritual rationality, preventing philosophy from recognizing, that nature is not biology but *physis*, i.e. the power to appear by itself (Being), and that what characterizes the human being is not being a rational animal, but its exceptional relation to this *physis*, that Heidegger defines as human "openness to the world".

According to the analysis of human being, which Heidegger terminologically calls *Dasein* ("Being-There"), the human openness to the world is based on what he calls *Befindlichkeit* or *Stimmung* ("state of mind" or "mood"). This "state of mind" in which the world primarily appears us, is prior to all rational "understanding", because every "understanding always has its mood" (Heidegger 1967, 142).

> "Ontologically, we […] obtain as the first essential characteristic of states-of-mind that they disclose Dasein in its thrownness, and – proximally and for the most part – in the manner of an evasive turning-away" (Heidegger 1967, 136).

"Thrownness" means the "facticity" of *Dasein*, the fact "that it is and has to be" (ibid., 134). By facticity Heidegger means, that prior to all rational understanding, we are thrown into a world, into a historic-cultural net of relations and meanings, which determines the way in which singular entities appear to us. But in our everyday-life, in our practical managing of the "equipment ready-to-hand" or in the theoretical contemplation of the mere present "objects present-at-hand", the world, the background of all meaning, is never explicitly at the center of our attention. This is so because in our everyday-life we are normally completely absorbed by "innerwordly entities" surrounding us, so that the horizon of references, their background, which is constitutive for the way they appear, that is for the way they are, does not directly occur to us. The notion of "mood" can be seen as an aspect of Heidegger's concept of *physis*, nature or "Being" as that which appears by itself. In fact Heidegger's emphasis on the "thrownness" of *Dasein*, opposed to the will of the classical metaphysical subject, points in the direction of the primacy of *physis*/Being, "[…] for the mood brings Dasein before the 'that-it-is' of its 'there', which, as such, stares it in the face with inexorability of an enigma" (ibid., 136). The "mood" reveals, therefore, not only the world as the ground on which inner-worldly entities appear, but also *physis*/Being, i.e. the groundless origin of *Dasein* conceived as "Being-in-the-world". The unforeseeable arise of "moods" in which we experience the world thus reveals itself as an aspect of the more general "unavailability", of *physis*/Being, i.e. nature: "A mood assails us. It comes neither from 'outside' nor from 'inside', but arises out of Being-in-the-world, as a way of such Being" (ibid., 136).

A special "mood" which according to Heidegger allows us to experience *physis*/Being/nature in the mentioned sense of that which appears by itself, is "profound boredom". Actually in his lecture on the *Fundamental Concepts of Metaphysics* the mood of "profound boredom" according to Heidegger causes a loss of meaning of the particular entities we normally deal with and thus leads to the revelation of their mere being or naturalness, i.e. there appearing by themselves.

According to Giorgio Agamben it is exactly this "boredom" which against what Heidegger thought, links human being to the animal. In *The Open: Man and the Animal* Agamben argues that the "daze" or "captivation" of the animal, i.e. its being completely merged with its environment, has, against Heidegger's own intention, a lot in common with the Heideggerian characterization of human "boredom" as privileged access to *physis*/Being. Agamben concludes that the captivation of the animal should not be juxtaposed with the disclosedness of *Dasein*. Instead Agamben proposes to consider human openness to *physis*/Being as interruption, or suspension of the captivation of the animal. This leads Agamben to a new definition of the relationship between human being and animal, insofar as the difference between human being and animal is then no longer a radical difference but only a gradual one. Whereas for Heidegger the human being-animal relationship had to remain an insoluble enigma – in his *Letter on 'Humanism'* (1976) Heidegger asserts that even the essence of the divine is less enigmatic than that of the animal – in Agamben's view human openness is only a different modus of the captivation of the animal, so that to him human being and animal are much more similar than Heidegger thought:

> "Being, world, and the open are not [...] something other with respect to animal environment and life: they are nothing but the interruption and capture of the living being's relationship with its disinhibitor [von Uexküll's term for environment]. The open is nothing but a grasping of the animal not-open. Man suspends his animality, in this way, opens a 'free and empty' zone in which life is captured and abandoned in a zone of exception" (Agamben 2004, 79).

Agamben's peculiar interpretation of the human being-animal relationship allows him to maintain the exceptionality of human being without being forced to negate its biological relationship to animal, a fact that for Heidegger was bluntly incomprehensible. Agamben argues:

> "At this point, two scenarios are possible from Heidegger's perspective: (a) posthistorical man no longer preserves his own animality as undisclosable, but rather seeks to take it on and govern it by means of technology; (b) man, the shepherd of being, appropriates his own concealedness, his own animality, which neither remains hidden nor is made an object of mastery, but is thought as such, as pure abandonment" (Agamben 2004, 79).

What this pure abandonment on the threshold between human being and animal may look like is described by Agamben, taking into account a painting by Titian exhibited in the Kunsthistorisches Museum in Vienna. The work depicts a Nymph and a Shepherd in post-coital serenity. According to Agamben the topic of this painting is the "saved night" Walter Benjamin mentions in one of his letters, meaning a night which does not expect another day to come, a time which is fulfilled, which is in no need of any goal (of history) anymore to be meaningful. The "saved night" Benjamin is speaking about would be a world beyond alienation (and any kind of action) and would permit a form of existence which does not search for its meaning in another, transcendent reality and therefore resemble the world beyond "truth" and "appearance" Nietzsche speaks about. Because if we abolish the invisible Platonic-Christian "true World" of ideas and values – the one which according to the tradition of metaphysics is the essence of the "appearing world", we experience with our senses – what remains is not the mere appearing world, but reality beyond the metaphysical distinction between "truth" and "appearance". What remains is pure presence without any future, without any exterior meaning. Who lives in this "saved Night", expects nothing, does not project himself into the coming, but is completely closed in a sort of lasting presence, very similar to the way the animal is "captured" in his environment, albeit not exactly the same, as Agamben stresses:

> "To be sure, in their fulfillment the lovers learn something of each other that they should not have known – they have lost their mystery – and yet have not become any less impenetrable. But in this mutual disenchantment from their secret, they enter, just as in Benjamin's aphorism, a new and more blessed life, one that is neither animal, nor human. It is not nature that is reached in their fulfillment, but rather […] a higher stage beyond both nature and knowledge […]" (Agamben 2004, 87).

To understand what Agamben wishes to illustrate with this description of the lovers and their fulfilled time beyond the partition into past, presence and future, it is necessary to go back to the first pages of his book *The Open*, as there Agamben outlines the astonishing fact that in an illustration of the *Vision of Ezekiel* in an ancient Hebrew Bible kept at the Biblioteca Ambrosiana in Milan the remnant of Israel, the righteous, that is the men who have reached perfection, are depicted with animal heads:

> "It is not impossible, therefore, that in attributing an animal head to the remnant of Israel, the artist of the manuscript in the Ambrosiana intended to suggest that on the last day, the relations between animals and men will take on a new form, and that man himself will be reconciled with his animal nature" (Agamben 2004, 3).

Considering the current developments in the field of biotechnology, however, humanity seems unlikely to reconcile itself with its animality, but rather to embrace the other possible option mentioned by Agamben: the replacement of natural development with technical production, i.e. the philosophy of transhumanism.

Transhumanism and (Human) Nature

In the words of Nick Bostrom:

> "Transhumanism is a loosely defined movement that has developed gradually over the past two decades, and can be viewed as an outgrowth of secular humanism and the Enlightenment. It holds that current human nature is improvable through the use of applied science and other rational methods, which may make it possible to increase human health-span, extend our intellectual and physical capacities, and give us increased control over our own mental states and moods" (Bostrom 2005, 203).

As Bostrom himself stresses in this passage, the core-concept of transhumanism dates back to Renaissance humanism and the ideals of the Enlightenment. In his *Oration on the Dignity Of Men*, a sort of humanist manifesto published in 1486, the Italian philosopher Pico della Mirandola wrote:

> "The Great Artisan […] made man a creature of indeterminate and indifferent nature, and, placing him in the middle of the world, said to him 'Adam, we give you no fixed place to live, no form that is peculiar to you, nor any function that is yours alone. According to your desires and judgment, you will have and possess whatever place to live, whatever form, and whatever functions you yourself choose. All other things have a limited and fixed nature prescribed and bounded by our laws. You, with no limit or no bound, may choose for yourself the limits and bounds of your nature […]. We have made you neither of heavenly nor of earthly stuff, neither mortal nor immortal, so that with free choice and dignity, you may fashion yourself into whatever form you choose. To you is granted the power of degrading yourself into the lower forms of life, the beasts, and to you is granted the power, contained in your intellect and judgment, to be reborn into the higher forms, the divine'" (Pico della Mirandola 1990, 4).

This "humanistic" approach defines human being as "animal rationabile," as Immanuel Kant puts it, that is, the animal that is able to achieve humanity and more than humanity, showing that the essence of humanism since its very beginning seems to be transhumanism or, as John Harris asserts:

> "It is doubtful that there was ever a time in which we ape-descended persons were not striving for enhancement, trying to do things better and to better ourselves" (Harris 2007, 13).

In Kant, the main figure of 18th century Enlightenment, the transformation of the human animal into human being, which is the history of civilization, is conceived as "emancipation" from "nature". In this model, humanity, identified with rationality, emerges from nature, which moreover is largely identified with the body and its biology.

Until recently, despite all efforts at educating humankind and controlling their souls and bodies, no one really questioned the stability of humanity's biological basis. Until the rise of pharmacology, genetics and prosthetics, human nature was thought to be unchangeable. To speak of something's nature meant to speak of its eternal given essence. Now this last line of objectivity is gone. Humans have definitively lost their essence. Since the work of Sigmund Freud at the latest, we are aware of the fact that our soul and subjectivity are nothing we can rely on; due to the astonishing achievements of biotechnologies, we are also forced to accept that nothing is given in our biological nature and objectivity. There is no natural boundary for what humans can be, no intrinsic essence of humanity, neither in the human soul nor in human biology. Thus, biotechnology carries the promise of finally transforming the human animal into the free being the Renaissance dreamed about. To reach this goal, transhumanism advocates the enhancement of three human "central capacities" to a "post-human" level, i.e. a level unimaginable for humans (which has nothing to do with the philosophical position of posthumanism discussed in the previous chapter):

> "*healthspan* – the capacity to remain fully healthy, active, and productive, both mentally and physically
>
> *cognition* – general intellectual capacities, such as memory, deductive and analogical reasoning, and attention, as well as special faculties such as the capacity to understand and appreciate music, humor, eroticism, narration, spirituality, mathematics, etc.
>
> *emotion* – the capacity to enjoy life and to respond with appropriate affect to life situations and other people" (Bostrom 2008, 107).

For bioethicists inclined towards transhumanism and liberalisms, the improvement of this central characteristics of the human being is not only unproblematic, but desirable, as these features represent in their view not "positional goods" – "whose goodness for those possessing them depends on other subjects not possessing them" (Bostrom/ Savulescu 2009, 11) – but "absolute goods", which "are good for people not because they confer advantages on some but not on others" (Harris 2007, 29).

Without going into detail, troubling questions arise, because whereas the meaning of an enhanced health-span seems sufficiently clear, posing only the question of whether we want to live in a world without "nativity" (see Arendt 1998) and the freshness of the youth – as a society of health-span enhanced people would have to agree to limit reproduction to a minimum –, it seems much more difficult to define what it would mean to enhance cognition, emotion and behavior. Do we really want to remember everything? What consequences would a generally increased IQ generate? What kind of society would a society of Mr. Spocks be, in which everybody has complete control over his impulses and moods? And finally: what would an enhancement of our spirituality consist of?

Hence, although it may be good for posthumans to be posthuman, i.e. heaving capacities simply unimaginable from our human point of view, the question we have to answer first is whether it is good for us to become post-human, as it is us who have to decide whether we want to embrace enhancement technology or ban it. In his paper *Why I want to be a Posthuman When I Grow Up* (2008), Nick Bostrom tries to argue that posthuman values are actually human values and that we have some sort of moral obligation to become posthumans, but as humans. But how could we value the transformation of humanity into posthumanity if humans are by definition incapable of even imagining how it would be to be posthuman? Concerning this question, Bostrom discusses a dispositional theory of value, which identifies the good, as that, which we would value if we were perfectly acquainted with it.

> "The claim is that for *most* current human beings, there are possible posthuman modes of being such that it could be good for these humans to become posthuman in one of those ways" (Bostrom 2008, 108).

In the words of Nicholas Agar:

> "Consider a music lover who has never listened to Bach's B-minor Mass. The Mass may be among his musical values if it were the case that he would enjoy it were he to be acquainted with it. The dispositional account enables Bostrom to say that posthuman values that seem beyond our comprehension may nevertheless fall within the ambit of our current dispositions" (Agar 2007, 15).

Against Bostrom's attempt to demonstrate that posthuman values are human values, Agar stresses the importance of "local values":

> "Local values are high on the list of those that contribute meaning to our lives. […] You wouldn't swap your child for another child, even if that child were manifestly smarter and better at sport. […] I value humanity because I'm human. I wouldn't trade my humanity for posthumanity even though I recognize that posthumans are objectively superior" (Agar 2007, 16).

According to Agar, even if we embraced posthuman values, which would be the case, if we were perfectly acquainted with them, it would not imply any moral obligation to accept enhancement. Whereas Agar thus sees no obligation to become posthuman, George Annas, one of the most outspoken opponents of transhumanism – famous for his equation of enhancement technologies with "weapons of mass destruction" (Annas 2000, 773) – is much more skeptical. Annas even launched a campaign for an international convention to ban transhumanist "species alteration", as this may endangers human nature and dignity:

> "There are limits to how far we can go in changing our human nature without changing our humanity and our basic human values. Because it is the meaning of humanness (our distinctness from other animals) that has given birth to our concepts of both human dignity and human rights, altering our nature necessarily threatens to undermine both human dignity and human rights. With their loss, the fundamental belief in human equality would also be lost […]. If history is a guide, either the normal humans will view the 'better' humans as 'the other' and seek to control or destroy them, or vice-versa. The better humans will become, at least in the absence of a universal concept of human dignity, either the oppressor or the oppressed" (Annas 2000, 773; see Silver 1997).

Enhancement and Human Dignity

The concepts of human nature and human dignity, emphasized by Annas and other "bioconservatives", as Bostrom labels them, are fundamental to the debate on transhumanism.

Although human dignity is a very controversial concept (see Resnik 2007), it plays a key role in debates on bioethics and is adduced as the basis of several important legal treatises and conventions. Among the numerous interpretations of "human dignity" put forward, three have been most influential: the Kantian, the naturalistic, and the religious (Judeo-Christian).

All three approaches to human dignity mentioned share the notion of human dignity as an expression of the exceptional moral value of the human being, forming the basis for its undeniable rights:

> "Human dignity is the idea that human beings have inherent moral value or worth. The 18th century German philosopher Immanuel Kant, who has developed the most influential view of human dignity, distinguished between two types of things in the world: things with a price and things with a dignity. Things that have dignity have a moral value that cannot be measured in terms of a price. […] According to Kant, dignity entails special treatment: one should not treat humanity (whether in one's own self or in another person) as having only an instrumental (market) value but always as having inherent, moral worth. […] Moral duties toward human beings imply moral rights: human beings have rights to life, liberty, property, due process and so on" (Resnik 2007, 215).

Whereas the exponents of this kind of personalistic approach to human dignity thus do not reject enhancement in principle, but express doubts concerning the possible legal consequences for the unenhanced (see Buchanan 2009), the partisans of the naturalistic model of human dignity try to maintain the concept of human nature (human biology) as some sort of unchangeable norm, although the arguments often differ considerably. Whereas Francis Fukuyama's position, for instance, is openly naturalistic, Jürgen Habermas' criticism of liberal eugenics focuses more on the consequences that manipulating the human genome may create on the social level.

Fukuyama's naturalistic approach is revealed in his definition of human nature. In *Our Posthuman Future* he states:

> "[…] human nature is the sum of the behavior and characteristics that are typical of the human species, arising from genetic rather than environmental factors" (Fukuyama 2002, 130).

Fukuyama identifies human nature with our specific genetic assets – i.e. with our biology – that determine our interaction with the environment, especially our emotional reactions. This pattern of emotional response encoded in the genome of the human species and transmitted from generation to generation represent for Fukuyama a sort of safe haven, as in his view, our emotional reactions are the common ground of human behavior and therefore the basis of all social interaction. According to Fukuyama, emotion – and not reason – is the grounds on which social interaction and politics are based. Emotions rather than arguments guarantee the peaceful co-existence between humans, or at least between members of the same ethnic group to which one feels viscerally attached "by nature." Interference in this relatively well-functioning system of instinctive behaviour could lead to disastrous consequences. Strangely enough, for Fukuyama the possible victory of the mind over the body, represented by biotechnologies, carries a risk of ending in a situation of general violence, a violence that today is restrained because of our inherited instincts.

A second problematic outcome of genetic enhancement advocated by transhumanism and picked up by Fukuyama is the danger that it allegedly poses to democracy, as it threatens to undermine the basic equality of humans. Fukuyama fears that the genetically modified…

> "[…] will look, think, act, and perhaps even feel differently from those who were not similarly chosen, and may come in time to think of themselves as different kinds of creatures" (Fukuyama 2002, 157).

Jürgen Habermas shares this fear. For him, the great difference between genetic inequality and all other possible inequalities (economic, social and political) between people is, that in contrast to all of these traditional inequalities, genetic inequality is not reversible. Whereas all social and political differences are contingent – because at least in theory the relationship between master and slave can be reversed – the relationship between the "Enhanced" and the "Naturals" is irreversible. For Habermas, the problem with liberal eugenics is that it threatens to fix power relations once and for all.

A second problematic consequence of genetic enhancements in Habermas' focus concerns the image that genetically modified people may have of themselves. According to Habermas, a genetically modified person who is aware of her condition, would no longer be capable of seeing herself as solely responsible for her actions, as she would always have in mind that perhaps she acts the way she does only because someone else made her that way. According to this argument, a genetically modified person would be incapable of conceiving of herself as an autonomous subject and therefore also as someone capable of making responsible decisions. From this Habermas concludes that with any but a natural origin – the German word Habermas uses is *Naturwüchsigkeit* – no person would be able to conceive of herself as an equal and autonomous individual. Thus, according to him, biotechnologies risk undermining the two most important pillars of liberal democracy: equality and autonomy. According to Habermas, a manipulated individual who becomes aware of the aims her parents pursued with her creation will lose the capacity to see herself as an autonomous and equal individual:

> "We cannot rule out that knowledge of one's own hereditary features as programmed may prove to restrict the choice of an individual's life, and to undermine the essentially symmetric relations between free and equal human beings" (Habermas 2003, 23).

As liberal democracy is possible only as an association of autonomous and, at least theoretically, equal citizens, germline interventions, according to Habermas, therefore endanger the very foundations of our liberal democracies.

Similar to Habermas, Michael Sandel also fears that transhumanist enhancement technologies "may cause […] loss of openness to the unbidden" (Bostrom/ Savulescu 2009, 6). And like Habermas, Sandel also stresses that the liberal approach to enhancement, expressed by Nozick's famous plea for a "genetic supermarket" (1974) is not essentially different from the old fashioned state-organized eugenics:

> "What, after all, is the moral difference between designing children according to an explicit eugenic purpose and designing children according to the diktats of the market?" (Sandel 2009, 85)

But the most interesting point in Sandel's criticism of human enhancement perhaps consists in his thoughts about the possible consequences that it may have for the notions of personal responsibility and solidarity:

> "If bioengineering made the myth of the 'self-made man' come true, it would be difficult to view our talents as gifts for which we are indebted, rather than as achievements for which we are responsible. This would transform three key features or our moral landscape: humility, responsibility, and solidarity. […] Suppose genetic test-

ing advanced to the point where it could reliably predict each person's medical future and life expectancy. […] The solidarity of insurance would disappear as those with good genes fled the actuarial company of those with bad genes. […] A lively sense of the contingency of our gifts – a consciousness that none of us is wholly responsible for his or her success – saves a meritocratic society from sliding into the smug assumption that the rich are rich because they are more deserving than the poor" (Sandel 2009, 86).

Sandel's preoccupations are shared by Eric T. Juengst, who stresses that the dangers of the new technologies lie not in the alleged manipulation of human nature (its biology), but in their amplification of pre-existing social divides:

"It is the social perception of genetic difference, not the actual biological differences that fuel human rights abuses. […] To the extent that this wave of post-genomic work accentuates perceived genetic differences between human groups already socially sorted by their mutual power relations (like the 'races'), it will feed draconian 'public health' infringements on reproductive freedoms, oppressive DNA identification and data banking programs, neo-eugenic immigration policies, economic discrimination practices, and at the extreme, biological warfare strategies" (Juengst 2009, 56).

Habermas, Annas, Buchanan, Fukuyama, Sandel and Juengst, alarmed most of all by the possibly disruptive social consequences of enhancement, argue for a ban on enhancement technologies and advocate abstaining from enhancing human nature and from forgetting that once we have the possibility to intervene in the natural lottery of genes, there is no way to escape responsibility. But even if we decide not to manipulate our genome, we have to actively make this decision (see Bayertz 1994). Once technology confronts us with the possibility of enhancing our biological features, we have lost our innocence one way or another, as we are responsible for acting in the same way that we are responsible for abstaining from acting:

"Could not a child who later became interested in a musical career, but had only the modest talents of its parents, complain that they had opted for the natural outcome and rejected it. In context, letting nature take its course is no longer a neutral response" (Coady 2009, 175).

Transhumanism and the Co-creation of Nature

Against the objections put forward by the "bioconservatives", the transhumanist position embraces enhancement as ultimate liberation and emancipation from human nature – i.e. the biological boundaries – that obstruct human freedom, which for this position is the very essence of human being and therefore his true "nature". In this view, the human animal represents only a transitory stage in the evolutionary history of this species, which has not yet come to an end. The human animal is not yet what it has to be, but must achieve its very essence by enhancing its proper nature (biology).

However, in this respect, transhumanism is, as we have already seen, not different from classical humanism, which identifies human being as the animal whose specific essence consists in not having a given essence at all. Human being is the only being that is not what it is, but, since essentially free, has to decide for itself what to be. According to Gregory Stock if humanity is not actively pursuing the goal of genetic enhancement, the possibility will come forward as a side effect of already widely accepted therapeutic practices:

> "The fundamental discoveries that spawn these coming capabilities will flow from research deeply embedded in the mainstream, research that is highly beneficial, enjoys widespread support, and certainly is not directed toward a goal like human germline engineering. The possibilities of human redesign will arrive whether or not we actively pursue them" (Stock 2003, 40).

In agreement with Kurt Bayertz (1994), Stock points out that the very concept of a given "natural nature", with which human being ought not to interfere, is quite problematic, as it is based on the assumption that human being himself is not part of nature. This distinction between the realm of nature (*physis*) where things develop on their own on the one hand, and human being and his technical products (*techne*) on the other, dates back to Aristotle. In the latter's work, the term nature is used to designate the realm of life, the realm of the beings, which have the principle of their motion within themselves, as we have mentioned above. Christianity takes on the Aristotelian distinction between *physis* and *techne*, with the difference that nature is then conceived as God's creation, seen in contrast to human being and his products (technology), since after the Fall of Man, humanity in a certain sense was no longer part of the created universe.

But there is also a different interpretation of the relationship between human being and nature. The concept of being created in the image of God is generally connected with the idea that human being shares with God the features of personhood and freedom, which again are central to human dignity. But human being, created in the image of God, has a relationship not only to the divine but also to nature. In the history of the three great monotheistic traditions (Judaism, Christianity and Islam), the relationship of human being to nature has taken three main forms: domination, stewardship, and co-creation (see Coady 2009), of which the latter is of particular interest in the context of the enhancement debate. Thus, for Eric Parens…

> "[…] according to Genesis, and it seems to me much of Judaism, our responsibility is not merely to be grateful and remember that we are not the creator of the whole. It is also our responsibility to use our creativity to mend and transform ourselves and

> the world. As far as I can tell, Genesis and Judaism do not exhort us to choose between gratitude and creativity" (Parens 2009, 189).

The idea of human co-creation, well known in Christianity (see Rahner 1970), is especially important in Judaism. Here human being is seen as being as natural as everything else and therefore a fundamental part of creation. And if human being is part of created nature, his products are as well. Rabbi Barry Freundel, a consultant with the United States Presidential Commission on Cloning, states:

> "If G-d has built the capacity for gene redesign into nature, than He chose for it to be available to us, and our test remains whether we will use that power wisely or poorly" (Freundel 2000, 119).

Here the idea that human being is the image of God results in the conception that human being, as poor as he is, has to be creative himself (see Prainsack 2006).

> "I do not find [human beings gaining control of their own evolution] to be any more troubling than discussing any other human capacity to alter the natural world. I take this position as a result of Judaism's teaching that human beings are the most important part of G-d's created universe […]. G-d has entrusted this world to humankind's hands, and the destiny of this world has always been our responsibility and our challenge. Whether or not we live up to that challenge is our calling and essential mission" (Freundel 200, 119).

Secularizing the Judaic vision of the God-nature-man relationship, which essentially means eliminating the notion of God, Stock states:

> "To some, the coming of human-directed change is unnatural because it differs so much from any previous change, but this distinction between the natural and the unnatural is an illusion. We are as natural a part of the world as anything else is, and so is the technology we create […]. Remaking ourselves is the ultimate expression and realization of our humanity" (Stock 2003, 197).

Bibliography

Adorno, T.W./ Horkheimer, M. (2002): Dialectic of Enlightenment. Stanford: Stanford University Press.

Agamben, G. (2004): The Open: Man and Animal. Stanford: Stanford University Press.

Agar, N. (2007): Whereto Transhumanism? The Literature Reaches a Critical Mass. In: The Hastings Center Report 37(3), 12-17.

Annas, G. (2000): The Man on the Moon, Immortality and Other Millennial Myths: The Prospects and Perils of Human Genetic Engineering. In: Emory Law Journal 49(3), 753-82.

Arendt, H. (1998): The Human Condition. Chicago: University of Chicago Press.

Bayertz, K. (1994): GenEthics: Technological Intervention in Human Reproduction as a Philosophical Problem. Cambridge: Cambridge University Press.

Bostrom, N. (2005): In Defence of Posthuman Dignity. In: Bioethics 19(3), 202–214.
Bostrom, N. (2008): Why I Want to be a Posthuman when I Grow Up. In: Gordijn B./ Chadwick, R.F. (eds.): Medical Enhancement and Posthumanity. Dordrecht: Springer, 107-136.

Bostrom, N./ Savulescu, J. (2009): Human Enhancement Ethics: The State of the Debate. In: Savulescu, J./ Bostrom, N. (eds.): Human Enhancement. Oxford et al.: Oxford University Press, 1-22.

Buchanan, A. (2009): Moral Status and Human Enhancement. In: Philosophy and Public Affairs 37(4), 346-381.

Coady, C.A.J. (2009): Playing God. In: Savulescu, J./ Bostrom, N. (eds.): Human Enhancement. Oxford et al.: Oxford University Press, 155-180.

Freundel, B. (2000): Gene Modification Technology. In: Stock, G./ Campbell, J.H. (eds.): Engineering the Human Germline: An Exploration of the Science and Ethics of Altering the Genes We Pass to Our Children. Oxford et al.: Oxford University Press, 119-122.

Fukuyama, F. (2002): Our Posthuman Future: Consequences of the Biotechnological Revolution. New York: Farrar, Straus & Giroux.

Habermas, J. (2003): The Future of Human Nature. Cambridge: Polity.

Harris, J. (2007): Enhancing Evolution: The Ethical Case for Making Better People. Princeton et al.: Princeton University Press.

Heidegger, M. (1967): Sein und Zeit. Pfullingen: Neske.

Heidegger, M. (1976): Brief über den 'Humanismus'. In: Heidegger, M.: Wegmarken. Gesamtausgabe (Vol. 9). Frankfurt am Main: Klostermann.

Heidegger, M. (1998): On the Essence and Concept of Physis in Aristotle's Physics B, I. In: McNeill, W (ed.): Pathmarks. Cambridge: Cambridge University Press.

Jonas, H, (1984): The Imperative of Responsibility: In Search of an Ethics for the Technological Age. Chicago et al.: University of Chicago Press.

Jonas, H, (1985): Technik, Medizin und Ethik. Frankfurt am Main: Suhrkamp.

Juengst, E.T. (2009): What's Taxonomy Got to Do with It? 'Species Integrity', Human Rights, and Science Policy. In: Savulescu, J./ Bostrom, N. (eds.): Human Enhancement. Oxford et al.: Oxford University Press, 43-58.

Kant, I. (1993): Grounding for the Metaphysics of Morals. Indianapolis: Hackett.

Nozick, R. (1974): Anarchy, State, and Utopia. New York: Basic Books.

Parens, E. (2009). Toward a More Fruitful Debate About Enhancement. In: Savulescu, J./ Bostrom, N. (eds.): Human Enhancement. Oxford et al.: Oxford University Press, 181-198.

Pico della Mirandola, G. (1990): De Homins Dignitate. Hamburg: Meiner.

Prainsack, B. (2006): Negotiating Life: The Regulation of Human Cloning and Embryonic Stem Cell Research in Israel. In: Social Studies of Science 36(2), 173-205.

Rahner, K. (1970): Zum Problem der genetischen Manipulation aus der Sicht des Theologen. In: Wagner, F. (ed.): Menschenzüchtung: Das Problem der genetischen Manipulierung des Menschen. München: C. H. Beck, 135-166.

Resnik, D.B. (2007): Embryonic Stem Cell Patens and Human Dignity. In: Health Care Analysis 15(3), 211-222.

Sandel, M.J. (2009): The Case Against Perfection: What's Wrong with Designer Children, Bionic Athlets, and Genetic Engineering. In: Savulescu, J./ Bostrom, N. (eds.): Human Enhancement. Oxford et al.: Oxford University Press, 71-90.

Savulescu, J. (2009): The Human Prejudice and the Moral Status of Enhanced Beings: What Do We Owe the Gods?. In: Savulescu, J./ Bostrom, N. (eds.): Human Enhancement. Oxford et al.: Oxford University Press, 211-250.

Silver, L.M. (1997): Remaking Eden: Cloning and Beyond in a Brave New World. New York: Avon Books.

Sloterdijk, P. (1999): Regeln für den Menschenpark. Frankfurt am Main: Suhrkamp.

Stock, G. (2003): Redesigning Humans: Choosing our Genes, Changing our Future. New York: Mariner Books

Evolution

Steve Fuller

1. Posthumanism and Transhumanism as Alternative Takes on Evolution

My understanding of the difference between *posthumanism* and *transhumanism* turns on a point of logic. Whereas posthumanism is normally presumed to be a general movement of which transhumanism is a specific version, I treat the two movements as mutually exclusive. The typical starting point for a discussion of post- or transhumanism is a general dissatisfaction with the current state of humanity and a feeling that – for better or worse and by design or not – we are on the verge of an ontological step-change, on the other side of which will be beings fundamentally different from ourselves. In this context, the "transhumanists" are simply those who take deliberate steps in this direction through, say, various forms of "enhancements". My rather different take on the matter comes from grounding the distinction in a normative rather than an empirical premise: In particular, transhumanism, which I broadly support, involves a desire to intensify and extend uniquely human properties beyond their normal physical parameters, whereas posthumanism, which I broadly oppose, involves an indifference if not hostility to the original humanist project. Starkly put, posthumanism is *anti-humanist*, while transhumanism is *ultra-humanist*. My paradigm case for each in today's world is, respectively, Peter Singer and Ray Kurzweil.

Four questions may be asked to distinguish *posthumanists* and *transhumanists*:

(1) What is your default attitude towards humanism? Do you believe that it was always a bad idea, the narcissistic ideology of an elite that only served to alienate and subordinate not only most so-called humans but also the rest of nature? Or, do you believe that humanism's historic excesses merely reflect the arrested development of a fundamentally sound ideal that will be more fully realized once we manage to reorganize ourselves and the environment, perhaps involving a scientifically informed sense of global governance?

(2) What is the source of the conflict between science and religion that has been so prominent in the modern history of the West? Do you believe that it lies in the Abrahamic religions' continued privileging of the human as the locus of meaning in nature, despite the successive displacements of human uniqueness wrought by Copernicus, Darwin and Freud? Or, do you believe that the conflict is simply a reflection of science's increasing capacity to deliver on the promises of the Abrahamic religions by demonstrating how we might turn nature, including our own animal natures, to realize our divine potential?

(3) How do you see Homo sapiens in the context of evolutionary history? Do you believe that the highly developed cerebral cortex that marks our species is little more than an entrenched genetic quirk that will eventually undermine our descendants, once the environment turns that quirk into a liability? Or, do you believe that the special powers enabled by our cerebral cortex provide an opportunity for us to break free from biological evolution altogether, say, by developing means for our uniquely human qualities to migrate from their current carbon-based containers to more hospitable, possibly silicon-based ones?

(4) Is there some normatively desirable intentional relationship in which a successor species should stand to us and our ancestors? Do you believe that evolution is so blind that it would make as little sense for a successor species to think of itself as improving upon what we had been trying to do as for us to think that we are advancing projects initiated by our simian ancestors? Or, do you believe that the legitimacy of any future transformation of the human condition, however fundamental, depends on the counterfactual prospect that we and our illustrious ancestors would recognize it as contributing to realizing our deepest aspirations?

In response to each question, *posthumanists* take the *former* option, *transhumanists* the *latter*. The differences may be epitomized as one of historiographical perspective. The "transhumanist" supposes that life is purposeful not simply at any given moment for a given organism but in its entirety – it has an overall direction. In this context, "humanity" is the name used to personify the leading edge of this overall process. In contrast, the "posthumanist" supposes that "humanity" simply names a transient species within life's flow that, to be sure, has its own perspective on the overall process but no special vantage point. As a first pass, this distinction reproduces the two main modern evolutionary frameworks – the teleological Lamarckian one (transhumanist) and the non-teleological Darwinian one (posthumanist).

2. Is Evolution Something that One Overcomes or to Which One Submits?

The above distinction in evolutionary perspectives also resonates with two different thresholds one might set for "consciousness": *intentionality* (i.e. thought reaching beyond itself to something desired) and *sentience* (i.e. thought as a self-satisfying experience). The former veers transhumanist, the latter posthumanist. However, as the Italian postmodern theorist Giorgio Agamben (1998) has argued, distinctions of this sort have been historically difficult to uphold. In particular, the more one has believed that the purposes of humanity extend beyond living human bodies, the greater the tendency to treat those (including our own) bodies instrumentally and perhaps even inhumanely. Indeed, today's ethical trans- and posthumanist struggles were already prefigured in 16th century diplomatic controversies over actions taken against individuals for "reason of state".

Both sides of the legal debate claimed to speak on behalf of "humanity", yet what the proto-posthumanist defenders of the integrity of the individual called "torture", the proto-transhumanist defenders of state prerogative termed "sacrifice". In this context, Hobbes' *Leviathan* appears as a blueprint for "Transhumanism 1.0", namely, the corporate android, the literal "body politic" whose cells, tissues and organs are perpetually regenerated by each new generation of individual humans who agree to be bound by the social contract. Kant may be seen as a Hobbesian who justifies the psychic transformation of successive generations of citizens who internalize the state perspective as their own, so as to interpret sacrifice as a personal obligation to embrace pain in the name of a higher, if not ultimate, sense of self-realization.

Today's trans- and posthumanist struggles are perhaps more recognizably traced to the vivisection movement championed by Thomas Henry Huxley in the 1870s on behalf of Britain's emerging biomedical establishment, but opposed by the Society for the Prevention of Cruelty to Animals (SPCA). Posthumanists follow the SPCA in taking the metaphysical backdrop of Darwin's original formulation of the theory of evolution by natural selection more seriously than did his great defender Huxley: No matter how much we may succeed in turning other species and the environment to human advantage, we are ultimately overwhelmed by nature. While this perspective, familiar from Epicurus and his followers in the ancient world, enables one to be open to the welfare of other creatures subject to a similar fate and humanity's affiliations with them (including quite unconventional "hybrid" ones), there is no sense that significant long-term change will come from the sort of concerted human intervention normally associated with implementing a long-term, large-scale plan. Here the denial of human *control* should not be confused with the lack of human *impact*, which posthumanists easily grant, especially when bemoaning "anthropogenic" climate change.

The emphasis that posthumanists place on Darwin's own understanding of evolution is reminiscent of "Primitive Christianity", whose legitimacy rests on accessing an "original" understanding of Christ's message stripped of clerical and theological baggage. The secular analogue of such baggage is an exaggerated faith in our "biotech century" (see Rifkin 1998) born of the history of the biomedical sciences *after* Darwin. *On the Origin of Species*, it should be recalled, was published a half-century before the rediscovery of Mendelian genetics and a century before the discovery of DNA's double-helix structure. Darwin himself was pessimistic about our ability to fathom the inner workings of life and arguably did not believe that life was tractable to mechanistic explanations at all, let alone the sorts of computer simulations of evolutionary history on the cutting edge of Neo-Darwinian research (e.g. Lenski et al. 2003). His own view of humanity's fate was probably rather close to that of the late Stephen Jay Gould, whose own research expertise followed Darwin's in stressing the field over the laboratory. To underscore our ephemeral cosmic status, Gould (1989) notoriously claimed that were the tape of evolutionary history replayed, *Homo sapiens* would probably not feature in it at all.

Posthumanists reject the historically most powerful reason for believing that humans might exceed other creatures in their control over nature – namely, the biblical doctrine of *imago dei,* i.e. that humans are created in image and likeness of the creative deity. The biblical prerogative is asserted even in the opening paragraph of the supposedly secular *Leviathan*, and perhaps unsurprisingly this unquestioned adherence to species chauvinism, or "speciesism", has been invoked by posthumanists to explain the failure of Marxism as a political project (see Singer 1999). For the posthumanist, the sense in which "natural selection" is an extension of "artificial selection", the means by which humans have domesticated nature, is merely *analogical*, not *univocal* – to recall the distinction that the medieval scholastics drew with regard to the semantics of God-talk. In other words, natural selection (formerly God) should not be seen as simply a much more powerful version of our plant and animal breeding practices (i.e. univocally), which might suggest that humans are uniquely placed to acquire nature's own powers in the future. Rather, the way we breed plants and animals gives us an intuitive sense of how patterns of biological descent *might* have arisen in nature – but it does not license any deeper sense of identity in the *modus operandi* of the two modes of selection. It is thus unclear exactly which, if any, of the surface similarities between artificial and natural selection are meant to be indicative of a common causal source (e.g. an overlap between human and divine intelligence).

It is worth observing that the original Protestant reformers derided the analogical approach of the Catholics as "equivocal" because it served to allay doubts in the faithful about God's existence and efficacy without empowering them to decide how to act on their understanding of God. Nevertheless, such uncertainty bred by an analogical sensibility helps to explain Darwin's refusal to endorse the "positive" eugenics schemes of his cousin Francis Galton, which aimed to increase the likelihood of humanity's epistemically progressive traits. Galton's more univocal, transhumanist perspective on evolution may be dubbed "Genetically Modified Darwinism", whereby we come to beat nature at its own game by mastering the laws of heredity. Indeed, the underground prehistory of transhumanism includes various attempts – say, from US developmental psychologist James Mark Baldwin to the UK animal geneticist Conrad Waddington – to simulate Lamarckian evolution by strictly Darwinian means (see Dickens 2000). Their broad common goal was to explain the apparent inheritance of acquired traits as a macro-level consequence of selection pressures on a population by proposing that those individuals already capable of expressing the requisite traits in a changed environment are reproductively advantaged. Thus, over time economic classes could morph into biological races that amount to a caste system.

Of course, the meaning of "inheritance of acquired traits" has become more fluid with recent advances in gene therapy and other forms of biotechnology that permit strategic intervention (what theologians might regard, perhaps with some consternation, as "intelligent design") at both ante- and post-natal stages. In this context, one nowadays often speaks of a revival of the early modern idea of "epigenesis" through the emerging science of "epigenetics" (see Shenk 2010). In its original 18th century context, epigenesis was one side of a dispute about how to interpret microscope-based experiments concerning an organism's pattern of development. The other side was preformation. At stake, we might now say, was whether development was "matter-led" (epigenesis) or "form-led" (preformation). In the former case, the organism as it matures is open to multiple paths of development, which in the end is determined by environmental input. In the latter case, the organism has a predetermined path of development that ultimately overcomes whatever interference the environment provides. In the language of systems theory, classical epigenesis was committed to "plurifinality", preformation to "equifinality".[1]

The two great 19th century evolutionists, Lamarck and Darwin, both more concerned with the natural history of entire species than the life trajectory of particular individuals, may be seen as having held opposing combinations of these two views. Lamarck was an epigenesist about individual lives but a preformationist about natural history as a whole: He believed that individuals could improve upon their inheritance in ways that brought their offspring closer to some ideal state of being. In contrast, Darwin was normally read as a preformationist about individual lives but an epigenesist about the overall course of natural history: For him, the largely genetically fixed nature of organisms discouraged any hope for indefinite survival, let alone improvement, against an en-

---

1 In the context of historiography, Fuller (2008) has referred to "underdetermination" versus "overdetermination".

vironment possessing no concerns of its own, let alone those of particular organisms.

The emerging science of epigenetics renders the workings of epigenesis more transparent and hence more controllable. Unlike the 20th century-style "Genetically Modified Darwinism" discussed above, epigenesis-based policies favouring transhumanism need not be limited to realizing individual genetic potential by matching the right genomes to the right general environments. Rather, they can draw on the finding that genomic expression as such requires exposure to the environment, especially via the chemical process of "DNA methylation", which has been experimentally induced in animals to switch specific genes on and off (see Borghol et al. 2012). By undergoing this specific process, so say today's epigenesists, organisms come to possess determinate traits, which they then maintain in the face of subsequent environmental changes and their offspring find easier to express.

At first glance, epigenetics appears to shift the evolution's horizons away from Darwin's back to Lamarck's, except that Lamarck portrayed animals as deliberately changing their genetic makeup through willed effort, whereas epigenetics is, strictly speaking, about the completion of one's genetic makeup, which at birth is still not fully formed. In this respect, epigenetics challenges an assumption shared by Lamarck and Darwin – namely, that we are born with a determinate genetic makeup. This shared assumption underwrote Galton's 1874 christening of "nature" and "nurture" as the two independent variables involved in an organism's development. However, epigenetics would have us revisit the older debate between epigenesis and preformation. It was concerned not with the extent to which an organism can overcome its genetic load, but rather the extent to which an organism constitutes a relatively open or closed system. From this standpoint, transhumanists differ from posthumanists in their willingness to engage in epigenetic interventions to reach a desirable closure to the genome's makeup, whereas posthumanists doubt the long-term efficacy of such efforts at strategic closure. For them all living systems are irrevocably open.

But of course, in trying to better realize specifically human properties that happen to have originated in our carbon-based history, transhumanists may find persisting along strictly biogenetic lines unduly limiting. It would be as if someone in the late 19th century were to argue that the best way to secure personal transport in a world that increasingly values speed and mobility is to breed faster and more agile horses rather than abandon animal conveyance altogether and invent something entirely different (e.g. the automobile) that can achieve these aims at a lower cost. In that respect, Al Gore may not have been so wide of the mark when he spoke of the internet in the 1990s as an "information superhighway". However, he probably did not anticipate that it would involve radically refashioning ourselves as more efficient transport vehicles. In particular, I mean the migration of that ontic talisman of humanism – "consciousness" – from the carbon-based bodies of our birth to some more durable medium identified as a cyborg, android or perhaps even a simulated "second life".

3. Evolution's Normative Implications in a Post- and Transhumanist Key

The increasing salience of the post- and transhumanist distinction suggests that had Galton not been Darwin's cousin, Darwin might never have been associated with eugenics at all. After all, Darwin coupled an empirically comprehensive account of natural history with a world-view that denies our capacity to direct its future significantly. The lumping together of Darwin, Spencer, T. H. Huxley and Galton as "Social Darwinists" reflected Ernst Haeckel's omnibus importation of their ideas to Germany, which spread through the "racial hygiene" movement that flourished in medical schools in the half-century prior to Hitler (see Proctor 1988). However, from today's standpoint, we would say that the more *laissez faire* Darwin and Spencer were "posthumanist evolutionists", whereas the more interventionist Huxley and Galton were "transhumanist evolutionists". At stake in their late Victorian heyday was the soul of "liberalism", the political ideology most closely aligned to humanism: Should it stand for nature taking its course or for us to steer an otherwise directionless nature? In the 20th century, the former veered right (e.g. Hayek) to neo-liberalism, the latter veered left (e.g. Keynes) to welfare statism (see Fuller 2011, chap. 5).

Of course, Galton himself did not succeed in mastering the laws of heredity, but 20th century genetics was populated by some rather heterodox Christians who interpreted the charge of "playing God" as a literal extension of our divinely mandated stewardship of the Earth: e.g. Ronald Fisher, Sewall Wright, and most notably Theodosius Dobzhansky (1967). We might even reach back to Gregor Mendel, the long-neglected Moravian monk who first demonstrated heredity's most basic statistical laws. His mentor was a devotee of the Unitarian preacher and radical chemist, Joseph Priestley, who clearly tied human emancipation from its fallen animal state to our impending control over the forces of nature (see Wood/ Orel 2005; Fuller 2011, chap. 4). Moreover, the two figures most closely associated with the original mid-20th century usage of "transhumanism", Julian Huxley (grandson of Thomas Henry) and Pierre Teilhard de Chardin (1961 [1955]), saw the transition from Christian theology through evolutionary science to an evolutionary humanism as a seamless process of divine self-realization (see Fuller 2007b, chap. 5).

In this context, Jesus symbolizes the continuing need to attend to persistent features of the human condition – notably poverty and injustice – that inhibit our divine potential. The difference between Huxley, who called himself a "humanist", and Teilhard, who called himself a "Christian", was that Huxley treated universal self-consciousness as an emergent feature of the evolution of matter, whereas Teilhard retained the Abrahamic idea that God pre-exists matter but creates by steering the evolutionary process. But in both cases, each human being is presumed to be of value as a unique participant in a superorganism, typically modelled on a world-brain, what Teilhard called the "noösphere". The idea was already present in Condorcet's defense of increased human population growth as a vehicle for the "hominization" of the world, the ultimate materialization of Enlightenment ideals (see Fuller 2006, chap. 13). Historians have tended to treat this continuity between Christianity and the Enlightenment as a mere atavism, what Carl Becker (1932) famously called "the heavenly city of the eighteenth-century philosophers". However, it is perhaps better understood as a moment in Christianity's evolution to transhumanism, in which Hobbes' absolute sovereign, Comte's positivist church and perhaps even the Marxist ideal of a global Communist order also serve as way stations.

Clearly, unlike the posthumanist and much more than the classical humanist, the transhumanist sees our overdeveloped cerebral cortex – the seat of intelligence – as less an biological accident than a harbinger of things to come. In the transhumanist case, it might even involve abandoning biology for technology as the relevant medium for our evolutionary future. But how are we to understand this promised advance in intellectual powers? Without resorting to science fiction, the most natural place to look is to the self-transcending forms of cognition that have been put forward by philosophers and theologians, especially when defining the overlap between human and divine being. Perhaps the clearest secular philosophical residue of this line of thought is so-called *a priori* knowledge, which supposedly enables us to grasp basic structural features of reality with relatively minimal sensory input, as if our being were not confined to our animal bodies.

Great claims have been made about the reach of such knowledge, usually inspired by the universal applicability of mathematics (see Wigner 1960). Thus, Leibniz held that through "intellectual intuition" one might infer the laws of nature by feats of heroic abstraction tantamount to adopting God's standpoint, the proverbial "view from nowhere". Kant famously debunked such alleged powers of mind as empirically unsubstantiated assumptions that nonetheless may be psychologically required to underwrite our continuing faith in science. However, Kant's strictures were rendered obsolete within a century as the empirically unrestricted mathematical imagination managed to anticipate forms of experience (e.g. non-Euclidean geometry, transfinite set theory) that resulted in revolutions in physics and logic in the early 20th century. Moreover, the increasing migration of scientific inquiry to the virtual reality of computer simulations in the late 20th century adds to the sense that perhaps our capacity for intellectual intuition needs to be taken more seriously (see Horgan 1996).

Health policy provides a prism from which to witness the different evolutionary assumptions of post- and transhumanists in action. Humanists, influenced by the Abrahamic privileging of our species being, have supported scientific research and clinical practice designed to keep the entire human body functioning as long as possible, regardless of cost. Of course, this principle has been applied across the age spectrum from the unborn to the very old, including the multiply disabled. Clearly, then, humanism is ideologically promiscuous: Both the Left and the Right can claim its arguments. The same promiscuity applies to posthumanists, who are more concerned with the promotion of life as such than human life specifically. They have supported both the traditional medical idea of a "good death" (once a "good life" can no longer be led) and the more modern idea of life's efficient servicing by treating everyone as potential "organ donors", including to other species, where appropriate. The practical implications of the posthumanist ideal – perhaps with a jibe at Peter Singer – are vividly on display in Utilitaria, one of the destinations of the fictional Professor Caritat (Condorcet's family name) in Steven Lukes' (1996) recent update of *Gulliver's Travels*. For their part, transhumanist visitors to Utilitaria would be less troubled by the radical utilitarian framework for welfare provision, with its apparent disregard for the integrity of organisms, than Utilitaria's normative commitment to a steady-steady ecology whereby life is simply recycled but never improved.

In contrast, a good entry point into transhumanist health policy is to recall the special value attached to human intelligence. Thus, a premium would be placed on preserving a recently deceased human brain, perhaps cryogenically or attached to some suitable electro-chemical medium, for future resurrection. In the long run, transhumanists would like to overcome the leakage problems of "wetware" altogether by enabling one's world-view, if not personality, to be uploaded to a silicon chip that is then implanted in an android. Once again, they prove themselves to be much less carbon-fetishists than either humanists or posthumanists – and hence happier to deviate from the Darwinian sense of biological evolution.

Indeed, transhumanists would prefer to keep the DNA of various species, including *Homo sapiens*, on tap for discretionary use than sustain the fully matured bodies of such species in well-policed ecologies. In the end, these ecologies amount to no more than global projections of zoological and botanical gardens – exactly how Linnaeus originally saw them in the 18th century, when promoting their construction in order to re-instate humanity's biblical prerogative, which he took to involve recovering the conditions that had obtained in Garden of Eden (see Koerner 1999). While today's transhumanists can hardly object to Linnaeus' anthropocentric biosphere, as beneficiaries of subsequent developments in genetics and molecular biology, they are more likely to look to the storage facilities of laboratories than outdoor gardens, however well-managed, to house organic paradigms for technologies that enhance our own capacity for survival and extension – a field nowadays known as "biomimetics" (see Benyus 1997).

Finally, a key site for exploring the transhumanist evolutionary sensibilities is so-called interspecies research, which ranges from the implantation of human stem cells in a mouse embryo to the transplantation of organs from a genetically modified pig into a human body. In the former case, the mouse is used as a breeding ground for human organs; in the latter, the pig is actually bred to provide those organs (see Bonnicksen 2009). At first glance, both humanists and transhumanists can support interspecies research because of the priority it gives to the promotion of human welfare. But humanists would be less eager than transhumanists to license an open-ended exploratory approach to transgenic organisms, which may result in new living beings, so-called "chimeras" and "hybrids" that threaten to impose new ethical burdens on humans. Such qualms would not arise for transhumanists, who take a more instrumental attitude towards animal embodiment, reflecting a generally demystified attitude towards the very idea of an organism.

However, the prospect that these transgenic entities may be ends in their own right – and not mere means to human ends – engages posthumanists in the moral discussion surrounding interspecies research, in which they become the protectors of "life itself". One prospect on the horizon that would bring together transhumanist and posthumanist conceptions of evolution is the rise of "systems" or "living" architecture, in which organisms are embedded – and in some cases engineered – to complement the lifecycle of ordinary construction materials, so as to provide for more ecologically integrated buildings capable of literally repairing themselves with minimal human intervention (see Armstrong 2009). This would be an instance of a posthumanist sensibility embedded within a transhumanist one that in the short term supports our lingering commitment to humanism.

Bibliography

Agamben, G. (1998): Homo Sacer: Sovereign Power and Bare Life. Palo Alto(CA): Stanford University Press.

Armstrong, R. (2009). Protocells and Plectic Systems Architecture. In: Sophia 3, 17. http://www.ucl.ac.uk/~ucbpeal/sophia/issue3-web.pdf (accessed July 14, 2013).

Becker, C. (1932): The Heavenly City of the Eighteenth-Century Philosophers. New Haven(CT): Yale University Press.

Benyus, J. (1997): Biomimicry. New York: William Morrow.

Bonnicksen, A. (2009): Chimeras, Hybrids and Interspecies Research: Politics and Policymaking. Washington, D.C.: Georgetown University Press.

Borghol, N, et al. (2012): Associations With Early-Life Socio-Economic Position in Adult DNA Methylation. International Journal of Epidemiology 41(1), 62-74.

Dickens, P. (2000): Social Darwinism: Linking Evolutionary Thought to Social Theory. Milton Keynes: Open University Press.

Dobzhansky, T. (1967). The Biology of Ultimate Concern. New York: New American Library.

Fuller, S. (2006): The New Sociological Imagination. London: Sage.

Fuller, S. (2007a): New Frontiers in Science and Technology Studies. Cambridge: Polity.

Fuller, S. (2007b): Science vs. Religion? Intelligent Design and the Problem of Evolution. Cambridge: Polity.

Fuller, S. (2008): The Normative Turn: Counterfactuals and a Philosophical Historiography of Science. In: Isis 99(3), 576-84.

Fuller, S. (2011): Humanity 2.0: What It Means to Be Human Past, Present and Future. London: Palgrave Macmillan.

Horgan, J. (1996): The End of Science. Reading(MA): Addison-Wesley.

Koerner, L. (1999): Linnaeus: Nature and Nation. Cambridge(MA): Harvard University Press.

Lenski, R., et al. (2003): The Evolutionary Origin of Complex Features. In: Nature 423, 139-144.

Lukes, S. (1996): The Curious Enlightenment of Professor Caritat. London: Verso.

Proctor, R. (1988): Racial Hygiene: Medicine under the Nazis. Cambridge(MA): Harvard University Press.

Rifkin, J. (1998): The Biotech Century. New York: J.P. Tarcher.

Shenk, D. (2010): The Genius in All of Us. New York: Doubleday.

Singer, P. (1999): A Darwinian Left. London: Weidenfeld & Nicolson.

Teilhard de Chardin, P. (1961 [1955]): The Phenomenon of Man. New York et al.: Harper & Row.

Wigner, E. (1960): The Unreasonable Effectiveness of Mathematics in the Natural Sciences. In: Communications on Pure and Applied Mathematics 13(1), 1-14.

Wood, R./ Orel, V. (2005): Scientific Breeding in Central Europe in the Early Nineteenth Century: Background to Mendel's Later Work. In: Journal of the History of Biology 38(2), 239-272.

The Body

Francesca Ferrando

The 21st century has ushered in a redefinition of the body by cybernetic and biotechnological developments. As we[1] shall see in this article, the concept of "human" has been broadly challenged, while "posthuman" and "transhuman" have become terms of philosophical and scientific enquiry. Physicality no longer represents the primary space for social interaction: the decentralization of the self into virtual bodies and digital identities has turned Baudrillard's simulacra into ultimate hyper-realities, as the growing issue of internet addiction seems to suggest. Human cloning has approached bioethical disputes and surrogate motherhood is deconstructing natural conception. The semantic demarcation between humans and cyborgs[2] has blurred. On one side, electronic pacemakers, high-tech prostheses, and plastic surgery have become accepted practices of body reconfiguration. On the other, following the route opened by Project Cyborg 2.0,[3] a growing number of people have begun inserting RFIDs under their skin, in a pioneer experimentation towards technological enhancement.[4] Are these scenarios, which characterize some hyper-technological macro and micro societies of planet Earth,[5] inducing a paradigm shift in the ontological and epistemological perception of the human body? If so, will gender, race, age and class among others, represent significant categories of reformulation? More radically, from a futuristic perspective: will posthumans need any embodiment at all? Posthumanism and transhumanism offer different answers to these questions. Before presenting them, I first need to analyze key concepts such as "human", "body" and "embodied self." I will delve into each of them independently, in order to trace a rhizomatic map of intellectual exploration and academic rigor.

---

1 The use of "we" is strategically employed not to fall into the illusionary suggestion that this text is somehow non-human centric. According to the feminist policy of "situating": I was born in a human body, I am writing in a human language, and I am expressing a human body of thoughts to other human readers. Still, humans radically differ from each other on a social, political, and individual level.

2 The term "cyborg" was coined in 1960 by Manfred Clynes and Nathan Kline, and refers to a being constituted by both biological and artificial parts (see Clynes/ Kline 1960).

3 On March 2002 a one hundred electrode array was surgically implanted into the left arm of Professor Kevin Warwick (see Warwick 2004).

4 There is not enough data available yet to determine the long term side effects of such implants on humans.

5 I would rather use this geo-political characterization instead of broadly applied "Western societies", to indulge into a more precise account of glocalized (the survival of local specificities in a globalized world) policies.

The Body

"Body" is an English term used to define a broad human notion which describes, amongst other meanings: "the physical structure and material substance of an animal or plant, living or dead", "a person", "a collective group." Still, when we think of bodies, the human body is the first signified to come to mind, exposing the human-centric dialectics of the term. Do animals,[6] plants and machines have bodies as humans do? "Body" is a human concept created in a human language. While its connotations may vary depending on context and association (i.e. the animal body, the plant body, the mechanic body, that is, the automata), the denotation of the body *is* the human body. And still, such a denotation manifests itself as an assemblage of different connotations. Phenomenologically, the human body appears multiple and situated. Its symbolic meaning and social reception might shift depending on its gender, race, age, ethnicity, physical – plus intellectual – capabilities; and on cultural, historical and economic contexts. The body itself is constantly reshaping and defining its boundaries – think of the pregnant body, the menstruating body, the aging body, the sick body. Signifier for an extensive range of signifieds (including apparent dichotomies such as dead/alive, person/group; and relevant differences such as human/animal/plant), the body reveals its inner dynamics as well as its absolute centrality to the construction of taxonomical accounts; its ontological configuration can hardly be separated from detecting its epistemes[7] and epistemological outfits.

How We Became Humans

The word "human" derives from Latin "humanus", an adjective cognate to "humus" meaning "earth[8], ground, soil", on notion of "earthly beings" whose symbolic realm would mark the border with the one of the celestial gods. The Earth is the third planet in order from the Sun. Evidence suggests that life on this globe has existed for about 3.5 billion years. There is no scientific consensus on how it originated, but all known life forms share fundamental molecular mechanisms, supporting the hypothesis of the last universal ancestor (LUA), a primor-

---

6 For a philosophical account on the animal as a homogeneous set deprived of the *logos* – from Aristotle to Heidegger, from Descartes to Kant – see, for instance, Derrida (2008).

7 I am referring to the use of the term, as elaborated by Michel Foucault in *The Order of Things*: "the epistemological field, the episteme in which knowledge […] manifests a history which is not that of its growing perfection, but rather that of its conditions of possibility" (1970 [1966], xxii).

8 Not to be confused with "Terra", the Latin translation for Earth – which, at the time, was not yet conceived as a planet.

dial single cell organism from which all life forms would descend[9]. In the evolutionary history of life, which focuses on the evolution of living and fossil organisms, the term "human" refers to the *Homo* genus, and includes not only modern humans (*Homo sapiens*), but other species closely related and now extinct. From a posthumanist perspective, it is important to observe that the earliest evidence of stone tool usage precedes the paleontological advent of *Homo*: technology is not something separated from the human, but can be seen as a mode of biological revealing.[10]

Still, the scientific classification of humans has considerably changed over time and its exact makeup is constantly under debate, blurring the lines between the ontological, epistemological and methodological dimensions of human cognition. A notable date in this genealogy is 1758,[11] when Carl Linnaeus coined the binomial name "*Homo sapiens*" (Latin for "knowing man"), referring to the only living species in the *Homo* genus. Paralleling, Linnaeus also coined the term "*Mammalia*", addressing the group of animals named after their mammary glands. For the first time in Western history, humans were placed in a system of biological classification like any other animal or plant species. Yet, this terminology – which is still in use today – clearly reflects sexist biases. As Londa Schiebinger has pointed out:

> "[…] the mammae are 'functional' in only half of this group of animals (the females) and, among those, for a relatively short period of time (during lactation) or not at all. As we shall see, Linnaeus could indeed have chosen a more gender-neutral term, such as *Aurecaviga* (the hollow-eared ones) or *Pilosa* (the hairy ones)" (Schiebinger 2000, 11-12).

While the term "mammal", which is related to female biology and stresses human specificities,[12] is used to place the human species into the larger natural system; the term *Homo sapiens* emphasizes the human cognitive functions within a

9 Note that the hypothesis of LUA can also be based upon non-unitarian origins (see Woese 1998).

10 While technology is still often addressed as an external source which might guarantee humanity a place in post-biological futures, the non-separateness between the human and the techno realm shall be investigated not only as an anthropological (see Gehlen 1980 [1957]) and paleontological issue (see Leroi-Gourhan 1943; 1993 [1964]), but also as an ontological one (see Heidegger 1977 [1954]; Stiegler 1998).

11 1758 is the date of the tenth edition of *Systema Naturae* (first edition: 1735), which is considered the starting point of modern botanical and zoological taxonomy.

12 Human children have the longest infancy in the animal kingdom.

male frame,[13] and is applied to mark the distinction between humans and other primates, revealing the inner sexism and speciesism of both notions.

Which Humans are Human?

Historically, the recognition of the human status has been regularly switched on and off. In the American system of slavery, for instance, captives were considered property to the extent that, in some cases, owners had legal rights to kill them.[14] In Nazi Germany (1933-1945), this pattern reached a dramatic apex. The Nazis, as stated by Kete:

> "[…] abolished the line separating human and animal and articulated a new hierarchy based on race, which placed certain species – races – of animals above 'races' of humans – eagles and wolves and pigs in the new human hierarchy were placed above Poles and rats and Jews" (Kete 2002, 20).

The dissolution of the animal/human divide was sealed in blood. The Nazis exterminated approximately six million[15] European Jews and millions of others, including: Germans with mental and physical disabilities, homosexuals, Roma ("Gypsies"), Poles, Jehovah's Witnesses, and Soviet prisoners of war. European witch trials in the Early Modern period, which ended in an estimation of sixty thousand[16] executions (a large majority of women), proved another discontinuity within the human frame: not only the lives of those humans considered inferior could be taken, but also the ones of those who were assumed to be supernatural shall be sacrificed, in order to keep the human realm safe. The witch-hunt proved superstition as one of the hidden forces behind law making apparatuses, next to biological determinism, scientific racism and ethnocentrism. Rosi Braidotti points out the superstitious roots of teratology. She redefines the figure of the monster as "a process without a stable object" (Braidotti 1996, 150), historically attributed to different embodiments and to different causes, such as women's power to create – and consequently deform – life. Freak shows were expected to shock the viewers by exhibiting uncanny bodies pertaining to the

13 In Latin "homo" means "man" as "person" or "human", whereas "vir" indicates "man" as opposed to woman or child. Still, it is grammatically expressed strictly in the masculine form, exposing the sexist outline of the Latin language itself.

14 In 1740 South Carolina passed the *Negro Act*, which made it legal for slave owners to kill rebellious slaves.

15 Although it is impossible to determine the exact number of Jewish victims, six million is the round figure accepted by most authorities.

16 This estimate is problematic. Since the murders were not systematically recorded and many of the archives which existed have been lost, the number of deaths could be much higher. Consequently, historians have not settled on a figure.

liminal zone of the human; in Braidotti's words: "we all have bodies, but not all bodies are equal: some matter more than others; some are, quite frankly, disposable" (Braidotti 1996, 136). Geo-historically situated, the human body stands as a symbolic text of cognitive and social processes. The establishment of a discourse of perversion (see Foucault 1998 [1976]) and the consequent practices of normalization of the perverse, such as the Nazi genocide, the witch-hunt and the discipling of the maternal body instrumental to scientific teratology, are embedded to its genealogy, in a recurring paradigm of human abjection.[17]

While the monster and the supernatural stand as social and mythical archetypes delimiting the domain of the comprehensible body, it can be argued that human identity *tout court* has formed, historically and theoretically, through the construction of the "Other": animals, automata, children, women, people of color other than white,[18] queers[19] etc. marking the shifting borders of what would become "the human" through a process of performative rejections. Race being one of the canons, Yancy states:

> "The Black body has been historically marked, disciplined, and scripted and materially, psychologically, and morally invested in to ensure both white supremacy and the illusory construction of the white subject as a self-contained substance whose existence does not depend upon the construction of the Black qua inferior" (Yancy 2008, 1).[20]

If the black body has symbolically and physically represented the working shadow necessary to validate white existence, in this configuration of the human, women have represented the body as the locus of original sin; in the cartesian split, an ontology of metaphysical irrelevance. As Price and Shildrick maintain:

> "At the risk of misleading simplification, it can be argued that the denial of corporeality and the corresponding elevation of mind or spirit marks a transhistorical desire to access the pure Intelligible as the highest form of being" (Price/ Shildrick 1999, 2).

In Western traditions, but not only, the symbolic body of this dualism was female and had two simplified variables of representation: the primordial body (the mother), and the sexual body (the prostitute). On the other side, the body as the norm in biological and medical sciences has been unequivocally male: "Woman, considered a monstrous error of nature, was studied for her deviation

17 And still: the abject is neither subject nor object, but precedes the symbolic order (see Kristeva 1982).

18 For an extensive reflection on the "racial Other", see Goldberg (1993).

19 For a critical reading of the human rooted in queer theory, see Butler (2004, 2), where she states: "If I am a certain gender, will I still be regarded as part of the 'human'?"

20 Thanks to Prof. Jean-Marie, for bringing this text to my attention.

from (the) male norm" (Schiebinger 1999, 27), in a schizophrenic attempt to pose a symbolic body with a sex but without organs, and a clinical body with organs but without sex – neutral, that is, white[21] and male.

Embodied Selves

Humans are embodied, and so is human thought, human language and human phenomenological reception. The 1970s marked a blast of critical approaches to "the neutral subject". In the historical and philosophical frame of postmodernism, feminist, black, gay and lesbian, postcolonial theorists, together with differently abled activists and other outsiders, pointed out the partiality of the construction of the discourse.[22] Irigaray has brilliantly used the image of the "Speculum" (see Irigaray 1985) to refer to the symbolic Woman of this structural account as the dark continent, the irrational, the unknowable. The Seventies also marked the official birth of animal rights, for which animals should be viewed as non-human persons and members of the moral community. In this context, the term "speciesism" was popularized (see Singer 1975) to name the practice of privileging humans over other animals. Ecofeminism marked a new wave of environmentalism based on parallels between the oppression and subordination of women and nature in Western cultural traditions (see Merchant 1980), while accounts of different societies based on matriarchy and worshipping the Goddess began to nourish archeological research as, for instance, in the work of Marija Gimbutas (1974). In 1970 Shulamith Firestone published *The Dialectic of Sex*, which offered a philosophical twist to technophobic feminist perspectives: technology could actually open new exciting possibilities by "freeing women from the tyranny of reproduction" (Firestone 1970, 221). Firestone's theoretical approach marked the birth of technofeminism. But could women rely on technology and science? The Nineties saw the rise of Feminist Epistemology. Scientists such as Sandra Harding, Evelyn Fox Keller, and theorists such as Patricia Hill Collins and Helen Longino, argued that objectivity is situated and embodied. In Haraway's words: "Feminist objectivity means quite simple *situated knowledges*" (Haraway 1996, 253). Traditionally, scientific observations have been elaborated from a specific standpoint, which has been: white, Western, economically privileged, heterosexual and male. Technology and science

21 For an account on the role played by race in the production of medical knowledge, see Harding (1993), among others.

22 I am referring not only to the Foucaultian use of the term as a way of constituting knowledge, social practices and power relations (see Foucault 1998 [1976]), but also to the phallogocentric *logos* (see Irigaray 1985 [1974]), and the symbolic order (see Kristeva 1984).

are not free from sexist, racist and Eurocentric biases; their social construction is embedded in their methods and practice.[23]

Posthuman Bodies

Humans are embodied. What about posthumans?

> "Here, at the inaugural moment of the computer age, the erasure of embodiment is performed so that 'intelligence' becomes a property of the formal manipulation of symbols rather than enaction in the human lifeworld" (Hayles 1999, XI).

Following Katherine Hayles' criticism of the erasure of embodiment by the computer age, will the posthuman body still be shaped in terms of gender, race, age, class, (dis)ability and sexuality among others? Namely, will posthumans need to take into account the histories and herstories which have determined the historical configuration of the human body? Posthumanism itself was actually generated from the radical deconstruction of the "Human", which began as a political project in the Seventies and turned into an epistemological one in the Nineties. Posthumanism came along within and after postmodernism. Although the term is already present in *Prometheus as Performer: Toward a Posthumanist Culture?* (see Hassan 1977), posthumanism grew out of literary theory in the 90s, and made its way into philosophy by the end of the 20th century, enacting a thorough critique of humanism and anthropocentrism (Braidotti 2013). And still, posthumanism refers not only to an academic critical position, but also to a perception of the human which is transhistorical.

The hybrid has been part of human symbolic and cultural heritage since the beginning of recorded civilization: from the lion-headed figurine of the Hohlenstein Stadel[24] to the Egyptian sphinx; from Ganesha – the hindu deity with the elephant head – to the biblical devil embodied as a snake in the garden of Eden. The chimera, the masculine minotaur and the feminine harpy are just a few characters of the very fecund Greek mythological parade. Alternative embodiments are contemplated in psychological, spiritual and religious domains. Islam has a foundation in dream initiation: the Isra and Mi'raj – the Night Journey during which Mohammed ascends to heaven and speaks to God – has been described as both a physical and spiritual journey. Altered states of consciousness, trance rituals and psychoactive substances form part of shamanic practices in different traditions, and are aimed to achieve spiritual elaborations of the self

---

23 On the sociology of scientific knowledge, see Latour (1979; 1987).

24 Determined to be about 32.000 years old, this is the oldest known zoomorphic sculpture in the world.

through a mediated perception of the physical body. The Jungian collective unconscious and the paranormal activity can be viewed as other terms of speculative embodiments. What about virtual bodies as contemporary interpretations of the other selves? Following McLuhan's definition of the media as "extensions of man", (see McLuhan 1964) online identities have been regarded as extensions of the self, and as "the second self" (see Turkle 1984). In cybernetics, an avatar indicates one (of many) graphic representation of a user, while its etymology suggests a transcendental nexus: in Sanskrit "avatar" refers to the appearance or manifestation of a deity from heaven to earth, and it is widely translated into English as "incarnation". Extending its enquiry over the boundaries of the scientific domain, and so opening to different types of knowledge and understanding, posthumanism offers a theoretical invitation to think inclusively, in a genealogical relocation of humanity within multiversality ("post-humanism" as a criticism of humanism, anthropocentrism and universe-centrism), and alterity within the self ("posthuman-ism" as a recognition of those aspects which are constitutively human, and still, beyond human comprehension). In this double sense, "posthuman" is becoming a key concept for the past,[25] not only for the present and the future.

Posthumanism radically opens to alterity and extensions of diversity, and thus reflects on alternative human embodiments. More extensively: will *Homo sapiens* evolve into a number of subspecies, as Warwick (1997) predicts? This question leads to conjectures. In the near future some people might migrate to planets other than Earth; due to adaptation, generation after generation their DNA may mutate. Other humans might radically merge with technology and machines, with their descendents evolving specific traits and, ultimately, turning into what has been called "*Homo cyberneticus*." Due to its postmodern roots, posthumanist accounts adopt a strong critical approach, trying to keep *historia magistra vitae* in mind and to dislocate human-centric perspectives. Obviously, since posthumanism is thought by humans, that may prove a hard task. Still, this strong criticism of humanism is crucial for posthumanist reflections, as much as this decentralization does not end in a new structure which simply reverses the traditional one. More than one century ago, Dubois was wondering about race:

> "What shall be its functions in the future? Manifestly, some of the great races of today – particularly the Negro race – have not yet given to civilization the full spiritual message which they are capable of giving" (Dubois 1897, 11).

Emphasizing a comprehensive genealogy of humanity, which strives to dethrone previous monopolies of social identities historically based on hierarchical tax-

---

25 Some authors, for instance, have started to produce posthumanist readings of Plato, Dante, Shakespeare (see Joy/ Dionne [eds.] 2010).

onomies of bodies, posthumanism seems congenial to the social and spiritual realization envisioned by Dubois. We still have to take into account all of human perspectives, in order to praise diversification and not sadomasochistic new accounts of the conflicted, but still egocentric, symbolic white man.[26]

Transhuman Bodies

Just like posthumanism, transhumanism[27] arose as a movement in the late 80s / early 90s, orientating its interests around similar topics. But the two movements do not share the same roots nor perspectives (see Ferrando 2013). While posthumanism comes out of postmodernism, transhumanism seeks its origins in science and technology, especially early ideas about human evolution. It recognizes the Enlightenment as one of its sources, and thus it does not expropriate rational humanism. The concept of posthuman itself is interpreted in a specific transhumanist way. In order to greatly enhance human abilities, transhumanism opts for a radical transformation of the human condition by existing, emerging and speculative technologies (as in the case of regenerative medicine, radical life extension, mind uploading[28] and cryonics); it suggests that diversity and multiplicity will replace the notion of existing within a single system, such as a biological body.[29] For transhumanists, human beings may eventually transform themselves so radically as to become "posthuman." According to Kurzweil:

> "We will continue to have human bodies, but they will become morphable projections of our intelligence. […] Ultimately software-based humans will be vastly extended beyond the severe limitations of humans as we know them today" (Kurzweil 2005, 324-325).

In his democratic transhumanism, Hughes calls for an equal access to these technological enhancements, which could otherwise be limited to certain socio-

---

26 This generic definition mainly refers to the symbolic subject of Western official discourses, assuming that not every embodied white man in history has shared such schemata.

27 The term was coined in 1957 by biologist Julian Huxley.

28 Also defined as "whole brain emulation", mind uploading describes the hypothetical process of transferring or copying a conscious mind from a brain to a non-biological substrate, with the onto-epistemological risks of dualism and mechanism that such a view entails.

29 It is interesting to notice that transhumanists value the human body and advocate self-responsibility in maintaining health and well-being, in order to live longer and keep the biological body alive until other options might become available – I thank Dr. Natasha Vita-More for her input and clarification on this point.

political classes and related to economic power, consequently encoding racial and sexual politics (see Hughes 2004).

Max More defines morphological freedom as "the ability to alter bodily form at will through technologies such as surgery, genetic engineering, nanotechnology, uploading" (More 1993). Natasha Vita-More has been working on the design of a posthuman body for more than ten years. Her project is one of a visionary mind:

> "Affected by this state of progress, human nature is at a crossroads. [...] We are questioning our human biology and challenging what it means to be biological" (Vita-More 2004).

Still, the table that represents some of the differences between the human body and the 21st century Primo Prototype is only part of the story. Primo Prototype figures as "ageless", with "replaceable genes" and "upgrades." The human body, instead, is defined by "limited lifespan", "legacy genes", and by the fact that it "wears out", among other terms. Gender is marked as "restricted" (compared with Primo Posthuman's "changeability"). Race is not mentioned. Age must be overcome. But this human body does not seem to be situated, nor to belong to a genealogy. Most transhumanist accounts on the body lack in philosophical deconstructionism as a theoretical practice. Talking of human embodiment as an outfit which can be conveniently reshaped reveals a reductionist approach, based on the Cartesian body/mind dualism. My question to this seemingly "neutral" body being redesigned is: how are the histories and herstories of the historical human body going to affect our posthuman future? The body, as a biological and figurative locus of socio-political interactions, is hardly neutral; reaffirming its discontinuities, emphasizing differences rather than erasing them when delivering phenomenological accounts of embodied humans, will set a more strategic *terminus a quo* to envision forthcoming posthumanities.

Conclusions

Presenting the ontology of the human body as a performative and pluralistic process interdependent with its taxonomies and epistemologies, provides a theoretical ground and analytical tool to speculate on posthuman bodies. Yet, such a framework might not offer a full spectrum approach to depicting future embodiments. On one side, the concept of "body" is human and, inevitably, human-centric. On the other, "human" is a shifting etiquette which has been historically sustained through generative reformulations of the symbolic "Other"; it has been consequently ascribed within the frame of: speciesism, racism, sexism, heterosexism, ethnocentrism, classism, ageism, elitism and ableism, among other

-isms. Furthermore, it might be unnecessary to think in terms of "post" when referring to the future of humanity, if concepts such as "technology" and "tools" are symbiotic to the biological manifestation of the human itself, blurring the traditional divide nature/culture. Still, the term "posthuman" reveals a hidden value in social comprehension of narrative representations of knowledge. Not only does it imply a historical perspective on the human, but also, due to its newness to the common vocabulary, intrigues people to rethink on the meanings of the human. A historical and biological site of intersectional differences, the human body appears multiple. Humans are situated: born from a specific female body, in a certain era and geo-political arena; an individual out of one of many species inhabiting the earth. Humankind is no longer at the center of the universe, not only because posthumanism has decentralized the human, but also because the universe itself might have no center. On one side, we might be living in a multiverse;[30] on the other, our own organism shall be conceived as an assemblage of organs and different forms of life.[31] And still, everything is connected. Biodiversity is a measure for the health of ecosystems: "health" etymologically derives from proto-Germanic "hælþ", which means "whole."

Contemporary scientific and bio-technological discourses are carving the future into a broader spectrum of alternative human embodiments, proposing a scientific revisitation of mythological chimeras, in a generic and all-inclusive posthuman horizon. But the same Western traditions which are now debating post-embodiments, have culturally and politically theorized the human body in terms of exclusion. How much emphasis do we need to give to the past in order to reflect on the present and on the forthcoming time? The best way to predict the futures is to think about them. Envisaging posthuman bodies is a philosophical and a political task, involving human agency. Histories and herstories of the human body are herstories and histories of the cyborg. Not only contemporary posthumanist and transhumanist thinkers shall freely refer to them, but future generations of humans, post-humans and intelligent machines will have to process them, in order to access a deeper understanding of themselves.[32] Denying feminism, race studies, postcolonialism and all accounts made by subjects who have been historically located outside of hegemonic discourses, will offer a very

---

30 For a scientific revisitation and a theoretical reflection on the multiverse, see, for instance, Randall (2005). For a historical account on the notion of the multiverse, from quantum physics to cosmology, see Greene (2011).

31 Humans have ten times more bacteria than human cells; still, we don't think of "them" as "us" (Keller 2009).

32 In his classic study *Mind Children*, Moravec (1988, 1) stated on AI: "it will be in our artificial offspring's power, and to their benefit, to remember almost everything about us, even, perhaps, the detailed workings of individual human minds".

limited notion of the human, and will stand as one more repetitive ego trip of the omniscient neutral subject, lacking on providing an accurate representation of humanity as an evolving life form rich in diversity.[33] My future is posthuman, but my posthumanism is rooted in a comprehensive critical account of what it means to be human.

Acknowledgements

I am grateful to Prof. Achille Varzi, Dr. Natasha Vita-More, Prof. Vivaldi Jean-Marie and Prof. Luisa Passerini for their precious comments on this article; to Prof. Patrick Millard, Ellen Delahunty Roby and Thomas Roby for their helpful proof-reading; to Prof. Francesca Brezzi, Dr. Stefan Lorenz Sorgner and Luca Toledo for their constant support.

Bibliography

Braidotti, R. (1996): Signs of Wonder and Traces of Doubt: On Teratology and Embodied Differences. In: Lykke N./ Braidotti R. (eds.): Between Monsters, Goddesses and Cyborgs: Feminist Confrontations with Science, Medicine and Cyberspace. London: Zed Books, 135-152.

Braidotti, R. (2013): The Posthuman. Cambridge: Polity Press.

Butler, J. (2004): Undoing Gender. New York: Routledge.

Clynes M.E./ Kline N.S. (1960): Cyborgs and Space. In: Astronautics 14(9), 26-7, 74-6.

Derrida, J. (2008): The Animal That Therefore I Am. New York: Fordham University Press.

Du Bois, W.E.B. (1897): The Conservation of Races (The American Negro Academy Occasional Papers, No.2). Washington D.C: The Academy.

Ferrando, F. (2013): Posthumanism, Transhumanism, Antihumanism, Metahumanism, and New Materialisms: Differences and Relations. In: Existenz 8(2), 26-32.

Firestone, S. (1970): The Dialectic of Sex: The Case for Feminist Revolution. New York: Quill William Morrow.

Foucault, M. (1970 [1966]): The Order of Things: An Archaeology of the Human Sciences. New York: Random House.

Foucault, M. (1998 [1976]): The History of Sexuality (Vol. 1: The Will to Knowledge). London: Penguin.

Gehlen, A. (1980 [1957]): Man in the Age of Technology (European Perspectives). New York: Columbia University Press.

Gimbutas, M. (1974): The Gods and Goddesses of Old Europe: 7000 to 3500 BC Myths, Legends and Cult Images. Berkeley et al: University of California Press.

33 According to Gould, evolution is not driven towards complexity, but towards diversification (Gould 1996).

Goldberg, D.T. (1993): Racist Culture: Philosophy and the Politics of Meaning. Cambridge(MA): Blackwell Publishers.

Gould, S. J. (1996): Full House: The Spread of Excellence from Darwin to Plato. New York: Three Rivers Press.

Green, B. (2011): The Hidden Reality: Parallel Universes and the Deep Laws of the Cosmos. New York: Random House.

Haraway, D. (1996): Situated Knowledges: The Science Question in Feminism and the Privilege of Partial Perspective. In: Keller, E.F./ Longino, H.E. (eds.): Feminism and Science. New York: Oxford University Press, 249-263.

Harding, S. (1993): The "Racial" Economy of Science: Toward a Democratic Future. Bloomington et al: Indiana University Press.

Hassan, I. (1977): Prometheus as Performer: Toward a Posthumanist Culture? In: The Georgia Review 31(4), 830-850.

Hayles, N.K. (1999): How We Became Posthuman: Virtual Bodies in Cybernetics, Literature, and Informatics. Chicago et al: The University of Chicago Press.

Heidegger, M. (1977 [1954]): The Question Concerning Technology and Other Essays. New York: Harper Torchbooks.

Hughes, J. (2004): Citizen Cyborg: Why Democratic Societies Must Respond to the Redesigned Human of the Future. Cambridge(MA): Westview Press.

Huxley, J. (1957): Transhumanism. In: Huxley, J.: New Bottles for New Wine. London: Chatto & Windus, 13-17.

Irigaray, L. (1985 [1974]): Speculum of the Other Woman. New York: Cornell University Press.

Joy, E.A./ Dionne, C. (eds.) (2010): When Did We Become Post/human? In: Postmedieval: A Journal of Medieval Cultural Studies 1(1-2).

Keller, E.F. (2009): Society and Health (Presentation at The Darwin 2009 Festival, Cambridge University). http://www.coursehero.org/lecture/evelyn-fox-keller-society-and-health-tue-7-july (accessed August 3, 2013).

Kete, K. (2002): Animals and Ideology: The Politics of Animal Protection in Europe. In: Rothfels, N. (ed.): Representing Animals. Bloomington et al.: Indiana University Press, 19-34.

Kurzweil, R. (2005): The Singularity is Near: When Humans Transcend Biology. New York: Viking.

Kristeva, J. (1982): Powers of Horror: An Essay on Abjection New York: Columbia University Press.

Kristeva, J. (1984): Revolution in Poetic Language. New York: Columbia University Press.

Latour, B./ Woolgar, S. (1986 [1979]): Laboratory Life: The Social Construction of Scientific Facts. Princeton: Princeton University Press.

Latour, B. (1987): Science In Action: How to Follow Scientists and Engineers Through Society. Cambridge(MA): Harvard University Press.

Leroi-Gourhan, A. (1943): L'Homme et la Matière. Paris: Albin Michel.

Leroi-Gourhan, A. (1993 [1964]): Gesture and Speech. Cambridge(MA) et al.: MIT Press.

Linnaeus, C. (1758): Systema Naturae per Regna Tria Naturae: Secundum Classes, Ordines, Genera, Species, cum Characteribus, Differentiis, Synonymis, Locis – Editio Decima, Reformata. Holmiae: Laurentius Salvius.

McLuhan, M. (1964): Understanding Media: The Extensions of Man. Cambridge(MA) et al.: The MIT Press.

Merchant, C. (1980): The Death of Nature: Women, Ecology, and the Scientific Revolution. New York: HarperCollins.

Moravec, H. (1988): Mind Children: The Future of Robot and Human Intelligence. Cambridge(MA): Harvard University Press.

More, M. (1993): Technological Self-Transformation: Expanding Personal Extropy. In: Extropy #10, 4(2).

Price, J./ Shildrick, M. (eds.) (1999): Feminist Theory and the Body: A Reader. New York: Routledge.

Randall, L. (2005): Warped Passages: Unraveling the Mysteries of the Universe's Hidden Dimensions. New York: HarperCollins.

Schiebinger, L. (1999): Theories of Gender and Race. In: Price, J./ Shildrick, M. (eds.): Feminist Theory and the Body: A Reader. New York: Routledge, 21-31.

Schiebinger, L. (2000): Taxonomy for Human Beings. In: Kirkup, G. et al. (eds.): The Gendered Cyborg: A Reader. New York: Routledge, 11-37.

Singer, P. (1975): Animal Liberation: A New Ethics for Our Treatment of Animals. New York: New York Review.

Stiegler, B. (1998): Technics and Time, 1: The Fault of Epimetheus. Stanford: Stanford University Press.

Turkle, S. (1984): The Second Self: Computers and the Human Spirit. New York: Simon & Schuster.

Vita-More, N. (2004): The New Genre: Platform Diverse Body / Substrate Autonomous Persons – (e.g. Primo Posthuman) (Presentation at Ciber@RT Conference, Bilbao). http://www.natasha.cc/paper.htm (accessed August 3, 2013).

Warwick, K. (1997): The March of the Machines: The Breakthrough in Artificial Intelligence. London: Century.

Warwick, K. (2004): I, Cyborg. Urbana(IL) et al.: University of Illinois Press.

Woese, C. (1998): The Universal Ancestor. In: Proceedings of the National Academy of Science of the United States of America 95(12), 6854-6859.

Yancy, G. (2008): Black Bodies, White Gazes: The Continuing Significance of Race. Lanham et al: Rowman & Littlefield Publishers.

Bioart

Andy Miah

For over a century, science fiction has gripped the attention of audiences worldwide, with some of its most successful achievements furnishing the world with utopian and dystopian narratives about the progress of science and the limits of humanity's ability to understand its own complexity and place in the world. However, it is only in the last 30 years that ideas of transhumanism and posthumanism have become part of the intellectual influences of various *other* art forms that engage with similar subject matter. It is even more recent that posthumanist and transhumanist scholars have interpreted the work of many pioneering artists and designers as manifestos for their ideas, or as rejections of the possible futures their ideas imply. This is not to say that transhumanist and posthumanist thought is absent from art works that precede this period, but that the explicit link between theories of post- and transhumanism and such artwork has only recently been made.

This chapter makes explicit the association of certain art forms and art works to trans- and posthumanist ideas, which have become constitutive of the political, cultural and philosophical differences and similarities that exist between these concepts. It discusses a range of art practices with a view to identifying themes within trans- and posthumanist art, while also articulating some of the foundational contributions in this field. It begins by advancing a definition of bioart to capture the common ground between transhumanist and posthumanist art. It then considers interpretations of such works and rejection of their collective definition, by drawing attention to their socio-political and bioethical context. Finally, I consider how one may read bioart from the perspective of transhumanist and posthumanist thought. Throughout, some of the defining artists in the fields of transhumanist and posthumanist art are considered.

Defining Bioart

Over the years, posthumanism and transhumanism have enjoyed slightly different intellectual trajectories (see Miah 2008) and this is true also of how their ideas are present or absent within certain forms of work that may be collectively defined as *bioart*. To this extent, it is misleading to claim that artists, whose works may be interpreted as either trans- or posthumanist, have intended to make any explicit connection with these concepts. Indeed, these terms are two, among many others, that are engaged within artwork that explores how scientific and technological changes may alter the nature of biology. For instance, the pioneering work of Stelarc is visibly engaged with the concept of the cyborg, at least as much as it is concerned with the idea of the posthuman. As an artist, Stelarc's work is exceptionally useful to theorists since he also provides written accounts of his ideas, which allow greater insight into his influences and intentions as an artist (see Stelarc 1997; 2005). Yet, it would be difficult to claim that Stelarc's work can be neatly described as typical of either trans- or posthumanist thought. Equally, it is untrue to claim that those artists whose work may be associated with trans- and posthumanist thought are necessarily engaging with them as separate, unrelated concepts. Rather, when examining bioart, one is quickly made aware of how these two concepts are intertwined, if not through the artist's intentions, then through the many interpretations that follow from it.

For simplicity, I propose that art practices which advocate the transgression of biological boundaries as more typical of transhumanist art, while those work focuses on scrutinizing biopolitical relationships are more characteristics of posthumanist art. The common ground that is occupied by each of these terms may be the only justification for unifying such artwork under the common banner of *bioart*. Indeed, it may be the only justification for utilizing the term bioart at all. In this respect, the crucial difference between transhumanist or posthumanist art is that the former is focused on provoking debate about the merit of disrupting biological continuity via science and technology and the latter is interested in expressing the socio-political consequences of such changes.

My explanation of their difference also helps to explain why they are often conflated within the literature. In this respect, the moral philosophical issues arising from transhumanism are often subsumed within debates about the political implications of such transformations. Nevertheless, both concepts are united in their interest to consider what may change about humanity – and the broader biosphere that people inhabit – if people develop and accept a range of technological modifications. This interpretation may betray a prima facie explanation of their meaning, as ideas that are simply focused on either a) states of human transition (transhumanism) or b) defining the conditions of our species, once the concept of Homo sapien ceases to have meaning (that is, once we have become posthuman). Indeed, this more literal explanation of their meanings is also a reasonable indication of how many artists have engaged with them through their work. Thus, some art is more simply preoccupied with imagining a future where the category of the human species ceases to exist – once humanity has transcended its species-typical functions, either through becoming enhanced or by developing new capacities. For example, Dunne & Raby's *Foragers* (2009) imagines how humans may redesign themselves biologically to "maximise the nutritional value of the urban environment", in a world of nearly no resources and an inability for governments to resolve. Alternatively, Michael Burton's

(2007) *biophilia clinic*, builds on scientist Edward Wilson (1984) and James Lovelock (1989) to consider what kind of attachment people may have to the experience of illness, in a world where all disease has been eradicated. He imagines that people would check-in to such clinics, just to undergo an experience where they are made more fragile and need to experience the otherwise absent forms of suffering that would describe future of humanity. Such examples often make no recourse to either post- or transhumanist thought, but the ideas presented by them are certainly related.

Yet, this view of trans- and posthumanism also neglects a final interpretation, which focuses on the concept of *humanism*, rather than the *human species*, as the primary site of contestation. In this case, the interest is less about exploring the implications of an evolutionary break from the category of Homo sapien and more about how one might regard the state of being human without recourse to ideas that defined the age of humanism. In this respect, post- and transhumanism are unified in their intention to scrutinize humanism and challenge its integrity as a valued interpretation of the human condition.

Given these conditions, one may define bioart as a set of hybrid practices that 1) have drawn on both trans- and posthumanist thought, 2) explore biological boundaries, and 3) involves the manipulation of biological matter through scientific or technological means. Such art work is often made possible by collaborative endeavour and the utilization of mixed media, a further modus operandi of the media art genre to which many contributors in this field are most closely associated (see Hauser 2008; Miah [ed.] 2008). Moreover, each of these definitions of the distinctions between trans- and posthumanism may be found in varying degrees between artistic genres and even within the life's work of any artist.

A good example of how artists operate across the spectrum of such definitions is, again, Stelarc, an Australian artist whose work has spun such a range of performances that it would be challenging to limit the boundaries of his work to either one particular form or another. His early works included body-hook suspensions and, while challenging the limits of the body's resilience to pain and undertaking a modification to his body by inserting hooks into his flesh, one could not really claim that the work explored new scientific knowledge or technologies. Admittedly, this may yet be a controversial claim, since one could argue that constructing an architecture of suspension hooks that can perfectly balance a human body in a specific position also requires a playful encounter with physical principles, mathematics, and an understanding of the limits of biology. Yet, this early work is very different from his more recent *Extra Ear* (2008) project, which involves partly using stem cells to create an artificial ear on his arm created from his own tissue. The career of such artists as Stelarc may also be seen has having defined the field of bioart. Thus, while his earlier works may not be seen in this way, they may be explained as steps towards defining a now reasonably clear set of practices that bioartists undertake in their work.

Rejecting Bioart

Despite these conditions, many contemporary artists, whose work has been characterized as bioart, also reject this term for a variety of reasons. First, one may argue that the concept of bioart fails to acknowledge the multi-faceted social roles that artists and artists' works play. For instance, limiting the definition of a bioartist's contribution to just art, may overlook the broader function of art and artists within political debate about the teleology of science, or may fail to recognize the way that an artist's practice can advance scientific understanding. Second, this definition of bioart fails to acknowledge that what defines bioart may be less the employment of biological matter within the work – some artists do not use biological matter at all, but still express ideas associated with bioart – and more about the interest to explore the technical and cultural boundaries of biology.

A third rejection of bioart is expressed by Eduardo Kac, who instead utilizes the term *transgenic* art to describe his work, considering the concept of bioart too generic to capture any unique contribution made by artists who actually disrupt biology, rather than just contribute to its visualization (see Kac 2000). Perhaps the most well known exemplar of Kac's transgenic art is *GFP Bunny*, also known as *Alba*, which was an albino rabbit born via transgenic expression that created a fluorescent quality to its skin. When placed under fluorescent light, the rabbit would glow in the dark. In this example, it is the specific biotechnological practice of transgenesis that defines the work, rather than any broader categorization as bioart.

A fourth, more general, rejection of the term bioart is that it neglects to consider the broader conditions that define the work of such artists, which are more adequately described as *new media art* – created by artists whose practice is defined largely by the desire to experiment with new artistic media. On this basis, what defines this artistic community is less the category of biological matter or its transgression through scientific or technological means and more its currency as a medium through which to create artwork. Thus, such artists as Stelarc or Kac may be defined more adequately as new media artists insofar as their career has been defined by an on-going experimentation with new forms of media. On this basis, the consequent interpretation of work as trans- or posthumanist is merely incidental. In the past, while such artists might have relied on developing sophisticated robotic devices or artificially intelligent prostheses, their more recent work uses the newest biotechnological methods through which to explore the boundaries of the body and mind.

To this end, the value of defining bioart may be limited, especially since some artists – whose work it is supposed to describe – reject the term. However, I will yet argue on behalf of its use, as a way of delimiting art that engages with trans- and posthumanist ideas, more focused on interpretations of individual works than defined as a set of practices or ways of working. In so doing, this definition also requires that such work actively engages with the relocation of biological matter within the art, either through its being performed, manipulated or re-situated. In this respect, the present definition would encompass Kac's bunny, Stelarc's ear and may even encompass Stelarc's body suspensions. However, it would not include artwork that engages people with ideas about biological transgressions, without undertaking a biological transaction within the work itself. In this respect, it is sufficiently broad to encompass such works as Jenny Saville's photography, Damien Hirst's dead animals in formaldehyde, and perhaps even Bill Viola's still life, slow motion video art. However, it should be narrow enough to not encompass Lucien Freud's portraiture, even though it is part of a history of artistic practice that has reimagined ways of seeing our humanity. The term transaction here is admittedly fuzzy, but would principally involve work that invites interpretations that have to do with questioning biological boundaries.

In short, the term bioart may be utilized to distinguish any artistic practice that involves the *resituating of biological matter* to create works that are principally forms of artistic practice. While one may argue that many forms of human-centred art work involves a biological transaction of some kind, or a resituating of biology so as to provoke thoughts about biological transgressions, for present purposes, bioart involves either the physical alteration of biological matter or situating an artist's physical presence within the art work so as to engage such ideas.

While bioart often involves the disruption of some biological boundary – and thus may be seen as trans- or posthumanist – this need not always mean the alteration of biological matter. For instance, in Kira O'Reilly's *Falling Asleep with a Pig* (2009) – her performance involves co-habiting with a sheep for some days – spending every minute of the day side by side in a gallery – literally a "companion species" (see Haraway 2003). Her work provokes onlookers to consider their relationship to non-humans and animals, a prominent theme within posthumanist literature and an increasingly pertinent biotechnological theme as pig organs are used increasingly to help humans survive. Yet, it also reminds urban dwellers of the intimacy between shepherds and their flocks that continues to exist, along with foregrounding life within more rural environments. Other artists, such as Catts and Zurr have scrutinized the need for humanity to farm animals, at a time when environmental activists point out the vast amount of energy needed to sustain one animal life and the harmful gases generated by such life forms. As an alternative, they have developed *victimless meat* (Catts/ Zurr 2008) a new kind of food grown from cell cultures, which has the neat consequence of also attending to animal rights concerns, since there is no sentient life to speak of that is harmed by the consumption of such products.

In closing, there is also often a performative dimension to bioart, notably where the artist plays a crucial role in its physical manifestation, either as the canvass of the work itself or as the facilitator of critical engagement with the artwork. For example, the French performance artist Orlan undergoes cosmetic surgery to alter her appearance in a way that challenges the commercial industry of body modification. In creating non-standard modifications to her body, she invites onlookers to consider how else we might imagine our bodies to look, outside of standard notions of beauty that are typical of the fashion industry. Alternatively, John O'Shea's work on *Pig's Bladder Football*, envisages the possibility of creating sustainable leisure technology by cultivating football bladders made from his own cell tissues, so as to combat the reliance on synthetic materials. In contrast, Gina Czarnecki's *Palaces* project considers the wasted biological materials that people discard, but which may be useful to people for research, repair or exhibition. In this case, milk teeth donated by children – including teeth from her children – are used to build a "tooth fairy palace". *Palaces* reveals how bioart need not involve utilizing body modification or technology at all, but simply utilizing biological matter that naturally separates from us. In each of these works, it is unclear that either trans- or posthumanist ideas has shaped the vision of the artist, but the interpretation of their work may certainly find itself closer to either one or the other of these ideas.

Interpreting Bioart

Given the blurred boundaries around the definition of bioart, identifying how transhumanism and posthumanism may have shaped such work – or, in turn, how it may be shaping these ideas – also requires acknowledging how other disciplines of creative expression have contributed to these works. For it is unlikely that contemporary manifestations of bioart can be divorced from the broader media culture in which they are created. Consider Orson Welles' radio play *War of the Worlds*, which was a hoax public broadcast designed to convince listeners that aliens were coming to Earth. Compare this with a more recent public broadcast hoax, this time propagated by a Dutch broadcast called *The Great Donor Show*, a programme that purported to be auctioning a human kidney in a live reality television format where viewers would vote to decide which of the contestants who were in need of a kidney was most deserving to receive it from the donor on the show.

While these examples may seem to stretch the above definition of bioart too far – perhaps instead towards "mediated spectacle" (see van Dijck 2003) – they are part of the public context within which contemporary forms of bioart take place, as practices that have become mechanisms of public engagement with science and technology and the moral predicaments that arise from (the promise of) new innovation. Indeed, *public engagement with science* has become a research discipline of its own in recent years and is a crucial dimension of what many bioartists do when performing their work for an audience. This is made evident by the way that scientific and medical research organizations like the UK's Wellcome Trust fund such work. On this basis, bioart allows scientists to relocate their research into an accessible, public space. Moreover, art utilizes of a non-scientific language as a device through which to engage people with the implications of innovation, which – when done well – serves an important translational role from science to a wider public. This is not to say that such public engagement work is principally about promoting understanding of the science, but that it often endeavours to engage people with the practice of science and its relation to broader society. By implication, given the interest of science to promote public understanding and, by implication, public compliance with the progress of science, one may also recognize a potentially challenging role for artists, many of whom may not align their work with such goals.

While some artists embrace this public communication task and have capitalized on occupying this translational social function, others have interrogated their role as mediator of scientific knowledge and have engaged with playful public deceptions through, often, satirical creative projects. For example, biodesigners James Auger and Jimmy Loizeau created a prototype called *Audio Tooth Implant*, which was reported on the cover of TIME magazine in 2002. This telephone tooth implant resembled a conventional cavity filling and its function would be to allow a user to permanently be connected to their mobile device. The project may be interpreted as a critique of pervasive mobile culture, but it also alludes to the transhumanist theme of integrating biology and digital technology. Moreover, their interventions may be seen as a critique of how the media engage with science and technology, both calling to attention the inadequacy of some forms of scientific journalism and the need for wider debate beyond newspaper headlines and sensationalized reporting. After all, these designers had no intention of producing the technology, but convinced others that it would soon be widely available.

This theme also finds a place within the field of artificial intelligence, another area that is at the border of bioart. Composer and scientist Eduardo Miranda (2011) has developed artificially intelligent robots that teach each other to sing, thus perhaps extending the idea of manufactured music to its logical end. Miranda's work addresses the last bastion of human relevance; after having successfully automated physical and intellectual labor, Miranda's robots suggest how human creativity and the capacity to make art may also be automated. To this end, his work provides insight and meaning that forces people to consider what matters to us about being human (see Miah 2011). In a world where the creation of music may no longer require participation from humans, then humanity must accept that its unique selling proposition has been compromised, save perhaps for the capacity to care and express emotions. Miranda's work also engages with the ideas of transhumanist scholars such as Ray Kurzweil (2005), perhaps the most famous transhumanist proponent of the *singularity* – a moment when computer intelligence overtakes that of the human species. In this respect, one may interpret it as a form of transhumanist art. However, far from envisaging a future that is absent of humans, Miranda's compositions provide reinterprets the future, suggesting how creative collaboration between machines and humans may provide a new chapter in our thoughts about artificial life forms and inter-species co-habitation.

Miranda's work may be seen as a critique on society at large – and on transhumanism – but many artists find their contributions subject to vehement criticisms from the popular press who are confounded by their propositions, labelling them as "sick" or a waste of "tax payers money" (see Daily Mail 2006). Such public disdain for art is sometimes directed at the worth of art generally, but especially conceptual art that challenges such fundamental values as the sanctity of life. Consider Guillermo "Habacuc" Vargas's *Starving Dog*, which consisted of a live, stray dog which was caught and situated in a gallery accompanied by the text "Eres Lo Que Lees" ("You Are What You Read"). The achievement of this work was forcing on-lookers to confront their feelings about the limits of artwork and what art galleries ought to exhibit. It also reminded people of how animals are exploited across society in various ways, either through domestication which can be to the detriment of an animal's general health, or through humanity's consumption of animals to fulfill various, non-necessary human needs.

Reactions to this work were aggressively angry towards the festival, which chose to exhibit the dog. Yet again, the curators were deliberately attempting to provoke thought via the ambiguity of perceptions that people experience when confronted with any artwork. Thus, despite the outward appearance of this exhibit, the gallery's director stated that the dog was, in fact, not starving at all and was adequately cared for during its exhibition. While its emaciated condition led viewers to express outrage at the work and to campaign for its removal, this was a staging effect. In this example, we see the crossover of bioart, performance art and live art. The work may also be seen as a commentary on society's neglect for animals or the contractions in their treatment. Moreover, like Kac's fluorescent rabbit, bringing the starving dog into a gallery space is less about objectifying life and more about placing viewers in an uncomfortable position, reminding them of what is happening outside of the gallery space. Exhibiting such work takes the risk of being subject to public outcry and facing widespread political condemnation, while also succeeding in making artwork reach populations that, without the controversy, would be completely unaware of what takes place in novel edge art practice.

There is also a broader political interpretation to the work of many bioartists, which is that it forces a reconsideration of how original knowledge should be created and valued within society. Artist collectives such as SymbioticA (Australia), The Arts Catalyst (UK), Dunne & Raby, enact a form of biopolitics that is focused on creating collaborative relationships between scientists and artists/designers. An integral part of this praxis has been the infiltration of scientific laboratories by artists, in pursuit of creative expression and the development of new knowledge about the boundaries of biology. Yet, it is not just natural or physical scientists whose work may engage with bioartists. For instance, the work of designers Dunne & Raby undertakes a sociological survey of the future, by working with groups to imagine what kinds of decisions they would make about their lives if certain technological opportunities were available to them. This is true of their *Evidence Dolls*, which involved participants considering how genetic testing would influence their decisions over romantic relationships (see Dunne et al. 2008). This work asked people to consider whether the ability to genetically test their potential partners for a range of characteristics would lead to its use as a condition for entering into a relationship. By envisioning new forms of biological transformation and utilization, artists' ideas become constitutive of the landscape in which debates about biological change take place. However, by utilizing sociological methods, their work demystifies the idea that insights for artistic practice rely solely on individual creative vision. Admittedly, the example may reveal the difference between how artists and designers work, but the crucial point is that bioart often involves similar kinds of consultation and empirical inquiry to inform the work. Equally, a number of bioartists are active within the field of bioethics and regularly write for ethical periodicals. This includes Natasha Vita-More (2010) whose own theorizations on transhumanist art are inextricable from the ethical contexts where decisions about their legitimacy take place.

To this end, bioart, body art, and biodesign also scrutinize contemporary bioethical issues and scientific practice, such as the utilization of embryonic stem cells, or the development of transgenic species. However, it is unclear whether all artists intend to resist such processes. Indeed, some are seeking their propagation in order to make their art possible. For example, Stelarc's own body modifications convey the body's obsolescence in an era of synthetic biology and stem cell regeneration (see Smith 2005). The use of stem cells within his *Extra Ear* project is still not the end stage of the work, which next aims to implant an auditory device within the ear and for it to be remotely connected to the internet, so web browsers can hear what the ear hears creating a distributed auditory system. If this were not enough evidence of how bioartists may sometimes celebrate the transformative aesthetic potential of biotechnology, then consider Julia Reodica's collection of synthetic hymens, which go beyond genital piercing and tattoo, but which resonates with these similar tribal motifs. This work invites us to consider the role of virginity and its loss in the 21st century, a theme that may be interpreted as intimately connected to the biotechnological era, as the contraceptive pill is one of the most transformative technologies of the late 20th century.

Some aspects of bioart are not especially new; biology has been a medium for artists for some time. Everything from saliva to human excrement has entered the play space of artists over the years. The differences among many of these new works is that artists are only now beginning to experiment with cutting edge scientific applications, such as stem cells, cosmetic surgery and biotechnology generally to produce work. Such biological matter is a medium that is generally inaccessible for the non-specialist to use without suitable qualifications and the artist's use of it disrupts the boundaries between science and society. Indeed, the struggle of many artists to exhibit their work in galleries speaks to the inadequacy of social regulations to permit such biological matter to exist anyway but a laboratory. For instance, bioartist Tagny Duff was unable to get her *Viral Tattoos* work into the United Kingdom from Canada as part of the International Symposium of Electronic Art 2009. Alternatively, at the Foundation for Art & Creative Technology Liverpool, the sk-interfaces exhibition (see Hauser 2008) was unable to exhibit living genetically modified matter as part of Jun Takita's transgenic piece *Light, Only Light* (see Miah [ed.] 2008). Indeed, the exhibition of such content requires a license from the UK's Human Tissue Authority. These examples remind viewers of the political nature of the work. By testing the readiness of society to create opportunities for public engagement – for, without the gallery, there is nearly nowhere that such work could be seen

– artists, curators and gallery managers are party to a new kind of ethical terrain, which may be called public bioethics.

Additionally, the work of bioartists may be seen as an attempt to disrupt the knowledge economy, as many such artists are not interested simply in their creative means drawing on the work of scientists or revealing its beautiful complexity. Rather, the expectation is that the artist will become co-creator of original knowledge, a genuine research partner in the design and undertaking of scientific studies, to such a degree that some intellectual property over new discoveries or insights may be attributed also to the artist. In this sense, the gradual occupation of artists in labs raises important questions about how society is organized and understand our own humanity. For instance, why do societies privilege scientific knowledge over, say, aesthetic, as is evidenced by the way in which funding is skewed in favour of the former? Would humanity have been better off over the last 100 years or so if it had dedicated more of its resources to the so-called softer sciences, arts and humanities? Would societies have asked different questions, or sought different solutions to difficult problems? Admittedly, societies might have produced fewer technologies that would save lives and, perhaps would have failed to reduce suffering as effectively as they have through medicine, but then with fewer people on the planet, it might have been more effective at distributing goods more evenly. These are impossibly speculative questions, but which nevertheless expose the claim that hierarchies of knowledge systems affect the overall wealth in the world and that the scientific method need not have produced the least amount of suffering in the world.

By implication, one may argue that these collaborative bioart works should also be credited to the scientists involved and, indeed, they often are. While this may beg the question over ownership and the right to commercialize the work or benefit from its syndication in exhibitions or private sale, like all collaborative works, decisions about this are for the artist and scientist to negotiate in advance of and during the collaboration process. There are no fixed rules about who ought to be principal author, but equally it is often true that the scientist's terrain and the artists are distinct enough for all to benefit. Indeed, in the same way that an artist is unlikely to be in a position to capitalize on the scientific work, the same is true of the scientist in relation to the artistic presentation.

The work of these bioartists and designers also raises difficult ethical questions. For instance, it requires society to consider by what codes of ethics such work should be governed? This is often the initial response of critics who find such work disturbing, offensive or potentially illegal: how could a society permit the playful use of transgenic science simply to create a new aesthetic artefact? Many people might consider this to be a trivialization of scientific research and its proposed end goals to alleviate human suffering. However, there are good reasons for refraining from such judgments and this is because the aesthetic content of such works is only one way of evaluating their worth. The more relevant ethical view to take reveals itself when inquiring into some of the challenges that such artists have faced in the pursuit of their work. For instance, in 2004, US bioartist Steve Kurtz was pursued by the FBI under suspicion of bioterrorism, after petri dishes with biological matter inside them were found in his home (see Annas 2008). Such artists would want us to see them as acting on our behalf to make science more accountable to a broader public and for their work to engage us more fully on its long term goals and aspirations. Equally, some artists aim to highlight that the presumed end goals of such research for human benefit are often not present at the crucial, experimental stage. In this respect, experimental science can be considered similar to experimental art.

Conclusion: Bioart as Trans- and Posthumanist Thought

In conclusion, bioart aligns with transhumanism insofar as such work pursues the disruption of biological boundaries and this encompasses experimentation with many new scientific techniques, such as stem cell or genetic manipulation, or even the creation of new life forms. Yet, in so doing, such art also engages with the posthumanist critique of humanity's presumed omnipotence within the natural order and invites alternative questions to those that underpin scientific research. Thus, technological development to improve humanity's resilience or lifestyle is not the premise on which bioart may be justified. Rather, the value of such work is found in its capacity to generate new insights for humanity that may inform the kind of science humanity pursues and in the intrinsic value of creating new aesthetic encounters that may alter our appreciation of the world around us and humanity's role within it.

Yet even here, elements of posthumanist thought are apparent. Consider again Kac's fluorescent bunny, that concerns particularly a non-human life form. In this case, Kac's aspirations are to locate genetic engineering "within a social context" (see Kac 2000; Osthoff 2008). Moreover, Kac comments on the inadequacy of using such technologies to satisfy human desires, thus critiquing the transhumanist notion of humanity's entitlement to pursue modifications that it deems to be valuable:

> "The question is not to make the bunny meet specific requirements or whims, but to enjoy her company as an individual (all bunnies are different), appreciated for her own intrinsic virtues, in dialogical interaction" (Kac 2000).

Thus, the transgenic art of Eduardo Kac asks us to consider the limits of "Playing God" and he is quick to point out that scientists have already undertaken such experiments, we just do not hear very much about it, or it is cloaked in some vaguely communicated remote chance that the experiment will lead to knowledge that will assist humanity in some specific way. While *GFP bunny* reveals something about what is going on within experimental research that may have implications for humans, Kac's contribution is to reveal how advances in science occur via the sacrifice of non-human animals.

It is no coincidence that the rise of transhumanist and posthumanist art occurs alongside the rapid growth of biotechnology and the public anxieties over bioethics. Indeed, to the extent that artists often undertake work as a commentary on contemporary issues or an engagement with new media, the rise of bioart is intimately connected to this trajectory. However, it would be wrong to suggest that such art forms are principally supportive of the ways in which humanity may be reimagined and reconstituted by technological change. Moreover, it is not even clear that either trans- or posthumanist artwork aims to engage people with the range of ethical narratives that surround such developments, though some do. Rather, the biological medium is often principally a material device through which artists have explored aesthetic qualities associated with the idea of life after *Homo sapien* – and the presumed relationships with other species that this definition implies.

Bibliography

Annas, G.J. (2008): Bioterror and 'Bioart' – 'A Plague O' Both Your Houses'. In: Miah, A. (ed.): Human Futures: Art in an Age of Uncertainty. Liverpool: Liverpool University Press, 100-111.

Burton, M. (2007): Biophilia Clinic. http://www.michael-burton.co.uk/ (accessed July 22, 2013).

Catts, O./ Zurr, I. (2004): The Ethics of Experimental Engagement with the Manipulation of Life. In: da Costa, B./ Philip K. (eds.) Tactical Biopolitics: Art, Activism, and Technoscience. Cambridge(MA): MIT Press, 125-42.

Daily Mail (2006): It's Art, Says the Naked Woman Who'll Hug a Dead Pig on Stage. http://www.dailymail.co.uk/news/article-401165/Its-art-says-naked-woman-wholl-hug-dead-pig-stage.html (accessed July 22, 2013).

Dunne, A./ Raby, F./ Miah, A. (2008): Screening for Undesirable Genes: The Evidence Dolls Project. In: Miah, A. (ed.): Human Futures: Art in an Age of Uncertainty. Liverpool: Liverpool University Press, 62-75.

Dunne, A./ Raby, F. (2009): Foragers. http://www.dunneandraby.co.uk/content/projects/510/0 (accessed July 22, 2013).

Haraway, D. (2003): The Companion Species Manifesto: Dogs, People and Significant Otherness. Chicago: Prickly Paradigm Press.

Hauser, J. (ed.) (2008): Sk-interfaces. Liverpool: Liverpool University Press.

Kac, E. (2000): GFP Bunny. http://www.ekac.org/gfpbunny.html#gfpbunnyanchor (accessed July 22, 2013).

Kurzweil, R. (2005): The Singularity is Near. New York: Viking.

Lovelock, J.E. (1989): The Ages of Gaia. Oxford: Oxford University Press.

Miah, A. (ed.) (2008): Human Futures: Art in an Age of Uncertainty. Liverpool: Liverpool University Press

Miah, A. (2008): A Critical History of Posthumanism. In: Gordijn B./ Chadwick, R.F. (eds.): Medical Enhancement and Posthumanity. Dordrecht: Springer, 71-94.

Miah, A. & Rich, E. (2010): Bodies, Health & Illness. In: Albertazzi, D./ Cobley, P. (eds.): The Media: An Introduction (Third Edition). Harlow: Pearson Education Limited, 485-504.

Miah, A. (2011): Foreword: New Forms of Music. In: Miranda, E.R.: Mozart Reloaded. Sargasso Publishing.

Miranda, E.R. (2011): Mozart Reloaded. Sargasso Publishing.

O'Reilly, K. (2009): Falling Asleep with a Pig. http://www.kiraoreilly.com/blog/?cat=30 (accessed July 22, 2013).

Osthoff, S. (2008): Eduardo Kac: A Conversation with the Artist. In: Miah, A. (ed.): (2008) Human Futures: Art in an Age of Uncertainty. Liverpool: Liverpool University Press, 146-51.

Smith, M. (2005): Stelarc: The Monograph. Cambridge(MA): The MIT Press.

Stelarc (1997): Hollow Body/Host Space: Stomach Sculpture. In: Cultural Values 1(2), 250-251.

Stelarc (2005): Prosthetic Head: Intelligence, Awareness and Agency. In: CTHEORY. http://www.ctheory.net/printer.aspx?id=490 (accessed July 22, 2013).

van Dijck, J. (2002): Medical Documentary: Conjoined Twins as a Mediated Spectacle. In: Media, Culture, and Society 24(4), 537-556.

Vita-More, N. (2010): Aesthetics of the Radically Enhanced Human. In: Technoetic Arts: A Journal of Speculative Research 8(2), 207-214.

Wilson, E.O. (1984). Biophilia. Cambridge(MA): Harvard University Press.

New Media Art

Evi Sampanikou

In 1940, the founder of iconology, the study of the symbolic meaning of artistic images, Erwin Panofky published his famous essay *History of Art as a Humanistic Discipline* (1955), suggesting modern approaches and new theoretical directions for art history that had just been accepted as a vast, independent, synthetic, research field, much broader than connoisseurship, seeking for a distinct place among humanities. Based on the study of the Renaissance, Panofsky had underlined the strong relationship between art and classical humanism, making interdisciplinary cultural crossovers among literature, philosophy, history, poetry and music.

By the end of the 20th century, in the nineties and more specifically in 1995 and 1996, new theories on art, based on the emerging example and the possibilities of the new media, started to emerge. Erki Huhtamo (1996, 296-303; 2007), Peter Weibel (1996, 338-351; 2007) and Friedrich Kittler (1996; see also Gane 2005) among others, underlined the fact that there was a strong need for new directions and inclusions for the field of art history that had surpassed its humanistic period and limits and was seeking for a contemporary identity as both humanism and modernism belonged to a past that could not reproduce itself anymore. I have to underline here the great importance of one of the most influential for the 21st century books on new media in 1996 that also marked a continuity between new media and what was known as conceptual art, placing the new notion of art history somewhere between media studies, New Aesthetic Philosophy and new media theories (see Druckrey 1996). The eternally doubtful term "postmodernism", greatly served by well-known scholars as Arthur Danto (e.g. 2003, 103-124), offered a solution for some decades, it was however clear that it was never enough. Contemporary scholars and philosophers as Slavoi Žižek (1996), Jean Baudrillard (2001) and Paul Virilio (1991, 72) offered some additional help for the inclusion of art history into the field of both cultural studies and opened the doors to new emerging philosophies and media theories. During the last years and under the prism of the works of Lev Manovich (2001, 129-135), Oliver Grau (2003), Frank Popper (2007), Anne Friedberg (2006, 231-244) among others, a new shape of things has started being formed, whispering the notion of the end of postmodernism, while other scholars and artists as Louise K. Wilson (1996), Victoria Vesna (see Popper 2007, 322-324), Maurice Benayoun (see Grau 2003, 237-240; Popper 2007, 201-205) and others, although not stating it at all, led art to the path of posthumanism. Therefore, what can be accepted as a state of the art nowadays is that new media art – actually the continuity of conceptual art including performance, video and video installation – can now be examined as an independent posthumanistic discipline. To give a new definition, what can be conceived as posthumanist art nowadays, is the art that explores the notion of being human in an environment dominated by technology. At the same time, transhumanist art examines the countless possibilities of several "what ifs" on human enhancement, human-machine interaction, or completely new hybrid breeds.

The Heritage of Conceptual Art and Posthumanist Art

Conceptual Art appeared in the late 1960s, becoming a dominant trend in the 1970s. Focused on the dematerialization of art and the prevailing importance of *meaning*, conceptual art started being recorded mainly after the influential 1970 exhibition of MoMA (New York) entitled *Information* (see Arnason/ Prather 1998, 628-630). The title couldn't have been accidental. It actually drew the first contact line between art and information technology. The famous work of the American artist Joseph Kosuth (born 1945), *One and Three Chairs* (1965) was included into this exhibition. It was in fact an installation composed of one chair, a photo of this chair and a text, the dictionary definition of the word "chair". The emerging problem was rather philosophical, dated back to Plato years: what actually *is* a chair and how it can *really* be best illustrated? Photography is also playing a prevailing role into other conceptual artists' work, John Baldessari (born 1931), for example, leading scholars to start discussing about matters of "postphotographic practice." (Tomas 1996, 145)

Joseph Beuys: Conceptual Performance as an Ancestor of Posthumanist Art

In 1965 also, Joseph Beuys (1921-1986), a German artist that was never fully accepted and absorbed into the internationalist air of the *Fluxus* movement, staged one of his early performances that can now be viewed as early posthumanist art. However we have to underline here that when this performance was first shown to the public, it was conceived as part of *fluxus* expression or early conceptualism. Later, during the eighties such works were rather viewed as early "poststructuralist postmodernist" (see Foster et al. 2007, 596-598) declarations. In the Galerie Schmela in Düsseldorf Beuys created the installation/performance *How to Explain Pictures to a Dead Hare* (see Arnason/ Prather 1998, 631-632). A pilot in the Second World War, Beuys was shot down and rescued during a blizzard by Crimean locals (Tatars) that collected his injured and frozen body and applied animal fat all over it to keep him warm. Beuys returned as a pacifist who wanted to "rehumanize both art and life by narrowing the gap between the two" (ibid., 631). He also belongs to the generation of post-war German artists that were never familiarized with the idea of the denial of mourning for the Nazi's victims; therefore he expresses mourning in almost every occasion seeking reconciliation between human and animal beings and nature. In the previously mentioned performance, Beuys sat in an empty room in the gallery, surrounded by fat, felt, wood and wire, having his face covered by gold as a mask, holding a dead hear in his arms and whispering to the animal. In this performance, Beuys played the role of the shaman, the healer that could even bring the hare back into life. Beuys also created several sculptures of wood and fat talking about the transformation of the idea of sculpture and the widening of the notion of artistic creation (see ibid., 631-641). For Beuys these creations were "forms of thought" or "forms of speech" implying the fact that everything is under a process of continuous transformation and change (ibid., 631-632). The totality of his work can be characterized as life, death and art, in an early posthuman environment.

Nam June Paik: From Fluxus to Video Sculpture

The Korean American artist Nam June Paik (1932-2006) on the other hand, closely related to Fluxus during his first period and initially known for his humoristic approach, his body art performances and electronic art experimentations, was evolved into one of the leading video artists of our times with a strong belief that "the TV screen will permanently replace the canvas from now on" (ibid., 632). Fascinated by the power of the screen and the sovereignty of electronic and digital media that can easily change the reality of every image, Paik, sharing a lot of Baudrillard's thought, became a witness of the massive hallucination imposed by TV and the later electronic media like computers, the internet, 3D and virtual reality. In one of his famous video installations from the nineties, called *Electronic Superhighway: Bill Clinton Stole my idea* (1993-1995) (see Rush 2001, 117-118; Sampanikou 2008, 265-269), his participation in the 1993 Venice Biennale in the German pavilion, Paik had gathered "dozens of monitors packed from floor to ceiling" (Rush 2001, 118-119; images: 129-130) broadcasting images of the world's news and documentations: wars, politics, the Bill Clinton scandal, images from the nature, or disasters all over the planet, used as a record of contemporary world's state. This is a purely posthumanistic view of the media ruled world, in a notion of politicized posthumanism also underlined by the artist's declaration that his aim is "the humanizing of technology" (Elwes 2005, 144), met here with Fredric Jameson's later notion of postmodernism (2008, 377-380).

Bill Viola: From Experimental VHS Video to Digital Media Screening as Director

One of the most influential and most "contemporary" artists of our time is undoubtedly the American Bill Viola (born 1951). Moving into digital video after several years of TV and VHS video experimentations, Viola seems initially to be fascinated by the notion of the several *masculinities*, identity, family, man-woman, life-death. Starting from family relationships, a metaphorical *locus* into which he traces the shaping of his identity, in an unusual way for a male artist, Viola makes further steps to identify this experience as "part of a wider universal consciousness" (Elwes 2005, 71). However, this posthumanistic approach gets clearer into Viola's recent works (from 2000 and after), when he gets more and more inspired from Renaissance and the old masters and transforms their viewing into professional quality video works directed by him, with professional actors. His series of video works *The Passions*, a project that began in 2000 illustrate the above mentioned in the best way (see Walsh 2003).[1] In a deep research for the expression of emotions motivated by a year of studies (1998) at the Getty Research Institute as a guest scholar on the topic "The Representation of the Passions", Viola, who in the past had read Hindu, Buddhist and Sufi writers, had the opportunity to come into contact with Christian art and Christian literature of the later Middle Ages (St. John of the Cross, Meister Eckhart), as well as modern critical art history literature on medieval pictorial representation of feeling and the symbolic *language* and gestures used by the painters (see Walsh 2003, 31-32). Charles Darwin's views on facial expression and Victor Hieronym Stoichita's work on visionary experiences in Spanish painting influenced him most of all (see ibid., 31). According to Peter Sellars, what is revealed in "high-end American art" is the post-September 11th atmosphere. This atmosphere meets with the so-called "culture of mourning" in Viola's art, through an alternative proccess that has been underdeveloping for long in the work of a series of American artists (see Walsh 2003, 158-160). For Viola "art can have a healing function" as art is "for cultivating knowledge on how to be in the world" (Walsh 2007, 25). Viola's art is for arousing strong emotions of participation, empathy and passion to the viewer (see Townsend 2004, 8-14), a function almost forgotten by both the artists and the public during the 20th century.

1 More than 20 works by now, most of them are available on YouTube.

Shirin Neshat and William Kentridge: Posthumanist Sex and Identity and Humanism in Post-Humanist Disguise

Shirin Neshat (born 1957), the well-known Iranian origin video artist and the very important South African animator William Kentridge (born 1955) are two other alternative examples of posthumanist art. The first can in many ways be conceived as an American artist narrating the condition of being a woman in the country of her origin, while the second, who has never left his country, can in many ways be viewed as a humanist citizen of the world.

Neshat was born and raised by an upper middle class family in Tehran before the Islamic Revolution (1980). The Revolution found her in the States studying fine arts, therefore her stay in California became permanent. Returning to Tehran (where her family still lives) some years later, for a short visit, was a traumatic experience to her as everything had changed in a dramatic way, especially the place of women (see Grosenick 2003, 136-139; Friedberg 2006, 219). Her video work contains the sense of displacement she felt, as well as the unbalanced feeling of living between two worlds, seeking for an identity at a "third place". This "third place" is for Neshat a series of digital video narratives about Iranian men and women struggling to get over the limits of their world and condition. After a series of photographies called *Women of Allah* (1993-1997) and her earlier videos *Turbulent* (1998), *Rapture* (1999), *Soliloquy* (1999) (see Grosenick 2003, 139), *Fervor* (2000), *Passage* (2001) and *Tooba* (2002) (see Elwes 2005, 175-177), the screening of *Women Without Men*, is undoubtedly her most inspired work. The whole video project, that later became a movie (2009), consists of five video-installations, each narrating the story of one woman: *Mahdocht* (2004), *Zarin* (2005), *Munis* (2008), *Faezeh* (2008), *Farokh Legha* (2008) that live during the 1953 coup d'état. In these five parallel and intertwining stories, Iranian female characters of different class origin revolt in their own way against the political and social conditions (see Kafetsi 2009). The stories work like ancient drama sharing a feeling of *catharsis* in the end.[2] They can therefore be read as political posthumanist *texts*.

William Kentridge on the other hand is an artist very much engaged with humanist matters like the notion of freedom, violence and the transformations of society. His medium, animation, offers the artist, who permanently lives in Johannesburg and first appears between 1981 and 1987, a special look at such social problems as racism, and also an access to youth public. His art consists of "old fashioned" black and white obscured images made by carbon. Kentridge's technique consists of recording the process of drawing and deleting-correcting,

2 This project gave Neshat acceptance to a broader public. All her photographs and videos are accessible on YouTube.

as a moving image (see Foster et al. 2007, 652-653).[3] With German Expressionism as his immediate 20th century artistic influence (see Arnason/ Prather 1998, 141-170), but also Daumier, Goya and Hogarth (see Marian Goodman Gallery 2013), Kentridge creates a series of animated characters around the main two: Soho, the industrialist, always clad in a costume with stripes recalling the early industrial period and Felix, the anti-apartheid intellectual, naked most of the times, both personifications of the conflicting white South African consciousness. The artist describes himself as a member of a white elite who *knew* what was happening during the apartheid. According to Kentridge's own words, he is interested in "*political art* [...] the art of unfinished gestures and an uncertain end" (Tone 2003, 98-112). Among his famous works are: *Felix in Exile* (1994), *Stereoscope* (1999) and *Fragments for George Melies* (2007). Kentridge's humanistic approach and arguments make him one of the purest and most politicized posthumanists of our times.

Transhumanist Art: A Non-Humanistic Discipline?

Among transhumanist artists I could generally include H. R. Giger, as a forerunner, Stelarc, Orlan, Piccinini and Eduardo Kac, that are the commonly accepted paradigms. However, these artists give an emphasis to only one aspect of transhumanism: the *enhancement* or *transformation* (even the monstrous one) of the body. However, the bulk of the formerly called "electronic art" that has nowadays evolved to either digital or virtual art, fulfills the requirements of an analytical approach to the philosophical background of transhumanism, the meeting of the human brain with "the machine". Therefore, I would like to introduce here three major artistic examples that mainly deal with transhumanist matters: Karl Sims, Knowbotic Research and Jake and Dinos Chapman, all of completely different origin and background.

The biotechnologist and computer graphics artist and researcher Karl Sims, born in the sixties, became known with his *Galapagos* twelve-monitors interactive installation (1995, 1997-2000, Intercommunication Centre, Tokyo), inspired by Darwin's theory of natural selection (see Rush 2001, 205-208, images: 221-222; Popper 2007, 126). *Galapagos* is actually a computer graphics based visualization of Darwin's theory. 3D Graphics in this installation resemble to new organisms, "genetic" ones, developing into the environment of the computer. This development can be done by any visitor of the exhibition and consists of

3 Kentridge uses a rotating metal cylinder put in the middle of his papers on which his drawings are reflected and he then records these reflections on the cylinder (see Universes in Universe 2005).

random changes of either shape, or color/texture or other characteristics to convince the viewer that a new breed of creatures is actually happening (see Sims 1997). *Genetic Images* (1993) was the early version of this installation (Centre Pompidou, Paris). The artist considers the project a "collaboration between human and machine" for two reasons: its potential as a tool and the unique method it suggests "for studying evolutionary systems" (ibid.). It can however be a basis for discussing transhumanism in an open-minded way.

Knowbotic Research, a German-Swiss electronic art group established in 1991, is composed of Yvonne Wilhelm, Christian Hubler and Alexander Tuchacek.[4] Their work is according to Grau "developing hybrid models for digital representation of knowledge" and has already become the field of a very analytical critical approach by both Oliver Grau (2003, 213-217) and Frank Popper (2007, 345-350), while they were also recorded by other scholars (see Tribe et al. 2006, 56-57). Undoubtedly, their most prominent project is the virtual installation *Dialogue with the Knowbotic South* (1994-1997), a work that "processes scientific data from research stations' networked databases to create a changing abstract representation of Antarctica" (Grau 2003, 213). The data collectors are software agents, the knowledge robots or "knowbots". The knowbots interact with (human) visitors of the exhibition and poetic software machines, while the projected image resembles star constellations or supernovas (see Grau 2003, 213; Popper 2007, 249). This exchange of feelings, images and experience between human beings and knowbots is actually putting the development of this project in an early transhumanist discussion on the human-machine interaction and the possibility of new directions of developing (and enhance) knowledge.

I will end this text with the duet of the London-based brothers Jake and Dinos Chapman (born 1966 and 1962), of British-Cypriot origin, who belong to a series of "provocative" artists[5] of this century that create "hermaphrodites" with genetic anomalies manifested in absurd combinations of arms, heads, legs and torsos, with the nose, ears or mouth replaced by an anus, a vulva or an erect penis (*Fuck Face* 1994, *Cock-Shitter* 1997) (see Riemschneider/ Grosenick 1999, 98-101). Their example illustrates, in the best way, that art is becoming, more and more a post- and transhumanistic discipline, reminding us that biotechnology can not only "enhance" human species, but also "breed monsters", in Goya's terms. The reason Goya is mentioned, is no other than the Champan's respect to Goya and their straight influence by his engravings that are visualized by the

4 They share a Professorship for Art and Media at the University of the Arts in Zürich.

5 In 2008 the exhibition *If Hitler Had Been a Hippy How Happy Would We Be* (White Cube, London) showed thirteen watercolors by Adolf Hitler modified by Jake and Dino Chapman (see White Cube 2008).

artists' life-size sculptures made of resin and fiberglass. Their nightmarish work *Great Deeds Against the Dead, after Goya's etching* (1994), composed of fiberglass dismembered bodies tied in a tree's trunk and branches, exactly imitates Goya's *Grande hazana! Con muertos!* (A heroic feat! With dead men!). Chapmans' creatures are actually an irony to biotechnology or rather an irony to its possible unlucky experiment results. Their work, often accused as mere bad taste by several art historians, functions as a reflective mirror of the diachronical moral ugliness produced by human beings, with aspects of biotechnology being a part of it nowadays.

Bibliography

Arnason, H.H./ Prather, M.F. (1998): A History of Modern Art: Painting, Sculpture, Architecture, Photography (4th Edition). London: Thames and Hudson Ltd.

Baudrillard, J. (2001): Selected Writings. Oxford: Polity Press.

Danto, A.C. (2003). The Abuse of Beauty: Aesthetics and the Concept of Art. Chicago: Open Court.

Elwes, C. (2005): Video Art: A Guided Tour. London et al.: I.B.Tauris.

Foster, H. et al. (2007). I Techni apo to 1900: Monternismos, Antimonternismos, Metamonternismos. Thessaloniki: Epikentro Publishers.

Friedberg, A. (2006): The Virtual Window: From Alberti to Microsoft. Cambridge(MA) et al.: The MIT Press.

Gane, N. (2005): Radical Post-humanism: Friedrich Kittler and the Primacy of Technology. In: Theory, Culture & Society 22(3): 25-41.

Grau, O. (2003): Virtual Art: From Illusion to Immersion. Cambridge(MA) et al.: The MIT Press.

Grosenick, U. (ed.) (2003): Women Artists in the 20th and 21st Century. Köln et al.: Taschen.

Huhtamo, E. (1996): From Caleidoscomaniac to Cybernerd: Notes Toward an Archaeology of Media. In: Druckrey, T. (ed.): Electronic Culture: Technology and Visual Representation. New York et al.: Aperture, 299-303.

Huhtamo, E. (2007): Twin – Touch – Test – Redux: Media Archaeological Approach to Art, Interactivity and Tactility. In: Grau, O. (ed.): Media Art Histories. Cambridge(MA): The MIT Press, 71-101.

Jameson, F. (2008): Oi Archaeologies tou Mellontos: I Epithymia pou legetai Outopia (Vol. 1). Athens: Topos Publishers.

Kafetsi, A. (ed.) (2009): Shirin Neshat: Women Without Men (Exhibition Catalogue). Athens: National Museum of Contemporary Art..

Kittler, F. (1996): There is No Software. In: Druckrey, T. (ed.): Electronic Culture: Technology and Visual Representation. New York et al.: Aperture, 331-336.

Manovich, L. (2001): The Language of New Media. Cambridge(MA) et al.: The MIT Press.

Marian Goodman Gallery (2013): William Kentridge. http://www.mariangoodman.com/artists/william-kentridge (accessed July 22, 2013).

Panofsky, E. (1955): The History of Art as a Humanistic Discipline. In: Panofsky, E.: Meaning in the Visual Arts: Papers in and on Art History. Garden City(NY): Doubleday, 1-25.

Popper, F. (2007): From Technological to Virtual Art. Cambridge(MA) et al.: The MIT Press.

Riemschneider, B./ Grosenick, U. (eds.) (1999): Art at the Turn of the Millennium. Köln: Taschen.

Rush, M. (2001): New Media in Late 20th-Century Art. London: Thames and Hudson.

Sampanikou, E. (2008): Conclusions: What about the 'End of Art'? In: Sampanikou, E./ Kavakli, E. (eds.): Aspects of Representation: Studies on Art and Technology. New Technologies in Contemporary Cultural Expression. Mytilini: Univesity of the Aegean.

Sims, K. (1997): Galápagos. http://www.karlsims.com/galapagos/index.html (accessed July 22, 2013).

Tomas, D. (1996): From the Photograph to Postphotographic Practice: Toward a Postoptical Ecology of the Eye. In: Druckrey, T. (ed.): Electronic Culture: Technology and Visual Representation. New York et al.: Aperture, 145-153.

Tone, L. (2003): William Kentridge: Stereoscope. In: Kafetsi, A. (ed.): Synopsis 3: Testimonies: Between Fiction and Reality (Exhibition Catalogue). Athens: National Museum of Contemporary Art, 98-112.

Townsend, C. (2004). Introduction: Call me Old-Fashioned, But… Meaning, Singularity and Transcendence in the Work of Bill Viola. In: Townsend C. (ed.): The Art of Bill Viola. London: Thames and Hudson.

Tribe, M./ Jana, R./ Grosenick, U. (eds.) (2006): New Media Art. Köln et al.: Taschen.

Universes in Universe (2005): William Kentridge. http://universes-in-universe.de/specials/africa-remix/kentridge/english.htm (accessed July 22, 2013).

Virilio, P. (1991): The Lost Dimension. New York: Semiotext(e).

Walsh, J. (ed.) (2003): Bill Viola: The Passions (Exhibition Catalogue). Los Angeles: The J. Paul Getty Museum.

Weibel, P. (1996): The World as Interface. Toward the Construction of Context – Controlled Events – Worlds. In: Druckrey, T. (ed.): Electronic Culture: Technology and Visual Representation. New York et al.: Aperture, 354-365.

Weibel, P. (2007): It is Forbidden Not to Touch: Some Remarks on the (Forgotten Parts of the) History of Interactivity. In: Grau, O. (ed.): Media Art Histories. Cambridge(MA) et al.: The MIT Press, 21-41.

White Cube (2008): Jake & Dinos Chapman: If Hitler Had Been a Hippy How Happy Would We Be. http://whitecube.com/exhibitions/jake_dinos_chapman_if_hitler_had_been_a_hippy_how_happy_would_we_be_masons_yard_2008/ (accessed July 22, 2013).

Wilson, L.K. (1996): Cyberwar, God and Television: Interview with Paul Virilio. In: Druckrey, T. (ed.): Electronic Culture: Technology and Visual Representation. New York et al.: Aperture, 321-330.

Žižek, S. (1996): From Virtual Reality to Virtualization of Reality. In: Druckrey, T. (ed.): Electronic Culture: Technology and Visual Representation. New York et al.: Aperture, 290-295.

Literature

Marcus Rockoff

When Leon Kass opened the first session of the recently established US President's Council on Bioethics (PCBE) in 2002, he began his investigation into moral questions of modern biotechnologies with a joint reading of Nathaniel Hawthorne's short story *The Birthmark* (1843). Kass, chairman of the PCBE, maintained that the reading of Hawthorne should "deepen our understanding of the meaning of biomedical advance" (PCBE 2002).

Hawthorne's short story is about the brilliant scientist Aylmer who is married to a beautiful woman called Georgiana. She, being almost perfect, has a certain shortcoming, a birthmark on her cheek. This birthmark obsessively reminds Aylmer of her imperfection, which he desperately tries to eliminate. He persuades Georgiana to drink a potion he created in his alchemistic laboratory. This mixture should make her birthmark disappear and thus guarantee her complete perfection. However, the experiment fails and while the last signs of her birthmark fade completely, Georgiana dies.

The members of the PCBE read the story as a parable of human aspiration to gain complete perfection of our given nature and interpreted the ending as a warning sign for the risks of biotechnologies. Here, Georgiana's birthmark indicated human mortality and finitude. The described alchemistic procedure, which was supposed to fix her macule, as well as the subsequent failure of such project expresses essential human questions concerning our engagement with nature and the transhumanist aspirations "to improve this or to fix that" (PCBE 2002).

Kass' method was not uncontroversial. Harvard medical doctor and writer for *The New Yorker,* Jerome Groopman, notes that Kass exploits literature "to illustrate the consequences of scientific hubris and the dangerous quest for perfection, instead of using hard facts" (Stripling 2005, 48). Kass misused Hawthorne's work during the first session of the PCBE to illustrate allegedly timeless moral truths as a warning of possible dangers of human enhancement technologies. The described pursuit of perfection with all its fatal consequences is projected onto our biotechnological age. The tragic ending of Aylmer and Georgiana's love, however, is taken out of context (see Newman 2004, 3) and turned into an argument against the improvement of human nature by means of emerging technologies.

Still, Kass' reference to this piece of literature as a critique of transhumanist ideas is only one possible role literature can play in relation to transhumanism. In this article possible relations between literature and trans- as well as posthumanism shall be discussed. After a brief sketch of both movements in the first section, the second section will introduce and discuss three different classes of references to transhumanism in literary works. The third section illustrates a plurality of possible interpretations of transhumanist literature. By discussing Mary W. Shelley's novel *Frankenstein* (1818) and Aldous Huxley's *Brave New World* (1932), it will be shown how different plausible readings of the same fictional works could lead to contradictory evaluations of the transhumanist project. Finally, the fourth section examines the novels *The Elementary Particles* (2000 [1998]) by Michel Houellbecq and *Oryx and Crake* (2003) by Margaret Atwood, which are widely discussed in post- and transhumanist debates. In contrast to standard interpretations it will be argued that both novels not only deal with transhumanist ideas but also show elements of posthumanist thought.

Post- and Transhumanism

The question of literature and post- or transhumanism can be approached from two directions. On the one hand, literary work can be analyzed with regard to its post- or transhumanist themes and motifs. On the other hand, discourses on post- or transhumanism can be searched for references to literature and the importance of literature for the discourse itself. Approaching these two aspects, it is worth determining the concepts of post- or transhumanism. Even though both terms are frequently used interchangeably, they refer to a variety of distinct theories and movements. In particular "posthumanism" is distinguished by a plurality of meanings (see Miah 2008) and is (confusingly enough) sometimes used to refer to transhumanism, too.

In this paper transhumanism shall be perceived as the project to change and improve human nature…

> "[…] through applied reason, especially by developing and making widely available technologies to eliminate aging and to greatly enhance human intellectual, physical, and psychological capacities" (Bostrom 2003, 4).

This must not be seen as a purely theoretical and intellectual endeavor, but rather as a cultural movement. Transhumanists see themselves as successors to humanism and aim for redesigning human nature so far that it becomes posthuman. The most important transhumanist organization is Humanity+, which openly embraces such aspirations.

The concept of posthumanity in transhumanism describes a future stage of history where human beings will have taken evolution into their own hands and improve themselves so radically as to be "more than human", i.e. posthuman (see Bostrom 2005, 204). By the same token, most transhumanists envision that such a radical change of our biology would also turn the world into a better place (see, e.g., Bostrom 2008).

Transhumanist ideas as well as their political agenda have been under heavy attack by so-called bioconservative authors. Fukuyama, member of the PCBE under Kass, presents "the posthuman as a condition of threat posed by allegedly invasive new technologies to the integrity of human nature" (Wallace 2010, 692). The transhumanist aspirations for posthumanity, so the argument goes, would transform a common meaningful concept of human nature (Fukuyama 2002, 7). In contrast to transhumanism, the "posthuman" in Fukuyama's work is used in a pejorative sense. It is a symbol of bioconservative critique and points to some consequences of false belief in emerging technologies to alter human nature. New means of genetics, information technologies, cybernetics as well as neuroscience, which may eventually alter human nature and thereby transform human beings into posthumans, are not only perceived as an attack on our common nature but also pose threats to liberal western democracy (see ibid.).

From these debates on transhumanism and posthumanity, we can distinguish "posthumanism". Posthumanism is sometimes referred to as *cultural* posthumanism (see Miah 2008, 76) or *critical* posthumanism (see Simon 2003; Graham 2004; Wallace 2010) and can be seen as an umbrella term for postmodern theories in cultural studies and humanities. Unlike the posthuman in transhumanist and bioconservative literature, the "'post' of posthumanism need not imply moving beyond humanness in some biological or evolutionary manner" (Miah 2008, 72). Posthumanism in this sense should rather be seen as a critique on humanist concepts of "human being". It questions the deep-rooted anthropocentrism in Western culture that is distinguished by the…

> "[…] domination and subjugation to its externalized others – animals, machines, nature, the environment, nonindividualistic cultures and – in the case of the ambiguously generic 'man' – women" (Wallace 2010, 693).

This perspective rests on an insight that has already been embraced by Foucault (2005 [1970], 421) and Hassan (1977, 212). The (humanistic) "human" is, in fact, a self-made historical figure, which serves the purpose of dissociating the human from the nonhuman. This separation, however, has been scrutinized by the medical, bio- and information technological access to the human body during the 20th Century (see Waldby 2000). This event leads to the…

> "[…] apparent blurring of the boundaries by which 'the human' has traditionally been distinguished from 'the non-human': natural/artificial, biological/technological, real/virtual, organic/manufactured" (Graham 2004, 179).

The main focus of this article shall be the relation between literature and transhumanism, yet cultural or critical posthumanism will also be considered with respect to some central issues. The following sections will focus on identifying and systematizing transhumanist elements in different literary works.

Three Classes of References to Transhumanism in Literature

There are three classes of *transhumanist literature*, or, to be more precise, three classes of references to transhumanism that can be distinguished in literature. First, one can find the theme of specific, mainly technological methods and procedures in numerous novels that are of great relevance for the transhumanist project. These concern a fictional engagement with present and future technological possibilities, which are often in the focus of science fiction literature. They describe and extrapolate technologies that are either in an early stage of development or will be developed in the future. This is how a large amount of scenarios of various technologies such as genetic engineering, prosthetics, cryonics, cybernetics, neuro and nano science, AI research and robotics also inspires the transhumanist project.

The second class refers to mere thematological concepts, which can be understood as central ideas or key messages of the story. As for the references to transhumanism, it is the general idea of human enhancement or even human perfection. While there is certainly an overlap between this class of references and the first one, here the general motif of improving human beings is central rather than a specific reference to the technological means. This also allows for including literary works from periods of time when people did not even dream of today's biotechnical options. Mary Shelley's *Frankenstein; or, The Modern Prometheus* (1818), for instance, certainly shows transhumanist themes, while being far away from today's technological standard.

A third rather rarely used class of references could be seen in the theme of transhumanism as an active and present ideological movement.

References to Specific Technologies Relevant for Transhumanism

There are references to all kinds of emerging technologies in literature. From the perspective of literary studies these references can be seen as fictional reflection of real-world science and technologies. Most science fiction or cyberpunk novels make use of extrapolations of present and future technologies to optimize the human body. As a matter of fact science fiction literature rarely does without transhumanist elements.

One example for these elements is genetic engineering, used in various clone novels such as Kazuo Ishiguro's *Never Let Me Go* (2005) or Michael Marshall Smith's *Spares* (1996). In Bruce Sterling's novel *Schismatrix* (1985), two different rival posthuman species are described. The so-called *Shapers* – described as masters of biology and genetic engineering – have adapted their DNA to the environmental conditions, whereas their rivals, the *Mechanists,* have chosen the path of information technologies and mechanics to modify themselves into almost immortal cyborgs.

Another prime example is William Gibson's *Sprawl trilogy* with his famous first volume *Neuromancer* (1984). It contains numerous elements also known from transhumanist visions such as artificial intelligence or the determined modification of the human body through technology. Most people in Gibson's novel have been modified by microchips that make them more intelligent or have improved their physiology through implants and prostheses.

Another central topic is cryonics. James L. Haperin's novel *The First Immortal* (1998) tells the story of Benjamin Franklin Smith's preservation by cryonics, giving him the opportunity to celebrate his 200th birthday at the end of the book. After it is described how the main character has been preserved in 1988, the novel illustrates fictional scientific progress in medicine, genetic engineering, nanotechnology and information technology. Thanks to these forms of progress, mid-21st Century humans are not only enabled to revive preserved people, but also to delay their aging process.

In this way Haperin's novel describes a future world, where eternal youth and health are ubiquitous because of emerging technologies. Furthermore, the novel gives an interesting example of the interaction between fiction in literature and present ambition in science. In the novel's appendix one can find detailed scientific background to preservation by cryonics and references to organizations that either approach this method or already practice it. At the same time information material of real-world organizations, such as Alcor Life Extension Foundation (2014) or the Cryonics Institute (2014), refers to Haperin's novel as an effective start to learn about cryonics.

Common motifs and topics as much as the constant reflection on the possibilities, potentials and limitations of technological progress bring science fiction literature into the center of transhumanists' attention. Here science fiction literature, transhumanism and sciences can be seen as mutually stimulating discourses (see Dinello 2005).

Thematological References to the Transhumanist Idea of Overcoming Human Nature

The second class of references corresponding to transhumanism can be seen as so-called thematological references, which are often described as motifs, themes or basic narratological schemes (see Jost 1988). In the case of transhumanism they can be characterized as referring to the "transhumanist mindset".[1] Transhumanism is being described as a cultural or ideological movement that pursues the aim of improving the biological disposition of the human being by means of technologies. So this second class of thematological references points to the essential transhumanist idea of overcoming human nature by means of technology. It takes up the long and widely branched history of cultures and ideas, which itself states that humans can control their fate and progress through the use of technology.

In this regard, one can easily notice that even the earliest evidence of human culture includes transhumanist themes and ideas. The *Epic of Gilgamesh* is seen as the earliest documentation of transhumanist thought (see Bostrom 2005, 1): It tells the story of the protagonist's search for a plant, growing on the sea bed, which bestows eternal youth. Here Bostrom sees the permanent desire of humankind to overcome death by using "technologies" – in spite of a metaphysical understanding of the world promising redemption in the hereafter.

The transhumanist idea of human enhancement can also be found in numerous mythological narratives and figures such as *Daedalus* or *Pygmalion* (see Slusser 2009, 127). The most meaningful and significant, however, is the myth of *Prometheus*, in its countless variations and adaptions. The most common reception of this myth highlights human creativity, craftsmanship and technical abilities. Until today, Prometheus represents the symbol of human self-authorization to shape his environment and ultimately himself (see Stock 2003, 2).

In this context, the motif of the "artificial man" is often mentioned as an apparent precursor of transhumanist concepts. However, it has to be noted that the stories and tales of golems, homunculi, *doppelgangers* and human machines can only in part be associated with transhumanist ideas. The motif of the "artificial man" primarily focuses on the human desire to become his own creator. This happens by imitated divine creation, even without or against god's will, in a magical-mystical, mechanical-electronic or biological-chemical way.

Aspects of improvement or perfection of these first artificial beings, however, are of little importance for these stories. They must rather be read as a literary reflection on human's intellectual abilities to understand the functioning of (human) nature and on his craftsmanship to create the *man-made* human beings. On the one hand, the creation of these artificial beings illustrates human faith in his own central position in the world, which can also be found in Renaissance humanism. On the other hand, artificial human beings serve as instruments to

1 In these works of literature, however, references of the already mentioned first class can also be found.

gain knowledge of humanity. With the help of these beings, humans can question and understand their own – later also technologically manipulable – constitution.

Perhaps the first literary work that explicated genuine transhumanist thinking is Mary W. Shelley's novel *Frankenstein; or, The Modern Prometheus* (1818). With the figure of Victor Frankenstein not only the first modern transhumanist enters the stage of world literature. Furthermore, various innovations for the Prometheus motif, which are still important for contemporary transhumanist fiction, can be found throughout this piece of literature.

The project of Victor Frankenstein has striking parallels to transhumanism. In the transhumanist project three elements can be identified that are already present in Shelley's *Frankenstein*: (1) the specific diagnosis of the current human being as a defective existence; (2) the purposeful modification and improvement of humanity to free it from disease and limitations of the human life span (immortality), but also to "amplify human intelligence, increase emotional well-being, improve our capacity for steady commitment to life projects or a loved one, and even multiply the range and richness of possible emotions" (Bostrom 2003, 5); (3) the belief in rationality, science and technology as the main resources to improve humankind and make the world a better place.

Initially, the diagnosis of the current human conditions is a connecting factor to understand the importance of *Frankenstein* for transhumanist thought. Humans are imperfect in the view of transhumanism: they are defective creatures (see Gehlen 1988). This means not only that their mortality is perceived as a deficiency, but also that their current physical and mental abilities "do […] not represent the end of our development but rather a comparatively early phase" (Bostrom 2003, 4). Transhumanists share the belief that the current nature of the human cannot remain the same in order to meet the challenges of the present and the future successfully (see Huxley 1963, 5-6; Bostrom 2013, 46).

Although at the beginning of his project Victor Frankenstein focuses on the mere pursuit of knowledge and wisdom (see Shelley 2004 [1818], 62) as well as on the interest "to understand the hidden laws of nature" (Shelley 2004 [1831], 324), over time, while dealing with these issues, Frankenstein develops something that can be interpreted as a transhumanist belief. His perception of the current human being complies with the current transhumanist premise of man as a flawed being: "we are unfashioned creatures, but half made up, if one wiser, better, dearer than ourselves — such a friend ought to be — do not lend his aid to perfectionate our weak and faulty natures" (ibid., 319).

The ultimately successful search for the "principle of life" (Shelley 2004 [1818], 79) that has put him in a position to bring already dead matter back to life also leads to the research objective of overcoming the defective human, who is plagued by diseases and mortality:

> "[...] what glory would attend the discovery if I could banish disease from the human frame and render man invulnerable to any but a violent death!" (Shelley 2004 [1818], 69)

In the end the experiment succeeds and on a rainy November night Frankenstein creates a post-human being. Despite its terrible appearance, which causes Frankenstein "breathless horror and disgust" (Shelley 2004 [1818], 85), his creature is a genuine rational being (ibid., 238) with amazing capacities. Not only does the creature possess superhuman abilities regarding strength, speed and stamina. His intellectual abilities can be characterized as far developed, too. In less than two years the monster of the status of a newborn becomes an educated, sensitive and moral being (ibid., 152-153).

Thus, it becomes clear that Shelley's story – compared to other variants of the motif of artificial people – is not just eager to create human life, but also describes a redesign of the human species, which is so profound that it can be considered as a new post-human species:

> "Life and death appeared to me ideal bounds, which I should first break through, and pour a torrent of light into our dark world. A new species would bless me as its creator and source; many happy and excellent natures would owe their being to me" (Shelley 2004 [1818], 81-82).

The third aspect of a clear reference to transhumanism in the novel is the scientific creation of the being. Frankenstein's monster is a product of the modern natural sciences and thus a child of applied technology and scientific-empirical methods. As it is written in the text, his emergence as a living being is not due to the work or influence of a god, a demon, or any occult or magical powers. Accordingly, the novel is also often placed at the beginning of the history of the science fiction genre (see Aldiss 1988, 19). With the transition from alchemy to science, Shelley's *Frankenstein* is also the first literary document in which the human species is to be improved by a modern understanding of knowledge and science (see Vasbinder 1984; Rowen 1992).

The most famous aspect for which Shelley's novel is notorious, however, is the reading that *Frankenstein* presents "a story of technology out of control" (Bostrom 2005, 8). Thus the work becomes a "fundamental literary myth of neo-Luddism, a tale about the dangers of technology" (Jones 2006, 106), which is, until today, expressed most evidently in the presentation of the *mad scientist motif*. Its clout is so relevant for the transhumanist literature that it is constantly renewed in different contexts, with new technologies, or updated goals. The core of the story, however, always remains the same: A brilliant scientist wants to control nature or change human nature. However, the experiment goes out of control and turns against its creator (Haynes 1994).[2]

The assessment of *Frankenstein* as a story about technology out of control requires a critical review. Before approaching this issue, a third class of transhumanist references in literature will be presented.

References to Transhumanism as an International Movement

Transhumanism as a cultural movement refers to the group of scientists, artists and intellectuals that evolved during the 1980s. These thinkers are united in their aspiration to change the human condition radically. Many transhumanists are organized in groups such as *Humanity+* to give their ideas and interests a political force (see Tirosh-Samuelson 2011). The third class of references explicitly points to this movement, addresses transhumanism as a cultural phenomenon or illustrates figures that can be recognized as transhumanists.

Significant in this context is especially Dan Brown's bestselling novel *Inferno* (2013), which introduces transhumanism along with its worldview to a wide audience. In Brown's novel Robert Langdon, symbologist know from *The Da Vinci Code* (2003) and *The Lost Symbol* (2009), is facing the chemist Bertrand Zobrist. The latter is described as a member of a militant faction of transhumanism, who is convinced that mankind is doomed due to overpopulation. Therefore Zobrist, in the tradition of the mad scientist motif, develops a pathogen, "a Transhumanist Black Death" (Brown 2013, 366), in order to curb the uncontrolled distribution of the human species. It is up to Langdon to prevent this by – typical for Brown's style of writing – searching for "puzzle pieces" in the literary and cultural history to find and stop Zobrist.

During the course of the plot not only the transhumanist movement and its central theses are portrayed, but the Humanity+ Summit 2010 in Los Angeles, the h+ magazine, which belongs to the Humanity+ network, and transhumanist thinkers such as Fereidoun M. Esfandiary (FM-2030) are mentioned, too. The

2 A similar story can also be found in H. G. Wells' *The Island of Dr. Moreau* (1896). In the novel the brilliant scientist Dr. Moreau moves into the loneliness and social isolation of a South Sea island retreat to create human-animal chimeras by means of vivisection. Based on the theories of Charles Darwin, the evolution of life is seen as a huge experiment and Moreau attempts to create a new super race by combining different characteristics of different species. Here again, the created beings rebel against their creator. In Karel Čapek's *R.U.R.* (1921), Aldous Huxley's *Brave New World* (1932), Michel Houellebecq's *The Elementary Particles* (1998) and Margaret Atwood's *Oryx and Crake* (2003) or, as already mentioned, *The Birthmark* (1843) by Nathaniel Hawthorne, we also find traces of this fundamental conflict of human self-empowerment over nature.

narrator also leaves little doubt that he sympathizes with transhumanism. In fact, the end of the novel just reads like a plea for the transhumanist project:

> "[...] we as humans have a moral obligation to participate in our evolutionary process [...] to use our technologies to advance the species, to create better humans – healthier, stronger, with higher-functioning brains. Everything will soon be possible" (Brown 2013, 377).

A similar militant transhumanist comparable to Brown's Zobrist is presented in Zoltan Istvan's widely discussed[3] novel *The Transhumanist Wager* (2013). The protagonist of this novel, Jethrow Knights, is fascinated and equally obsessed by the idea of becoming immortal with the help of various technologies such as cryonics, cloning, genetics, neurotech and artificial intelligence. In the novel Knights develops an transhumanist philosophy, which is called *Teleological Egocentric Functionalism* (TEF). The central point of this philosophy is the so-called *transhumanist wager* that provides an imperative for achieving immortality:

> "We love life and therefore want to live as long as possible – we desire to be immortal. It's impossible to know if we're going to be immortal once we die. To do nothing doesn't help our odds of attaining immortality, since it seems evident that we're going to die someday and possibly cease to exist. To attempt something scientifically constructive towards ensuring immortality beforehand is the most logical solution" (Istvan 2013, 46).

According to such imperative, every attempt by conservatives, religion or anti-transhumanists to intervene or to stop this process must be seen as "*manslaughter*" (ibid., 22). In the end there are violent acts of war between conservative critics of transhumanism, such as political and religious leaders of several nations, and progressive transhumanists, who already live in their utopian-like *Transhumania* under the leadership of Knights. This conflict intensified because Knights represents an "extreme, nearly militant version of the radically libertarian formulation of transhumanism championed by the Extropy Institute in the 90s" (Prisco 2013).

Nothing can stop these transhumanists from becoming immortal and egoistic "omnipotenders" (Istvan 2013, 42). Their success depends on the transhuman morality that is not distinguished by kindness, altruism, love, religion and human value (ibid., 67). Their morality is "defined and decided by the amount of time [they] have left to live" (ibid.) and the decisions necessary to become omnipotent.

---

3 See various extensive reviews on this novel by Prisco (2013), Searle (2013), Stolyarov II (2013).

The novel is an interesting piece of literature concerning the transhumanist movement and ideas. We can easily identify current debates about the pros and cons of transhumanism in our society. But we also recognize an idiosyncratic concept of transhumanism, styled in warrior-like crusade against "society's addiction to illogicality, egalitarianism, historical culture, blind consumerism, and religion" (ibid., 70). In the novel these cultural phenomena are seen as the main obstacles preventing the posthuman future.

Finally, a last work of fiction should be mentioned. Richard Powers' novel *Generosity: An Enhancement* (2009) tells the story of the Algerian woman Thassadit Amzwar – now living in Chicago – who despite terrible and violent experiences in her childhood is still an extremely happy and generous person. Various scientists try to figure out the secret of her happiness, which is probably linked to a genetically caused abnormality, a Hyperthymia (see Powers 2009, 67). In the novel Amzwar's *happiness genes* (see ibid., 183) serve as a narrative to discuss recent and upcoming possibilities of human enhancement technologies in general.

In *Generosity*, the most significant reference to transhumanism can be seen in the depictions of the scientist Thomas Kurton. He is described as a geneticist and entrepreneur of various biotechnology start-ups. Remarkably, Kurton writes "ecstatic pieces about the coming transhuman age" in his spare time (ibid., 23). In fact, he must be seen as a champion of transhumanism. Kurton believes "in the one nonarbitrary enterprise, fairer than any politics, truer than any religion, deeper than any artwork: measurement" (ibid., 271). Furthermore, he is convinced that "given enough time and creativity, we humans [can] make ourselves over into anything we want" (ibid., 23).

The quest for Amzwar's happiness as well as the possibility to identify the biological cause of her generosity and eventually sell it on the market sets the stage for the confrontation between transhumanist ideas and its critics. This dispute recalls C. P. Snow's famous "Two Cultures" distinction originally mentioned in his popular lecture at Cambridge (see Snow 2001 [1959]). While the scientist and transhumanist Kurton argues that if Amzwar's happiness and generosity are heritable we might be able to understand the phenomenon and make use of it to enhance ourselves, the nameless critic, represented by a novelist, responds that the "remodeling of human nature will be as slapdash and flawed as its remodelers. We'll never *feel* enhanced. We'll always be banned from some further Eden. The misery business will remain a growth industry" (ibid., 141).

Considering the story of *Generosity* we find illuminating references to the transhumanist movement situated in a society that resembles modern Western democracies. On the one hand we find the pursuit of happiness, brought forward by transhumanists. Here the novel reveals a questionable mixture of transhumanist ideas with hidden commercial interests, which want to shape consumers' attitudes. On the other hand there is a deep-seated skepticism concerning the technological means to achieve such a never-ending feeling of bliss. This reminds us that, despite all scientific fantasies of human enhancement, every human is still the architect of his own fortune.

Everybody's Darling: Using Literature to Illustrate the Pros and Cons of Post- and Transhumanism

Shelley's Victor Frankenstein, Wells' Dr. Moreau as well as Brown's Bertrand Zobrist are all descendants of the mad scientist motif. The mad scientist symbolizes the central dilemma of our technological age. On the one hand these characters present the human confidence that we will be able to improve the current and future civilizations by technological means. This view is emphasized by transhumanists' readings of such literature. On the other hand there is hubris. This literature can be read as a warning sign of possible risks and dangers related to emerging technologies. Critics of transhumanism emphasize this view.

While we find a one-sided reading of the mad scientist by transhumanists as well as bioconservatives, this motif does not determine one ultimate interpretation. This is because literature is ambiguous. If we think about the meaning of literature there is no easy way to employ terms like right or wrong. We are rather forced to use terms like plausible and implausible or convincing and unconvincing only. Thus, transhumanists and bioconservative critics should be careful of using literature to illustrate possible or potential dangers of technology.

In this way Shelley's *Frankenstein* is not only "a story of technology out of control" (Bostrom 2005, 8). A close reading shows that the experiment actually succeeded but Frankenstein's project fails in a different regard. Reading *Frankenstein* as a plain critique on technological progress, we fall for a one-sided, even deceptive interpretation. The evil of the monster, for which it later gained fame in pop culture and cinematic reception, does not stem from the nature of the creature itself. The disaster, which is expressed in the extinction of all the people dearest to Frankenstein, derives mainly from the environment and social relations in which the monster was placed. Eventually the experiment fails neither because of technical difficulties nor because of religious or ethical considerations. It fails because of a lack of tolerance and acceptance of others. The creature says:

> "[…] still I desired love and fellowship, and I was still spurned. Was there no injustice in this? Am I to be thought the only criminal, when all human kind sinned against me?" (Shelley 2004 [1831], 243)

Taking these suggestions into account *Frankenstein* as a story of technology out of control gets a whole new meaning. It raises the ethical question "whether humanity is mature enough to deal with very fast technological progress, particularly if it radically alters the human condition" (Coenen 2007, 163).

Another novel where we find the mad scientist motif is Aldous Huxley's *Brave New World* (1932), which is mainly referred to by bioconservatives to criticize the transhumanist project. In *Brave New World* the mad scientist is not a distinct figure. We rather see this motif in the illustration of the World State, a technocratic government dominated by the logic of science where control of human nature is state doctrine.

In Shelley's *Frankenstein* a scientifically controlled intervention in human biology has the ambition of producing happy and noble creatures. In Huxley's *Brave New World* this intention is not only industrialized and put under state control, but it has also become a part of the socio-political environment. Humans will no longer be born, the Bokanowsky Process will produce them; humans will no longer be educated, they will be normed by pharmacological procedures and Pavlovian conditioning. In the novel it all began with the idea that controlling the environment and human nature can enrich people's lives. This project, however, did not stop at this point and went out of control. The biotechnologies used have influenced people's lives and their bodies with the aim of *producing* individuals that are highly productive and well customized for the work in a *Ford-like* production process. In the end it seems that "the people in *Brave New World* may be healthy and happy, but they have ceased to be *human beings*" (Fukuyama 2002, 6).

For critics of transhumanism (see Kass 2001; Fukuyama 2002) Huxley's novel is a warning against the dehumanizing potential of technology. The outcome of the broad socio-biological experiment in Huxley's story is seen as a prediction for the transhumanist project. In their view this project is risky because it undermines human nature (see Fukuyama 2002, 149).

Compared to this reading, transhumanists do not interpret *Brave New World* as "a tale of human enhancement gone amok", but rather as a "tragedy of technology and social engineering being deliberately used to cripple moral and intellectual capacities", and hence as "the exact antithesis of the transhumanist proposal" (Bostrom 2005, 206). They are not convinced that the transhumanist project will unavoidably lead to a dystopia like *Brave New World* (ibid.).

According to the transhumanist reading biotechnologies in *Brave New World* are used to suppress humankind in a totalitarian world-state. This, however, is not the envisioned future of the transhumanists because it violates central elements of their project: morphological and reproductive freedom, i.e. "that individuals get to consult their own consciences as to what is right for themselves and their families" (ibid.).

Insofar as Bostrom refers to a liberal understanding of freedom as a basic premise of the transhumanist project, he, by the same token, underestimates possible dangers related to biotechnological manipulations, which might eventually undermine individual freedom. A careful reading of *Brave New World* reveals that it is not open and brutal terror that forces the fictious population of the World State to use biotechnological manipulationes. It is rather the prospect of living a happy and fulfilling life by means of all these technologies which makes people voluntarily give up their individual freedom. Even if transhumanists correctly point out that Huxley's society is based on state-controlled eugenics and thus runs counter to the liberal and libertarian use of biotechnologies affirmed by transhumanism, one has to take into account that genetic control, Soma and so forth, lead to a stable and peaceful society, which is of great interest for the people. Hence, the novel reminds us that individuals, searching for a happy and peaceful life may ignore that certain technologies and practices could have consequences for their individual freedom as well as their autonomy. As Huxley in *Brave New World* states:

> "People were ready to have even their appetites controlled then. Anything for a quiet life. We've gone on controlling ever since. It hasn't been very good for truth, of course. But it's been very good for happiness. One can't have something for nothing. Happiness has got to be paid for" (Huxley 1932, 269-270).

Questioning Our Perception of Humanity by Reading Literature

Works of fiction that contain transhumanist topics should neither be read as naive techno-futuristic visions as done by some transhumanists, nor as warning horror tales as done by some bioconservatives. Both readings will make future scientific and political debate between the two camps more difficult. Instead we should use literature "to help us think about problems, to test our systems and our assumptions, and to expand our imaginations" (Annas 2010, xx-xxi). But we should also keep in mind that in case of the difficult questions raised by the transhumanist project, works of literature often do not give any or no simple answer.

For instance Michel Houellebecq's *The Elementary Particles* (2000 [1998]) and Margaret Atwood's *Oryx and Crake* (2003) operate with a similar basic structure of the mad scientist motif. Here again, we find a genius scientist who, with the help of his extraordinary knowledge, improves human nature to prepare humanity for the future. In both novels the transhumanist project starts with a critique of the current social circumstances, which are perceived as extreme commercialism and egoism. Both novels see the cause of this decline in human nature, in the genetic makeup of humans. The diagnosis in *The Elementary Particles* is that "this unique genetic code – of which, by some tragic perversity, we were so ridiculously proud – was precisely the source of so much human unhappiness" (Houellebecq 2000 [1998], 269).

The diagnosis in *Oryx and Crake* is that humanity due to its intellectual capacities always adheres to the dream of immortality:

> "They put their energy into staying alive themselves until times get better. But human beings hope they can stick their souls into someone else, some new version of themselves, and live on forever" (Atwood 2003, 120).

This leads to the problem that humans, despite diminishing resources, do not reduce the population by adjusting their rate of reproduction: "the less we eat, the more we fuck" (Atwood 2003, 120). The inability to live in harmony with nature eventually will doom humanity.

In both novels the opportunities of modern biotechnology are seen as a possibility to rebuild humanity from scratch. In *The Elementary Particles* a nameless, sexless and peace-loving posthuman species is created, which reproduces itself by means of cloning technologies. In Atwood's novel there are the *Crakers*. This is a nearly human transgenic species, which, thanks to their catlike hyoids, has a very good and fast self-healing process. They can also keep away enemies with the help of special urine and have a biologically restructured sexuality. As a consequence of this, there is "[n]o more prostitution, no sexual abuse of children, no haggling over the price, no pimps, no sex slaves. No more rape" (Atwood 2003, 165) in their community. Thus, the Crakers live as a small group in harmony with the surrounding natural paradise and are also characterized as highly moral beings who do not know lies, deceit, or even hatred.

In Atwood and Houellebecq the mad scientist motif finds a revaluation. In both novels the transhumanist project does not lead to rejection of technology. There is no rebellion of the creation against its creator. The transition from the human to a genetically optimized posthuman species rather happens without any fight and, in particular in Houellebecq's *The Elementary Particles,* the process of overcoming humanity takes place calmly:

> "It has been surprising to note the meekness, resignation, perhaps even secret relief with which humans have consented to their own passing" (Houellebecq 2000 [1998], 273).

Accordingly, humans themselves have considered the disappearance of their own species.

To read these novels as a naïve techno-futurism, however, does not seem appropriate (see Coenen 2007, 142-143). One could rather interpret both novels as literary reflections on the possibilities of transcending the humanist framework, which is essential for transhumanism. In the epilogue of his novel Houellebecq describes "that humanity in its current state could and should control the evolution of the world's species – and in particular its own evolution" (Houellebecq 2000 [1998], 268) and thus also create the conditions to replace humanity (ibid., 272).[4] By shifting to asexual reproduction, individualism and egoism, the reasons for human suffering on earth, will be eliminated and replaced by "a mysterious fraternity" (ibid., 269). At this point the novel secedes from humanistic concepts of individuality and autonomy, which are so important for transhumanism (see Morrey 2013, 158-162).

In *Oryx and Crake*, the *Crakers* can also be seen as a critique of such a concept of humanism. They are a fictional formulated criticism of the humanistic self-image of the human, which claims that human beings possess a special status in the world. This delusion of human supremacy, as it is suggested in Atwood's novel, leads to the human inability to live in peace and harmony with nature. The transgenic species of the *Crakers* presents an alternative and a replacement of humanity. Their main feature is that they do not have the typical human deficit: "To stay human is to break a limitation" (Atwood 2003, 269). Their nature is altered and enhanced with a variety of animal functions and characteristics so that they can live in harmony with nature. This transgenic species represents a dethronement of current humanity.

It seems reasonable to perceive Houellebecq and Atwood's "literary experiments" with humans as a way of thinking that resembles critical or cultural posthumanism. This can be seen as a challenge to the modern human – in both its biological features as well as its cultural and social life. These novels do not celebrate a transhumanist techno-futurism. Further, the stories do not present cautionary examples of technology out of control. By using fictional imaginations, both works reflect and question concepts of the (post)human against the background of aiming for a better and happier world. This is, however, realized in different ways: In *The Elementary Particles* the posthuman is searched in the idea of the "taming of men" (Sloterdijk 2009, 15). With the help of biotechnology the individuality, egoism and thus the animal side of human nature will be wiped away. In *Oryx and Crake* the road to the posthuman leads through the "barbarization" of humanity, which gets closer to animals and nature. By the same token, this marks the end of human's superior position in the order of the world.

4 The humans are "the first species in the universe to develop the conditions for its own replacement" (Houellebecq 2000, 272).

Summary

Insofar as literature addresses questions, hopes and ideas of enhancing human nature in many different ways, it is a highly relevant subject for the discussion of transhumanist and posthumanist issues. As for transhumanism it has been argued concerning references in literature that three different classes can be distinguished: First, there are references to technologies that might be used to overcome limitations of human nature and which are also on the transhumanist agenda. Sometimes fictional work and transhumanist discourses even inspire each other mutually, as we see in the case of cryonics.

Second, there are references to the transhumanist mindset of overcoming human nature. These references can be found throughout literary history where we find several narratives, motifs and figures, which deal with ideas that resemble transhumanism. Above all the myth of *Prometheus*, Shelley's *Frankenstein* and the mad scientist motif are highly relevant for this class.

Third, in some literature we find explicit mentions of transhumanism as an actual and present movement, as well as references to (fictional) characters that belong to this movement. In contemporary novels like Richard Powers' *Generosity* or Dan Brown's *Inferno* these references not only deal with transhumanist ideas but also reflect on the role of the transhumanist movement in current society.

Especially for the moral and political debate about the transhumanist project, literature provides a large amount of material for transhumanists and their critics. While the latter read selected works of literature as cautionary tales to warn against the dehumanizing potentials of biotechnologies, supporters of transhumanism refer to literature to illustrate the desirability and inevitability of a biotechnological future. Most remarkably, both camps often believe to find support for their positions by refering to the same works of literature.

This, however, is not a surprise considering the fact that literature does not allow an ultimate interpretation. It does not make sense to speak in terms of truth or untruth. We should rather refer to the plausibility or implausibility of an interpretation. Thus it is possible that the very same text of literature evokes several conflicting and even contradicting readings.

Posthumanist issues can also be found in many literary works. In some fictional scenarios of transcending human nature it becomes obvious that literature does not only reflect on the chances and risks of biotechnologies for human nature. Some works of literature also focus on the concept "humanity" in particular. They draw our attention to the blurry boundaries between nature and technology and thus can be read as a critique of the humanist concept of a "human being". In this regard novels like Atwood's *Oryx and Crake* or Houellebecq's *The Elementary Patricles* contribute to and represent posthumanist thinking.

As a medium of reflection, literature is of great importance. With the help of fictional texts we can think through different scenarios, possible chances and risks of transhumanism in a narrative framework as well as possible consequences of our common concepts such as "humanity" or "human nature". Nevertheless, since literature is open to various possible interpretations, it is problematic to attribute exclusive validity to a specific perspective. Thus, literature proves to be a difficult terrain for gathering arguments for or against the transhumanist project or posthumanist ideas. This is also true, if critics or advocates of post- and transhumanism try to abuse certain works of literature by refering to them within arguments for allegedly timeless truths or as trend-setting scenarios of an inevitable future.

Bibliography

Alcor Life Extension Foundation (2014): The Alcor Library. http://alcor.org/Library/index.html#onlinebooks (accessed April 25, 2014).

Aldiss, B.W. (1988): Trillion Year Spree: The History of Science Fiction. London et al.: Paladin.

Annas, G. J. (2010): Worst Case Bioethics: Death, Disaster, and Public Health. Oxford: Oxford University Press.

Atwood, M. (2003): Oryx and Crake. New York et al.: Doubleday.

Bostrom, N. et al. (2003): The Transhumanist FAQ: A General introduction (Version 2.1). http://www.transhumanism.org/resources/FAQv21.pdf (accessed April 10, 2013).

Bostrom, N. (2005): In Defence of Posthuman Dignity. In: Bioethics 19(3), 202-214.

Bostrom, N. (2008): Letter from Utopia. In: Studies in Ethics, Law, and Technology 2(1), 1-7.

Bostrom, N. (2013): Why I Want to be a Posthuman When I Grow Up. In: More, M./ Vita-More, N. (eds.): The Transhumanist Reader: Classical and Contemporary Essays on the Science, Technology, and Philosophy of the Human Nature. Oxford: Wiley-Blackwell, 28-53.

Brown, D. (2013): Inferno. New York: Bantam.

Čapek, K. (1921): R.U.R. (Rossum's Universal Robots). Adelaide: University of Adelaide.

Coenen, C. (2007): Utopian Aspects of the Debate on Converging Technologies. In: Banse, G. et al. (eds): Assessing Societal Implications of Converging Technological Development. Berlin: edition sigma, 141-172.

Cryonics Institute (2014): Cryonics Institute Resource Library. http://www.cryonics.org/resources/ (accessed April 25, 2014).

Dinello, D. (2005): Technophobia: Science Fiction Visions of Posthuman Technology. Houston: University of Texas Press.

Foucault, M. (2005 [1970]): The Order of Things: An Archaeology of the Human Sciences. London et al.: Routledge.

Fukuyama, F. (2002): Our Posthuman Future: Consequences of the Biotechnology Revolution. New York: Douglas & Mclntyre.

Gehlen, A. (1988): Man: His Nature and Place in the World. New York: Columbia University Press.

Gibson, W. (2004 [1984]): Neuromancer. 20th Anniversary Edition. New York: Ace Books.

Graham, E. (2002): The Representation of the Posthuman: Monsters, Aliens and Others in Popular Culture. Manchester: Manchester University Press.

Graham, E. (2004): Bioethics after Posthumanism: Natural Law, Communicative Action and the Problem of Self-Design. In: Ecotheology 9(2), 178-198.

Groopman, J. (2002): Science Fiction. In: The New Yorker. http://www.newyorker.com/archive/2002/02/04/020204ta_talk_groopman (accessed April 10, 2013).

Haperin, J. (1998): The First Immortal: A Novel of the Future. New York: Del Rey.

Hassan, I. (1977): Prometheus as Performer: Toward a Posthumanist Culture? In: Benamou, M./ Caramello, C. (eds.): Performance in Postmodern Culture. Madison(WI): Coda Press, 201-207.

Hawthorne, N. (1921 [1843]): The Birthmark. In: Perry, B. (ed.): Little Masterpieces. Garden City(NY), Toronto: Doubleday, Page and Company, 21-51.

Haynes, R. D. (1994): From Faust to Strangelove: Representations of the Scientist in Western Literature. Baltimore et al.: Johns Hopkins University Press.

Houellebecq, M. (2000 [1998]): The Elementary Particles. New York: Knopf.

Houellebecq, M. (2006): The Possibility of an Island. New York: Knopf.

Huxley, A. (1932) Brave New World. London: Chatto & Windus.

Huxley, J. (1963): The Future of Man: Evolutionary Aspects. In: Wolstenholme, G. (ed.): Man and his Future: A Ciba Foundation Volume. Boston: Little, Brown and Company, 1-22.

Ishiguro, K. (2005): Never Let Me Go. London: Faber & Faber.

Istvan, Z. (2013): The Transhumanist Wager. Future Image Publishing.

Jones S. (2006): Against Technology: From the Luddites to Neo-Luddism. New York et al.: Routledge.

Jost, F. (1988): Introduction. In: Seigneuret, J.-C. (ed.): Dictionary of Literary Themes and Motifs (Vol. 1). Westport(CT): Greenwood Publishing Group, xv-xxiii.

Kass, L. (2001): Preventing a Brave New World. In: The New Republic (May 21, 2001), 265-276.

Miah, A. (2008): A Critical History of Posthumanism. In: Gordijn, B./ Chadwick, Ruth F. (eds.): Medical Enhancement and Posthumanity. Dordrecht: Springer, 71-94.

Morrey, D. (2013): Michel Houellebecq: Humanity and its Aftermath. Liverpool: Liverpool University Press.

Newman, W. (2004): Promethean Ambitions: Alchemy and the Quest to Perfect Nature. Chicago: University of Chicago Press.

PCBE (2002): Science and the Pursuit of Perfection (Transcripts Session 2, January 17, 2002). http://bioethics.georgetown.edu/pcbe/transcripts/jan02/jan17session2.html (accessed April 10, 2013).

Prisco, G. (2013): The Transhumanist Wager and the Terrifying Struggle for the Future. http://io9.com/the-transhumanist-wager-and-the-terrifying-struggle-for-510012440 (accessed December 20, 2013).

Powers, R. (2009): Generosity: An Enhancement. New York: Farrar, Straus and Giroux.

Rowen, N. (1992): The Making of Frankenstein's Monster: Post-Golem, Pre-Robot. In: Ruddick, N. (ed.): State of the Fantastic: Studies in the Theory and Practice of Fantastic Literature and Film. Westport(CT): Greenwood Press, 169-77.

Searle, R. (2013): Betting Against The Transhumanist Wager. http://ieet.org/index.php/IEET/more/searle20130916 (accessed December 20, 2013).

Shelley, M.W. (2004 [1818]): Frankenstein; or, The Modern Prometheus. In: Macdonald, D.L./ Scherf, K. (eds.): Frankenstein; or, The Modern Prometheus. 2. ed. Peterborough: Broadview Press, 45-244.

Shelley, M.W. (2004 [1831]): Frankenstein; or, The Modern Prometheus. In: Macdonald, D.L./ Scherf, K. (eds.): Frankenstein; or, The Modern Prometheus. 2. ed. Peterborough: Broadview Press, 316-359.

Simon, B. (2003): Introduction: Toward a Critique of Posthuman Futures. In: Cultural Critique 53, 1-9.

Sloterdijk, P. (2009): Rules for the Human Zoo: A Response to the Letter on Humanism. In: Environment and Planning D: Society and Space 27, 12-28.

Slusser, G. (2009): Dimorphs and Doubles: J. D. Bernal's "Two Cultures" and the Transhuman Promise. In: Westfahl, G./ Slusser, G. (eds.): Science fiction and the Two Cultures: Essays on Bridging the Gap Between the Sciences and the Humanities. Jefferson(NC): McFarland & Co, 96-129.

Smith, M.M. (1996): Spares. New York: Bantam.

Snow, C.P. (2001 [1959]): The Two Cultures. London: Cambridge University Press.

Sterling, B. (1996 [1986]): Schismatrix Plus. New York: Penguin.

Stock, G. (2003): Redesigning Humans: Choosing Our Children's Genes. London: Profile Books.

Stolyarov II, G. (2013): Thoughts on Zoltan Istvan's "The Transhumanist Wager": A Review. http://ieet.org/index.php/IEET/more/StolyarovII20131106 (accessed December 20, 2013).

Stripling, M. (2005): Bioethics and Medical Issues in Literature. Westport(CT): Greenwood Press.

Tirosh-Samuelson, H. (2011): Engaging Transhumanism. In: Hansell, G.R./ Grassie, W. (eds.): H±: Transhumanism and Its Critics. Philadelphia: Metanexus, 19-54.

Toffoletti, K. (2007): Cyborgs and Barbie Dolls: Feminism, Popular Culture and the Posthuman Body. London et al.: I.B. Tauris.

Vasbinder, S.H. (1984): Scientific Attitudes in Mary Shelley's Frankenstein. Ann Arbor: UMI.

Waldby, C. (2000): The Visible Human Project: Informatic Bodies and Posthuman Medicine. London: Routledge.

Wallace, J. (2010): Literature and Posthumanism. In: Literature Compass 7(8), 692-701.

Wells, H.G. (2005 [1896]): The Island of Dr. Moreau. London: Penguin.

Science Fiction Literature

Domna Pastourmatzi

When in 1985 in her *Cyborg Manifesto* Donna Haraway asserted that "the boundary between science fiction and social reality is an optical illusion" (Haraway 1991, 149), she was diagnosing a new phenomenon in American culture, namely the conflation of the scientific and the science-fictional modes of thinking that had also gotten hold of the Reagan administration and the U.S. military establishment. At the same time she noted the incursion of science fictional creatures (like the cyborg) in the real world. Despite her insistence that her blasphemy was laden with irony and that it was meant to be "a rhetorical strategy and a political method" (ibid.), many took her final words "I would rather be a cyborg than a goddess" (ibid., 181) as an endorsement of posthumanity as lived experience. When N. Katherine Hayles in 1999 tried to give an account of how Americans became posthumans (both culturally and scientifically) she linked the theories of American scientists (Norbert Wiener and Hans Moravec) to the same assumptions informing the fictional scenarios of *Star Trek*. In the post-World War II years, American science and science fiction were regular bed-fellows influencing each other. Notable scientists (Edward Teller, Freeman Dyson, Stephen Hawkings, Marvin Minsky and others) have been "heavy-duty SF fans" and "some even wrote it" (Benford 2000, xi). Indeed, many American "scientists make their own culture through SF" and American science in general "feels the genre at its back, breathing on its neck in the race into the future" (ibid.). NASA physicist and science fiction writer Gregory Benford points out that "the central lesson of SF as a medium is that the highway between it and science runs both ways" (ibid., xii). Academic Sharona Ben-Tov has demonstrated that much of American hard science fiction is "a source of images that gratify national pride in U.S. technology" and at the same time both "*reproduces* the ideologies that formed modern technology" and "engages the readers in *reenacting* those ideologies" (Ben-Tov 1995, 5; emphasis in the original). Thomas M. Disch also acknowledged "that the future represented by SF writers continues to be an American future" (Disch 1998, 2).

Starting out (in the United States in the 1980s) as an obscure minority, some futurists and fervent supporters of technology (members the baby-boomer generation nurtured in science fiction) began to organize, to launch their own political agendas and to construct a variety of schools of thought under the umbrella label of transhumanism. Since then they have worked systematically to enlist into their ranks scientists, academics, philosophers, technocrats, policy-makers, and businessmen in order to widen their influence on the western power-centers and eventually – technology-permitting – to steer the course of biological humanity toward a type of perfectibility that reeks technological determinism. With the attainment of the posthuman condition as their main goal, transhumanists have engaged "in foresight, activism and promotional activities" in order to solicit support for their "way of life" (Dvorsky 2008, 62). As a matter of fact, the consorted efforts of transhumanists have been somewhat successful, for the number of supporters in the West and around the world has increased to such a degree that it allows transhumanists to currently boast that theirs is not just a "burgeoning lifestyle choice and cultural phenomenon" (ibid.), but also an international social movement and a philosophy that rivals the dominant but outdated systems of thought. Nicholas Agar reports that checking the web site of the World Transhumanist Association (founded in 1998 by philosophers Nick Bostrom and David Pearce) revealed that its global membership in the last decade was close to 4,000 (see Agar 2007, 12). Despite its universalizing rhetoric and its posture as a global new philosophy, transhumanism (and its spin-offs like extropianism) is actually a historically-specific, culture-specific, masculinist, technocentric, American-inspired, capitalist framework with roots in the two-hundred-year-old industrial-military-scientific complex. In many respects, transhumanism (or Humanity+ or reversible destiny theory) is a re-invigorated version of humanist ideals intended to erase the nihilistic impact of postmodernist philosophies. Ardent champions like Simon Young engage in meme wars in order to restore the damaged reputation of an allegedly philanthropic technoscience and defend it against the biases of anti-transhumanists, bio-Luddites, nature-lovers, environmentalists and other (in his opinion) cultural throwbacks.

Perceiving the human species as a limited, substandard and defective life-form, and viewing human nature "as a work-in-progress, a half-baked beginning" they would like to "remold in desirable ways" (Bostrom 2005, 4), transhumanists have embarked on a campaign to first conceptually implant their science-fictional vision of posthumanity into the popular imagination and secondly to lead the willing members of humankind toward an unprecedented metamorphosis; to become literally a distinctly nonhuman species, which in the long run will itself engineer such an incompatible 'essence' or condition that this will automatically preclude interbreeding with its human predecessors. From the transhumanist perspective, the already moribund *Homo sapiens* must and *will be* superseded by the superior *Homo cyberneticus*. Unlike its pitiful and enslaved ancestor (the victim of his own selfish genes and of an evolutionary program for self-destruction), unparalleled *Homo cyberneticus* "will be the steersman of his own destiny" (Young 2006, 22); in fact he will literally be a self-made metaman, created in Man's own image. Further, choosing an "artificial-evolutionary path" toward an irreversibly posthuman future, according to transhumanists "suits humanity better then remaining as the species we have been" (Seidel 2008, vii). In the words of spokesman Max More, "We have decided that it is time to amend the human constitution" (More 2009). Pronouncing technology as "a natural extension and expression of human intellect," Max More asserts that this futuristic monopath is the inevitable fate of the species: "We will co-evolve with the products of our minds, integrating with them, finally integrating our intelligent technology into ourselves in a posthuman synthesis" (ibid.). American roboticist Hans Moravec was among the first to predict that what awaits us is...

> "[...] a future which, from our present vantage point, is best described by the words 'postbiological' or even 'supernatural'. It is a world in which the human race has been swept away by the tide of cultural change, usurped by it own artificial progeny" (Moravec 1988, 1).

Whereas transhumanists crave the literal enhancement of human beings via cutting-edge technologies, extol techno-transcendence as the solution to biological limits and mortality, perceive life as infinitely malleable, and defend a social order based on laissez-faire individualism, scholars and theorists (in the humanities and social sciences) engage in a different kind of critical posthumanism. Bart Simon defines it as...

> "[...] an interdisciplinary perspective informed by academic poststructuralism, postmodernism, feminist and postcolonial studies and science and technology studies" (Simon 2003, 2-3).

Interested in undermining the assumptions and rationale of various philosophical humanisms and the liberal legacy of the Enlightenment on the discursive and representational levels, critical posthumanists also investigate the prospects, the limits and the politics of various popular versions of transhumanism and of the ultra-scientism disseminated by the writings of various scientists. Since the mid-1990s the term 'posthuman' has been employed as a critical tool with which (among other goals), to challenge the essentialized accounts of 'human nature', to deconstruct authoritative representations of human identity, to reveal the exclusionary functions of the signifier 'human' and to knock *Homo sapiens* from its privileged position on the top of the species-scale. As a new theoretical model, posthumanism is burdened with "different and irreconcilable definitions" (Wolfe 2010, xi). It may mean the demise of humanist perspectives; it may mean the convergence of technology and biology into one indistinguishable force shaping humankind. For Katherine Hayles, the posthuman is a point of view. For Catherine Waldby the term evokes "a general critical space" in which the "stability of the categories 'human' and 'nonhuman'" can be called into question (Walby 2000, 43). For Cary Wolfe, posthumanism is a mode of thinking which engages "directly the problem of anthropocentricism and speciesism" (Wolfe 2010, xix). For Elaine Graham, who prefers to use the term 'post/hu instead of adopting the widely used convention of the 'posthuman', the term is a device of interrogation. In her words, "The post/human is that which both confounds but also holds up to scrutiny the terms on which the quintessentially human will be conceived" (Graham 2002, 11). Her objective thus is to use the term to question a) "the inevitability of a successor species" and b) the myth of any "consensus surrounding the effects of technologies in the future of humanity" (ibid.). She contends that "the logic of erosion, dehumanization and obsolescence are simply metaphors for, not predictions about, post/human development" (ibid., 14-15). Despite the flourishing of posthumanist approaches in the scholarly investigations of normative representations of the 'human' in technoscience, in popular culture and in the arts, a weariness and disillusionment has already set in. Cultural theorist Donna Haraway has turned her back on the concept of the 'posthuman' and admits that she has "stopped using it" because, in her words, it has been "too easily appropriated by the blissed-out, 'Lets all be posthumanists and find our next teleological evolutionary stage in some kind of transhumanist technoenhancement'" (Gane 2006, 140) type of projects. She emphatically adds that the reason she went to companion species theory "is to get away from posthumanism" (ibid.). In a similar mood, Neil Badmington, who has written extensively on the subject and has contributed to "the long battle against those who would defend the glory of 'Man'" has "lost faith, even blasphemous faith, in posthumanism" (Badmington 2010), because of the re-insertion of the distinctly humanist matrix of Cartesian dualism in the "apocalyptic or complacent posthumanism" (Badmington 2004, 111), the kind Hans Moravec, Marvin Minsky, Ray Kurzweil and other like-minded transhumanists espouse.

The Use of Science Fiction

Among the cultural tools that transhumanists utilize in their campaign to steer humankind toward posthumanization – at least conceptually in this early phase of their enterprise – is the popular genre of science fiction. Admittedly, there is a plethora of utopian, dystopian, skeptical, as well as hyper-technophilic, science fictional narratives which compete with each other for the attention of the general public. Of course, not all have the same degree of success. Nevertheless, Anglo[illegible] science fiction (particularly in the United States), has become a [illegible] f influence and persuasion; under the guise of entertainment, the [illegible] nd posthumanist agendas are being explained, scrutinized, ex[illegible] ed, materialized or debunked. Each writer, depending on his/her [illegible] ies, either explicitly or implicitly, promotes, rejects or express[illegible] attitude toward genetic and cybernetic enhancements and the

expected transition from the biological present to a metaphysical, techno-transcendent future.

Thought experiments structured upon the "what if" line of speculation abound both in philosophical debates and in science fictional narratives. Indeed, "some of the best science fiction tales are in fact long versions of philosophical thought experiments" (Schneider 2009, 2). In our technological epoch, there are "a number of key areas in philosophy where the interplay between philosophy and science fiction is rich"; both cultural discourses "are converging upon a set of shared themes and questions" (ibid.); both explore the concepts of identity, subjectivity, embodiment, consciousness, the relationship between body and mind and the notion of autonomous agency and free will in a world pervaded by technological determinism.

Undeniably, philosophical frameworks can be difficult to follow (especially if they are grounded in abstract language and permeated with the jargon and theories of seasoned philosophers), often requiring the mediation of an expert to become comprehensible, whereas many science fiction tales with a philosophical orientation are far more approachable.

> "At the fundamental level, this genre explores the human condition – what it is and what it might become – while pushing us to consider what lies beyond the horizon of the present" (Nichols et al. 2009, 1).

Leading us to new conceptual realms and alternative imaginary universes, science fiction "prompts us to reflect critically upon the fundamental beliefs and the future of our species" (ibid., 2) and asks us to mull over the proposition that the technologically-mediated or artificially-enhanced existence constitutes the good life. In other words, science fiction does a superb job in helping the non-expert to understand the various challenges and dilemmas that spring from the implementation of advanced technologies and to assess the high price humankind has to pay if it collectively indulges in the techno-fantasies disseminated by technophiliacs. Indisputably, …

> "[…] science fiction is particularly suited to exploring the question of the posthuman because it is a discourse that allows us to concretely imagine bodies and selves otherwise" (Vint 2007, 19).

The conceptualization of the human body as a mere assemblage of parts and pieces, infinitely malleable by technical means, and the fantasy of extracting the self, mind or consciousness from the flesh in order to achieve cybernetic immortality are recurrent themes, often employed as the springboard to investigate the perennial question of what it means to be human.

Because of its primary focus on a technology-driven world, science fiction complements western philosophy in scrutinizing a set of questions and ethical issues which in the last few decades have become the focus of intense debate. Often written in a straightforward, realistic style, as well as in a palatable and easily comprehensible language, philosophical science fiction enables even the most ignorant reader (who lags behind in tracking current scientific developments or fails to adequately grasp difficult and complex knowledge) to become enlightened about various aspects of the controversy over the immanent and inevitable Singularity that is said to be arriving on our planet. Aubrey de Grey admits that "dry academic arguments" do not resonate in the hearts of people; that is why transhumanists "need a populist approach" (de Grey 2006, 10). In short, science fiction has become the literary forum par excellence through which to popularize, disseminate and critically examine the wild proposals concerning human enhancement and invasive prostheses as well as the rationalizations that bolster the advent of the posthuman as a life-enhancing and life-saving phase in the evolution of humanity.

Whether saturated with transhumanist values and posthumanist perspectives or indulging in sober philosophical meditations over the nature of humankind as a species or merely constructing metaphors for the interrogation of traditional dualisms and normative paradigms, science fiction offers a panoramic window from where to gaze and assess critically the vistas both of the present moment and the near future. Mainstream authors who have tried to tackle the repercussions of a posthuman future usually resort to the conventions, devices and motifs of science fiction in order to speculate appropriately on the issues. Cultural theorists, future-oriented scientists and authors of non-fictional works often frame their arguments in science-fictional terms. "Both Baudrillard and Haraway have explicitly associated their theoretical work with SF" (Csicsery-Ronay 1991, 389). So have Gilles Deleuze, Felix Guattari, Rosi Braidotti, Teresa de Lauretis, and Fredric Jameson among others. As Jameson points out, science fiction renders concrete technofantasies about the future with "an apparent realism or representationality"; at the same time it functions to "defamiliarize and restructure our own experience of our own *present*" (Jameson 2005, 286; emphasis in the original). Its target is frequently "the here and now"; in fact this form of narrative and form of knowledge, Jameson argues, does not actually…

> "[…] attempt to imagine the 'real' future of our social system. Rather, its multiple mock futures serve the quite different function of transforming our own present into the determinate past of something yet to come" (Jameson 2005, 288).

Although Jameson diagnoses that Anglophone science fiction has suffered from an "atrophy of the utopian imagination" and is characterized by a tendency to weave apolitical, private and "libidinal fantasies of all kinds" (ibid., 289; 292), we cannot ignore the fact that there are exceptions to this rule. Philosophicallyinclined and/or politically-informed serious science fiction writers do perform an invaluable social service by mobilizing this popular genre to makes us confront the ramifications of an ultra-capitalist, consumerist techno-mode of thinking; they do help the common reader gauge the impact of an unrestrained technological progress by speculating on the possible negative outcomes that may adversely impact our 'real' lives; they do assist us to envision the various possible trajectories of human evolution and they do try to alert us to the fact that certain western power-centers are trying to tip the scales by promoting one specific future over another. In other words, there are science fictional thought experiments (utopian or dystopian) that scrutinize the practices of western institutions, of economic and political systems, the theories of human nature as well as the moral and political principles of dominant cultures; they do offer "concrete applications of theoretical assumptions for our evaluation" (Little 2007, 17). Finally, several writers do ascribe to the belief that "the central message of science fiction is this: 'Look with a skeptical eye at new technologies'" (Sawyer 2005a, 154). Literature by definition is anthropocentric and science fiction is no exception. Even the most extreme scenarios cannot conceal a lingering anxiety stemming from the possible dangers and unanticipated consequences that lurk if the transhumanist desire of turning the human being into a posthuman entity finds a wholesale application.

The Transhuman and Posthuman Condition in Science Fiction

Having provided a rationale why science fiction is an indispensable intellectual tool, offering insightful commentary on current technological trends and scientific paradigms, as well as illuminating the premises and aspirations of transhumanists and posthumanists, I would like now to refer to selected stories and novels. The avid readers know that the pages of Anglophone science fiction were brimming with nonhuman creatures spawning new evolutionary paths long before the recent advances in technoscience have led to the actual production of clones, hybrids, cyborgs, avatars, digital personas and other posthuman techno-bodies. But in the last thirty years, English-speaking authors have deluged the market with short stories and novels which graphically depict a variety of posthuman futures as well as a wide range of existential conditions very different from the ones we are familiar with in our daily lives. Extraordinary or weird posthuman ontology has become a staple (if not the norm) for some science fiction writers.

One of the earliest short stories offering "a vivid and lyrical look into the life of a posthuman" (Dozois 2002, 66) is *Halfjack* (2002 [1979]) by American Roger Zelazny. Long before Haraway talked about the seamless combination of the organic body with technological components, and long before Hayles expressed her anxiety about a culture that regards the body as a fashion accessory rather than ground of being (see Hayles 1999, 5), Zelazny envisioned the deliberate transformation of the (male) body into "a body glove" through a procedure he called "Lateral hemicorporectomy." The cyborgian nature of the male hero retains aspects of the humanist subject; the markers that encode and sustain Jack's humanness and manhood are both biological and universal. As Jack says, "I need a stomach and balls and lungs, because I have to eat and screw and breathe to feel human" (Zelazny 2002 [1979], 68). Zelazny's story was written before the "flesh-eating 90s" (Kroker as cited in Hayles 1999, 5), before the influence of the transhumanist movement and before the proliferation of the cyborgian and posthuman icons that saturate Hollywood movies and postmodern science fiction. Zelazny's portrait of the posthuman neither erases the flesh entirely nor debunks as redundant what he assumes to be essential biological needs (food, oxygen, sex) of humanity. A few decades later, Canadian Robert J. Sawyer, in *Mindscan* (2005b), will present a male hero incarnating the radical transhumanist (Cartesian) vision which privileges the disembodied mind as precious and debunks the mortal body and the pleasures of the flesh as unessential, thus giving up all biological gratifications for the sake of becoming an immortal posthuman.

Rehearsing familiar transhumanist arguments favoring positive eugenics and the scientific production of optimal children, Australian Greg Egan, in *Eugene* (1995 [1990]), speculates about parental choices and the ensuing responsibility to offspring in the context of a technologically-driven world, faced with acute environmental problems, climactic changes and political turmoil. One of the philosophical questions Egan asks the reader to think about is whether infertile parents with sufficient funds (since creating a superchild is a very expensive business) should indulge their personal desire to "purchase" an extraordinary, intelligent, charismatic and creative child from the highly specialized reproductive industry or whether they should reassess their priorities with a humanitarian, disinterested perspective and disburse their money to charitable worthy causes, such as feeding the millions of starving people or combating the "abysmal infant mortality" (Egan 1995 [1990], 48) in third world countries. Egan urges us to weigh the personal benefits of bringing superchildren to an ecologically "crippled planet" against the wider social benefits resulting from unselfish acts which may alleviate the dreadful human condition of the already living. Egan pits the claims of "the best reproductive specialist money could buy" – who defends the beneficence of genetic engineering and readily dismisses as unfounded the fears of opponents who wrongly accuse molecular biologists as being "intent on creating a world of Aryan supermen" (ibid., 49; 52) – against the counterarguments, choices and actions of the ideal child-construct. Further, Egan speculates whether bioethics (human-made ethical guidelines for scientific conduct) can guarantee non-breachable moral lines when powerful interests lurk behind specific techno-objectives. The reader can probe the effects of brain implants, posthuman transformations and cybernetic immortality in Egan's first collection *Axiomatic* (1995), which contains a series of stories that interweave technological with psychological and social questions in their imaginary scenarios.

Since the 1990s, Greg Egan has emerged as one of the most provocative writers, whose philosophical science fiction deals systematically with the impact of computer technology, the digitization of the human mind, and simulated life in cyberspace. Asking fundamental questions about (post)human identity, the nature of consciousness, the impact of computational speeds and other related issues, Egan depicts a variety of transhuman futures populated by diverse posthuman entities and superhuman autonomous agents of a cyborgian or a cybernetic nature. From his first novel *Quarantine* (1992), through *Permutation City* (1994), to *Diaspora* (1998 [1997]) *to Schild's Ladder* (2001), to *Incandescence* (2008), Egan has traversed the bridge from cyberpunk to singularity fiction, has replaced Newtonian physics with quantum mechanics, and has vindicated the belief that the pure self (as encoded information) can be transmitted like a signal to the remote places of the galaxy and be uploaded into virtual constructs or downloaded into physical or robotic embodiments. Egan's vision of electronic cloning in a postbiological, nonphysical universe is informed by the arguments of the strong AI hypothesis. Flirting with the idea that consciousness is a property of certain algorithms, or merely a matter of computation, Egan approaches posthumanization as a purely scientific question. Indeed, Egan is "perhaps SF's most committed rationalist in the mould of Richard Dawkins. If it cannot be measured, weighed and analyzed, for Egan it does not exist" (Harvey 2008). Mainly a cerebral than an affective writer, Egan seriously probes the nature of personal identity, of subjective experience and of techno-solipsism in works containing fascinating ideas; however, many of his posthuman characters are cold and mechanical and leave the ordinary reader unmoved and disenchanted. Large sections of his narratives may entail difficulties for the uninitiated, since they become a dumping ground for detailed expositions of scientific paradigms. Without doubt, Egan's mathematical approach to existence and his intensely transhumanist perspective render his work a part of a major trend in cyberpunk that Rosi Braidotti identifies as "a 'post-human' techno-teratological phenomenon that privileges the deviant or the mutant over the more conventional versions of the human" (Braidotti 2002, 197).

Death seems to be the number one enemy of transhumanists, aging being the second in line. John Harris purports that "[m]ost people fear death, and the prospect of personal extended life-span is likely to be welcomed." He also adds, that the "new 'immortals' would neither be old, nor frail, nor necessarily retired." According to Harris it "is unlikely that we can stop the progression to increased life-spans and even 'immortality' and it is doubtful that we can produce coherent ethical objections" (Harris 2000, 59). Therefore, until western technoscience finds a way to annul the irreducible fact of death, Harris advises us to start indulging in immortality at least cognitively. That is exactly what American James L. Halperin has done by writing his novel *The First Immortal*. Published in 1998 (two years earlier than Harris's advice), this technophilic account of the good life dramatizes as well as predicts the wonders of a posthuman future awaiting fortunate mortals, who do not scoff at the idea but take advantage of the new consumer service of cryonic suspension. Fervently endorsing the transhumanist dream of physical immortality, Halperin invents an all-America male hero (by the name of Benjamin Franklin Smith) and uses him as a vehicle to first familiarize the reader with the appropriate steps that need to be taken if one wants to become a client of Alcor (the corporation offering cryonic suspension services). The promises and drawbacks of the freezing procedure are discussed in detail. This intensely Americano-centric novel, saturated with unrestrained techno-hype, functions as a barker for transhumanism. Carefully researched and written in a straightforward, comprehensible language, Halperin's novel tries to convince the readers that physical immortality, accompanied by eternal youth, good health, and long-lasting beauty is a done deal in the not so remote American-made future. One should not expect a literary masterpiece but should approach *The First Immortal* as a good introduction to cryonics and nanotechnology (since Halperin takes pains to make them intelligible even to the most uninformed person) and to the controversies surrounding them. It is an unabashed hymn to the inexorable march of technology and material progress, to American ingenuity, to liberal individualism, and to a globalized ultra-capitalist, market-economy glutted with consumerism.

On the other hand, Canadian Robert J. Sawyer offers a more skeptical and deeply philosophical approach with which to ponder the effects of the transition to posthumanity. His novel *Mindscan* (2005b) explores the transhumanist idea of achieving personal immortality via the technique of uploading one's scanned mind (and consciousness) into a robotic body. Sawyer's in-depth look into this form of posthuman eternal life enables the reader to grasp the interpersonal, legal, economic and political implications that ensue after a person's transformation into a posthuman entity. The reader is guided to delve into the questions: *what makes us human, what differentiates the human from the posthuman,* and *do posthumans deserve personhood and civil rights*? Sawyer, trying to be fair, gives voice to the multiple arguments of both advocates and opponents, concerning the identity and social status after a human being becomes a digital copy of his/her former self. He also delves into the motives and psychological profiles of would-be-posthumans, people who will intentionally choose to replace their biological with a mechanical embodiment. Unlike Halperin, Sawyer is not a "techie cheerleader"; he does not trade in utopia but rather agrees with William Gibson that "the job of the science fiction writer is to be profoundly ambivalent about changes in technology" (Sawyer 2005a, 154). This reluctance to embrace wholeheartedly the techno-Eden promised by transhumanists has begun to characterize the attitude of several writers (including William Gibson) as well as cultural critics who have become weary of the uncritical techno-capitalistic thrust of futuristic agendas and the ongoing commodification of human subjectivity.

In *Oryx and Crake* (2003), Canadian Margaret Atwood paints with a grim mood the nightmare in store for the frail and vulnerable humanity, when a male misanthropic scientist decides to end the human dominance on the planet earth by engineering a lethal virus and releasing it from the laboratory in order to create a world-wide epidemic. Humanity's deliberate extermination is the first step toward the realization of Crake's ultimate objective: bequeathing the planet to a successor species, called the Crakers, that is genetically improved superhuman prototypes. These innocent posthuman creatures (created in the laboratory according to the male scientist's designer-specifications) are raised in an artificial environment and testify to Crake's godlike omnipotence. Unlike Marvin Minsky, Hans Moravec or Ray Kurzweil, who may not live long enough to see their vision of bequeathing the planet to their beloved Mind Children, fictional scientist Crake has the chance to materialize the transhumanist dream of a Second Creation and to die with the knowledge that he has matched the creative powers of the Biblical God.

Among the critically acclaimed novels which portray the emergence of new posthuman intelligences, the evolution or splintering of humanity into a variety of nonhuman subspecies, the scientific construction of new creatures, superhuman immortality (biological, mechanical, electronic or cyborgian), the obsolescence of *Homo sapiens* and in general a variety of issues directly relevant to transhumanism and posthumanism are: *Software* (1982) by Rudy Rucker, *Blood Music* (1985) by Greg Bear, *Schismatrix* (1985) by Bruce Sterling, *Synners* (1991) by Pat Cadigan, *Accidental Creatures* (1998) by Anne Harris, *Altered Carbon* (2002) by Richard K. Morgan, *Natural History* (2003) by Justina Robson and *Accelerando* (2005) by Charles Stross. Finally, the ant
men: Tales of the Posthuman Future contains excellent stories wi
ist themes. Among them, Robert Charles Wilson's *The Great G*
dramatizes the separation of humanity into "two very distinct h
(Wilson 2002 [2000], 449) and tries to bridge the generatio

evolutionary divide" with mutual acceptance and familial ties. The story realizes the posthuman exodus to the galaxies. The dream to engineer a posthuman species that it will be able to withstand the pressures of space and thus spread itself into the galaxies has its scientific grounding in the paper *Cyborgs and Space* when in 1960 scientists Clynes and Kline proposed "altering man's bodily functions to meet the requirements of extraterrestrial environments" as a solution to the problems facing space travel projects. Becoming a cyborg was not meant to be an end in itself or the desired next evolutionary stage of humanity (as many transhumanists claim) but only a means, a technofix, to facilitate space conquest "*without alteration of heredity*" (Clynes/ Kline 1960, 26; emphasis in the original). In *A History of the Human and the Post-Human Species* (2002 [2000]), physicist Geoffrey A. Landis who works for NASA, conceptualizes an elaborate scheme which gives rise to new species and attributes this divergence to "the intense pressure of evolutionary forces." Bruce Sterling, in *Homo Sapiens Declared Extinct* (2002 [1999]), entertains the idea that the days of humankind are numbered. He begins his narrative with an official declaration of humanity's extinction in the year AD 2380.

When we turn to African American or feminist writers – who tackle the racial, gender, class and political dimensions of a (white) technocratic futurism – we find profoundly alternative posthuman futures then the ones promulgated by tech-addicted transhumanists. For example, Walter Mosley's *Futureland* (2001) is a *tout de force* narrative which exposes the politics behind the American vision of a liberating techno-Eden and challenges the assumption that posthumanization would put an end to old human vices (such as injustice, inequality, enslavement, poverty, exploitation, segregation) and of diachronic interracial conflict. In a recent interview, Mosley has soberly asserted:

> "I think that the idea that technology is going to liberate us is false. All you have to is look at the fifty-year span between 1950 and the year 2000. The amount of technological advance in those years that should open up people's lives is immense. […] It certainly didn't liberate us" (Mosley as cited in Perez 2011, 109).

To conclude, science fiction is a vehicle of ideas and a forum for debate; it may facilitate the reception or boost the critical evaluation of new scientific paradigms and radical technocratic movements, which primarily enthrall techno-enthusiasts (like the employees and scientists in Silicon Valley and NASA). Philosophical science fiction actively engages in current controversies and contributes to social awareness. The multiple and diverse perspectives registered in the plethora of imaginary narratives via dramatization and speculation enable readers to understand that although the human future is theoretically open, there an ongoing intellectual battle and systematic efforts by some circles in western culture to prepare the ground for a posthuman future favored by powerful technocratic elites. In general, speculative literature, like any other intellectual activity, can be exploited by writers with an ideological agenda to promote, challenge or debunk the fantasies, convictions, and values of highly trendy movements like transhumanism and posthumanism.

Bibliography

Agar, N. (2007): Whereto Transhumanism? The Literature Reaches a Critical Mass. In: The Hastings Center Report 37(3), 12-17.

Atwood, M. (2004): Oryx and Crake. London: Virago.

Badmington, N. (2004): Alien Chic: Posthumanism and the Other Within. London et al: Routledge.

Badmington, N. (2010): Man Saved by Wolfe. In: Electronic Book Review. http://www.electronicbookreview.com/thread/criticalecologies/savedbywolfe/ (accessed September 2, 2013).

Benford, G. (2000): Introduction: The Science Fictional Century. In: Benford, G. (ed.): Nebula Awards Showcase 2000. San Diego: Harcourt.

Bostrom, N. (2005): Transhumanist Values. In: Journal of Philosophical Research 30 (Issue Supplement - Ethical Issues for the Twenty-First Century), 3-14.

Braidotti, R. (2002): Metamorphosis: Towards a Materialist Theory of Becoming. Cambridge: Polity Press.

Clynes M.E./ Kline N.S. (1960): Cyborgs and Space (Reprinted by the New York Times). In: Astronautics 14(9), 26-7; 74-6. http://nytimes.com/library/cyber/surf/022697surf-cyborg.html (accessed September 2, 2013).

Csicsery-Ronay, Jr. I. (1991): The SF Theory: Baudrillard and Haraway. In: Science Fiction Studies 18(3), 387-404.

de Grey, A. (2006): Foreword: Forever Young. In: Young, S: Designer Evolution: A Transhumanist Manifesto. Amherst: Prometheus Books, 9-10.

Disch, T. (1998): The Dreams Our Stuff is Made of: How Science Fiction Conquered the World. New York: The Free Press.

Dozois, G. (2002): Prologue. In: Dozois, G. (ed.): Supermen: Tales of the Posthuman Future. New York: St. Martin's Griffin, 66-67.

Dvorsky, G. (2008): Better Living through Transhumanism. In: Journal of Evolution and Technology 19(1), 62-66. http://jetpress.org/v19/dvorsky.htm (accessed September 2, 2013).

Egan, G. (1992): Quarantine. New York: Harper Prism/ Harper Collins.

Egan, G. (1994): Permutation City. New York: Harper Prism/ Harper Collins.

Egan, G. (1995): Axiomatic. London: Millennium.

Egan, G. (1995 [1990]): Eugene. In: Egan, G: Axiomatic. London: Millennium, 41-59.

Egan, G. (1998 [1997]): Diaspora. New York: Eos/Harper Collins.

Gane, N. (2006): When We Have Never Been Human, What is to Be Done? Interview with Donna Haraway. In: Theory Culture & Society 23(7-8), 135-58.

Graham, E.L. (2002): Representations of the Post/Human: Monsters, Aliens and Others in Popular Culture. New Brunswick: Rutgers University Press.

Halperin, J.L. (1998): The First Immortal. New York: Del Rey/ Balantine Books.

Haraway, D.J. (1991): Simians, Cyborgs and Women: The Reinvention of Nature. New York: Routledge.

Harris, J. (2000): Intimations of Immortality. In: Science 288(5463), 59.

Harvey, C. (2008): Review: Quarantine and Teranesia. In: Strange Horizons. http://www.strangehorizons.com/reviews/2008/06/quarantine_and_.shtml (accessed September 2, 2013).

Hayles, K.N. (1999): How We Became Posthuman: Virtual Bodies in Cybernetics, Literature, and Informatics. Chicago: The University of Chicago Press.

Jameson, F. (2005): Archaeologies of the Future: The Desire called Utopia and Other Science Fictions. London et al: Verso.

Landis, G.A. (2002 [2000]): A History of the Human and the Post-Human Species. In: Dozois, G. (ed.): Supermen: Tales of the Posthuman Future. New York: St. Martin's Griffin, 444-448.

Little, J.A. (2007): Introduction. In: Little, J.A. (ed.): Feminist Philosophy and Science Fiction: Utopias and Dystopias. Amherst: Prometheus Books, 13-34.

Moravec, H. (1988): Mind Children: The Future of Robot and Human Intelligence. Cambridge(MA): Harvard University Press.

More, M. (2009): True Transhumanism. In: Global Spiral. http://www.metanexus.net/essay/h-true-transhumanism/ (accessed September 2, 2013).

Mosley, W. (2001): Futureland. New York: Aspect/Warner Books.

Nichols, R. et al. (2009): Philosophy through Science Fiction: A Coursebook of Readings. New York: Routledge.

Perez, H. (2011): Walter Mosley Talks Technology, Race, and His Return Trip into Futureland. In: Brady, O.E. (ed.): Conversations with Walter Mosley. Jackson(MS): University of Mississippi Press, 107-111.

Sawyer, R.J. (2005a): The Future is Already Here: Is There a Place for Science Fiction in the Twenty-First Century?. In: Anders, L (ed.): Projections: Science Fiction in Literature and Film. Austin(TX): Monkey Brain Books, 153-169.

Sawyer, R.J. (2005b): Mindscan. New York: Tor/Tom Doherty Associates.

Schneider, S. (2009): Introduction: Thought Experiments – Science Fiction as a Window into Philosophical Puzzles. In: Schneider, S. (ed.): Science Fiction and Philosophy: From Time Travel to Superintelligence. Oxford: Wiley-Blackwell, 1-14.

Seidel, A. (2008): Inhuman Thoughts: Philosophical Explorations of Posthumanity. Lanham: Lexington Books/Rowman & Littlefield.

Simon, B. (2003): Introduction: Toward a Critique of Posthuman Futures. In: Cultural Critique 53, 1-9.

Sterling, B. (2002): Homo Sapiens Declared Extinct. In: Dozois, G. (ed.): Supermen: Tales of The Posthuman Future. New York: St. Martin's Griffin, 442-443.

Vint, S. (2007): Bodies of Tomorrow: Technology, Subjectivity, Science Fiction. Toronto: University of Toronto Press.

Waldby, C. (2000): The Visible Human Project: Informatic Bodies and Posthuman Medicine. London et al.: Routledge.

Wilson, R.C. (2002 [2000]): The Great Goodbye. In: Dozois, G. (ed.): Supermen: Tales of The Posthuman Future. New York: St. Martin's Griffin, 449-450.
Wolfe, C. (2010): What is Posthumanism? Minneapolis: University of Minnesota.
Young, S. (2006): Designer Evolution: A Transhumanist Manifesto. Amherst: Prometheus Books.
Zelazny, R. (2002 [1979]): Halfjack. In: Dozois, G. (ed.): Supermen: Tales of The Posthuman Future. New York: St. Martin's Griffin, 66-70.

Movies

Dónal P. O'Mathúna

This chapter will examine where posthumanist and transhumanist ideas occur in movies. The analysis will be selective because of the frequency with which science fiction movies touch on these themes. The focus will be primarily on mainstream movies as these most directly impact popular culture. Some have questioned how well such movies represent posthumanism since they are enmeshed within the ideologies posthumanism critiques (see Lacey 2006). As the discussion will show, they are at least raising the major issues of concern to posthumanism and transhumanism.

Identifying movies as transhumanist or posthumanist is challenging. Sometimes movies will both support and disagree with transhumanist and posthumanist ideas. Many movies present a complicated (and sometimes contradictory) picture of technology and its impact on humans. While transhumanism has been defined succinctly, posthumanism continues to elude one concise definition (see Wolfe 2010). This creates further challenges in identifying posthumanism in movies. In addition, posthumanism has a more complicated relationship with emerging technology than transhumanism.

A final challenge arises from the nature of filmmaking. While there is much interest in philosophy and movies, it must be remembered that movies, especially mainstream movies, are primarily entertainment (see Falzon 2007). Some, certainly, are written to communicate a specific message. Other movies are made with a goal of not providing a clear and obvious meaning. The *Vanilla Sky* DVD (2001) included a documentary which stated that the movie is "a story, a puzzle, a nightmare, a lucid dream, a psychedelic pop song, a movie to argue over" with a goal that "every time you look at it you might see something different."

Rather than declaring movies to be posthumanist or transhumanist, I will identify ways in which movies engage with prominent themes in these philosophies. Readers will likely disagree with my selection of movies or where I detect posthumanist or transhumanist ideas. My suggestions are presented to contribute to on-going discussions about posthumanism and transhumanism. These may help us decide if we accept "that posthuman life [...] is better than either current human life, or human life given its best possibilities as human life" (Seidel 2010, 1).

Fiction helps stimulate the imagination so that we can envision whether projected futures are likely to contain better lives, better communities, or better people. Such futures should then cause us to reflect on the ethical values and character traits we accept and affirm today. It can also help reveal whether such visions are so fraught with problems that we ought to look elsewhere for guidance and direction.

Technology

Transhumanism is more straight-forward to detect in movies. The central premise of transhumanism is that humanity can and should use technology to enhance human physical, cognitive and emotional capabilities. Such developments are motivated by the desire to eliminate disease and suffering and extend human life-span indefinitely. According to Humanity+, formerly the World Transhumanist Association, the ethical use of technology should "enable everyone to enjoy *better minds, better bodies* and *better lives*. In other words, we want people to be *better than well*" (Humanity+ 2009; emphasis original).

Arguably the clearest presentation of this vision is in the television series and movies, *Star Trek*. First aired on US television in 1966, the way philosophical issues have been examined has varied. However, the series has remained generally committed to a positive portrayal of humanist ideals.

> "*Star Trek*'s narratives explore and uphold the principles of progress, reason, individualism and tolerance [...] a world in which science renders possible the realization of human dreams and aspirations" (Graham 2002, 134).

Such themes track well with transhumanism as it "encompasses many principles of modern humanism" (World Transhumanist Association 2002).

In *Star Trek*, technology exists to assist and serve humanity. It has brought about moral progress and improvement in humanity and, by association, the alien races the crews encounter. Rare among popular science fiction, the utopian society displayed in *Star Trek* shows unparalleled human well-being and control over nature.

> "Freed by science and technology from most physical and social ills, these people are able to devote themselves entirely to the acquisition of knowledge, to missions of scientific investigation, and to their own development and self-improvement" (Falzon 2007, 187).

Such is the world many transhumanists seek. Short-term developments could include prostheses like that which allows the blind chief engineer Geordi La Forge to see. The matter compilers which produce food on demand might be developed by nanotechnology and would, in the transhumanist vision, eliminate all shortages. Developing the technology to allow extended space travel is a long-term goal, but is in keeping with the transhumanist desire to overcome our confinement on Earth (see World Transhumanist Association 2002).

Anthropocentrism

Star Trek, even within the microcosm of its Bridge, shows that racial and cultural divisions between humans can be eliminated. At the same time, clear boundaries remain between humans and non-humans. Lieutenant-Commander Data is an android with many human characteristics and raises the possibility of machines becoming persons. In keeping with humanism, this is never accepted in *Star Trek* where reasons to maintain clear boundaries prevail (see Graham 2002). Emotion plays a large role in these accounts, exploring the lack of emotion in machines and the problems emotions would generate if they emerged in machines.

This affirmation of human distinctiveness and uniqueness contrasts with posthumanism. Instead, new technologies "have called into question the immutability of boundaries between humans, animals and machines, artificial and natural, 'born' and 'made'" (ibid., 1-2). Digital representations in movies further blur these boundaries. Movies like *Blade Runner* (1982) play on lack of clarity between the humans and the machines. Rather than worry about this, posthumanism calls on us to accept that we are all cyborgs and that we should take pleasure in the lack of boundaries (see Haraway 1985).

Transhumanists advocate the well-being of all sentience, whether artificial, human or non-human. On this point, they are in agreement with posthumanism. While one concise definition of posthumanism does not exist, foremost amongst the agreed aspects is a critique of humanism and its overemphasis on rationality. The privileged position taken by humans is seen as fostering an arrogance and disrespect towards other life and the environment.

Posthumanist claims are supported by new findings about the lives of animals which make it untenable to view them as wholly "other." Developments in genetic manipulation, cloning and implants make the boundaries between human and non-human species difficult to defend. Technological developments in robotics and artificial intelligence raise the necessity of considering the rights of robots and intelligent machines.

Such concerns regularly arise in movies. In *Bicentennial Man* (1999), the essence of human nature is explored. Although initially unsuccessful, the robot Andrew Martin is eventually declared human after he accepts mortality. This topic is also explored in *I, Robot* (2004), where the plot revolves around suspicion that Sonny, a robot, murdered his creator, Dr Lanning. Most humans think this is impossible because robots do not have free will. As the movie develops, Sonny displays more and more human attributes, especially emotions and free will. The decision to "decommission" Sonny highlights the central ethical quandary. Might Sonny have developed to where he is conscious? If so, he could entitled to at least some of the rights of personhood (see Coleman/ Hanley 2009).

Dr Lanning narrates the deep questions that concern transhumanists and posthumanists.

> "There have always been ghosts in the machine. Random segments of code that have grouped together to form unexpected protocols. Unanticipated, these free radicals engender questions of free will, creativity, and even the nature of what we might call the soul."

This exemplifies why posthumanism is "nowhere [...] explored more passionately than in contemporary speculative fiction" (Hayles 1999, 247).

Problems with Technology

While *Star Trek* highlights the beneficial sides of technology and humanism, other movies point to limitations, e.g. *Metropolis* (1927), which in a H+ article on the best transhumanist movies by Treder (2010) was ranked as number two and refered to as the grandfather of all science fiction movies. Made in 1927, missing scenes have only recently been rediscovered and restored. Metropolis highlights problems as society becomes more dependent on technology. The majority are enslaved, becoming literally cogs in the wheels, so that the minority enjoy technology's benefits. As such, it critiques capitalist industrialization and its resulting dehumanization and social inequality.

In keeping with posthumanism, *Metropolis* points to problems with rationalist humanism. Its central message is that the head (the rich rationalists) and the hands (the workers) need someone with heart to mediate between them. Freder starts as the spoilt son of the Master of Metropolis, but matures to become the saviour of the workers' children and mediator between head and hands. In keeping with humanism, however, Freder's development comes from him accessing core human characteristics, like courage and faithfulness. Central to this is his falling in love with the wise and just Maria. She claims their society's problems originate in the humanistic proclamation, "Great is the world and its Creator! And great is Man!" Posthumanism would affirm that our problems lie in such an over-exaggerated view of humanity.

The complex web of human interaction with technology is also explored.
[illegible]ang, builds a robot and imbues her with life stolen from Ma-
[illegible]ia is evil, and leads a rebellion to destroy the machines. But
[illegible]hich they are enslaved are also essential to their lives. Reject-
[illegible] not the answer. This lies in head and heart becoming recon-
[illegible]ediator. As such, *Metropolis* is saturated in biblical imagery.

Many movies continue to appeal to humanist values when crises hit. Freder was generous to a manager his father fired, and a common worker. Later, they return his kindness to get him out of tight spots. Similarly in *Star Trek*, Hugh, one of the Borg, is won over by being treated humanely (see Graham 2002). For some, human virtues and character can be developed through "a humanistic, literature-centred culture" (Falzon 2007, 202). Posthumanism disagrees because "a successful ethics is not possible, given human nature as presently constituted" (Seidel 2010, 20). Human nature itself needs to be changed, which is only possible "if as a species we undergo an appropriate […] controlled evolution" (ibid.).

Controlling Evolution

Metropolis critiques the attempt to control evolution and create life. The same general message comes through in classics like *Dr Jeckel and Mr Hyde* (1886) and *Frankenstein* (1818). These cautionary tales warn transhumanism and posthumanism about attempts to control human evolution. Whether described as playing God, or Promethean hubris, the constant striving for technological progress inevitably leads in movies to more problems than benefits.

For example, *I am Legend* (2007) begins with the confident declaration that science has found the cure for cancer. The cure is effective, but its side-effects almost annihilate humanity. While such movies typically blame humanistic scientism, they also can be taken to suggest that transhumanist and posthumanist futures may not be reached without creating serious problems along the way.

Of more direct relevance to transhumanism are the potential problems with intelligent machines. The number one transhumanism movie in Treder's rankings is *2001: A Space Odyssey* (1968). Space exploration has arrived, ultimately assisted by Hal, the 9000 series computer. But human confidence in Hal is misplaced when an error is detected. As the human astronauts act more like automata, Hal discusses his feelings and worries. When Hal learns that he may be unplugged, his survival instincts take over and he starts killing humans.

The depiction of intelligent machines turning on their human creators is a regular theme in science fiction. This was viscerally and popularly exemplified in the *Terminator* series. While human reliance on technology (in this case, for security) leads to the problem, humanism is not rejected completely. The rise of the machines is coupled to human character development. John Conner goes from being a sniveling thief to inspirational leader of the human resistance. Humanity's position at the center of the universe was in trouble, but not relinquished. More generally, as posthumanism developed in philosophical circles, Hollywood revealed cracks in the inevitable progress proclaimed by humanism.

However, "Man, the films insisted, would survive: this was destiny, the law of nature" (Badmington 2000, 8).

Avatar (2009) paints a different picture. While film critics found much to fault in *Avatar*, new technological heights were scaled in making the movie which many moviegoers enjoyed. The worst of modernism and humanism are presented as humans exploit the natural resources of the planet Pandora. Genetic technology is used to make avatars from mixing the DNA of humans and natives, the Na'vi. More technology allows the human mind to be connected to the avatar. We see here the transhumanist vision of transferring consciousness into other bodies and machines. The Na'vi body is larger, stronger and more durable. But the humans can only see them as non-humans: "blue monkeys" without rights, getting in the way of progress and wealth. *Avatar* also raises issues of embodiment, to be discussed below.

The humans attack the Na'vi viciously. Their technological superiority appears to guarantee human victory. But the Na'vi have retained their link with nature and Spirit. As a result, they enlist resources not "seen" by the humans, even with all of their scanning technology. Those with a deep respect for all species and the environment overcome the rational materialists. Not only is humanity defeated, but as they are marched off Pandora, they are declared the aliens – and sent back to their dying planet. Then the hero, Jake Sully announces that this is his birthday, when he gives up his human body and is born again as a Na'vi. Might this represent something like the human transition to the posthuman?

Injustice

Avatar reminds us that technological development alone will not remove racism and discrimination. Concerns are raised that posthumanity will inevitability lead to injustices. Seidel notes that "a richer, more joyful existence awaits those fortunate enough to make [the] transition" from human to posthuman (Seidel 2010, vii). Enhancement pharmaceuticals are likely to be the first step in this direction, but only people "who can afford [them] […] will have them" (ibid., 4).

Transhumanists deny the inevitability of social inequalities and injustices, but science fiction regularly depicts human enhancement leading to discrimination and enslavement. In *The Time Machine* (1885), selective breeding leads to a future where the Morlocks hunt and dominate the unenhanced Eloi. In *Brave New World* (1998), reproductive technology allows the Alphas to rule over the Betas, and both use Deltas as little more than slaves. In *Gattaca* (1997), genetic testing and reproductive technology are used to separate the "in-valids" from the "valids," who are granted many more opportunities in life. Our history of racism, sexism, slavery and abortion argues strongly that the strong will tend to dominate or eliminate the weak – unless we develop a powerful ethic of defending the vulnerable, a value not obvious within transhumanism.

In response, some transhumanists predict that social harmony will be maintained by strong rulers. In common with many Enlightenment thinkers, we would need "a society ruled by a rational, scientifically informed administration, a strong ruler who imposed reforms and progress upon the population" (Falzon 2007, 188). Among transhumanists, Nick Bostrom is a prominent and prolific promoter of transhumanism and has described such a ruler as a "singleton." For humans to take control of their own evolution…

> "[…] would require the development of a 'singleton,' a world order in which at the highest level of organization there is only one independent decision-making power (which may be, but need not be, a world government)" (Bostrom 2004, 341-2).

Everyone would initially agree to this global authority, but once in place it would have no external competitors and internal challenges to its constitution would not be permitted.

We see this exemplified in *Brave New World* (1998) by Controller Mond. In *Gattaca* (1997) likewise, order is kept in place by an elite who deny some people access to all of society's benefits. However, movies tend not to be as positive as Bostrom about this development. In *Brave New World*, drugs keep people happy but numb, and Mond bans the reading of old books. In *Gattaca*, personal privacy is intruded upon to ensure "in-valids" don't access privileged positions. Such benevolent, totalitarian rulers typically turn out negatively.

Embodiment

According to Cary Wolfe, embodiment is an important theme that distinguishes posthumanism from transhumanism. For him, "the fundamental anthropological dogma associated with humanism" (Wolfe 2010, xiv) is that the essence of being human is achieved by "transcending the bonds of materiality and embodiment altogether" (ibid., xv). This view is carried into transhumanism, but rejected by posthumanism.

The movie *Surrogates* (2010) exemplifies this issue. Virtual reality has developed to where people stay at home and "plug in" to their robotic surrogates. The androids go out to work and play, allowing people to experience everything from the safety of their homes. The technology relies on the assumption, made by transhumanists, that consciousness and the full human experience can be transferred electronically. The ultimate transhumanist vision is that our minds can be downloaded into computers or robots, and the human body done away with altogether.

Wolfe and some posthumanists claim that this humanist and transhumanist search for disembodiment and autonomy is a fantasy. For posthumanism, human beings are embodied and embedded in the biological world and the technological world. *Surrogates* points to some fundamental problems with transhumanist transference. As embodied beings, something is missing from disembodied experience. Bruce Willis plays a policeman who is deeply dissatisfied because something fundamentally human is missing from his relationship with his wife. He wants to be with her person-to-person, in the flesh, in spite of the messiness this brings.

Other humans in *Surrogates* have the same misgiving. These protestors are led by The Prophet, and live in surrogate-free reservations. Once again, the enhanced separate themselves from the unenhanced, left to fend for themselves in poverty. The transhumanist vision is that a better life will result from better bodies. The Prophet rejects this notion as lacking meaning. Just because we run faster, or know more, or live longer, our lives will not necessarily be more meaningful – or have any meaning. Materialistic humanism rejected meaning as something merely religious. Transhumanism continues in that vein, offering more life with no inherent meaning. Pleasure, beauty and security are available (for some), either via surrogates or soma. Hence the portrayal of enhanced humans in many movies is of those who are missing something deeply human. Many plots center around the few who engage in quests to find what has been lost, as in movies from *Brave New World* to *Surrogates*.

Movies that are more posthumanist than transhumanist point to the importance of embeddedness. In *Avatar*, the Marine General acts like a humanist in believing that Jake Sully's consciousness can move unaffected from his human body to his Na'vi avatar and back. But Jake does not simply collect information in his mind and deliver it back to his boss. He learns through his feelings, experiences and relationships when embodied as a Na'vi. He is changed by his embodiment in and with the Na'vi.

While transhumanists seek the technology to make this possible, posthumanists like Wolfe say this is neither possible nor desirable. Like the people plugged into their surrogates, the human experience disconnected from the body is not the same as an embodied experience. Something vital is missing.

Embodiment is also a central theme in *Vanilla Sky* (2001). The lead character, David Aames, is a rich and handsome bachelor whose life is thrown into turmoil. A car accident leads to serious facial disfigurement and other injuries. The doctors offer him surgery, pills and a mask, which can be taken as a critique of modernist scientific medicine. They fail to recognize his deeper pain arising from his bodily injuries which have fragmented his identity.

As noted above, the movie's meaning is deliberately unclear. Sprinkled throughout the movie are TV ads about life extension technologies. David has accepted a transhuman future, where his body is cryopreserved and his consciousness disembodied. He now lives through his mind, in a life of his own creation. He controls the people who appear in his "life" because, as tech support tells him, "You are their God."

The humanist and transhumanist assumption that rational consciousness is in control turns out to be wrong. As posthumanists would point out, embodiment must be taken into account. The dream turns into a nightmare because, as the psychologist in *Vanilla Sky* declares, "The subconscious is a powerful thing." Bodily memories from his heart and soul keep invading his experience, creating confusion and terror. In the end, David chooses to be unfrozen and return to a physical body. Having lived in a postmodern dream where he is God, creating his own reality, he prefers the real world, with no guarantees. Such is the human experience.

Conclusion

Movies with posthuman(ist) and transhuman(ist) themes raise many issues, but are unified in asking questions about human nature and technology. They point out problems in humanism's emphasis on rationality, scientism and lack of meaning. They question the distinctiveness of humans and human value. They look to a future which brings "a period of human empowerment and evolution – even divinization" (Graham 2002, 5).

The movies discussed here regularly raise the God question. Not, as might be expected, in terms of whether emerging technology is playing God. Instead, the question comes up as embodied consciousness searches for meaning and identity. The search for God is one response to the question of why we are here and how we should live. The creature in *Frankenstein* is driven to find his creator. The replicants in *Blade Runner* want to find their maker to understand (and prevent) death. Transhuman technology allows David Aames to act like God, but he discovers he is not fit for the task.

Longer lives with enhanced capacities leave questions of meaning unanswered. In *Surrogates*, The Prophet points to a different source of meaning.

> "When you sacrifice your own personal desires for a greater cause, a greater good, you never die. You never disappear. That is what it means to be human [...]. We sacrifice many modern pleasures and conveniences to feel truly connected, not with

> machines, but with ourselves. This is the human condition. This is what gives life meaning."

The surrogates offer a life of comfort and convenience, not sacrifice.

In humanism, the greater cause is often the preservation of humanity. Posthumanism questions why this is good, especially given the pain and destruction humans have caused. "I believe that what we currently understand about human nature is sufficient to show that a successful ethics is not possible, given human nature as presently constituted" (Seidel 2010, 20). Transhumanists and some posthumanists agree that the answer lies in humans undergoing some sort of "controlled evolution" (ibid.) to a new nature. How that might be done is where much of the debate lies.

All the movies question whether humans are capable of bringing about the needed change in human nature without causing huge problems. All of the technologies featured in these movies turn out to have glitches and problems, or to inherit or transmit negative aspects of human nature. For this reason, some movies turn to the need for something superhuman to change human nature.

The Road (2009) and the *Book of Eli* (2010) are similar apocalyptic stories but with very different endings. Both are set after humanity has almost destroyed itself. *The Road* ends with hopelessness and no certainty that humanity will survive. The *Book of Eli* ends with a community of people who have hope. They have found supernatural guidance, which they believe, can save humanity. They agree with the posthumanists that human nature is broken and needs transformation. But they disagree that controlled evolution or developing technology will solve the problem. As Vaclav Havel stated, we need "a transformation of the spirit and the human relationship to life and the world" (Havel as cited in Annas 2005, 39).

Spirit-work takes us to another realm, where divine action is needed to remove the old nature and make it into something totally new. This appears to be what is happening at the end of *Avatar*. This is not superficial acceptance of doctrine or adherence to religious rules. This is the death of the old self, the renovation of the heart, and the creation of a new creature. Science fiction raises the oldest questions of life. What does it mean to be human, and how can we become the people we are meant to be? Post- and transhumanism are the latest in a long line of proposals.

Bibliography

Annas, G.J. (2005): American Bioethics: Crossing Human Rights and Health Law Boundaries. Oxford: Oxford University Press.

Badmington, N. (2000): Introduction: Approaching Posthumanism. In: Badmington, N. (ed.): Posthumanism. New York: Palgrave, 1-10.

Bostrom, N. (2004): The Future of Human Evolution. In: Tandy, C. (ed.): Death and Anti-Death, Volume 2: Two Hundred Years after Kant, Fifty Years after Turing. Palo Alto(CA): Ria University Press, 339-371.

Coleman, S./ Hanley, R. (2009): *Homo Sapiens*, Robots, and Persons in *I, Robot* and *Bicentennial Man*. In: Shapshay, S. (ed.): Bioethics at the Movies. Baltimore(MD): Johns Hopkins University Press, 44-55.

Falzon, C. (2007): Philosophy Goes to the Movies: An Introduction to Philosophy. New York: Routledge.

Graham, E.L. (2002): Representations of the Post/Human: Monsters, Aliens and Others in Popular Culture. New Brunswick(NJ): Rutgers University Press.

Haraway, D. (1985): A Cyborg Manifesto: Science, Technology, and Socialist Feminism in the Late Twentieth Century. In: Socialist Review 80, 65-108.

Hayles, N.K. (1999): How We Became Posthuman: Virtual Bodies in Cybernetics, Literature and Informatics. Chicago: University of Chicago Press.

Humanity+ (2009): Better Than Well. http://www.transhumanism.org/index.php/WTA/constitution/ (accessed June 24, 2013).

Lacey, N. (2006): Postmodern Romance: The Impossibility of (De)centring the Self. In: Brooker, W. (ed.): The Blade Runner Experience: The Legacy of a Science Fiction Classic, 190-201.

Seidel, A. (2010): Immortal Passage: Philosophical Speculations on Posthuman Evolution. Lanham: Rowman & Littlefield.

Treder, M. (2010): Top Ten Transhumanist Movies. In: H+ Magazine. http://www.hplusmagazine.com/editors-blog/top-ten-transhumanist-movies (accessed June 24, 2013).

Wolfe, C. (2010): What is Posthumanism? Minneapolis: University of Minnesota Press.

World Transhumanist Association (2002): The Transhumanist Declaration. http://www.transhumanism.org/index.php/wta/declaration (accessed June 24, 2013).

Music

Stefan Lorenz Sorgner

Most academic treatments of post- or transhumanism and the arts have concerned the fine arts, science fiction, performance arts or bioart. The genre of music has been rather neglected in this context, even though the use of technologies and a new immanent or relational and non-dualistic understanding of human beings can be seen as particularly widespread within the realm of contemporary music, both popular as well as classical to use some outdated modes of classifying music. It starts with the DJ who can be seen as a Cyborg musician, continues with the use of amplified instruments in concert halls and can be found in the use of iPhones in iPhone ensembles or together with traditional music instruments (e.g. Ólafur Arnalds). There are connections and traces of both trans- and posthumanism in all of the diverse musical pieces mentioned here. In the following reflections, I move in between the conceptual and theoretical level concerning reflections on trans- and posthumanism, and the practical level of performing and composing music. Thereby, various movements which analyze the impact of our new technologies are supposed to be associated with clearer concepts and description, and at the same time, the wide spectrum of contemporary musical genres, which deals with questions related to the attempt to move beyond humanism are supposed to be hinted at.

By humanism, I am referring to a type of humanism, which is associated with the affirmation of categorical dualities, reason and the passions, nature and culture, or mind and body. Both transhumanism as well as posthumanism are movements which transcend this type of humanism. Even though many transhumanists regard themselves as being in the humanist Enlightenment tradition, this is not necessarily the case in all respects (see Hughes 2014). Enlightenment humanism is associated with an affirmation of categorical dualities like the immaterial soul and the material body. Kant's philosophy represents a paradigm case of a humanist enlightenment philosophy and his philosophy is based upon the aforementioned understanding of body and soul (see Sorgner 2010, 82-108). However, given this metaphysical basis, he rather ought to be seen as a philosopher whose philosophy is built upon a Christian metaphysics while at the same time trying to hide it. Most transhumanists, however, uphold a this-worldly, immanent, Buddhist or a naturalist understanding of the world, which implies the rejection of the humanist metaphysics and which is related to there being a material body and an immaterial soul. Hence, transhumanists move beyond the aforementioned understanding of humanism. The same applies to posthumanists whereby the question whether or not they attempt to transcend Enlightenment humanism is less problematic than in the case of transhumanist's. Given that the main goal of posthumanist's is to transcend categorical dualities and humanists affirm this type of dualities, they are bound to move beyond Enlightenment humanism. However, the word "posthuman" on which the term "posthumanism" rests is a problematic one and can easily be misunderstood. By claiming that we are already posthumans and as human beings have always been posthumans, it does not imply that in a phylogenetic sense we have ever been human beings, but it implies that in a cultural sense we have been human beings and that we have moved beyond this understanding of human beings. So, the posthuman is not a step within the evolutionary process. The posthumanist concept of the "posthuman" refers to human self-understanding within a certain culture. After Darwin, Nietzsche and Freud, many people understand themselves as non-dualist entities, who are not constituted out of a material body and an immaterial soul, but have always been both cultural and natural beings. Hence, we are posthumans not in a phylogenetic sense, but in a cultural sense. As contemporary beings we classify ourselves as non-dualist entities. During the Enlightenment, the human self-understanding was different. Then, it was widely acknowledged that human beings have a material body and an immaterial soul and Enlightenment philosophers such as Descartes and Kant are the leading representatives of such an anthropology. However, the use of the term "posthuman" is problematic for further reasons, as it is also used by transhumanists who use the term in several other ways. In order to avoid misunderstandings and misleading connotations I suggested employing the concept "metahuman" instead to refer to our self-understanding as non-dualist entities, such that the concepts of the trans- and posthuman can still be used in the transhumanist senses, which implies that transhumans and posthumans represent stages within human evolutionary development (see Sorgner 2013a, 85-100). Today, many human beings understand themselves as metahumans, e.g. as non-dualist entities, which are gradually different from other animals. Transhumans are a type of metahumans which are on the way of becoming posthumans, who are even further developed and might belong to a different species. However, the differences between the various types are merely gradual, not ontologically categorical ones.

At this stage, I could be criticized in my way of representing humanism and posthumanism, because of the words I am using like immaterial and material, soul and body and so on. In addition, I could be seen as someone who is creating a categorical distinction between posthumanism and humanism, which implies that I ought to be a humanist myself, due to my analysis being built upon dualistic categorizations. What could I do to avoid this problem? Either, I could invent a new language so that the words no longer have the metaphysical implications our words have, which was the path Heidegger took, or I could explain that a dualistic metaphysics seems to be embedded within our grammatical and intellectual systems which does not have to mean, however, that it corresponds to the world, but that by using our common language, it needs to be stressed that everything we say is bound to be problematic (or metaphorical) and is in need of further explanations and specification, which is Nietzsche's solution. I decided to choose the second option, which means that I am using a clear, academic, and traditional language, which implies also that for my judgments to be grasped appropriately a permanent process of interpretation, specification and explanation is needed. However, this approach has the advantage that both trans- as well as posthumanists might be able to relate to the content I intend to convey. I think that post- and transhumanists have more in common than what they themselves recognize and acknowledge. The main challenge for a successful communication between trans- and posthumanist's is a matter of style. Transhumanists have a linear and scientific way of communicating, but posthumanists employ a rather dialectical and artistic way of doing so. I regard myself both as a weak transhumanist and a weak posthumanist and attempt to bridge the discursive barrier between these two movements by moving in between (*meta*) them. In the following reflections, I aim to bring out more clearly, too, that trans- and posthumanists have more ground in common than many members of both communities seem to believe (see Sorgner 2011b).

Posthumanism is associated with the dissolution of categorical dualities, and thereby with the dissolution of the special status of human beings which becomes obvious in contemporary works of art, too. Wolfgang Welsch, a leading contemporary philosopher of art, refers to the relevance of non-dualities in contemporary works of art. According to him, it can be found in all genres of art. However, elsewhere I put forward some reasons for holding that as a sensual experience, this quality is particularly associated with music (see Sorgner 2012). Thereby, I do not claim that music is in any absolute sense superior to the other arts, but merely that with respect to the sensual experience of the dissolution of the special status of human beings, music as a genre is best suited for bringing it about in their listeners. This judgment implies that the same quality can be expressed and can manifest itself in other artistic genres, too, but in a different form, e.g. in literature in a more intellectual form.

In contrast to myself, Welsch refers to this phenomenon as the transhuman perspective, which is his way of referring to the integration of human beings into nature, as a widespread phenomenon in contemporary works of art (see Welsch 2004, 100-114). The transhuman perspective has nothing to do with transhumanism or the concept of the transhuman in transhumanism. It is his idiosyncratic way of describing the phenomena in question. As the characteristics he employs are posthumanist ones, I suggest referring to them as a posthumanist perspective. In any case, Welsch is correct in stressing that there is a strong link between Eastern thinking and this perspective. Consequently, he does not regard it as a coincidence that artists like Cage or Feldmann, who present such a perspective in their works, according to him regard themselves as particularly related to Eastern thinking. In the Eastern tradition human beings are not as seen in opposition to the world but as participants in this one world which possesses a bigger than human measurement. Hence, it is supposed to be more common for this tradition to present, represent and create such a perspective than it is for the Western tradition, according to Welsch (2004, 110). He also reveals the importance of the dissolution of the special status of human beings, as there could not be a close connection between human beings and nature, if human beings were radically separated from this world. In his article *Art Beyond Aestheticism*, he suggests some descriptions of how this perspective can be perceived within the works of arts of the above-mentioned artists. When we listen to the music of John Cage and Morton Feldman, then he describes the experiences connected to this perspective as follows: "We experience ourselves like beings welcomed and participating in a world that is not on a human scale" (Welsch 2004, 67). In this article he refers to further examples. His list however could get expanded further: One could include other composers like Philip Glass, too. Later on, I will explain it further why this is the case from my point of view. In addition, it needs to be pointed out that it was Nietzsche, who already described the possibility that human beings are not in opposition to this world but are regarded as participants in this one world within his early work *Birth of Tragedy,* and connects this perspective to Dionysian works of art, which are created by Dionysian artists. In contrast to Welsch, he does not regard all the arts as equally able of expressing this perspective, but makes clear that it is music in particular which represents best the Dionysian perspective. I agree with Nietzsche in this respect (see Sorgner 2012).

However, the philosophical issue mentioned last is one which needs to be stressed in this context. Posthumanism is related to the dissolution of absolute hierarchies. If it is the case that music as artistic genre is actually best in sensually expressing the doubt concerning the categorical special status of human beings in this world, then there would be a new hierarchy of the arts and the old battle between the arts, the *paragone*, would be renewed: Concerning the ability to sensually expressing the doubt of the categorical special status of human beings in this world, music would be best, and opera and ballet might follow on some of the next places. Would it contradict some of the basic attitudes of posthumanism to make such a judgment? I, who uphold a weak version both of post- and of transhumanism, doubt that this is the case. To doubt the possibility of absolute hierarchies and categorically separate distinctions does not necessarily exclude the possibility of having criteria for making a distinction or a judgment. However, even though it is possible from my perspective to have a criterion for creating a hierarchy, this does not mean that such a position falls back into traditional, conservative philosophical Platonism, far from it actually. Affirming a criterion does not imply that the criterion is universally valid or valid at all. Affirming a criterion from a posthumanist perspective merely means that I affirm the criterion at the moment. Given new data or information, I might revise my position, alter it and accept a different one. An affirmation of a criterion is consistent with posthumanism as long as one does not claim that it is a universally valid criterion, and that it is not subject to revision.

The posthumanist perspective is merely one aspect of this paper, as I am also dealing with music from a transhumanist point of view. A central aspect of transhumanism is the affirmation of the use of technology to enhance human beings so that the likelihood increases that the posthuman comes about. Hence, the use of technology and the positive attitude toward this use seem necessary features of music which becomes classified as transhumanist. Several works of Michael Nyman are concerned with the use of enhancement technologies. However, they also imply a rather skeptical attitude concerning the use of these technologies. Maybe, they ought to be seen as anti-transhumanist musical pieces. However, in one of the movies for which he wrote the score, *Gattaca*, a piece turns up which could get classified as a transhumanist one, as for it to be performed a piano player with six fingers on each hand is needed. Such a person could be referred to as trans- or maybe even posthuman. I will make some further remarks concerning the movie *Gattaca* later on.

The "Eyeborg", Neil Harbisson, might be a suitable already existing example for a transhumanist composer. In cooperation with an engineer, Harbisson – who is color-blind – developed a device which enables him to hear the colors of the objects on which he focuses, and uses these audial experiences for composing works of music. It might also be appropriate to talk about transhumanist music, if the latest or newly created computer based instruments are being used to create the necessary sounds. *The Reactable* is an excellent example of such an instrument which was first used in a concert in 2005. It was developed by the Music Technology Group from the Universitat Pompeu Fabra in Barcelona (see Wilson 2010, 122-123). Björk also integrated it into her songs during her 18-month world tour entitled *Volta*. A further example of transhumanist music are musical pieces performed by computer played drums or guitars, and the Japanese art unit Maywa Denki has created some spectacular examples of such instruments (see Miah 2008, 278-279). Their pieces are being referred to as "products" by the members of the group and a performance of such a piece is called "a product demonstration". This use of words implies many philosophical questions concerning the status of these works of art. Chico MacMurtrie and his group Amorphic Robot Works also cooperate to create robotic events, performances and installations. Their piece the *Drumming and Drawing Subhuman* from 1993 is a particularly well known example (see Wilson 2010, 110).

A further aspect of transhumanism is the analysis that the border between humans and machines has become blurred, even though it is also this aspect which is characteristic of some central posthumanist traditions. One option concerning the future of human beings is that the posthuman will exist in the digital realm. Another option is obviously that of a genetic evolution towards the posthuman. The blurring of the boundary between human beings and machines has been dealt with from the perspective of dance and music artists. The dance artist Garry Stewart, Louis-Philippe Demers, a multi-disciplinary artist, a video artist, Gina Czarnecki and costume designer Georg Meyer-Wiel created an extraordinary piece entitled *Devolution* which confronts us with a world full of dance and music in which the traditional relationship between machines, robots and human bodies is being challenged (ibid., 111).

A related topic can also be found in the works of artists who are more closely connected to posthumanism. Particularly fascinating examples are the various metaformances of the metahumanist artist Jaime del Val (see Tuncel 2011, 1-4). In contrast to posthumanist accounts, he presents a relationalist ontology of becoming which implies the immediate interaction and close connection between sounds, and movements (see del Val/ Sorgner 2011). In one of his metaformances, he walks the streets of Madrid by night as Pangender Cyborg. Thereby, it becomes clear what a dissolution of categorical dualities and an affirmation of relationalism can mean. There are cameras at various parts of his otherwise nude body. Furthermore, he wears a projector so that the new and unsusual perspectives upon his body, postanatomical representations, can be projected upon the wall in front of him. Depending upon his own movements, the projections get altered and have an effect back upon his movements. In addition, he wears loud speakers and a microphone by means of which the sounds he is making get altered and amplified. These sounds again have an effect upon his movements and the projections of his movements which again alter how he moves and which sounds he makes. Hence, the traditional subject-object-distinction gets blurred and the same applies to the separation between the metaformance artist and the composer. There are many further philosophical aspects related to this metaformance.

By continuing to focus on the dissolution of categorical distinctions, which is associated with posthumanism, another work of music has to be mentioned: *Exurbia* by David Cecchetto and William Brent from 2011. It is a web-based installation of sound samples which can be uploaded by whoever becomes part of this project. These sound samples can be used by all project participants to create further musical works. However, all participants also have the chance of editing existing sound samples such that the alterations cannot be undone which again effects the works by all the other artist's in whose pieces the sample has been used. Thereby, the internet is being used for creating musical pieces without there being a specific composer and a finished work. There are merely musical pieces which are permanently subject to change.

Returning to the musical works of Philip Glass, there are several posthumanist trends in them. Firstly, the doubt concerning rigid separations of formerly categorically distinguished entities, e.g. the dissolution of the subject-object-separation which has been dealt with in the former paragraphs. *Koyaanisqatsi: Life out of Balance* is a film directed by Godfrey Reggio with film music composed by Philip Glass (see Kostelanetz 1997, 131-151). It is the first film of the *Qatsi-Trilogy*, which has been created by the same two artists, Reggio and Glass. "Qatsi" is a word from the Native American Hopi language and means "life". *Powaqqatsi: Life in Transformation*, and *Naqoyqatsi: Life as War* are the titles of part two and three of the trilogy. Each of the films represents different aspects of life, the world and in particular the wide spread dominance of technology today, and the score is composed to support the visual images of the films. Without the artists explicitly wishing to convey a specific meaning by means of the films, one issue becomes clear immediately, and it comes out strongest in *Koyaanisqatsi: Life out of Balance* from my perspective: the music draws us into the film, makes us aware that we are a part of the world shown in the movie. The inter-connectedness between technology, nature and human beings and the loss of any rigid and clear separation between these domains is the initial standpoint from which the relations of life manifest themselves. When watching and listening to the film, the audience is being drawn into the world and confronted with the central philosophical and ethical issues of today. Hence, watching and listening to this movie can be seen as a starting point for posthumanist reflections.

Three aspects, which are particularly significant for posthumanist philosophies, can be referred to within some of the most successful of operas by Glass, too: 1. An interest in scientific and technological issues, e.g. *Einstein on the Beach* (see Kostelanetz 1997, 152-166); 2. An affirmation of Eastern, non-dualist thinking, e.g. *Satyagraha* (ibid., 176-188); 3. A rejection of rigid and absolute categories and a relatedness with a way of thinking which rejects the categorical ontologically special status of human beings, e.g. *Kepler*. A detailed analysis of each of the three operas would reveal central philosophical issues related to posthumanism. In another article of mine, I analyzed at least some posthumanist traces within his opera *Kepler* (see Sorgner 2011a). However, further studies will most certainly reveal several more specific aspects not yet mentioned here.

From the aforementioned paragraphs, it has become clear already that the world of technology and the natural sciences has entered the realm of opera during the most recent decades. Two of the operas referred to previously even mentioned a scientist within their titles: Einstein and Kepler. However, Glass is not the only living composer who has been occupied with these issues. The aforementioned Nyman takes these issues at least as seriously as Glass. In contrast to Glass, who is most closely related to posthumanist reflections, Nyman is more intimately connected to transhumanist issues. I am not claiming here that either Glass or Nyman claim or wish to be associated with one of these movements. I am merely pointing at structural analogies between the basic premises of these movements and themes within the works of the two composers.

With respect to the music of Michael Nyman, I have referred to the movie *Gattaca* only so far. Besides the example mentioned already, there are further topics to be explored concerning the musical themes and the topics dealt with within the movie. Of particular relevance is a question, which has entered the transhumanist discourses under the tile "Gattaca argument", because the plot raises the question whether genetic enhancement by selection leads to two class society in which only posthumans or postpersons have the option of access to the socially better ranked positions and jobs whereas the lower ranked jobs are the only option for regular born human beings or persons. Both the transhumanist James Hughes in his excellent introduction to transhumanism entitled *Citizen Cyborg* (2004) as well as the bioethicist Lee M. Silver in his article *Genetics goes to Hollywood* (1997) have dealt critically with the movie. The title already reveals that the genes and the ethical relevance of their impact and of their alteration are being dealt with in the movie, as the title GATTACA is constituted out of the initial letters of nucleotides (Guanine, Adenine, Thymine, Cytosine) which being put together in a sequence form the genetic information in an encoded form of the DNA molecule which again is responsible for the development and the functions of many viruses and all known living organisms. RNA, DNA and proteins are the three major macromolecules of all known forms of life. By intensifying the emotional challenges related to the plot, Nyman's music ideally supports the plot of the movie.

After this brief excursion to *Gattaca*, the relevance of scientific and technological issues within operas can be dealt with again, as many transhumanist topics are being considered in two of Nyman's operas: *Facing Goya* and, in some respect also, *The Man who Mistook his Wife for a Hat*.

The opera *The Man who Mistook his Wife for a Hat* is based upon a book with the same title by neurologist Oliver Sachs in which he describes case histories of selected patients (see Siôn 2007, 115-146). A man with visual agnosia is the basis of the description used as foundation of the one act chamber opera composed by Michael Nyman which premiered 1986. The libretto was adapted from the Sachs story by Chistopher Rawlence. Thereby, a medical case history was turned into an opera.

A more explicit example of transhumanist reflections, which turn up in an opera, is the case of *Facing Goya* (see ibid., 197-212). However, the opera suggests rather an anti-transhumanist standpoint. *Facing Goya* is a four act opera composed by Michael Nyman with a libretto by Victoria Hardie, which premiered in the year 2000. The plot is concerned with the long-lost skull of Goya and the desire to create Francisco Goya's clone. The various singers of the opera represent perspectives concerning genetic engineering, cloning, and eugenics. An art banker and specialist in Goya's works wants to patent Goya's talent gene, raising the ethical question of gene patenting. A soprano represents someone obsessed with science who deciphers the human genome. A further soprano stresses the danger of "genoism" associated with the control and knowledge of genes. The word "genoism" was created by the writer of the film *Gattaca*, Andrew Niccol, and means an immoral ethical genetic discrimination. The tenor takes the role of an entrepreneur who affirms eugenic practices and wishes to create the first clone of a human being. The final leading role has a baritone who represents a fatalistic perspective of a thinker or a philosopher who does not uphold the special status of human beings. Hence, financial, scientific, ethical, entrepreneurial, and philosophical perspectives concerning the challenges related to eugenics are represented within the leading roles of this opera. In contrast to transhumanists who affirm the use of genetic enhancement so that the likelihood increases that a trans- or a posthuman comes about, the general vision of Nyman's opera *Facing Goya* is an anti-transhumanist one, as it was the case with the movie *Gattaca*, too.

Most examples from the realm of opera with which I dealt here have rather been critical concerning transhumanist ideas. This is not the case, if historical examples are also being taken into consideration. Within this text, I primarily focused upon contemporary musical pieces. However, it is possible to find both post- as well as transhumanist themes within the history of opera. The composer and intellectual Richard Wagner is probably the best example in question, as both trans- and posthumanist themes are widespread within his oeuvre. It is important to note that the Gods within his masterpiece *Ring des Nibelungen* are dependent upon the golden apples for keeping their strength and ongoing youth. In the opera *Rheingold*, the gods have to face the serious challenge of them no longer having access to these enhancement technologies, as there is the risk of them losing Freia, who takes care of these apples, to the giants Fasolt and

Fafner. Besides the structural analogy between Wagner's Gods and posthumans of transhumanists, there are also many posthumanist traces in Wagner's musical dramas, e.g. his use of words. The words, Wagner draws upon, sound strange for contemporary Germans, however, they have been unusual for Wagner's contemporaries, too. Like Nietzsche, Wagner was aware that language carries a world-view, and the German language seems to have a particularly close affinity to a metaphysical way of thinking with a clear categorical division between the subject and the object. Wagner was affirmative of evolutionary thinking and an immanent ontology. Hence, his intention was to move away from dualist ways of conceptualizing human beings. In order to avoid the dualist implications of German grammar, he developed his own personal and metaphorical language which can be found in all of his musical dramas (see Sorgner 2013b, 193-200).[1] By moving in between post- and transhumanist concepts, Wagner can be seen as an ancestor to metahumanist thinking.

Still, it needs to be noted that even though there are traces of metahumanism in Wagner's music dramas, the general social, political and ethical implications of his creations move into a more problematic direction (see Sorgner 2013b, 193-200). This is not the case for the most fascinating contemporary German composer Sven Helbig, whose musical drama *Vom Lärm der Welt oder Die Offenbarung des Thomas Müntzer* (world premiere at the 28th of March 2014 in Weimar) lies in the tradition of the Gesamtkunstwerk. Nevertheless, it successfully avoids the potentially totalitarian connotations of this tradition, both by stylistic means as well as by the plot of the libretto. Like Wagner's operas, this musical drama is concerned with central metaphysical, ethical, and political issues. Yet, this work does not remain within the mythic realm, but relates philosophical reflections to contemporary bioethical and religious challenges. How should one's religious believes be related to someone's political engagement? Which ethical norms are appropriate for beginning of life issues like abortion? Should utopian thinking play any role for day to day political decisions? The demons in the final scene of the music drama stress that we are doomed, if we follow a utopia, a general order and strong ideas. Thereby, the relevance of a radical type of pluralism gets stressed, and it is also being affirmed that the ethical nihilism of our times is an achievement rather than a loss (see Sorgner 2010, 242-243). This is the reason why this total work of art can be classified as a metahumanist one. In addition, by means of his use and integration of emerging technologies, new media and an accessible musical language, Helbig successful-

1 I was particularly happy about a personal conversation with John Deathridge in which it became clear that he also sees many posthumanist themes in Wagner's ideas and musical pieces.

ly avoids that the reception of this work remains limited to a specialized audience.

The above web of composers, musicians, and musical pieces related to post- and transhumanist reflections only provides a brief glimpse into the great variety of such works which have been produced. Historically the German band Kraftwerk is certainly a landmark for the interplay of technology, science and music. The role of the DJ as sonic cyborg prosumer could have been analyzed further, too. A prosumer is someone who simultaneously produces and consumes music. However, the goal of this article was to provide a broad survey of central post- and transhumanist themes within the musical genre, which can serve as a basis for further more specific studies, and to show that this topic deserves further academic investigations.

Bibliography

del Val, J./ Sorgner, S.L. (2011): A Metahumanist Manifesto. In: The Agonist 4(2), 1-4.

Hughes, J. (2004): Citizen Cyborg: Why Democratic Societies Must Respond to the Redesigned Human of the Future. Boulder: Westview Press.

Hughes, J. (2014): Politics. In: Ranisch, R./Sorgner, S.L. (eds.): Post- and Transhumanism. An Introduction. Frankfurt et al.: Peter Lang.

Kostelanetz, R. (ed.) (1997): Writings on Glass: Essays, Interviews, Criticism. London et al.: University of California Press.

Miah, A. (ed.) (2008): Human Futures: Art in the Age of Uncertainty. Liverpool: Liverpool University Press,

Silver, L.M. (1997): Genetics goes to Hollywood. In: Nature Genetics 17(3), 260-261.

Siôn, P. ap (2007): The Music of Michael Nyman: Texts, Contexts and Intertexts. Aldershot: Ashgate Publishing.

Sorgner, S.L. (2010): Menschenwürde nach Nietzsche: Die Geschichte eines Begriffs. Darmstadt: WBG.

Sorgner, S.L. (2011a): Nietzsche als Ahnherr des Posthumanismus in den Künsten: Reflexionen zum Verhältnis von Bild, Wort und Ton. In: Reschke, R. (ed.): Bilder-Sprache-Künste: Nietzsches Denkfiguren im Zusammenhang. Berlin: Akademie Verlag, 45-58.

Sorgner, S.L. (2011b): Zarathustra 2.0 and Beyond: Further Reflection on the complex Relationship between Nietzsche and Transhumanism. In: The Agonist 4(2), 1-46.

Sorgner, S.L. (2012): Music, Posthumanism and Nietzsche. In: The Agonist 5(1), 1-26.

Sorgner, S.L. (2013a): Evolution, Education, and Genetic Enhancement. In: Sorgner, S.L./ Jovanovic, B.-R. (eds.): Evolution and the Future: Anthropology, Ethics, Religion. Frankfurt am Main: Peter Lang, 85-100.

Sorgner, S.L. (2013b): Wagners (un)zeitgemäße Betrachtungen: Reaktionare oder progressive Uberlegungen zum Musikdrama? In: Loos, H. (ed.): Richard Wagner: Persönlichkeit, Werk und Wirkung. Markkleeberg: Sax Verlag, 193-200.

Tuncel, Y. (2011): Review of Jaime del Val's 'Metaformance'. In: The Agonist 4(2), 1-4.

Welsch, W. (2004): Art Beyond Aestheticism. In: Bindé, J. (ed.): The Future of Values: 21st-Century Talks. New York et al.: Berghahn Books, 64-68
Wilson, S. (2010): Art and Science Now: How Scientific Research and Technological Innovation are Becoming Key to 21st-Century Aesthetics. London et al.: Thames & Hudson.

List of Contributors

Curtis D. Carbonell is an Assistant Professor of English at Khalifa University of Science, Technology, and Research (United Arab Emirates).
Web: http://www.kustar.ac.ae/pages/dr-curtis-carbonell

Sascha Dickel works at the Friedrich Schiedel Professorship for Sociology of Science, Technische Universität München (Germany).
Web: http://www.saschadickel.de

Francesca Ferrando, Ph.D. in Philosophy, M.A. in Gender Studies, is a philosopher of the posthuman, an award-winning scholar, and an Adjunct Faculty at New York University (USA).
Web: http://www.theposthuman.org

Trijsje Franssen recently finished her Ph.D. at the University of Exeter (UK) with a thesis on the relation between human enhancement, philosophy and myth.
Web: http://exeter.academia.edu/TrijsjeFranssen

Andreas Frewer is Professor at the Institute for History of Medicine and Medical Ethics at the University of Erlangen-Nürnberg (Germany).
Web: http://www.igem.med.uni-erlangen.de/english/employees/andreas-frewer.shtml

Steve Fuller holds the Auguste Comte Chair in Social Epistemology in the Department of Sociology at the University of Warwick (UK).
Web: http://bit.ly/q3GBmi

Michael Hauskeller is Associate Professor of Philosophy at the University of Exeter (UK).
Web: http://socialsciences.exeter.ac.uk/sociology/staff/mhauskeller/

James J. Hughes is the Executive Director and Co-Founder of the Institute for Ethics and Emerging Technologies, and he teaches health policy at Trinity College in Hartford Connecticut (USA).
Web: http://www.ieet.org

Andy Miah is a Professor in Ethics & Emerging Technologies and Director of the Creative Futures Institute in the Faculty of Business & Creative Industries at the University of the West of Scotland (UK).
Web: http://www.andymiah.net

Dónal P. O'Mathúna is Senior Lecturer in Ethics, Decision-Making & Evidence, School of Nursing & Human Sciences, and an Affiliated Scholar, Institute of Ethics at Dublin City University (Ireland).
Web: http://www.bioethicsireland.ie

Domna Pastourmatzi is an Associate Professor at the School of English, Aristotle University of Thessaloniki (Greece), where she teaches science fiction.
Web: http://www.enl.auth.gr/staff/pastourm.htm

Thomas D. Philbeck is a Global Leadership Fellow at the World Economic Forum in Geneva (Switzerland), and is currently co-editing the Palgrave Macmillan Handbook on Posthumanism in Film and Television.

Robert Ranisch is a philosopher and Research Associate at the International Centre for Ethics in the Sciences and Humanities, and Research Assistant at the Chair for Ethics in the Life Sciences, University of Tübingen (Germany).
Web: http://www.ranisch.com

Marcus Rockoff, M.A. in German Literature from the University of Jena, is currently working as a Research Assistant at the International Centre for Ethics in the Sciences and Humanities, University of Tübingen (Germany).
Web: http://www.esureblog.com

Evi (Evangelia) Sampanikou is Associate Professor in Art History and Contemporary Visual Culture at the University of the Aegean (Greece), Department of Cultural Technology and Communication, and Co-Founder of the Beyond Humanism Network.

Stefan Lorenz Sorgner is a metahumanist philosopher, Director and Co-Founder of the Beyond Humanism Network, and Fellow of the Institute for Ethics and Emerging Technologies.
Web: http://www.sorgner.de

Hava Tirosh-Samuelson is Professor of History, Irving and Miriam Lowe Professor of Modern Judaism, and Director of Jewish Studies at Arizona State University (USA).
Web: http://jewishstudies.clas.asu.edu

Yunus Tuncel teaches philosophy in New York City (USA), and serves on the Board of Directors of the Nietzsche Circle, and on the Editorial Board of its electronic journal, The Agonist.
Web: http://www.philomobile.com

Martin G. Weiss is Assistant Professor of Philosophy at the University of Klagenfurt (Austria), and working on the ethical and political implications of biotechnologies.
Web: http://martingweiss.tumblr.com

BEYOND HUMANISM: TRANS- AND POSTHUMANISM
JENSEITS DES HUMANISMUS: TRANS- UND POSTHUMANISMUS

Edited by / Herausgegeben von Stefan Lorenz Sorgner

Vol./Bd. 1 Robert Ranisch / Stefan Lorenz Sorgner (eds.): Post- and Transhumanism. An Introduction. 2014.

Vol./Bd. 2 Stephen R. L. Clark: Philosophical Futures. 2011.

Vol./Bd. 3 Hava Tirosh-Samuelson / Kenneth L. Mossman (eds.): Building Better Humans? Refocusing the Debate on Transhumanism. 2012.

Vol./Bd. 4 Elizabeth Butterfield: Sartre and Posthumanist Humanism. 2012.

Vol./Bd. 5 Stefan Lorenz Sorgner / Branka-Rista Jovanovic (eds.). In cooperation with Nikola Grimm: Evolution and the Future. Anthropology, Ethics, Religion. 2013.

www.peterlang.de